# THE REALITY OF GLOBAL CRISES

To Francis Scott-Morgan

*my partner of choice through* any *crisis*

DR PETER B SCOTT–MORGAN

THE

# REALITY

OF

# GL BAL

# CRISES

Why good beginnings are ending badly and
leaving world-leaders increasingly powerless

ISBN-13: 978-1470115425

ISBN-10: 1470115425

# CONTENTS

# LIST OF FIGURES

# A NOTE ON CONFIDENTIALITY

Over the last twenty-five years I have had the privilege of being granted unique access around the world to a complete cross-section of the corporations, institutions, government organizations, secret societies, associations and informal groups that together make up the international community. That work opened doors for me that many times were opened for no one else, and I find myself in the position of being one of very few that has been fortunate enough to gain so much confidential insight into the hidden inner-workings of such a wide-ranging sample of the world economy. My problem now is how much I can legitimately reveal.

On every past analysis I ended up learning far more about concealed activities, counterintuitive behavior, unwritten rules and unexpected implications than I can reasonably release. Some of the insights I gained related to issues that those officially in control were unaware even existed, and to this day I remain the only person to know all the details because – although I typically fed-back to the most senior leaders the patterns behind the systemic threats that concerned them – I never revealed precise sources, nor the details of any instances that might be tracked to specific individuals, nor the particulars of similar examples I had seen elsewhere. All that, understandably enough, must remain utterly confidential.

But although the *details* from those assessments will in their entirety remain undisclosed, I have used as background to this book (supplemented by additional analyses conducted during the writing period) the overall *patterns* I observed across my investigations. These metatrends and common-denominators are not restricted by the terms of the many confidentiality-agreements I signed over the years. Similarly, although I have not in general been able to name organization-specific illustrations – in particular relating to banking, pharmaceuticals, IT, public utilities, the oil industry, the media, some religious sects, government bodies and the UN – I have felt able selectively to incorporate *some* confidentially-obtained details of specific organizations that, through other sources, have already reached the public domain.

*Peter Scott-Morgan*
*Torquay, 2012*

*Turning and turning in the widening gyre*
*The falcon cannot hear the falconer;*
*Things fall apart; the centre cannot hold;*
*Mere anarchy is loosed upon the world,*
*The blood-dimmed tide is loosed, and everywhere*
*The ceremony of innocence is drowned;*
*The best lack all conviction, while the worst*
*Are full of passionate intensity.*

**William Butler Yeats, 1920**

# HIDDEN CONSEQUENCES OF AN INTERCONNECTED WORLD

Our inability to see how complex world issues interlink or what underlying drivers they share or why even anticipated threats are so hard to avoid – makes escalation of current global crises inevitable

WE CANNOT SEE the Forest for the Trees. When it comes to threats to the world economy, any single major issue on its own is usually sufficient to crowd out all the others from our thinking. Even when the threats are well-recognized, we tend to consider each in isolation. We address each in turn. Categorize each to a separate part of our minds. Escalating global-economic threats from various forms of over-borrowing seem in every way different from escalating planetary threats such as global warming from too much $CO_2$. Threats to ancient institutions (such as schisms in religion over women's and gay rights) seem poles apart from threats to modern industries (such as the clamor for tighter press-regulation following abuses by tabloid journalists).

That is the problem. In reality, there *are* important but hidden links. As for the obscured ultimate causes of global crises – many are remarkably similar. Below the surface of everyday-life, these apparently distinct threats are often deeply interconnected. Many have common origins. Several have similar solutions. Just as importantly, buried deep within the complex inner-workings of the international community, it turns out that the worst threats to our collective progress in fact derive from the very same positive elements on which the world economy completely depends.

Our inability to see, let alone understand, this big picture is placing corporations, institutions, governments, whole industries, entire countries and the overall world economy – all at risk. Revealing the most important hidden connections within our global system, decoding their implications, and defining how to avoid the worst of the nasty surprises buried within them has now become vital. And that is what this book is all about.

## THE TREES

It is easy to understand why we all tend to keep global crises split apart: If we try to look at more than one major threat or opportunity at a time we lose focus. After all, the branching interlinkages of cause and effect within just one of these vast metaphorical trees – say, Middle-Eastern conflict – are already pretty much incomprehensible and impenetrable. As a result, it is perfectly natural that most of us view things like uprisings in distant autocratic regimes as being largely irrelevant to our everyday lives and certainly to our work lives. It is easy to classify these sorts of disruptions as little more than remote experiments in democracy that might temporarily impact fuel prices. Totally divorced even from local politics. And in a different universe to breakthroughs in stem-cell research. Yet they are all linked.

Despite being a truly-global society we nevertheless tend to segregate each of our major global threats one from the other. Worrying book titles are marketed to readers concerned about Ecology or Business or Politics or Religion but never all together. We do the same with major opportunities. Journalists specialize in reporting innovations in Science or Architecture but rarely both. In just the same way, senior politicians – other than Presidents and Prime Ministers – head departments that focus on specific Negatives such as bioterrorism or energy scarcity or food security that are themselves largely isolated from those departments focusing on what are seen as Positives like healthcare or business-development or education.

It is within this context of neatly-separated individual global threats and individual sources of opportunity that we all just get on with our work, conveniently removed from any but the worst turmoil. Often it is only outside of work – when we are catching up on The News – that most of us even get to hear all the pre-packaged snippets of what is going on in the world. In one item after another we gain hermetically-sealed insights into the continued world economic downturn, continued religious conflicts, another flu pandemic, another tsunami, threats to the Euro, threats to the polar bear, minimal progress on tackling global warming, minimal progress on tackling overfishing, increases in oil-price, increases in civil unrest, heightened alerts for terrorism and – quite separately – heightened alerts for cyberterrorism. Each is presented as a legitimate quantum of information. Yet they are all linked.

Completely independently, often from totally different sources, we also learn about the latest breakthroughs in science, technology and medicine.

# Introduction

Once again, each item is efficiently pre-tagged with its appropriate ID. Each is ready to be conveniently placed into its respective pigeon-hole in our brains. Yet they are all linked.

Not realizing that, we tend to treat the majority of global crises as being – at most - potentially relevant to our wider lives but not necessarily to our everyday work. That is a mistake. We also consider the developments that drive the overall progress of society as being almost the complete opposite to the slew of global crises that too-easily can feel like harbingers of growing chaos – almost as if the two were opposed forces battling each other. That is a serious mistake. On top of everything, we treat any superficially-similar clusters of threats (such as Economic Instability, Global Warming, Food Security or Religious Conflict) as being such major themes in their own right that we do not tend even to have the energy to *want* to understand if an overriding theme encompasses them all. That is a potentially fatal mistake.

## THE BLINDNESS

Despite the way we see our international community, it is not made up of 'isolated trees'. Instead, the branches of a global forest are intertwining at an accelerating pace. As the complexity and interconnections explode, so our collective blindness and inability to see the forest that is really there is becoming increasingly dangerous. It means that those of us within businesses and institutions and governments and social communities miss the linkages. So we miss the worst potential threats. It also means there can be no joined-up thinking. So we not only miss finding effective ways to counter the risks that threaten our organizations' survival, but those actions that we do take are misaligned and bring unintended consequences we can never anticipate.

It is all these mistakes together that now threaten to undermine established industries, major international institutions, and entire countries. They are mistakes that – once made – rapidly become contagious and risk pulling down other industries, institutions and countries. And that is why they are mistakes that increasingly threaten to destabilize not just every organization and community we are part of, but the world economy as a whole. The consequences of each individual mistake would be bad enough. Yet they are all linked too.

# THE REALITY OF GLOBAL CRISES

## THE FOREST

Those who work in mining, oil and energy corporations cannot see that the same mechanism that led to the Arab Spring risks forming a backlash against their own industries – along with many others. Government officials condemning the latest extremist outrage nevertheless cannot see that the reasons behind something like the 9/11 attack on the Twin Towers are very similar to why the general public holds politicians in low esteem and increasingly threatens a backlash against them.

Meanwhile, journalists indulging in a bit of Banker Bashing cannot see that financial institutions got into trouble for many of the same reasons as News Corporation did three years later – and that (along with politicians, the police and even the judiciary) the news media themselves currently risk far greater backlashes in the future. Likewise, Chinese and Indian businesses cannot see the associated causes between depleting water and the threats of structural backlashes that in the medium-term risk undermining their national economies.

And worldwide, key people cannot see that the crucial lesson to be learned from the United Nations' inability to prevent certain species being hunted near extinction is that leaders throughout businesses, institutions and political organizations have a vested interest to rise to the challenge of fundamentally changing how their respective industries and institutions operate – before a major wave of backlashes forces far-less-attractive sanctions upon them anyway.

## THE SEEDS

Thirty years ago, the threats addressed in this book did not yet exist. Even five years ago they had not fully developed. What has happened that has so changed everything since the 1980s? In a phrase: the continued explosion of High-Tech. The seeds of chaos that have now grown into many of the Major Concerns of the modern world have all germinated as a result of this sustained explosion. But then so has almost everything that we are proud of as well. Human progress over the last thirty years has become dominated by the intertwined growth of a handful of deeply-established trends that if you cluster them together you can loosely think of as 'High-Tech' (including not just IT-based products and services but all of the science and technology and medicine and consumer devices and commercial systems that now derive from them).

# Introduction

The reason these trends have become so extremely important is that over several decades they have continued to grow *exponentially* – that is, the better their performance, the faster it has become even better. That sort of sustained explosion is why these High-Tech trends have now outstripped everything else to become the dominant drivers of world progress. And there is a very important implication to that: The transformations between now and 2040 will *not* be equivalent to the changes felt since Ronald Reagan and Margaret Thatcher came to power; they will likely be equivalent to the progress made since Queen Victoria was in power.

## THE REALITY OF OUR GLOBAL FUTURE

If you are interested in exploring in depth the combined impacts of the largely-obscured High-Tech drivers of the world economy (Digitization, Networking, Miniaturization and Simulation), they are fully examined in the short companion-volume to this book – *THE REALITY OF OUR GLOBAL FUTURE: How five unstoppable High-Tech trends will dominate our lives and transform our world* – which acts as a detailed Appendix for those readers who want to understand specifics of how technology is set to dictate the development of the international community over the next thirty years. The book also explains the role of the emerging *fifth* dominant-driver of the world economy: Boundaryless People-Power. It is this trend in particular that is set to trigger an escalation of increasingly powerful global backlashes. Its book reference is ISBN-13: 978-1470115487.

Such an exploding rate of progress is already throwing up turbulence and causing all kinds of frictions. But that instability has very recently started to get worse. In only the last couple of years a new exponential trend has spontaneously emerged from High-Tech that is set to trigger an escalation of increasingly powerful backlashes throughout the world economy. For want of a better term I think of this new trend as Boundaryless People-Power. In 2011 we began to see its embryonic capabilities in the backlashes we call the Arab Spring as well as the lesser backlashes triggered by disclosure of *News of the World* abuses – neither of which have yet even begun to have their full impacts.

The emergence of Boundaryless People-Power is game-changing. This trend has almost unlimited potential. But it is not automatically benign. And it certainly does not tip the world economy toward stability – at least not in the short-to-medium term. In contrast, this new form of amplified feedback throughout the global economic system risks blasting some of our future prospects into destabilized oblivion.

## THE PATH

As I will explain in detail over the first four main chapters of this book, the High-Tech engine that continues to power the ascent of the world economy also necessarily impacts many otherwise-benign trends such as Capitalism, Industrialization, Population and even Religion. It is the cumulative effect of these sustained interactions that is in fact stirring up unintended consequences that we then observe as apparently-independent global crises. *Escalating global crises are a* side-effect *of the immensely beneficial High-Tech on which we all now rely.*

In the two chapters after those, I will show how – partly as a result of its continued central importance – High-Tech itself brings direct risks of crises to the economy. And I will explain how all these seemingly-separate crises are in turn strengthened and proliferated by Globalization – which opens camouflaged interconnections and which channels hidden complexity in ways that are completely unprecedented. In each of those first six chapters of the book I will reveal how various seemingly-distinct global crises all come from similar clashes of 'unstoppable' High-Tech against one or more 'immovable' components of the world economy. Even more importantly, I will also explain the specific approaches that each major sector must take in order to counter the threats that it particularly faces.

However, in the seventh and final chapter of the book I will show why ultimately all of these categories of global crisis *need* to be considered as one – why, if you like, this is one book and not six. The overriding reason is that the very best approach to avoiding all of the different kinds of crisis is remarkably similar across each of the six clusters. Whatever the specific primary causes of a given escalating threat of major destabilization – and whether that threat is to corporations, major institutions or governments –

# Introduction

all of them need to realign their operations in ways that allow them to address head-on the *root-causes* of systemic backlashes.

Crucially, the basic path they need to follow to achieve that is common to all of them. Inevitably it takes them outside their conventional scope of activities. It also takes them outside their comfort zones. But for genuine leaders that has always been the case. And with this path there is the incentive that, as we near its end, we at last have a chance to emerge from the forest.

# CAPITALISM CRISES overview

Important elements of Capitalism – such as competition – nevertheless cause increasingly dangerous lack of control across the world economy and require Unelected Responsibility as a counter-measure

- Escalating financial crises are inevitable because deeply-established systemic-threats in the banking system remain unchanged and largely unchangeable

- Unrelenting competition has addicted modern corporations to change initiatives of which 70% fail causing further damage such as change-fatigue – which makes it hard to avoid backlashes

- Unintended major distortions of perception caused by how the media have to report stories and interact with governments are warping political control

- Widespread misinterpretation of how competition optimizes the world economy risks crucially important long-term solutions being irretrievably lost

- Capitalism crises need UNELECTED RESPONSIBILITY – corporations fulfilling a duty of due care over communities they impact

*Threats of backlashes to: BANKING, NEWS-MEDIA and POLITICS*

*FINANCIAL BACKLASHES...*
*...PROGRESSIVE POWERLESSNESS...*
*...MEDIA DISTORTION...*
*...DISCONNECTED POLITICS...*

# CAPITALISM

# CRISES

# THE UNSOLVED PUZZLE OF THE BANKING CRISES

The realities of modern banking encourage individual chronic short-termism with little regard for long-term consequences or impacts on others

JUST AS WE were daring to think it was safe again – another tsunami of global financial backlashes has begun to rear over us. We have already experienced the credit-crunched Great Recession started in 2008. We are in the midst of the contagious Sovereign Debt Crises within the Eurozone. We will soon inevitably be engulfed by many more global economic backlashes. The fundamental reason is that – as I will explain – deeply-established systemic threats in the banking system remain unchanged and largely unchangeable.

Meanwhile, and apparently unrelated, in mid-2011 the News Media began to suffer a backlash triggered by the *News of the World* phone-hacking scandal. Already as a result, what was once the biggest-selling English language newspapers in the world has been shut down, the takeover of BSkyB (the largest pay-TV broadcaster in the UK) has been halted, the unquestioned-power of News Corporation (the world's second-largest media conglomerate after Disney) has been weakened, the roles of the press, the police and politicians have been brought into question, key establishment figures have resigned, some have been arrested.

And yet this is only the beginning of a slew of backlashes set to hit the press, broadcast and on-line media. As well as politics. And the police. Phone-hacking was merely the symptom of something far more deeply embedded into how the media work and their relationship to the Establishment. That complex interconnection applies worldwide. And, as with banking, it is extremely strongly reinforced. These two topical sets of backlashes seem as good a place as any to begin revealing how our deeply-interconnected world *really* works – and how entire industries and major institutions unintentionally create the very conditions that then inexorably lead to a debilitating succession of backlashes.

# Systemic threats in banking

## LEGACIES OF ENRON

Throughout the 1990s the large energy company Enron Corporation was praised as being the most innovative company in the USA. This was certainly true in as far as a tremendous amount of innovation was channeled into creative accounting. After Enron went bankrupt in 2001, its core management practices were found to have been little more than institutionalized fraud on a very grand scale.

Just after the disclosures regarding Enron's collapse I was warning the business community generally – and banking top-executives in particular – that, based on what I had seen over the previous several years, although the ethical issues of Enron were extreme, its lack of control over how it operated was not. In addition, I advised them, such lack of control carried inevitable and growing risks of unintended consequences that would eventually hurt them – and with them, everybody else. The general response to me from banking CEOs and their colleagues in 2002 onward was: 'Don't worry.'

Many financial institutions attempted to placate me with reassurances that those sorts of risks were now regulated by the stringent requirements of the newly imposed 'Sarbanes-Oxley Act' (or SOX, as it became known) that, in response to public concerns over scandals like Enron, was forced by regulators onto all financial corporations worldwide that were doing business with the USA. What is more, supposedly even more reassuringly, in 2004 the 'Basel II Accord' required banks around the world to keep more money in reserve – as a safeguard against bankruptcy – the more risk they undertook. 'Everything is under control' I was consistently told.

But SOX primarily focused on the details of how banking processes operated rather than on the big picture. And for Basel II to work, financiers needed to know the full risks they ran. Six years after SOX, and four years after the Accord, the financial markets collapsed because nearly all the players found themselves exposed to completely unknown levels of risk that originally emanated from suspect loans issued in the USA. That is not what anyone should call control.

As I will now explain, in many ways it was inevitable. As was what happened next. Although state leaders vowed that they would humble the 'greedy bankers' who had taken such 'irresponsible risks' with other people's money, only months after taxpayers bailed the banks out with packages that will take more than a generation to pay back, I learned that the new acronym on Wall Street and The City was B.A.B. – Bonuses Are Back. What was going on?

## BOOM AND BUST

The experience of the last several centuries suggests that unfettered capitalism can lead to huge wealth in the short term but that after each boom inevitably comes a bust. However, when analyzing history it is very difficult to compare like with like. Commentators tend to reel off a series of supposed examples that start with Tulip Mania in 17th-century Holland and the South Sea bubble in the 18th century, build up to the Great Depression following the collapse of Wall Street in 1929, and then offer the ultimate clincher of the Global Credit Crunch that followed the bankruptcy of Lehman Brothers in 2008. However, apart from the Boom and Bust pattern of each example, they are actually each very different when you analyze anything but the superficial drivers of people's behavior. And that means that the ultimate causes were importantly different also.

The simple answer is that the same factor that put the financial industry at such risk in the first place was what made it bounce back so quickly. And that same factor will make the financial sector extremely difficult to change in the future – whatever well-intentioned politicians believe. The fundamental driver of all these three circumstances is buried in something I observed throughout the financial sector from the mid-1980s to the present day.

Throughout this frenetic time, the previously rather traditional banking industry adopted management fads with increasing gusto as it moved from being boring and conservative to priding itself as being dynamic and aggressive. Radical deregulation under Reagan and Thatcher, reinforced by growing Eastern markets, and ultimately powered by High-Tech, led to a 24-hour frenzy of complex activity that few of even the bankers' newly-hired PhDs really understood.

In some ways banking became over-innovated – its slickness was not always matched by wisdom. But no one really cared. After all, everything was so busy and so successful, and it seemed like there had been so much change. Whereas in one very-important way – there had in fact hardly been any. The Legacy Effects in the industry (that is, heavily-reinforced ways of doing things left-over from the past) were very much deeper than most top bankers would accept. And the backlashes from these aspects of capitalism were about to bring the global economy to its knees.

## UNWRITTEN RULES OF MODERN BANKING

The cause was an apparently-minor aspect of banking that never really changed over twenty-five years. For nearly all high-flying bankers, their immediate boss was the only person of any real importance to them because it was he or she (nearly always he) who effectively decided their enormity of bonus – and defined their chances of a continued highly-paid career. And how did the boss in practice make those decisions? Despite what Human Resources claimed, in reality he almost exclusively based them on the high-flyer's clearly-visible personal contribution to achieving *the boss's* short-term financial performance targets for that year.

It seems almost irrelevant. But – even on its own – that simple combination of factors would have been sufficient to lead to the consistent pattern of 'unwritten rules' most bankers all slavishly followed: Keep your boss happy, Stand out from the crowd, Avoid association with failure, Achieve your immediate financial targets at all costs, Protect your own turf, and Do not worry about anything else.

That combination of advice – which conceptually a successful banker might give to a very close friend joining the business – is in no way unique to banking, but those particular unwritten rules can be *very* strong there. And in every case where they are, that blend leads to chronic short-termism with no real regard for long-term consequences, individualism over teamwork, and hardly any understanding (or interest) in the impacts of an individual's actions outside their own department.

*Of course* those sorts of deep-seated unwritten rules tempted high-flyers to get carried away with risky products like Sub-Prime Loans (or rogue trading or breaching ethical guidelines). And, as I know from innumerable top-level discussions across the banking industry at the time, *of course* the management teams of the banks – long before the credit crunch – were fully aware of the chronic short-termism and individualism and insularity endemic in their industry.

# CAPITALISM CRISES

## SHORT-TERM INDIVIDUAL INSULARITY

The side-effects of the unwritten rules in most banks tend to reinforce each other. For instance, if you are trying to *Stand out of the crowd* as well as *Protect your own turf* then genuine *Teamwork* is going to have an uphill struggle. But that side-effect is itself reinforced by *Keep your boss happy* because your boss will not want you 'wasting your time' helping to grow another boss's area. In fact, there may not really be any reason for you to care about long-term impacts of your actions outside your own department at all – whether they are beneficial or not.

But – despite what business analysts and politicians and news reporters said immediately after the 2008 crash – the specific reward systems themselves were never the root cause of why everything went so wrong. The reward systems were a symptom of a far deeper issue. The fundamental problem across financial-services as a whole was *why* the systems were as they were. In reality, the puzzle that explains the whole banking backlash can be unlocked with the answer to one simple riddle: Why did the reward systems never fundamentally get changed despite the shortcomings the top teams knew that those systems brought?

# REASONS ANY SENSIBLE BANK TRIES TO KEEP THINGS AS THEY ARE

## Although within the industry its shortcomings are well-recognized, on balance it suits banks to leave things as they are

THE BASIC REASON was this: It seemed safer *not* to tamper. Otherwise banks would have fundamentally (rather than just superficially, as in fact happened) overhauled their industry's reward systems just as they changed almost everything else in their Management Fad wardrobe. Prior to the near-financial-meltdown, I held one-on-one confidential discussions about this issue with hundreds of banking executives around the world, with every conversation taking around a couple of hours. Once each banker opened up, they tended to be highly consistent with what their colleagues in other banks also said – so it seems legitimate to share the overall *pattern* of what they said even though of course the detail must always remain strictly confidential. A fly-on-the-wall during any one of these secret discussions would have heard something like this:

*'Yes, successful traders can easily earn bonuses worth hundreds of times the annual salary of a qualified nurse, but look how much more that trader makes for our firm. That means they're a tremendously valuable asset. And if we don't pay them these figures, then our competition will. It's not an 'obscene' bonus. It's market forces.*

*'What's more, even if none of our immediate competitors were willing to pay those amounts, even if no one in New York, London or Tokyo was willing to pay those amounts, our top people would simply move to one of the growing financial centers that aspire to make it onto the top-table and those institutions would be willing to pay them almost anything to get their services. And to stop others from having access to them. So we put up with the arrogance, and we treat them like stars, and they make us a fortune.*

*'Outsiders, who don't understand why we do what we do, complain. But ultimately they're complaining because they don't earn what we do. They're jealous. But because that seems petty, they disguise their jealousy as*

*outraged righteous indignation. They start talking about Fairness – not for us, of course, but everyone else. Outsiders who comprehend what's going on – including those few politicians who actually understand macroeconomics rather than just spend their lives talking about it – won't do anything dramatic. Because if they do, they know they may kill the golden goose.*

*'And they can't ever risk doing that because they know perfectly well that they, their country, the whole global economy – utterly depend on us for their continued prosperity. OK, however we posture to politicians, we'll never actually leave Wall Street, the City or Kabuto-cho* [the financial center in Tokyo] *– but push us too hard and we will very seriously reconsider just how much taxable work we choose to do there rather than maybe Hong Kong or Geneva or somewhere in India...'*

## INDIVIDUAL INVULNERABILITY

That is only the tip of the iceberg – reasonably visible to anyone who looks carefully. But the unwritten rules go very much deeper than that. Everyone in the banking industry knows how the game is played. It can be a very tough life and someone does not remain a high-flyer for long unless they really aspire to climb. If they ever manage to join a financial-industries firm, young entrants quickly recognize that many of those who earn the mega-salaries do not often come across as touchy-feely team players. Impressionable new recruits also soon notice that if someone can take major risks and pull them off then they not only make a personal fortune but they become heroes. And the industry loves heroes.

Although someone will usually be fully accountable for failure (unless they can spread the blame) in reality there is usually only an upside to taking risks. After all, it is not their own money they risk losing. So the worst that is likely to happen is that they merely lose their job – and in normal times there are usually a lot of equally-highly-paid jobs to jump to. The best outcome is that they get filthy rich while they are still young enough to enjoy it. Even if they cross the line and indulge in some shady practices, and even if they get caught, the bank is hardly going to want to publicize the fact. Unless the regulator catches them and tries to make a public example of them, the bank will try to keep things quiet – just like they do when a computer hacker breaches their IT systems. They will probably even offer a bit of a sweetener so that their ex-colleague does not start talking to the wrong people. They might even give them a good reference to help them on their way.

## CAUGHT IN A CORROSIVE SYSTEM

It is important to stress something here. Although it may currently be unfashionable to say, most senior bankers in my experience are fundamentally good people. The vast majority are not unduly greedy – although they usually take full advantage of what is readily on offer. With very few exceptions, they are certainly not corrupt. But they are caught in a rather corrosive industry. There may be some bankers who throughout their careers have never acted in any of the negative ways I have just mentioned. But I know from my personal knowledge of all those strictly-confidential discussions, there are also many bankers around the world who at best throughout their careers have felt strong pressures to 'give in to the dark side' and at worst, upon occasion, succumbed.

To be realistic about it, so might have most members of the general public had they been lucky enough and clever enough to be in the bankers' shoes. The problem is not really the bankers. Nor even 'the system' within each bank. The problem is the *overall* financial system. That system stretches far wider than most people assume. And – despite all the new technology – it is a very *old* system.

## A BANK IS A BANK IS A BANK

In addition to the discussions I have personally held with bankers, I have frequently been brought in as an expert advisor to review and help synthesize the findings of confidential documented-discussions that I did not personally attend. Combined with my first-hand knowledge, this allows me to draw conclusions from more than a thousand highly-private and detailed discussions with bankers across the globe. The findings are all remarkably consistent. The banking world has become truly globalized.

That means that the legacy of the past is deep because the policies and processes and expectations and industry norms and all the unwritten rules that follow from them are inextricably interconnected like messy spaghetti. Regrettably therefore, overhauling the banking industry is going to be very much more difficult than many political leaders and financial correspondents believe.

# CAPITALISM CRISES

It will take far more than just attempts at 'tougher regulation' or 'caps on bonuses'. Indeed, when the full dynamics operating on banking high-flyers are analyzed in detail, even ensuring that bonuses are paid in stock-options rather than cash (the preferred solution proposed by many politicians) will *not* overcome the bias in the financial system toward individual short-term insular high-risk behavior – mainly because the assumption of most of the risk-takers is that their bank's stock will on balance go up in value because of the risks they take. If you feel that way then being paid in Options is, almost literally, like money in the bank.

As a result of the major hurdles to changing the banks, there will be occasion after occasion when the global banking industry, despite any coordinated international attempts to curb it, will appear to revert back to its old ways of doing things. That should not be a surprise. As I will now explain, the reality is that the reinforcements for those old ways stretch far outside the banking industry itself.

# WHY ESCALATING GLOBAL FINANCIAL CRISES ARE INEVITABLE

Governments and regulators have little freedom to change the banking system without risking triggering alternative financial crises themselves

TO SEE HOW broadly the problem reaches, you need only consider why no one in posts of authority was clamoring to put a global brake on the financial-services industry even as late as 2007 when US-property prices were already dropping and so putting at risk those 'sub-prime' loans deliberately made to borrowers least capable of paying them back. The reason was that while things were going well – just as so many bankers had already told me – no one wanted anything to risk 'killing the golden goose'. Naturally the whole of the financial sector did not want things to change. What is more, even if an in-house PhD did have the courage confidentially to tell a top executive, 'I think our collateralized debt obligations may be vulnerable,' what was the firm expected to do?

After all, I never found any top banking executives that actually understood the immensely complex mathematics behind some of the massive investments their banks were making. So while everyone else (other banks, regulators, rating agencies) seemed happy, it was very tempting to assume any internally-raised concerns were unduly alarmist. And even if they were not, if a CEO told the public that some of the firm's investments looked riskier than previously thought – the firm's share-price would drop. And the CEO would likely lose his job.

At the same time, the financial regulators were not trying to get things to change either. On both sides of the Atlantic they had been filled with relatively dutiful people who had been instructed by their respective governments to regulate with a light touch – because that is what most experts genuinely thought was best for the capitalist system. No one had encouraged the regulators to focus on the big picture of how the overall system was operating. It was another classic example of 'not seeing the forest for the trees'. Instead of trying to decode the hidden interlinkages across the world economy, regulators were instead preoccupied with the detailed elements of individual institutions specified by SOX and Basel II.

## COLLATERALIZED DEBT OBLIGATIONS

Prior to the Credit Crunch, CDOs had become a very fashionable type of financial product for big banks to invest in. The trouble was that only a very few PhDs really understood why CDOs were supposed to work. The reason they were so incomprehensible was that they wrapped together lots of investments (some risky and some not) in a statistically very complex way that supposedly reduced risk almost to nothing. In practice, rather than getting rid of the risk it *spread it around*. When house prices dropped throughout the USA, large numbers of home owners defaulted on risky mortgages ('sub-prime loans') that had been wrapped into CDOs. So instead of affecting only a few US mortgage providers, the drop in US house prices almost pulled down the whole global economy.

Meanwhile, the Credit Rating Agencies – relied on to indicate how safe or risky a given investment was – found themselves in a position that made it far more difficult to remain indifferent than everyone assumed. Banks could shop around and try to play one rating agency off against another in order to get a Triple-A rating for the latest financial product so as to reassure the market that the product was very safe. But only the rating agency that the bank chose – typically the one that would give the highest rating – earned a huge fee, in an industry in which earning huge fees for the firm translated into earning huge personal bonuses. With the best will in the world, that created a potential conflict of interest and an inappropriate pressure (whether or not individuals gave into it) to 'upgrade' products that did not actually deserve it.

It was not just the bankers and regulators and rating agencies that did not want to risk disrupting the capitalist system. Neither did the governments who were benefitting from the banking industry's taxes, jobs and growth. Nor did any of those top people in various governments who aspired to become highly-paid advisors or Board members to financial institutions later in their careers. Nor did the hundreds of millions of consumers benefitting from easy loans from the banks. Everybody went along for the ride. And ultimately that is what caused the initial crisis. It is what later led members of the general public to riot in countries such as Greece because they were being forced to take extreme 'austerity measures' without having previously understood just how much they and their country had in fact been living far beyond their means. And it is what continues to risk the future sustainability of the Eurozone (the second largest economy in the world) – and with it the stability of the global banking system.

Such problems are deeply embedded. In 2007, banks around the world with hidden exposure to Sub-Prime loans (mortgages to people with poor credit ratings) found themselves threatened when US house-prices fell and borrowers could not repay their debts, leading to the Credit Crunch of 2008 as banks cut back on lending. Three years later, many of them found themselves exposed to Sovereign Debt (money borrowed by national governments, in part to survive 2008) of countries that might now not be able to pay back all they had borrowed. Indeed, in August 2011 even the mighty USA lost its AAA credit rating for the first time ever – because they were close to political gridlock. It is only a matter of time before the threat of a major national default or, for instance, some form of reconstitution of the Eurozone, leads to another severe 21$^{st}$-century Credit Crunch.

After all, the structure of the Eurozone is inherently unstable: To operate successfully it requires far greater homogeneity; but its component parts are fundamentally (and, for many purposes, usefully) diverse. One size – for example, of Austerity Measures – cannot fit all. And to force such a fit would anyway be undemocratic, take much too long and would sacrifice too much national diversity. Risk of failure of the Eurozone as it is currently constituted is deeply embedded into its fundamental makeup, and has been ever since political idealism overrode disciplined pragmatism and allowed too many diverse countries to join. No subsequent 'treaty' can remove the legacy of deep inconsistencies built up since 1998.

As things stand, worldwide economic backlashes will continue. The inevitable consequence of the fully-global hidden interconnections across the financial system – tying in, as they do, every one of us – is that changing the future of banking by breaking the deeply entrenched written and unwritten rules of the bankers will prove a massive undertaking. It will not just involve breaking the rules of the banking industry. It will necessarily involve breaking the rules for everyone else as well.

## Entrenched Financial Systems

That is an incredibly difficult thing to do because those types of entrenched legacies last, and the whole of the ancient capitalist system is deeply intertwined with the legacies buried within the global banking system itself. The majority of already-old organizations within that industry have gone through so many changes, mergers, rebrandings and reorganizations that their deepest inner-workings are now so entangled that they are largely locked in position and, unseen, keep corrupting further attempts at change – diminishing still further the control of bank leaders and politicians. Many of the overarching risks that caused the 2008 crisis still remain buried and are immensely difficult to change.

As things stand, another global economic crisis is inevitable because nothing fundamentally has really changed in the complex inner-workings of banking. Some of the most influential unwritten-rules remain unaltered. Similarly, despite changes in political parties and policies, large numbers of governments in massive economies from the USA downward remain addicted to state borrowing. Tax revenues are not sufficient to buy the services (or, less charitably, the votes) that politicians want, so they borrow – conceptually by taxing future generations. National debts grow so large that the interest payments risk escalating out of control. And any future major draw on finances, for instance caused by another world economic crisis, threatens state insolvency.

Those kinds of Legacy Effects are so very deeply entrenched and entangled with the whole capitalist system that too-dramatic a change would result in major unintended side-effects that could themselves bring the system to its knees again. So no one is likely to risk interfering too much. Political rhetoric about 'banker bashing' will not be allowed to go too far. The planned implementation of Basel III around the end of 2012 will not in practice be allowed fundamentally to change how the markets work. That is what the top bankers assume. That is why they believe they maintain a degree of immunity to government intervention. That is why further worldwide financial backlashes remain inevitable. And that is why, despite everything, Bonuses Are Back.

# Systemic threats in banking

## 1. WHY SYSTEMIC RISKS FROM BANKING TEND TO CONTINUE

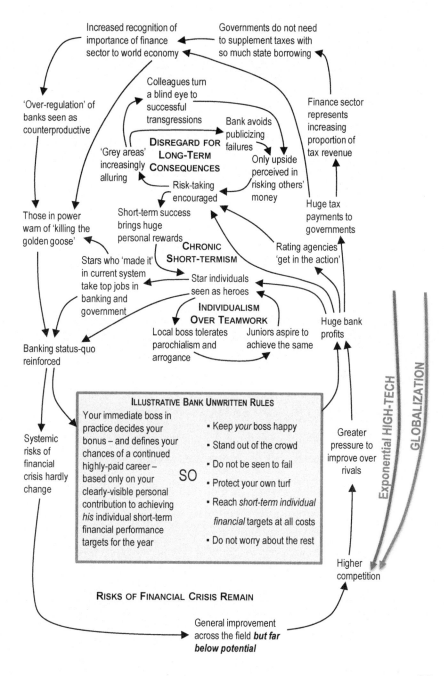

# CHANGING FASTER THAN THE COMPETITION

## Driven by international markets, today's corporations necessarily compete on being able to change faster and more effectively than their rivals

VERY IMPORTANT LESSONS can be drawn from Banking: The deeply-embedded pattern of behavior that over time unintentionally built the unrelenting backlashes we are experiencing today has little to do with Finance. Instead, as I will show over the following two subchapters, the behavior-pattern is a basic component of *Capitalism* – although usually it brings very positive outcomes. That fact alone carries major implications given that the world economy is inherently a capitalist system. After these subchapters I will show how exactly the same dynamic as in Banking has also caused the Media backlashes we are starting to experience.

To start, we will go back to basics so you can understand just why it is that, since the 1980s, High-Tech-Capitalism has been building hidden but increasingly dangerous threats of global crises.

### RUNNING UP THE 'DOWN' ESCALATOR

To make sense of what is going on, it is important to see the hidden reality of how capitalism actually works below the surface. Despite the way their political ideologies are normally portrayed, in terms of system-dynamics the fundamental difference between the reality of capitalism and socialism (and even more so, communism) is not so much 'who owns the means of production' but more 'who is encouraged to compete with whom'.

When the fundamental drivers of behavior in the rival economic systems are analyzed, it is the attitude to *competition* that really differentiates them. Even in the diluted forms of capitalism that most nations have these days adopted (and that even nominally-communist China is exploring), competitive behavior is fundamental to maintaining

# Addiction to change

the global economy. And it is that competition that has hidden implications that have been building in impact for the last thirty years.

By the end of the 1970s, capitalist competition was spawning whole new industries in electronics, computing and communications, as well as whole new industrialized nations such as Japan, Taiwan and South Korea. Meanwhile, people in the street were typically more knowledgeable, better off, and had higher expectations than ever before. All these transformations began to feed on themselves and by the mid-1980s, whether they knew it or not (and most of them did not), companies around the world were starting to compete on their ability to change and innovate faster and better than their rivals.

In publically-traded companies, the need to keep quarterly-results looking good for the stock-markets increasingly drove many top executives into an insatiable quest for instant gratification. Internal reward systems tended to follow suit, and much of Big Business progressively slipped into chronic short-termism. Management Consulting came into its own as Management itself became something of a fashion industry – with ambitious executives adopting one new fad after another as they chased after the elusive goal of sustained competitive advantage. But every time they changed something, so did the best of their competitors. That was when many executives first began to experience the symptoms of a global economy 'running up the Down escalator'.

By the 1990s the international business press was publishing around five new books *a day* on how modern organizations should operate, and even the public sector began to apply the techniques that were already so fashionable in the private sector. 'World-class management' was soon seen as synonymous with 'world-class management of competitive capitalist enterprises'. And that meant: Never-Ending Change.

Today it is what everyone takes for granted. Without us ever quite registering when it first started, we are all now increasingly subject to an inexorable pressure for superior lifestyle, greater freedom, more choice, protected rights, individual development, better housing, safer neighborhoods, improved education. And everything must be smaller, cheaper, grander – and above all – fast. Whether the innovation is national, multinational or global, and whether it is in healthcare, policing, education, banking reform, new products, new services or new technology – change has become the addiction of choice for the 21$^{st}$ century. And no addiction is without side-effects.

# CAPITALISM CRISES

## MANAGEMENT BY FAD

Early-1980s clothes fashion only had remnants of Punk competing with a transition from flared jeans and platform shoes to the New-Romantic look. Corporate Fashion in contrast had expert systems, TQM, Small is Beautiful, the Paperless Office, robots, quality circles, flexible automation, time-based competition and computer-integrated manufacturing. Just as with clothes – where each season there is a 'new' color – so it became with business as it adopted the same 'looks silly, looks cool, looks so last year' sequence that society adopts with any other fad. From the mid-'80s onward, each year there was a different word to add to an idea to make it seem impressive.

The sequence of fashion-accessory words from 1987 to 1993 went: '87 Quality, then in '88 the word became Excellence, then in '89 High-Performance, then in 1990 it became Team (and those yuppies who had been partying too hard and could not remember what year it was hedged their bets by referring to High-Performance Teams). Then in '91 it became Culture followed in '92 by Change (which, like wearing black, remains a safe bet). In contrast, 1993's word – Paradigm – definitely does not. At the same time as High-Tech shifted Capitalism into overdrive, the public-sector followed the private-sector's lead. Anyone, anywhere, who aspired to reach upper-management learned to become a fashion chameleon.

Each year a high-flyer could passionately love the Next Big Thing – and afterwards never be seen to use it again because it was not fashionable any more: Empowerment, Re-engineering, Downsizing, Right-sizing, Restructuring, Value Chain, Core-competencies, Outsourcing, Centralization, Decentralization, Balanced Scorecard, Enterprise Systems, Learning Organizations, Scenario Planning, Customer Relationship Management, Employee Relationship Management, Innovation, and then (in the exciting build-up to the new millennium) dot.com and e- everything followed by Pure Play, followed by Bricks and Clicks, followed by "I never believed all the hype anyway..." Having had their fingers burned, leaders began the 21st century with a 'return to basics' – but then quickly got ardently excited again about still-newer ways of competing ever-better.

# THE OPEN-SECRET THAT 70% OF CHANGE-INITIATIVES FAIL

## Lack of sufficient control means that most major change initiatives fail, leading to progressive change-fatigue and difficulties avoiding backlashes

ORGANIZATIONAL CHANGE-ADDICTION places Capitalism – and with it, many of the fundamental structures that underpin the global economy – under threat. Unlike for most of the last century, those risks do not arise from rival ideologies such as Communism or from a widespread rejection of the 'unfairness' or 'materialism' of an unplanned economy. On the contrary, for the foreseeable future most of the international community most of the time will strive to make themselves and their families financially better off than when they started. The collapse of communism as an ideology is *not* the type of threat that capitalism itself now faces.

Instead, it is the banking backlash almost two decades later – caused by the deeply-established reasons we have already examined – that best exemplifies how High-Tech-Capitalism is at greatest risk. That is because many potential backlashes are being made far worse *because of* capitalism's incessant change attempts. They are, paradoxically, making it far harder to change course and *avoid* future capitalism crises.

What is happening is a consequence of the ceaseless stream of change initiatives forced by modern competition. They are generating a form of Change-Fatigue. That phenomenon is not so much to do with people getting tired and stressed – though that can certainly happen. It is more to do with 'fatigue' in the same sense as 'metal fatigue'. In other words, it is the organizations themselves – rather than just the people within them – that are starting to suffer. They can no longer change as readily as they could before – even to avoid backlashes.

### LOSING CONTROL

The underlying reason is something that continues to astound me despite having spent twenty-five years analyzing the obscured reasons for it: Even

# CAPITALISM CRISES

within a very tightly-managed organization where the leader is apparently in control (say an efficient government department or a small privately-owned business) it can nevertheless sometimes prove *utterly impossible to make a change* even within just that group of people.

Many assume that such a relatively controlled environment ought to be trivial to alter. It is not as if the leader is trying to change the behavior of people outside the community – like an invading army tries to, or a business selling a new product to the general public tries to. The challenge is merely sustainably to modify the behavior of those people who are very largely under the thumb of the leader. This should be really, really basic stuff. The leader is in charge. The leader makes the rules about how people can act. It seems reasonable to expect that the leader could change those rules and so change behavior accordingly. Only it does not work that way.

## AVOIDING CHANGE

I have lost track of the number of Chairmen who have put on their Wise Voice and told me that 'people do not like change'. But that is actually a fallacy. In fact, in many ways the human species has only thrived *because* people were predisposed to change their behavior in response to things like ice-ages, animal extinctions and – in the last ten thousand years – major social innovations. From all the detailed analyses I have been invited to conduct, it seems far more accurate to say that: People do not like changes in which on balance they end up worse off, but they *do* like changes – even frequent changes – in which *on balance* they feel they are better off (even if on a few things they consider they have lost out).

The modern corporation is the easiest example to demonstrate this. A business organization provides the near-perfect conditions to persuade members of that community to do what their chief wants. Corporations have evolved to that end. The leader has no direct control outside the corporation (there the firm has to rely on Marketing and Advertising) but inside the corporation the circumstances are about as good as they get. Certainly, as I highlight in the subchapter on *Impossible challenges that governments nonetheless accept* (starting on page 383), they are far better

38

conditions than for a politician trying to get the general population to behave in a new way. Yet despite such ideal circumstances, the success rate of major change initiatives in companies is abysmal.

There is still something of a conspiracy of silence to the general public about the high failure rate of change programs in businesses. That silence has been maintained since the early 1990s. Over that same time period I have analyzed innumerable companies to explore the issue, as have many other change-experts. We all kept coming up with the same findings, namely that, in the judgment of the executives responsible, more than *two-thirds of all corporate change initiatives fail.*

That is staggeringly high when you think about it. But it also shows how difficult it is in practice to change things. If more than two out of three attempts fail within a tightly managed modern business – think how very much harder it is to influence those people outside the company in the relative chaos of the real world. The vast majority of all the attempts at significant change worldwide – fail.

But each time they fail, they leave a legacy. Certainly people are often left that bit more demoralized and cynical. But it is far more than that. For example, a bonus system maybe gets changed to encourage team behavior, but it is then out of alignment with other rewards (possibly promotion) that encourage people to stand out as individuals. Likewise, perhaps the targets for one part of the organization are successfully changed, but another department carries on pursuing its old goals – which are actually in conflict with the new ones. Maybe a new boss arrives every few years, but each one inherits the leftovers of partly-completed and often-inconsistent projects kicked off by a series of predecessors. Each of these echoes from the past creates unrecognized Legacy Effects that potentially disrupt any new initiative in unexpected ways.

As a result, even though leaders try to make changes, their organizations just do not react as expected. And the more the archaeological bands of failed change-initiatives accumulate, the worse they unpredictably disrupt things, and so the harder it becomes to make yet another major change. *That* is the sort of Change-Fatigue that is building up in today's global systems. Until the last few decades, major changes usually had time to work their way through a given organization. Inconsistencies got clarified. Mistakes got rectified. Gaps got filled. But given the modern pace of change-initiatives, there is not enough time. And as layer upon layer of unresolved misalignments builds up between leaders and their respective communities, so the corporate, political, religious and institutional organizations that make up society are slowly slipping out of control – just as we discovered with the banks in 2007-8. And that lack of control makes it increasingly impossible to avoid even *anticipated* global crises.

## REASONS FOR FAILURE

Legacy Effects arise when 'old' ways of doing things get tied into masses of other ways of doing additional things – which makes it hard to change any one of them. That is the main reason behind the 70% failure-rate for corporate change initiatives. Throughout history, leaders have tended massively to underestimate the power that Legacy Effects have to thwart attempts at transformation. Sometimes the change the leader attempts is at least 'possible' but simply is not seen as credible. An example may turn out to be the banking community changing its reward system to encourage longer-term more-responsible performance – coming as it does from those who climbed to the top by being individualistic risk-taking heroes. It is rather like parents attempting to counsel their teenage children against behaving in ways the children know their parents did themselves at that age.

On other occasions a new initiative just does not 'fit' with the attitudes of the individuals that have to adopt it. Many of the attempts to overhaul government departments and state-owned corporations using techniques from the private sector fall into this category. These approaches never reach their potential because it is a bit like bright children being sent to good schools that simply do not fit their personalities and learning styles. Everyone gets disenchanted.

And finally there are those initiatives that – even though no one may realize it – are in reality impossible to enact. A staid and caring charity that wants to keep all its existing volunteers but become 'lean, responsive and dynamic' would be an example. It may be a great strategy, just not for that community. It is similar to a young teenager aspiring to be a professional basketball player or ballet dancer but just not having the genetic makeup to grow into the right shape.

# Addiction to change

## ORGANIZATIONAL STRAIGHTJACKETS

Whatever they tell their shareholders, or electorate, or congregation, or trustees, modern communities are inherently far less manageable than their leaders would like to think or often care publically to admit. Stability and incremental change are long gone, replaced by turbulence and never-ending change. As a result of that, modern leaders face tremendous problems in achieving what they want. And avoiding what threatens to pull them down.

Of course there are still a few leaders left – including a disproportionate number in governments – who cannot accept that they have far less control than their official title suggests, so they carry on optimistically launching new initiatives with little ability to predict or influence success. And then those initiatives cause mini-backlashes that – because they are delayed, or show up in different areas, or are so complex – are treated as new problems in their own right that demand a slew of additional disconnected initiatives. In exactly that way, as mentioned at the start of this book, many of the global economy's apparently 'unrelated' backlashes are anything but.

Fortunately, such risky leadership is in the minority. Behind closed doors, most leaders that I meet readily admit to me they find it impossible to keep the different aspects of their community sufficiently in harmony. And a substantial number of the leaders privately acknowledge that they no longer really feel in control – even though they cannot publically admit the fact. Around the world, the goals of one government department end up in conflict with the needs of society as a whole. The ways volunteers interact do not fit with how a charity's computing system works. Informal rewards and peer-pressure in a Trade Union discourage members doing the very things that might help company bosses protect their workers' jobs. New overhauls in a nationalized industry are bogged down in the residue of old culture. And everyone, everywhere, is beginning to feel the pressure of 'initiative overload'.

Most leaders, in every field, are all-too-aware of how tough it is getting – and many are understandably feeling a little stressed. Never-ending change is, by definition, an on-going task. And for some large organizations it is already becoming sufficiently grueling that it is hard to imagine how the current pace can be sustained for many more decades. Since the 1980s, the competitive element that is inherent in capitalism has led to such levels of short-termism and change-addiction that – enabled by

High-Tech and strongly encouraged by the financial markets – leaders have steadily overloaded their ability to remain on top of things. As you will see later in the chapter on Population Crises, it is increasingly the fastest emerging economies (such as India and selectively-capitalist China) that are *most* at risk of cumulative change-fatigue and the relative uncontrollability and risk of backlash that accompanies it. But already, throughout the world economy, supercharged competition driven by High-Tech-Capitalism has taken its toll.

Nowhere is that straightjacket of Legacy Effects currently more visible than in bankers' and politicians' inability to overhaul the financial system that underpins the world economy. Those unrelenting backlashes will continue. Yet far less obvious – although equally dangerous – is the lack of political control that has arisen from the hidden reality of how supercharged competition in the Media industry works. Over the next three subchapters I will show you just how that has resulted in the first waves of what is set to become another unstoppable tide of crises.

## 2. WHY SYSTEMIC RISKS OF BUSINESS BACKLASHES ESCALATE

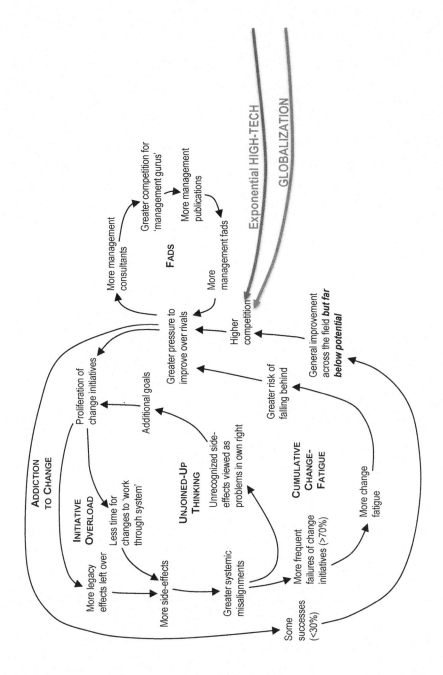

# Rolling News and the Unintended Distortions It Creates

## Developments like 24/7 Rolling News inadvertently cause gross misrepresentation of the true balance of what is happening in the world

UNINTENDED MAJOR DISTORTIONS of perception caused by how the media report stories and interact with governments are warping political control. It is far from obvious because, once again, it is hard to see the forest for the trees – complex interacting chains of cause and effect stretch across the apparently-separate realms of News reporting, government strategy, private investigation and even policing.

I should say from the start, this is not (just) a story of selective corruption. It is *far* more complex than that. Indeed, even if no journalist, politician, PI or police officer anywhere around the world ever does anything dubious ever again – we still have a major problem. The reason is that, largely unrecognized, the deliberate competition that capitalism encourages is in fact steadily and inevitably undermining the judgment of politicians, business heads and social leaders, as well as all of us – the general public. And that is because as human beings we all subconsciously build up an intuition of how the world works based on what we observe every day of our lives.

## OUR IMAGE OF THE WORLD

Throughout nearly all of history, people have almost exclusively learned from their interactions with those around them. But these days, most insights about how the world works are learned via News Media. That is building to be a serious problem because even if we only pay attention to 'serious' News – not that it is always easy to distinguish anyway – what we learn does not correspond with reality as much as we assume.

It might be expected that such misrepresentation would only to be true in those parts of the world where there is state censorship. But it actually applies everywhere. Although most of us today rely on the media for nearly all of our knowledge of what is happening in the wider world, what newspapers and news programs actually tell us is hopelessly and *necessarily* biased. Here is why.

No competitive form of News can get away with offering a balanced image of what is going on. People would rapidly lose interest if any media organization was ever naive enough to try. Many members of the general public think they want to read, hear or see an even-handed report of the state of the world. But in reality anyone would be bored stiff if they ever got that.

What people really want to learn about is what is wrong, what is different from expected, what is changed, what has happened to someone they 'know' (even though almost always the person concerned is in reality a celebrity that they have never actually met). What they do not want is an interminable list of all those things that are still fine, as expected, just as they were yesterday. Even in the early days of the first ever radio News broadcasts – when the evening announcers on BBC Wireless would (unseen) be dressed in dinner jackets to read the evening report because it was considered sufficiently serious – still the News was only about 'important' things.

Since the dawn of human history, reporting has been like that. Despite the way History is presented at school, for the vast majority of the last few millennia in reality very little of any importance ever happened. Typically things just carried on. What with hindsight is called History is not 'what happened' it is 'what dramatically changed'. What gets into history books is only those rare exciting bits.

## NEVER-ENDING NEWS

In the last few decades, however, something extra has been added to this age-old phenomenon. Rolling News. 24/7. Worldwide. And that changes everything. For a start, people's perception of the frequency of stressful events changes. Consider, for example: Were there *any* tsunamis before ten years ago? Even when they were incorrectly referred to as 'tidal waves' did they really occur as often as they do today?

The accurate answer is that although earthquakes and the tsunamis they can create do tend to cluster over a period of a few years in a particular earthquake zone, over longer periods they average out. Overall, tsunamis are no more common today than, say, a hundred years ago. But for many people it does not feel like that.

The immediacy of modern news coverage – complete with amateur video from mobile phones – has completely changed everyone's awareness of them. And our response to news has also adapted. Rapid news coverage when shared across a large population tends to exaggerate trends. If one or two people hear from their friend that their local bank has sought a loan from the government – perhaps for some quite benign reason – then little may change. If exactly the same information is broadcast on the evening News, then the next morning (even if the head of the bank has on-air tried to reassure its customers that nothing is wrong) there may well be a run on the bank and its future will be changed forever. Such reactions are a very-limited form of Boundaryless People-Power.

## WHEN THE BERLIN WALL ALMOST STAYED UP

Few know that in reality the night of November 9th 1989 got into the history books because of an administrative error. You have to feel for poor Günter Schabowski, the official who made the fateful mistake. He had just got back from vacation. He had not been properly briefed. And he was on live television. He told the world that henceforth East Germans could cross to the West. What his colleagues had *actually* decided was that starting the next day, during normal working hours, private individuals with the right paperwork could in a highly-organized fashion and with full identity checks cross the border into West Germany. What instead happened was that massive spontaneous crowds gathered demanding access to West Germany. The border guards initially refused to let them pass claiming quite truthfully that their patrol had not been given any instructions to that effect. The guards made frantic calls to their superiors. But it was getting a bit late in the day so not the easiest time to track people down. And no one whom they did manage to contact was willing to take the individual responsibility of ordering the use of 'extreme force' against the crowds. So the overwhelmed guards gave in and let the masses though with limited, if any, ID checks. It *was* the night the Berlin Wall effectively fell. But only just.

# News media and politics

The same phenomenon helped tear open the Iron Curtain in 1989 when a senior East German communist official took questions on a live television news conference and – in error – announced that effective 'immediately, without delay' East Germans would be allowed unlimited passage to West Germany. Within hours, tens of thousands had swept through Checkpoint Charlie and the other heavily fortified crossing points in the Berlin Wall. Having so publically opened the gates to what was in effect unregulated crossing, the communist regime found it could never close them again.

## COMPETITION FOR THE PUBLIC

The tendency of 24-hour news to exacerbate trends that might otherwise have little impact is tremendously amplified by capitalism-driven competition. Over the past few years I have had very many confidential discussions in newsrooms, and the truth is that today's reporters find themselves in an increasingly desperate and competitive arena. This is especially true in the UK where the press-industry has become far more cut-throat than in, say, the USA where most big newspapers have the comfort (and vulnerability) of city-wide monopolies. What is more, just as in financial industries, press regulation – typically in the form of 'self-regulation' – does not often work as advertised.

It is a little like the situation of primarily-good bankers caught in a corrosive wider system. 'Free speech' can be used to justify surprisingly major invasions of privacy, and rookie journalists quickly learn that there can be amazingly strong pressures to do almost anything to get a scoop. Illegally accessing someone's voicemail by hacking their mobile phone is only one (actually long-outmoded) example of the tempting but slippery slope that it can be tempting for a fearless journalist to edge along.

As competition grows, that temptation can get ever-stronger. It is currently very easy for an ambitious reporter to conclude that the real lesson of the backlash triggered by the 2011 *News of the World* phone-hacking scandal is that if it feels necessary to use illegal methods of gathering information then make sure you do so in a way that leaves you looking squeaky clean. Of course, so the logic goes, you still need to gather covert data. But please break the law in a 'safe' way.

Against that backdrop, it is misleading to fixate on some journalists' historical use of phone-hacking. It was only one of the so-called 'Dark Arts' typically learned from the Private Investigators. Those PIs continue to be regularly hired by respected banks, broadcasters and top newspapers to check people out. But these days it is far more tempting for them – and any of their eager pupils – to employ techniques such as Wi-Fi hacking in hotel lobbies, cafes, burger-diners and other public spaces.

After all, that is so very easy to do. It accesses so much more confidential data. And in practice it is often undetectable. It should go without saying that, given current sensitivities, many top executives have recently sent strong reminders to their employees that everyone must rigorously adhere to company policy and operate strictly within the law. But that does not prevent them continuing to use PIs. And the most 'resourceful' investigators tend to be the ones that keep getting rehired.

## PLAUSIBLE DENIABILITY

Journalists and others employing Private Investigators to run background-checks on individuals typically as a result end up providing themselves and their organizations with the potential defense of having 'rigorously adhered to strictly-lawful activity'. That is in reality very similar to what many top executives of major corporations have secretly told me they have to do when operating in countries where officials and others expect bribes – and where you simply cannot get the chance to compete in the market without illegally paying for the privilege. As far as I am aware, no household-names *ever* pay any bribes at all. But some do pay very healthy fees to respected local Agents and Consultancies that, somehow, manage to oil the wheels of commerce sufficiently to achieve the same effect.

Television is generally taking over from print news, so TV News around the world increasingly has to compete in the same way as Newspapers. Internet News will follow the lead of TV as it gets better funding mechanisms. However, even then there is the risk of distortion caused by a two-tier News system in which those subscribers who can afford high-speed lines will achieve a different level of insight (for example from video streaming) than those with only slow access (to stills and text).

Television brings its own type of extreme distortion. It is very different to the printing press because TV is so much more difficult and expensive to broadcast. That means it is primarily run by large corporations that need to make a profit – as well as occasionally keep certain politicians happy when cable or satellite or funding rights are being allocated. Under those circumstances, the pressures on newscasters are stronger than ever to select the news and present it in ways that keep the maximum number of viewers watching.

That brings unintended consequences far deeper than tabloid journalists sometimes feeling the pressure to bend or break the law in order to get material for an article. The most familiar impacts are 'sound-bites' and 'dumbing down'. Much less obvious is the trade-off between Entertainment and News. Few members of the general public appreciate what an incredibly small amount of total available video material is typically transmitted. Those few seconds that *are* shown are always highly selective. At best they represent what in the journalist's view best approximates 'the truth'. At worst they represent the best television.

## UNINTENTIONAL MISREPRESENTATION

That is an example of an inherent risk for all modern news coverage: High-Tech proliferation of media outlets means that however balanced it is that news editors attempt to be, it has now effectively become impossible for even the most professional to convey an accurate overall impression to the general public. For instance, when nearly all scientists were agreed that man-made global warming was a reality, half the news stories covering the topic still questioned whether it was. It made each story more interesting. It gave a feeling of balance within a given item. Even though the overall impact of all the coverage was *not* a balanced reflection of what the scientists rightly or wrongly believed. The same unintended overall misrepresentation often occurs with health-scares. Here is an example.

Hospital-acquired infections – such as from drug-resistant strains of bacteria like MRSA – are a serious problem in most Western nations. Throughout much of the last decade, someone was equally at risk of being visited by 'Mrs. A' in a US hospital as in a UK hospital. Yet, despite the fact that incidents have dropped in the UK by more than 80% from their peak in 2003-4, even today the British public tends to be far more scared about MRSA than US patients are. Why? Probably the press coverage.

Over ten years, the top UK newspapers published almost twenty-five times more MRSA articles than their US counterparts. Those articles tended to focus on named young children or pregnant women contracting infection, and yet the writers hardly ever mentioned the far more typical victims – namely the elderly or very ill. To be fair, in each case the journalist probably chose the angle that the news editor (and by implication the average audience) would find most compelling. And they each may have rigorously told the truth. They just edited out the more boring bits. No one can really blame them for that. But when so many journalists made so many similar choices then the collective result was something no individual journalist decided, no individual editor intended, and quite possibly no journalist, editor or reader actually wanted.

## MEASLES, MUMPS AND RUBELLA

In 1998, the respected medical journal The Lancet published a subsequently-discredited paper claiming possible links between MMR vaccine and autism in children. As the result of a later onslaught of media coverage, many parents – with no scientific background against which to judge the claims, nor even (thanks to the success of previous scientifically-based vaccination programs) any personal experience of measles, mumps or rubella – chose not to vaccinate their children and instead left them at risk of potentially fatal or permanently-damaging infection. Some of those vulnerable children later succumbed.

A similar dynamic occurred with the widespread reporting of alleged links between MMR vaccine and autism. The original isolated claim was subsequently ruled to be deliberately fraudulent – but by then large numbers of children had unnecessarily been placed at risk as a result of the numerous media reports that, when all taken together, unintentionally misled parents about the likely validity of the claim. In many countries infection rates increased substantially, public-health funds were wasted unnecessarily, and children died – largely as the unintended consequence of a 'good story'.

### INTENTIONAL MISREPRESENTATION

Inevitably, people get an even less accurate foundation on which to make up their minds when there is either bad science or deliberately misrepresented science involved. That applies to the book industry as much as the press. It is utterly extraordinary that some of the bestselling books on Diet and Nutrition do not have to carry their own health warnings.

And some of the Management Fad phenomenon is fuelled by books of very dubious scientific quality. There are even a few well-renowned Business School professors that do not seem to know the difference between Correlation and Causation. In other words, they observe characteristics in a selection of successful companies and then suggest that less-successful companies could improve by mimicking those same characteristics. Having myself analyzed the impact of many of the highly-expensive attempts corporations have made to try to follow such proposals, I have concluded that the advice in many of the bestselling business texts is analogous to telling an overweight amateur football-player that he will be able to jump as high as a prima ballerina if only he wears a tutu.

There is a real problem here. The vast majority of the general population, let alone politicians, are not scientific experts. So society as a whole in reality depends upon the media of all types to inform it enough to make up its mind on scientific issues. But some crucial issues – such as 'atomic-fusion research' – can come across as a bit academic or confusing, with the result that most people do not even want to spend time making up their minds about them. Far worse is when apparently scientific groups are funded by major organizations to issue deliberately misleading reports on issues such as climate-change or pollution – which is an approach some of the executives involved have claimed to me that they borrowed from the tobacco industry.

In an unprecedented move in 2006, the leading scientific body in the UK – The Royal Society – sent a letter to Esso UK Ltd (part of the US oil company ExxonMobil) complaining that ExxonMobil was presenting 'an inaccurate and misleading impression of the evidence on the causes of climate change that is documented in the scientific literature.' But this sort of informed push-back tends to get less coverage than any original deliberate misrepresentation. Under these circumstances politicians and the general public can be very easily misled. Which – as you will find detailed in the later chapter on Industrialization Crises – is exactly what some top executives have told me that they rely on.

It gets even riskier than that. Escalating competition has led to cut-backs and efficiency-drives across the media industries. As a result, while more and more news is being reported, less and less of it is being checked for factual accuracy. That vacuum has been willingly filled by PR Agencies. They send out Press Releases that are sometimes then published verbatim by reporters – not just because it saves so much time, but also because that way the journalist carries very little risk of being sued for misrepresentation. It is a win-win. And when the 'facts' involve any degree of Celebrity then it unofficially suits all parties to spread almost any story the PR Agency sets up – however orchestrated it may be. And as we will now examine in the next subchapter, few celebrities get more coverage than top politicians.

# BLIND LEADING THE BLIND

## Systemic distortions in reporting ultimately result in insufficient checks and balances for the political process as a whole

IF EVER THERE was a backlash just waiting to happen it was the one caused by the intersection of Entertainment News with Celebrity Politics. I first pointed the risks out to a media client in early 2004. But the genesis of the current furor stretches back far earlier even than that. In the last few decades, many countries have seen a rise in popularity of relatively superficial and emotional television – such as Reality TV shows – often at the apparent expense of shows offering more depth and reason. Some of the impact of this has rubbed off onto people's attitude to politics. Presentation is all.

Just as televised leaders debates have long been crucial in US Presidential elections, so in 2010 they for the first time also dominated the UK election process. The first televised debate of the main party leaders catapulted the largely unknown candidate Nick Clegg into such a prominent position in the public mind that a month later it seemed perfectly reasonable when he was made Deputy Prime Minister (as part of an unpredicted form of coalition parliament). But the election process is just the beginning. These days the political TV frenzy never ends.

There are obvious upsides and downsides to turning political leaders into TV stars – many more citizens have a chance to view them and hear extracts of what they say, but the way the leaders are actually presented risks favoring style over content and emotion over reason. However, in many ways those are minor (and certainly reasonably well-recognized) considerations. The far more important issue is that in any community, whether a village or a nation-state, well-informed citizens are meant to provide crucial checks and balances to those in power over them. Yet the reality of people basing their insights on even the best-intentioned modern news media is that, though they may think they are knowledgeable, their judgment is largely based on coverage than unintentionally completely warps reality.

That misrepresentation is not so much caused by *lack* of professionalism in the media as by the intense competitive demands of the profession itself. As just examined in the last subchapter, the more 'professional' that members of the media are the more detached from reality the rest of society risks becoming. The net result is that the public's collective views, and the resulting pressures they put on their political leaders, may or may not match up with The Truth. Manmade global warming? Risks from GM crops or nuclear power? The real beliefs of politicians? In practice it is extremely difficult for most of the population to find out 'the facts'. And very few have the time or inclination to try. The general public is not in a position any more to provide 'well-informed' checks and balances because no one *really* has an accurate sense of what is truly going on. As a result, citizens in modern democracies are in no more control of public policies than Politicians are in control of Banking.

## DISTORTED POLITICS

Contemporary politics is becoming progressively warped as a result of its relationship with 24/7 media. Politicians have always had a reputation of being notoriously opportunistic and sometimes very short-term in outlook. The daily news cycle combined with feedback from focus-groups can exacerbate that tendency still further. And the proliferation of media channels makes it far more difficult than it was in the past to influence the population in a coherent direction.

Some politicians have always coped with what can be a brutal calling by telling themselves 'It's all a game'. But today it can be easy also to feel that the only part of the game that really counts is performing – indeed *acting* – in front of a TV camera. The US Senate these days is largely unattended by other senators when it is not televised. The UK House of Commons degrades into tribal point-scoring during its weekly televised Prime Minister's Questions (and MPs typically defend their behavior as being something that 'the public enjoys' – as if that were complete justification for regularly wasting public money and politicians' valuable time by performing in a theatrical non-debate).

The media-distortion of modern politics goes far deeper than that. The daily news-cycle only has a certain amount of space. And it cannot *always* be filled by the most important issues because after a while even those stories risk becoming 'boring' if they are covered day-in and day-out. As a result, a skillful (or lucky) government press-office may overlap announcements of so many Difficult Issues that there simply is not time for all of them to be reported in depth.

Based on such an overload, the public may end up less incensed about a given issue and government plans may face less opposition overall. Just as effectively, the government may trial new ideas that, while controversial, are not in fact especially crucial to their overall goals. The media latch onto the controversy. Some of the public get enraged. The media report that. The government eventually 'listens' to the public mood and modifies or even backtracks on its proposals. The media report the alleged U-turn in full – and maybe even claim to have had a hand in helping the public voice to be heard. But all the time, the more-major on-going Difficult Issues were getting less coverage than otherwise they might have.

Another substantial distortion occurs in the run-up to important elections. Until the current media circus, political candidates achieved public office primarily by convincing their local electorate to vote for them based on what they said and how they performed. These days, mass media makes it far easier for the public to focus on the Parties and their Leaders rather than local candidates. Everything is much more centralized. Elections are dominated by TV News and TV advertising. Friendly crowds are bussed to photo-calls so that political leaders can be filmed surrounded by supporters – rather than risk having unchoreographed interactions with uncertified members of the local community. Focus-groups select which campaign policies will play best in those constituencies that have the most undecided-voters, and it is those messages that then flood the media even if they are not particularly representative of the party's political manifesto as a whole.

And throughout it all, depending on the style of the politician's Press Officers, journalists are either bullied or wooed, and often both – and it sometimes shows in their coverage. Which makes the politicians even more paranoid about the media than ever. Some end up permanently worried about putting a foot wrong. They live in thinly-disguised fear of triggering the press into retaliation. They may not know the term 'Boundaryless People-Power' – but they increasingly have a well-developed intuition about just what it can do.

## COVER-UPS

Even ten years ago, the pressure on politicians resulting from all the 24-hour News cycle was already high, but more recent internet-enabled services like Twitter and YouTube have led to a level of 'citizen journalism' that sometimes can feel claustrophobic. Only a certain character of Natural Celebrity politician finds it easy to cope. And increasingly, if politicians do not look good on camera, they find it hard to achieve (or keep) high office. Yet neither extroversion nor good looks particularly correlate with intellect, honor and statesmanship. At a time when a political career is far less alluring and respected than it was, and during an era when the highest abilities of political leadership will be needed to manage increasingly complex globally-defined threats, otherwise-excellent candidates are being arbitrarily blocked.

Primarily as a result of the 24/7 highly-competitive media that have automatically emerged from High-Tech Capitalism, society has unintentionally but dramatically restricted the selection criteria for those it allows to lead it. And now it is too late to change things very much. There is no longer sufficient time for a completely new type of politician to replace all those currently in power. The type of politician the public has today is largely the type it is going to have to rely on during the critical times ahead. They are what they are.

But although modern politicians come in for a lot of stick – some of it well earned – the truth is that under the best of circumstances it is a near-impossible task to persuade a widely-differing population to accept significant change. And no politician wants to lose any of that already-small influence because some earlier indiscretion is made public. Exposed to the unremittingly dazzling glare of the competitive media, it can become automatic to try to cover-up anything sensitive.

Even in countries where political leaders very largely strive to act with the public's best interests at heart, it is understandable why nevertheless some of those individuals cross the line in trying to stack the minimal odds a little bit more in their favor with regard the media in an effort to 'persuade' the general population to do what the politician honestly believes needs to be done anyway. Even if these days it is increasingly a very risky game to play.

# HOW POLITICIANS AND JOURNALISTS EACH DANCE WITH THE DEVIL

## Because the government and news media are both crucial to each other there can be increasingly risky conflicts of interest

POLITICIANS KNOW THAT the reality is that when the public are fed the right story at the right time and in the right way the government often gains support to take actions that the general population might never otherwise have wanted or even accepted. Armed conflicts are the most extreme examples – the invasion of Iraq in 2003 is unlikely to have gained even what support it did without the well-publicized claims on Weapons of Mass Destruction. But running up unprecedented budget deficits, and the subsequent austerity measures needed to claw them back, are other examples. That is why the media is now so crucial to politics, and political spin is now so endemic in the media. It is also why political journalists in truth play a very similar risky game to the politicians.

It is generally accepted that being a political reporter is a far less cutthroat profession than, for example, working on a tabloid newspaper. After all, much of the time is spent in the relatively rarefied atmosphere of The Corridors of Power. Days are often consumed interacting with none but a small and select cadre of important politicians. It might therefore be assumed that political reporting is largely immune to the risks of competition-driven distortion we have just been examining. However, it is the very nature of the elite interactions that brings its own distortions. This is summed up by the way everyone who is a modern politician or a political reporter has to learn to 'Dance with the Devil'.

A reporter can ask a really difficult question of a President or Prime Minister at a press conference. But then again it is the President and Prime Minister that point to a given journalist to invite them to ask questions at all. So if a member of the media makes their question *too* difficult then they may not get selected next time. Or be permitted to travel with the press corps on the next important trip.

## CLAIMS ABOUT WEAPONS OF MASS DESTRUCTION

Despite the various official inquiries into how it was possible for the claims of WMD in Iraq to have been so wrong, none of the reviews have explained to the general public how very easy it is – when multiple groups are involved in generating ideas – for conclusions to be 'warped' and 'biased' without any deliberate attempt at misrepresentation from anyone involved. In much the same way as the competitive media can collectively end up unintentionally distorting people's impressions about global warming or MRSA, so a false conclusion can emerge from a complex sequence of synthesis and editing without anyone in the chain necessarily being culpable. The only blame under those circumstances may be of no one in practice having sufficient oversight.

If presenters have their own radio or television Current Affairs program, they certainly have the option of developing the reputation of giving politicians a really hard time when they come on the show – but as a result it may become increasingly difficult to persuade top officials to appear with them in the future. In contrast, they can follow in the footsteps of some of the most famous television interviewers and offer a secret deal that if statesmen let *them* do an interview – rather than appear on a rival show – then although the guest may seem to be given a verbal beating it will not be too hard. Rival broadcasters may dismiss this approach as making a Pact with the Devil rather than carrying on dancing with him – but it is often the more 'respectful' broadcaster that the public will see consistently interviewing the great and the not-so-good throughout a long career.

The general public relies on reporters to ask the insightful questions that it would want asked if only it knew enough. The politicians rely on the fact that career reporters can only push so far, and so often. The journalist relies on the fact that the politicians increasingly depend on the media to convey their messages in a positive light (and therefore, at least in the politicians' minds, deliver votes – even if that is increasingly a myth). They also rely on the fact that most top politicians are sufficiently insecure as to be easily made paranoid that the media might turn against them as individuals.

That is the Dance with the Devil that both interviewers and politicians tread so knowingly – their ultimate defense being that each needs the other. It is the same dance as conducted by the Police – who likewise need the media to help solve crime as well as maintain trust in the Law. Meanwhile, journalists need stories and information. Sometimes they are willing to pay for it – if only 'in kind'. In turn, the Judiciary, usually in seductively exclusive surroundings, have their own form of Dance with the Devil – in their case with the Media *and* with Politicians – with all the risks that such behavior invites.

In all these Establishment dances, however much either partner believes that it is the other who is cast in the role of the Devil – PR is, and has always been, vital to amplifying the power of the state. Just as Marketing and Corporate Communications are crucial to maximizing corporate power. Just as preaching is to religions. Just as throughout history, all-powerful autocrats have always attempted to promote themselves, insulate the populace from any truth that might prove unflattering, and position themselves as the Protector of their people. Modern democratically-elected leaders still try to do the same. Which brings us to the final piece of media-enhanced political footwork that can trigger a global crisis.

## TURNING UP THE THREAT-LEVEL

There is one time when Leaders of State find the public a lot more manageable: whenever there is an External Threat. During a major international conflict – just as with a widespread national catastrophe – people pull together because, temporarily at least, they equate their own future with the future of the broader community. Under such circumstances, it is easy to see why it might sometimes be tempting for political leaders to feed the over-hungry media with sound-bites that encourage voters to focus on an external threat rather than problems at home. Put bluntly, if the public is in constant anxiety then its reason is distorted and for a while it is more amenable to extreme solutions.

It does not really matter whether it is the War on Terror or the Global Banking Crisis – either will tend to allow far greater political freedom to 'do what it takes'. And what about when those were not around? There was always the Cold War, or the Communist Threat, or the Threat of Nuclear

War. When any of those top-level crises waned, there were at least the externally-focused fallbacks of the OPEC Crisis, the Threat of Japanese Imports, and the ever-reliable Middle-East Conflicts.

Hardly any modern politician actually likes the idea of going to war. But playing-up external threats can often feel like no bad thing – even though overseas war is inherently so often destabilizing that it eventually builds inevitable political, economic and social backlashes back home, as seen recently in the USA and UK as a result of their wars in Iraq and Afghanistan. And throughout each of the world's conflicts, we see the same all-pervasive intertwining of politics and news.

Trying to emulate their ancestors, modern autocratic states still try to control their High-Tech media – and if necessary turn off their region's internet or block Twitter and other social media during protests – just as advanced democracies are increasingly tempted to do during uncontrolled riots. A modern army fighting to liberate people will, when invading a territory, aim to take control of radio, television and the press as soon as possible. And the main reason that Air Force One had to land after the September 11 attacks was that the President needed to broadcast to the US nation and the world.

## WHY GEORGE W WAS BROUGHT DOWN TO EARTH

In 2001, it became clear that a major shortcoming in the design of Air Force One – or more correctly, the two identical VC-25 aircraft, either one of which adopts that call sign when the President is on board – was that the President could not broadcast to the American public without landing. That has now been corrected.

In cold, logical terms, the autocrat's desire utterly to control the media is fully understandable – democratically-elected politicians often wish they could do the same. But because they cannot, their dependency on increasingly competitive media outlets progressively warps everything they say and do, even when it involves completely healthy media-competition with highly professional journalists who are doing nothing but excellent journalism.

# News media and politics

For today's politician, interacting with the media is like walking on eggshells. Other times it is more like walking through a minefield. Everyone in modern politics is constantly aware that even if the press does not turn against the government, media coverage can nevertheless be sufficient to stir up a political backlash by the general public. Any emotive topic might prove sufficient to breach a dam of sustained resentment and release a previously-constrained backlash of Boundaryless People-Power that reveals itself in anything from public outcry to full-blooded revolution or international terrorism.

## ENGINEERING A CRISIS

On various occasions I have had a variety of leaders quietly take me to one side and inquire whether they could 'engineer a crisis' so as to make their particular change easier to push through. The answer is always: 'Yes you could but no you should not.' Engineering a fake crisis is a short-term mugs game because it is inherently unsustainable and, quite rightly, risks destroying trust forever.

That is the problem. It can be anything: the collapse of Lehman Brothers in the USA, British tabloid journalists hacking the phones of non-celebrities, resentment against immigration within the European Union, child labor in Asia, embezzlement of foreign aid to sub-Saharan Africa, animals hunted toward extinction to satisfy the Chinese market, the huge disparity in wealth between India's financial elite and its sprawling rural and slum communities, unemployed Arab youths seeing that their counterparts are successfully rebelling. Any issue that the media plays up might go critical. The internet just makes things worse. All of that feeds political insecurity. And ups the tempo of The Dance.

## 3. HOW RISKS OF MEDIA AND POLITICAL BACKLASHES ESCALATE

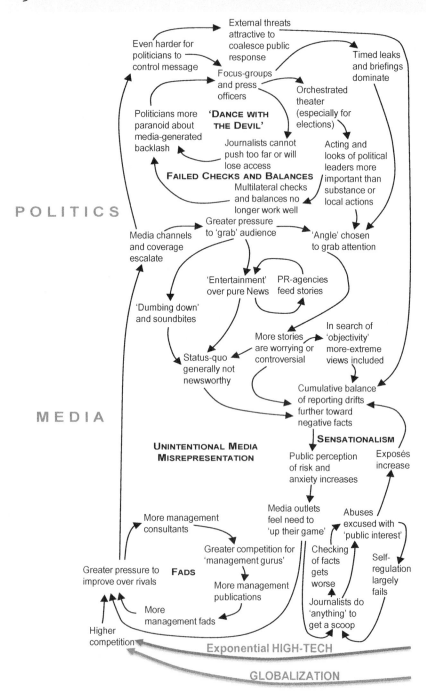

# THE FALLACY REGARDING HOW SURVIVAL OF THE FITTEST WORKS

## Widespread misinterpretation of how competition optimizes the world economy risks crucial long-term solutions being irretrievably lost

CAPITALISM HAS BEEN around a very long time. That means that it is very firmly established because it is deeply intertwined with the vast majority of global society. But it also means that when Capitalism interacts with another deeply-reinforced supertrend such as High-Tech then any backlashes that result are often themselves very powerful and very complex and interconnected. As you have seen so far, the prime examples of High-Tech-Capitalism crises are all side-effects of the inherent competition on which capitalism (and, it could be argued, much of civilization's progress) depends. But that competitiveness unexpectedly introduces a set of hidden risks.

The addiction of many countries to organizational change – inspired by the lure of ever-better competitiveness, fuelled by a competitive business press and largely made possible by High-Tech – is leading to widespread change-fatigue that makes it progressively harder to bring about each new change, even when that change is needed to avoid backlashes. Under the best conditions (a modern corporation) there is nevertheless a 70% failure rate for change. Modern organizations are nothing like as controllable as everyone pretends.

Strong competition in financial-services is what in many ways led to the 2008 collapse. And because the drivers of that competition have long been fossilized into the very bedrock of not just the banking industry but also every aspect of the global economy that banking serves, it is an awesome task to extract it and yet not undermine everything and so cause more harm than good.

Likewise, strong competition across the media industries, whilst bringing unprecedented levels of news coverage, nevertheless also inevitably – though in many cases unintentionally – results in increasingly wild distortions of reality and so a warping of the public's collective judgment. When combined with politics, this phenomenon is fundamentally changing the dynamics of how the public chooses its leaders, how politicians in turn try to manage society, and how both groups decide what is important to be done – based on insights that may or may not correspond with reality.

But there is a final and even more deeply-hidden backlash caused by High-Tech's impact on Capitalism. It too relates to competition. It links international banking, the world business community, political ideology and government. And it highlights a well-established but largely unrecognized example of Boundaryless People-Power. At the center of this growing backlash is the assumption widely-held by many politicians and economists that 'survival of the fittest' is in fact one of the healthiest aspects of the capitalist system.

## DARWINIAN CAPITALISM

As the original Industrial Revolution got going in England in the mid-18th century, whole communities fell apart because too many people had moved to the newly-forming cities where there was the promise of well-paid work. Utterly new jobs sprang up. Many old jobs, whether in spinning and weaving or in blacksmithing and pin-making, simply disappeared as they were mechanized almost overnight. Skilled craftsmen who had honed their trade throughout decades became redundant and starved.

The overall modern world is little different in this respect to rural 18th-century England. In a far slower way, and initially far-less-dramatic way, whole countries, even whole regions can fail within a world economy. As it was during the Industrial Revolution, High-Tech Capitalism means that global society faces a nation-sized version of 'survival of the fittest'.

Provided it is not *their* country that goes down, many politicians (and their citizens) might think that such a harsh by-product of Capitalism accelerated by High-Tech is an inevitable consequence of a system that ultimately nevertheless results in the best performing global economy overall. Some regions may dominate, some may respond to competitive pressure and be forced to improve, others may fail. But most people assume that the net effect of all the brutal competition is that the world as a whole is the best it could possibly be.

The more-compassionate might advocate that a limited amount of Foreign Aid is justified for humanitarian and long-term security reasons, but (many assume) if people are really hard-headed about it and discount any human suffering, the good news is that survival of the fittest is guaranteed to lead to the best eventual overall outcome. Unfortunately, that is completely untrue.

Familiar as everyone is with Darwin's concept of evolution by natural selection, politicians can all-too-easily assume that over time this form of evolution is the most effective type imaginable. It is not. Sometimes it is completely hopeless. The trouble is it can be even more chronically short-term and insular than a rogue banker. Whether in the depths of the Amazonian rainforest or the corridors of the Concrete Jungle, this form of selection only favors choices that *in the immediate short-term* are best suited to the *local* situation. Long-term, or further afield, those choices may prove a disaster.

Indeed, it may be that even in the medium-term an alternative choice – one that in reality gets culled – might have proved a very useful additional 'string to the bow' in case the first option started to go wrong. Survival of the fittest can end up completely ruling out those sorts of alternatives.

## DOBLE MODEL E

As late as 1930 people could buy a Doble Model E steam car that was so sophisticated that they could start it completely from cold with a flick of the ignition key and *thirty seconds later* could drive away. With no need for a gear shift, the Doble could rapidly and continuously accelerate up to speeds approaching 100mph, it could travel 1500 miles on a single tank of water and could be powered by a variety of fuels. It had no clutch, no transmission, and was virtually silent. Unfortunately the Doble company did not sell sufficient numbers to bring the price down enough to compete with the mass-produced Model T Ford. And today most people do not even know something like the Model E ever existed.

When the low-cost mass-produced Ford Model T killed off the highly-priced hand-built Doble Model E (which most people these days have never even heard of), it also destroyed the opportunity to develop steam cars as a radical alternative to the internal combustion engine. When the early 'reciprocating' automobile engine became well established it destroyed the option decades later of the potentially more attractive Wankel 'rotary' design ever being able to catch up. And when the oil cartel OPEC slashed the price of crude in the mid-1980s it effectively invalidated the cost-justification for nearly all research into energy-saving initiatives in the West – leaving the economy vulnerable to the massive price hikes in oil twenty years later.

Similarly, concerns over the safety of nuclear power generators led many countries severely to curtail their nuclear programs, but that also massively restricted their options for low $CO_2$ emissions thirty years later. And at the end of the 20th century, vested financial interests persuaded California to back down on quota requirements for green cars. In related moves, various automotive manufacturers pulled the plug on their electric vehicles, and some even refused to allow enthusiast drivers to buy their leased electric-cars but instead took them back and destroyed nearly all of them. Whatever the reasons behind these actions, they nevertheless seriously damaged a potentially attractive route to an alternative future.

Despite the evangelical preaching of some economists and politicians, unfettered capitalism does not in any way guarantee that *over the long-term* societies will end up with the best global economy that they could. On the contrary – raw capitalism has the foresight of a goldfish. It is constantly culling opportunities that might prove incredibly valuable in the long-term but are not the best local option in the immediate-term. And losing an opportunity can sometimes mean losing it forever.

## SHORT-TERM EDUCATION

A perennial example is very-long-term investments in education. Because of the impacts of the High-Tech supertrend, it is skills and knowledge that will increasingly be the only sustainable ways for individuals and nations to compete in a capitalist world economy – technology itself is often too easily copied. That means that for the foreseeable future appropriate Education is more important than ever.

The trouble is that it is too late to transform all of the current generation of teachers and curricula and students into something different. To a large degree the economy is stuck with the current crop of new entrants to the workplace who are destined to run things in a few decades. They face tremendous turbulence. For the even-younger generation still in school, changes will potentially be far more disruptive.

# Irretrievable losses

## DESTROYING OPTIONS FOR THE FUTURE

Options for the future are not only culled by the short-termism of raw capitalism. All your life you have been able to observe an equivalent process without necessarily being aware of what was going on. Think of the pop music that was playing when you were a young child. Now think of which songs from that period are played today. It is a very narrow selection of the original. It is not even all the songs that were top of the charts back then – only a few of them. And sometimes your very-favorite – the tune you just loved to hear as a kid – simply does not make it, and gets no modern air-time at all. Yet only those few old songs that commonly get played today have much chance of influencing young artists. Only they represent the legacy of the past that sustains into the future. The alternatives disappear.

The same is true even of our everyday memories of the past – our social history. It very quickly gets warped from reality. What car best represents the Swinging '60s in London? Obvious, it is the Mini or maybe the E-Type Jag. But what about the Bubble Car? I remember as a youngster in London at the start of the Sixties it was Bubble Cars that were really new and really Fab. The Isetta I once travelled in – driven by a young lady sporting an incredible 'beehive' hairstyle – had only three wheels and could only seat two slim people. But the whole front lifted up for you to climb in, and it was amazing to ride – very low, only a big windscreen between you and the traffic in front, a bit like a go-kart for groovy people. But no one filmed them enough. As a result people today do not get reminded just how iconic Bubble Cars were for a year or two. So they are getting written out of history, and in the process potentially destroying design ideas for the future.

Yet in most parts of the Western world governments have hardly even begun to invest sufficiently in preparing children for what they will have to face by 2040 – although that is less so in parts of India and East Asia; Taiwan, for example, produces students with some of the highest scores in mathematics and science in the world. In a world that will be utterly dominated by science and technology, most children in the West (and to be fair, most of their teachers) remain scientifically near-illiterate. And most, of both generations, are not even embarrassed by the fact. In universities, students are groomed for careers that are likely soon to be gone. As the clock ticks, most politicians talk about educational reform based on improving class-size and attendance rates. For many countries, and countless individuals, that is a recipe for disaster – primarily because it is very difficult to recover from.

## LIVING IN FEAR OF THE MARKET

Just as countries not investing in sufficiently upgraded education can lock themselves on course to a disastrous long-term destination, so can raw capitalism as a whole lock the world economy on a disastrous route. Capitalism left to its own devices is perfectly capable of going down a one-way-street. And too many examples of that could ultimately lead the whole capitalist system into a dead-end.

Survival of the fittest is how options for the future die. Yet many politicians are insufficiently aware of the facts behind how such a process works that they never even question what is being lost. Most other people do the same. The international community often acts as if it can if necessary retrace its steps after a backlash. Governments take collective gambles within the global economy based on the assumption that if things go horribly wrong then everyone can 'all learn from the mistake and do better next time'. There often is not a next time.

Moreover, the risks from largely-unregulated global capitalism have recently grown far more severe. And they are set to escalate. The reason is, once again, High-Tech. The danger of constantly culling options because they do not provide sufficient short-term benefits is not a new problem for Capitalism. However, the exponential growth of High-Tech combined with our global competition-driven addiction to change, means that those decisions are being made increasingly often and with far less opportunity for strategic thought (by governments or anybody). That would be disconcerting enough. But in reality things are much worse than that.

The Global Financial Market – institutions trading everything from stocks and currencies to commodities and government bonds – has now become so interconnected and so fast that *it has turned into a permanent channel for Boundaryless People-Power*. Indeed, although everyone talks of phenomena like the Arab Spring as being the best examples of Boundaryless People-Power, in reality it is The Market that is without doubt currently the most well-established and formalized channel for distributed action that exists anywhere on the planet.

## FLAMES THAT LIT THE FUSE OF AN ARAB EXPLOSION

It is an irony of the short attention-span brought by contemporary news coverage that already few members of the general public can even remember the name of the young man whose actions triggered the Arab Spring. At 11.30 on the morning of 17 December 2010, 26-year-old fruit-seller Tarek Mohamed Bouazizi deliberately set himself alight outside the offices of the Tunisian Governor in Sidi Bouzid. An hour earlier, a policewoman and two state officials had summarily confiscated Bouazizi's merchandise and scales because he would not pay them a bribe to continue trading. The total value of his wares was around $200 – but they were all he had to earn a living. Greedy and corrupt petty officials had now hassled and humiliated him into bankruptcy within a country that offered no safety-net. He had nothing more to lose. The flames did not kill him immediately. It took him two-and-a-half weeks to die. But dictators across the Arab world were about to find that the flames of resentment growing across a disempowered generation of young adults would not die as easily.

Financial markets as a concept are so old that those who work within them assume they are well-familiar with how they operate. But over the last two decades The Market has transformed into an incredibly High-Tech system. And, just like most other people, in the last couple of years individual traders have themselves become linked into the gossip of the internet, Facebook and Twitter. They are no more immune to the viral growth of particular ideas than anyone else. In fact, they are often on a hair-trigger – straining to see a trend ahead of their competition. That makes wild swings even more likely to occur than within the general population. And certainly more likely than, say, two decades ago.

Yet it is this increasingly unstable and untamed form of Boundaryless People-Power that now effectively rules the world. The Market is now so powerful that even the USA and the Eurozone live in fear of it. In 2011, the policies of politicians of small countries like Greece, Ireland and Portugal were effectively being dictated by The Market. Then it was larger countries like Spain and Italy that were forced to comply. By the summer, it was the whole Eurozone. Then the market, in effect, ousted the democratically-elected leaders of Greece and Italy and replaced them with technocrats.

Within the modern High-Tech version of The Market, the collective overreactions and heightened insecurities of individual traders all become channeled into what everyone then treats as being an all-powerful entity in its own right. The political leaders of nations and whole groups of nations find themselves forced to try get ahead of the curve of The Market, try to shock and awe The Market, try to reassure The Market. Because if they do not, then The Market will exact its cold, immediate and merciless sanctions. The Market is now viewed as an unstoppable force of nature. But it is not.

It is manmade. There is nothing preordained about how it is constructed. There is nothing inevitable about how it is allowed to operate. There is nothing behind the curtain of The Market other than a collection of individual fallible human traders each trying to make as much money for themselves as possible. If the overall result of their amplified rationalities and irrationalities was fundamentally beneficial to the world economy then it might make sense for politicians to maintain their long-established passive stance. And it might make sense for the financial institutions that make up The Market to encourage the politicians to do so.

But, for the same reasons as we have seen applies to *all* Darwinian Capitalism, the chronic short-termism of The Market can *never* be sufficient to maximize the long-term performance of the world economy. In fact, when The Market overreacts, it is extremely dangerous. The Market no longer just risks inappropriately culling 'experiments' that could turn into major opportunities in several decades' time. It can also wreck national economies in the short-term as well. And that risks pulling the world economy back into recession – again and again.

Just because there are immensely strong vested interests to leave the fundamental operation of The Market untouched does not automatically mean that it is wise to do so. What is more, those innumerable financial institutions at the core of The Market are themselves the ones that ultimately risk the greatest backlash from the public when – increasingly – the world economy no longer simply bounces back from a crisis every few years as it always did in the past.

# Irretrievable losses

The current negative view of Bankers by the general public is as nothing to what it could become. Ultimately, it is the leading financial institutions that will benefit from rethinking their role in The Market – just as much as governments, business and indeed everybody else will.

## 4. HOW SURVIVAL OF THE FITTEST RISKS IRRETRIEVABLE LOSSES

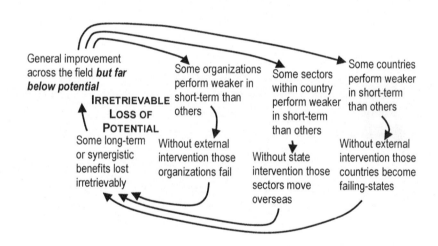

General improvement across the field *but far below potential*

**IRRETRIEVABLE LOSS OF POTENTIAL**
Some long-term or synergistic benefits lost irretrievably

Some organizations perform weaker in short-term than others

Without external intervention those organizations fail

Some sectors within country perform weaker in short-term than others

Without state intervention those sectors move overseas

Some countries perform weaker in short-term than others

Without external intervention those countries become failing-states

# Reducing the threats:
# UNELECTED RESPONSIBILITY

Capitalism crises need *Unelected Responsibility* – corporations fulfilling a duty of due care over communities they impact

OF THE ONE-HUNDRED largest economies in the world, about half of them are not countries at all – they are corporations. Huge companies like these have far deeper pockets than many of the member-states at the UN. They can lobby the governments of those countries for, basically, whatever suits them. And yet their leaders tend to be completely unelected. It used to be that increased power and wealth were viewed as a route to individual well-being. But one of the most important inventions of Capitalism has been the Company, which in law is typically treated as if it were an individual in its own right (legally distinct from the people who work within it or who own it). As a result, the power and wealth of a corporation is now often viewed as an end in its own right. Corporate success is seen as the route to securing a *corporation's* well-being – not directly aimed at any particular individuals at all.

It is that detachment that is heavily contributing to many of the Capitalism Crises examined in this first chapter of the book. To help counter these threats, international business must become more closely aligned with the collective smooth-running of the nations they cut across. However, there is something very important that must be recognized about such a shift: *Big Business realigning itself with its host nations is ultimately in its self-interest.* That is because Big Business has probably already become too powerful and too independent otherwise to avoid a concerted public and government backlash against it to stop it being allowed to continue to act as a leaderless independent state in its own right. As a result – ultimately for their own benefit – major corporations must realign their activities explicitly to include the additional strategic goal of *Unelected Responsibility*.

# Unelected Responsibility

The guiding principle of Unelected Responsibility is based on the recognition that – just like human beings – corporations are part of a community, even if that 'local community' has become so large that it is now in effect the whole of global society. That places responsibilities on a company that are greater than merely maximizing shareholder profit. In an isolated rural society, it would be impossible for even a powerful family to get away with consistently acting too selfishly – for example, risking the survival of the community as a whole by polluting the river upstream of where other villagers drew water. It would be no defense for the family to claim that the river was a common resource available to everyone to use in whichever way they chose.

Whatever 'the law', it is basic common sense largely to play fair in a tight community. We learn the same unwritten rules about how to fit into a community when we are at school – again, the overall social dynamics are pretty obvious. But the more abstract it is that people's relationships become, the easier it feels to disregard what under different circumstances would be basic rules of community living. Once someone gains a position within a corporate top-team it is easy to become so detached that it feels positively exhilarating to fixate on profit above all else – even if few around the table would necessarily choose to behave like that in front of their friends and family or in their local community. Having participated in many such meetings myself, I can confirm that on some of those occasions it is practically possible to smell the testosterone in the boardroom. It is the closest that most of the participants ever get to being in a war just before battle.

## GLOBAL ACCOUNTABILITY AND GLOBAL CONSEQUENCES

That natural tendency needs to be counterbalanced. Companies need to be held accountable for their overall impact – for good and for bad. But to be fair to everyone, *all* companies must be held to account wherever they are. Otherwise, those who act more responsibly risk being uncompetitive (at least in the short-term) in comparison with those who are more selfish – just as when whole countries overfish the oceans.

This is one of the areas in which (as detailed in the final chapter of this book) multinationals can benefit from helping set up shared mechanisms that play a direct role in even-handedly communicating to themselves, to governments and to the general public the best and the worst of what is happening – immune to lobbying and always guaranteed to be speaking from a fully-global, rather than national or corporate, perspective.

There is another crucial component to global accountability. Just because some corporations are so powerful and so important does not make it legitimate for them effectively to bully the international community by playing one country off against another. Global corporate regulation needs to be coordinated. Global tax regulation needs to be unified. And as a result, global accountability and its associated global consequences need to become unavoidable.

Although it is of course tempting for hugely-powerful multinationals to use their power exclusively to maximize shareholder profit – and therefore in general to lobby against increased regulation – that is an increasingly naive stance to maintain. Big Business has long had a reputation for pushing its weight around. And nobody likes a bully. Those who (fairly or unfairly) feel victimized wait for a chance to get their own back. And when that chance comes – when enough fellow-victims all push back at the same time – bullies get a taste of their own medicine. And, feeding on resentment too long pent up, such a retaliatory backlash can be unduly harsh.

## INDUSTRIES AS AGENTS – NOT VICTIMS – OF CHANGE

It is well-established that people are far more committed to altering their behavior if they feel they are themselves at least partly the originators of the change rather than just its victims. Consequently, in parallel with resolving universal issues such as global taxation mechanisms, the best ideas of how given industries should demonstrate (and regulate) Unelected Responsibility must ideally come from those industries themselves.

In so doing, corporations get a chance to reframe Unelected Responsibility in terms of, for example, Good PR. However, having once come up with such proposals, industries cannot then just expect to be left to regulate themselves in whatever way they choose. Self-regulation is often a popular and comfortable idea – I have just never found that it works particularly well unless it is given a bit of a prod first. There tend to be simply too many vested interests at play.

Instead, the proposals that industries come up with need to include ways by which the success of their proposals will subsequently be measured and policed. And if their ideas are not credible, then governments and the public need to question why. Regulation of capitalist enterprises is rarely best achieved through legislation. But neither does it come from toothless and incestuous self-regulation that can too-readily be wooed away from potentially-embarrassing issues. Ultimately, effective regulation needs access, independence and power.

## News Media after the Myth of Self-Regulation

Having industry-members devise their own reform – but avoiding unduly self-interested self-regulation – is particularly important for parts of the News Media. In the UK particularly, newspapers have become extremely competitive, with all the attendant consequences – including law breaking. To put that in context, it is important to remember that some exceptional investigative journalism has also taken place. Some of the journalists involved have indeed broken the law in pursuit of an important story that was truly in the public interest, such as the parliamentary expenses scandal in 2009. But almost everyone rightly accepts 'Public Interest' as a legitimate and important justification. However, in addition to concerns about illegality are the long-standing worries that impartiality, accuracy and even basic facts-checking too often have suffered. Those misleading stories then internet around the world. In addition, as already covered in the subchapter *Blind leading the blind* (page 53), the 24/7 News cycle encourages unintended bias because journalists and their editors have to choose the juiciest stories and then squeeze the pips out of them.

Concepts of Freedom of Speech and Freedom of the Press need to be brought up to date. They were devised – and for many countries (such as the USA) then cast in stone – at a time when no one had the same power to publish worldwide that is afforded to even the lowliest blogger today. High-Tech has changed what is reasonable and has significantly altered the balance that is fairest between individual freedom and collective security. What is more, as highlighted in the subchapter about *How politicians and journalists each Dance with the Devil* (page 57), there can be unfortunate side-effects that emerge from the interactions of news media and politics – and sometimes the police. In the modern world, there is a tremendous benefit from a free press being powerful enough to hold government to account, however embarrassing that may be. However, no unelected news organization should be so large – and therefore so powerful – that it can exert *undue* influence over elected governments. And, to avoid conflicts of interest, the revolving-door of career-moves and consultancy between Establishment bodies such as the media, politics and the police should not spin anything like so fast. Nor does it look good if too many individuals from appropriately-distinct branches of the establishment nevertheless drink at the same places or share membership of the same clubs. Or belong to the same Lodges.

Throughout history, there has always been a balance to be maintained across society. High-Tech has shifted the weight of power toward numerous forms of unelected media. That balance now needs to be corrected. The Media themselves are by far the best people to work out ways to restore equilibrium as well as improve the accuracy of how the public perceive complex topics such as global warming or medical risks or political trade-offs. But the Media will then need help to get their industry – and those that interact with them – actually to change.

## BANKS STEPPING UP TO A MORE-STRATEGIC ROLE

Banking similarly serves a vital purpose, but even so, the financial-services industry desperately needs reform. Banks are crucially important to stimulate and facilitate the global economy. However, they are not particularly helpful when they exaggerate trends by betting on whether something like a company's value, a currency or a commodity-price will go up or down. The unfettered Boundaryless People-Power of The Market has become too damaging and too unquestioned for its own good. Whatever traders typically claim to me, that sort of behavior is not always an example of 'corrections in The Market' – it is often pure guesses and gambling. And despite the argument that such well-considered bets uncover existing financial weaknesses and therefore help improve the world economy by removing those vulnerabilities, the reality is that such culling is chronically short-term and non-strategic.

As explained in the last subchapter, the net result can in fact be to lose forever potentially crucial options for the future. Genuine strategic investment in companies or countries, which as a result can grow better, is a win-win for both parties. But simply placing bets on them with the detachment of a spectator-sport risks being parasitic. Although the extremely clever people who analyze various financial markets and bet accordingly claim quite rightly to me that they have sometimes served a useful purpose by pointing out where the market has 'got it wrong', that skill would have proved more useful to the community at large (and their line of defense would be demonstrably less self-serving) if they had, for example, been working as analysts to assist the government rather than to line their own pockets.

Many traders go on to point out to me that they risk losing their shirts if they do not get their bets right. That sounds good on a TV interview, but it is usually far from the truth. More accurately, most of them only risk losing other people's money and their own bonuses. And when such casino-banking unnecessarily damages the effectiveness of the global economy as whole, it becomes unacceptably risky both for nations and for individuals.

## CASINO BANKING

Although the term 'casino banking' has recently become a common term to refer to high-risk speculative investment banking, it is a little unfair. Having analyzed the organizations behind both forms of speculation I can confirm that, unlike investment banks, casinos tend to have an extremely good grasp of the risks they run. Nor do they tend to over-borrow.

There is another problem with how The Market is allowed to operate. For the lauded 'market forces' to work, Capitalism requires orderly failure of some organizations in order that other more-competitive organizations can take their place – albeit, as just explained, it is in fact only those that are more-competitive in the immediate-term. That applies to banking as well. But modern banks have engineered a form of partial immunity because they tend to get the upside of economic booms while the taxpayer gets the downside (because the banks are too crucial to be allowed to fail). As a result, the financial institutions that constitute The Market do not live or die according to the same rules they insist apply to everyone else.

Even those banks that receive no formal government bail-outs nevertheless often benefit greatly from the tax payers in the country where they are headquartered. The reason is that everyone around the world assumes that the banks will, if necessary be protected by their respective governments, and therefore those banks are able to borrow money for less than they otherwise could. Thanks to the assumed protection afforded by potential bailouts funded by taxpayers, lending to most banks has long been seen as a very low-risk loan. So they are more profitable. So they have more money to pay themselves in the form of bonuses.

It is the general taxpayer who effectively pays for the implicit 'insurance' that the banks enjoy and that gains them privileged interest rates (and bonuses) unavailable to anyone else. Consequently, during a credit-crunch, when those same protected banks choose not to lend money to the very taxpayers that fund the banks' special privileges, it is hardly surprising that the resentment of a future backlash continues to build.

## CHANGING THE UNWRITTEN RULES OF THE MARKET ITSELF

Before some financial institutions become too big to save, governments and banks across the international community must address the current misalignments in the global capitalist system and realign their activities accordingly. They must re-evaluate just what The Market most usefully can be. And they must reassess how it is allowed to operate. This needs to have been sorted long before the inevitable stock-bubbles that will rise (just like the dot.com boom and bust) with biotech, nanotech and AI. And that is only possible with global agreements that *actually change the hidden logic that defines the Unwritten Rules of Banking* – in the same way as regulation aimed at Media and other sectors must also do.

By this measure, Basel 3 seems set to prove insufficient. And although bodies such as the G20 will be crucial in moving the debate forward, because ultimately they represent the interests of individual nations – not global interests as a unified entity – even they will not be sufficient unless they are supported by new powerful bodies that truly can take an independent view of the new world order. Ultimately, the political paralysis that often accompanies escalating financial crises needs to be addressed at source: the structure of The Market itself.

It is time to stop running scared of The Market. It is time to stop treating it as if it had some divine right to existence in its current form. And it is time to debunk forever the absurd myth that in the long-term The Market optimizes the world economy in the best possible way. In an analogous situation, until very recently, the apparent omnipotence of the dominant players in the global news-media remained unquestioned. Many politicians resented the situation – but felt there was in practice nothing they could do. All that changed. Very fast. Those who ride high on The Market's financial behemoths currently rampaging uncontested across the world economy would do well to take careful note. And then, in the furtherance of Unelected Responsibility, use their phenomenal collective power to change The Market – before others combine together to change it for them.

# CAPITALISM CRISES

**Important elements of Capitalism – such as competition – nevertheless cause increasingly dangerous lack of control across the world economy and require Unelected Responsibility as a counter-measure**

Escalating financial crises are inevitable because deeply-established systemic-threats in the banking system remain unchanged and largely unchangeable
- *The realities of modern banking encourage individual chronic short-termism with little regard for long-term consequences or impacts on others*
- *Although within the industry its shortcomings are well-recognized, on balance it suits banks to leave things as they are*
- *Governments and regulators have little freedom to change the banking system without risking triggering alternative financial crisis themselves*

Unrelenting competition has addicted modern corporations to change initiatives of which 70% fail causing further damage such as change-fatigue – which makes it hard to avoid backlashes
- *Driven by international markets, today's corporations necessarily compete on being able to change faster and more effectively than their rivals*
- *But lack of sufficient control means that most major change initiatives fail, leading to progressive change-fatigue and difficulties avoiding backlashes*

Unintended major distortions of perception caused by how the media have to report stories and interact with governments are warping political control
- *Developments like 24/7 Rolling News inadvertently cause gross misrepresentation of the true balance of what is happening in the world*
- *Systemic distortions in reporting ultimately result in insufficient checks and balances for the political process as a whole*
- *Because the government and news media are both crucial to each other there can be increasingly risky conflicts of interest*

Widespread misinterpretation of how competition optimizes the world economy risks crucially important long-term solutions being irretrievably lost

# Chapter summary

Capitalism crises need UNELECTED RESPONSIBILITY – corporations fulfilling a duty of due care over communities they impact

- *Just as legally a company is treated as a separate individual so it should also carry much the same social obligations as members of the broader community*
- *Global accountability and resultant global consequences need to be unavoidable even for corporations attempting to play one country off against another*
- *Each industry should itself propose the best ways to demonstrate and regulate Unelected Responsibility – governments and the public will anyway then ensure that they do*
- *The News Media must find ways to avoid competitive-pressures unintentionally leading to bias and misrepresentation – because it will increasingly be held far more accountable*
- *Financial-services must find how to play a truly-strategic role within the global economy – and not be incentivized toward short-term culling of temporary-weaknesses*
- *The success of self-regulation and external measures must be that they change the hidden logic that drives the 'unwritten rules' of The Market itself – otherwise they will fail*

## 5. How High-Tech Capitalism carries Systemic Risks

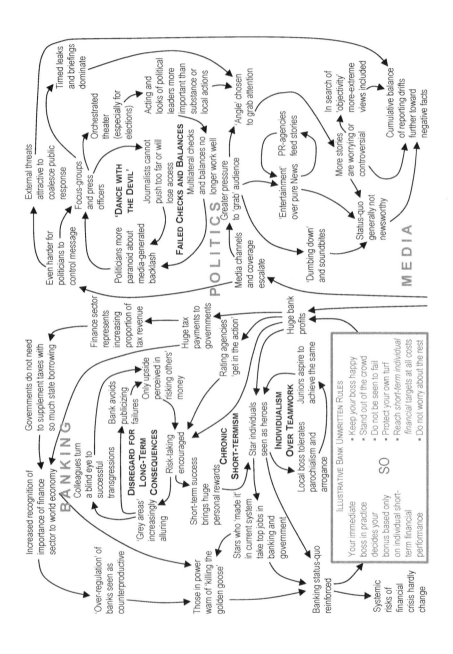

# Chapter summary

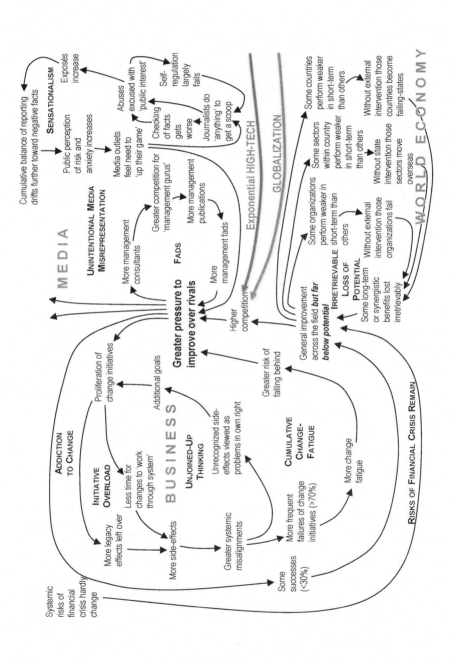

# INDUSTRIALIZATION CRISES OVERVIEW

Industrialization generates Pollution and Depletion side-effects that – starting with oil companies – are building major backlashes against those deemed responsible and require True Costing as a counter-measure

- The exceptional benefits of cheap sources of concentrated energy and carbon-based chemicals have left the world-economy addicted to fossil fuels

- For convoluted and partially-obscured reasons the genuine threats from climate change are being heavily misrepresented

- Energy producers feel unable to publicize that production of 'cheap' forms of crude oil is peaking and costs will on-balance escalate

- Governments know the economic threats from climate-change and peaking oil-production but find it close-to-impossible to change course

- Industrialization crises need TRUE COSTING – reflecting all the hidden costs and savings that different options ever bring

*Threats of backlashes to: MINING, OIL and ENERGY SUPPLIERS*

*ENERGY ADDICTION...*

*...POLLUTION...*

*...CLIMATE CHANGE...*

*...RESOURCE DEPLETION...*

# INDUSTRIALIZATION

# CRISES

# HOW ONE-TIME ENERGY GOT THE WORLD-ECONOMY ADDICTED

## The exceptional benefits of cheap sources of concentrated energy and carbon-based chemicals left the world-economy addicted to fossil fuels

THE UNTOLD HISTORY of Industrialization is a story of societies becoming progressively hooked on a small range of substances – each an increasingly more concentrated form of energy and exotic chemicals. To understand why this historical curiosity is set to cause such massive problems for the world economy, why it is contributing to backlashes against the scientific community and against politicians, why it is building up vastly greater backlashes against oil producers and energy suppliers, and why those backlashes are much the same pattern as will later also play out for those involved in mining and distributing other crucial commodities such as tin, lead, copper and phosphorus, you first must understand the fundamental link between the inexorable rise of Industrialization and how to make fire.

Even today many people around the world still burn wood to keep warm and cook food. What few of them realize is that they are actually using the wood like a storage battery that captured sunlight over (typically) several years but can be made to release the energy very quickly. While they are alive the plants grow by converting and storing solar energy, and that accumulated energy can later be released as heat by combining the wood with oxygen in the process we call fire.

Until a few hundred years ago, that was all that anybody ever needed to do to satisfy all their heating needs. But when the Industrial Revolution began in the mid-18$^{\text{th}}$ century, steam engines and iron smelting demanded more concentrated forms of energy than wood. They needed to become hotter, faster. As a result, early industry began using *fossilized* wood – in other words coal – which releases more energy when it is burned than the same quantity of wood ever can.

# Fossil-fuel addiction

That was sufficient for a hundred years or so, but by the 20<sup>th</sup>-century it was clear that if someone really needed concentrated solar-energy (for instance in order to power a horseless carriage or flying machine) then, instead of trying to use coal as the energy source, an even better idea was to use oil. This is the geologically-ancient remains of plankton and other living things that either directly absorbed the sun's energy in the early ages of the Earth or else ate those things that did. It is the most condensed form of fossilized solar-energy that exists.

That means it is also the most easily transported – which is why modern automobiles (and all powered airplanes ever built) do not run on wood or even coal but always on derivatives of oil. And there is an extra advantage to oil and the natural gas – primarily methane – that is often found with it. Because they originally came from living things, they contain a lot of carbon. For an industrial chemist, that is tremendously attractive because, more than anything else, carbon can combine with other elements to form a very-wide variety of substances. Science already knows of about ten *million* of these different carbon-based chemicals. Plastics are just one family of them.

## THE CHEMISTRY OF LIFE

Except for a very few simple substances that are historically excluded, the chemistry of carbon is known as 'organic' chemistry because of the long-recognized link between carbon and living organisms.

The special properties of irreplaceable fossil fuels have given civilization the one-time boost needed to create the modern world. Indeed, they have proved utterly vital. The amount of the sun's energy they contain – which is released when they are burned – is extraordinary. One liter (roughly one quart) of crude oil or gasoline provides the same amount of energy as a strong person working heavy labor for more than three days. The concentrated energy released from coal made the Industrial Revolution possible. The huge supplies of condensed energy – and also chemicals – trapped in coal, oil and gas have kept that revolution going for a couple of centuries.

# INDUSTRIALIZATION CRISES

Fossil fuels have literally powered the exploding growth of the global economy. Since Industrialization began, world output has expanded dramatically, most of it during the last century. And as wealth has increased, so too have populations that in turn depend on access to amounts of energy that are now far more than could possibly be generated by just using the energy that the Earth stores naturally each year in the form of new trees and plants.

Since about 1750 it has not been possible to sustain civilization without eating into the Earth's one-time store of fossilized solar-energy. The growing human population could not have satisfied the energy-demands of the 19$^{th}$ and early-20$^{th}$ centuries by burning wood alone any more than it could have satisfied the later-20$^{th}$ century's demand for plastics, artificial fertilizers and synthetic pesticides without deriving them from oil and natural gas. Largely as a result, the idea of apparently-unlimited 'extra energy' has become deeply embedded into every aspect of society – ranging from the inventions of suburbia and daily commuting to supermarket chains and international air travel.


## UNLIMITED OIL

Any early worries about how widespread oil was seem to have disappeared as soon as huge deposits were discovered around the world during the 1950s and 1960s. The Soviet Union then helped keep prices down by selling cheap oil in return for hard currency. Although the OPEC oil embargo in 1973 (in response to the USA resupplying the Israeli military during their Yom Kippur war against an Arab coalition) temporarily caused concerns about oil dependency, these were all-too-quickly forgotten when the oil began flowing again.


As already explained in the context of *The unsolved puzzle of the banking crisis* (page 20), throughout the last few decades the world economy has become addicted to never-ending change. But in reality that has only been possible because for the previous few centuries many societies were *already* deeply addicted to fossil fuels and the good times they provided. It is a habit that still feels great, and until recently it did not even cause many headaches. Yet national and global economies are increasingly at risk from

# Fossil-fuel addiction

this deep-seated craving because exponentially-hazardous threats are building around two fundamentally different side-effects. And those two threats have recently started to combine.

# CLOUDED INTERPRETATIONS
# OF POLLUTION

## Although the damage of local pollution from Industrialization has been obvious for centuries, the effects of airborne pollution remain far less clear-cut

EVEN FROM EARLY on in the process of Industrialization there were problems. During the Victorian summer the blinds on the Royal Train were required to be drawn down as the Queen passed through the North of England en-route to her Balmoral estate in Scotland – because she thought the industrial landscape had become so ugly. And winter 'pea-soupers' in London – caused by sulfurous coal fumes mixing with cold mists from the Thames – became so frequent that they were a common backdrop to the Sherlock Holmes stories as they swirled around 221b Baker Street. But yellowish smogs were gone by Spring and slag heaps were invisible a few miles up the track. In the Victorian Age, by-products of industrialization typically just seemed to disappear. They still do.

### PLASTIC, PLASTIC EVERYWHERE...

Recent research suggested that the volume of plastic in the oceans might have peaked in recent years – possibly as a result of tighter marine-pollution controls. More worrying explanations of the data are that the plastic is breaking into pieces too small to be caught by survey nets, that it is sinking to the bottom of the oceans, or that it is being ingested by marine life. A particular worry about that last explanation is that when small marine creatures eat plastic it can influence their bodies as if it were a hormone – interrupting breeding cycles and potentially collapsing vital elements of the food chain as a result.

# Climate-change misrepresentation

Yet much of that disappearing-act is an illusion. Every year, for several decades, millions of tons of plastic for example have found their way into the open oceans where large rotating currents called 'gyres' gradually gather together enormous flotillas. The largest is in the Eastern Pacific. A conservative estimate is that this floating garbage pack covers an area the size of Texas or France. By other criteria it is judged to be closer to the size of the whole of the USA. Either way, it seems to have doubled in size in the last decade.

Far less visible are the side-effects of apparently-beneficial industrial products such as synthetic fertilizers. These may be good for crops, but run-offs can for instance make their way to rivers where they fertilize the water causing huge algal blooms that, when they die, deplete the water of oxygen and kill fish as a result. In addition, as explained further in the discussion on superbugs (page 322), the damage to wildlife caused by powerful industrial pesticides such as DDT has been well-recognized for many decades. That sort of damage is created not just because insect-populations can build up resistance and become uncontrollable, but because birds that depend on eating the insects either die from hunger if the insects have been killed or else they absorb the pesticide themselves (which, for instance, can destroy their ability to lay proper eggs and as a result hatching rates drop).

Equally worrying is the release of long-lived pollutants from industrial activities such as chemical processing and mining. Mercury, for instance, is a by-product of gold mining, metal production, cement plants and especially coal-powered generators. Mercury compounds frequently get washed into the sea where they are absorbed by algae that are eaten by small fish that are themselves eaten by bigger fish. Although mercury is readily absorbed by animals, it then tends just to stay in them and accumulate. At each level of the food chain the mercury gets increasingly more concentrated, until in very big, long-lived fish – such as swordfish, shark and tuna – the mercury can build to levels that are fatally toxic to humans.

Similarly, although the risks from inhaling asbestos are well known, it is still a popular building material in rapidly-developing countries such as China and India. Attitudes to Health and Safety issues in those societies are often rather relaxed. As a result, both nations are at risk of severe escalations in asbestos-related illnesses over the next few decades.

# INDUSTRIALIZATION CRISES

## AIR POLLUTION

Any of the Pollution side-effects of Industrialization can potentially trigger a backlash against those deemed most responsible for things like progressive mercury poisoning or asbestosis. But above all else it is *air* pollution that is contributing to an imminent major backlash against oil and energy suppliers.

In much of the world, just as in Victorian London, air quality remains a problem. Back in the 1970s it was recognized that pollution from activities like burning coal formed small amounts of sulfuric acid and nitric acid in the atmosphere. The resulting 'acid rain' killed forests and destroyed whole lakes. Today, air pollution in cities is still poor. It probably causes more deaths than passive smoking, traffic accidents or obesity – even though it typically attracts far less political attention. Such pollution is estimated to reduce average lifespan of city-dwellers by more than half a year, and in the worst cities people with asthma may die almost a decade earlier than they would have with clean air.

One of the major culprits, hardly talked about, is Black Carbon – invisibly small particles of soot. In the developed world it is typically caused by incomplete burning of fossil fuels (whether gasoline in traffic-jams or coal in power stations). However, black carbon is often also a problem in developing countries because so many forests and grasslands are being burned. Although black-carbon particles are a direct health risk, they can also have an impact on climate because – before they get washed out of the atmosphere within a few weeks by rain – they absorb heat in a similar way to the far-more-talked-about 'greenhouse gases' like methane and carbon-dioxide ($CO_2$) that have a warming effect on the atmosphere.

## SOLVENT ABUSE

Other forms of air-pollution that are not themselves greenhouse gases can nevertheless also indirectly affect air temperature. For example, carbon monoxide caused by the partial burning of carbon-based fuels – as well as 'volatile organic compounds' (VOCs) such as the solvents in paints – both interact with other airborne pollutants to form heat-trapping compounds.

# Climate-change misrepresentation

Methane is often quoted as being about twenty times more potent than $CO_2$ as a greenhouse gas – although there is much less of it in the atmosphere. The facts are actually more complex than that. Methane stays in the atmosphere only about a tenth as long as $CO_2$ does, but while it is there it does a lot more damage. As a result, over a hundred-year period, methane's potential for global warming is indeed roughly twenty times the same mass of $CO_2$. Over a twenty-year period, though, its potential impact is many times that.

These days, leaks from landfill and natural-gas systems are increasing the concentration of methane in the air all the time. However, by far the greatest manmade contribution is actually from industrial-scale farming. Most people are aware that livestock such as cows produce methane in their guts. Less well known is that huge amounts of methane are also produced from the rice paddy fields that grew up during the $20^{th}$ century in Asia. We now know that microbes living in the water release large quantities of methane into the air.

Yet it is carbon-dioxide increases in the atmosphere that have attracted the greatest controversy over the last few decades. After all, modern Industrialization is already venting several tens of billions of tons of $CO_2$ every year – over a third from burning coal, forests and vegetation, over a third from oil, and much of the rest from natural gas. With countries like China building a couple of new power stations every week (and representing half of the entire world's coal consumption), pollution is set to increase dramatically. But just because more $CO_2$ is released into the atmosphere, will it actually change anything? After all, forests and oceans naturally absorb $CO_2$ – which is one of the reasons that China decided to lead the world in getting its citizens to plant new trees every year. So why cannot Nature simply absorb a bit more of the by-products from Industrialization than it already does?

And even if $CO_2$ levels *are* increasing – that does not prove that most of the rise is not natural. And anyway, even if Industrialization is the cause of rising concentrations of greenhouse gases, that does not automatically imply that it is the cause of global warming – even if there is any, which is not obvious. It is a convoluted web of issues that it is almost impossible for politicians and the general public not to get completely tangled up in. And that is exactly what a selection of powerful individuals has confidentially told me they are relying on.

## CHINESE WIND TURBINES

It is important to recognize that China is acutely aware of the potential polluting effects of its planned power plants and is working very hard to minimize them. A less-quoted statistic is that China builds a new wind-turbine *every hour*. What is more, it is only fair to point out that the average American is currently responsible for pollution levels that are maybe five or six times that of the average Chinese citizen.

# CLIMATE-CHANGE AND CONFUSION

## Politics, self-interest, complex science and unintentional media distortion are complicating interpretation of the manmade contributions to climate-change

WHEN IT COMES to decoding the overall backlash that will emerge from fossil-fuels (especially oil), it is completely misleading to try to explain something like 'climate change' only in terms of pollution. In reality, what will happen will be the result of a largely-hidden battle of contrasting vested interests in international politics, energy security, the media, private industry and oil multinationals.

I have been invited in to analyze the hidden workings of all of these areas, and when it comes to the oil corporations at the very center of this particular imminent global backlash I have worked in great detail with several of the largest. Partly as a result, I have built up an immense respect for many of them. But they are increasingly caught in a hugely interconnected jumble of conflicting incentives that risk trapping their industry – and all the rest of us – in serious trouble. So, throughout the remainder of this 'Industrialization Crises' chapter of the book I will try to tease out strand after strand of the hidden logic that is woven throughout the complex web surrounding fossil-fuel.

The initial strand is the misrepresentation of the science behind the climate-change debate. It is a deceptively important strand because that misrepresentation carries potential consequences that stretch far further than just oil, carbon-emissions and manmade global warming – it undermines trust in the self-same scientific community whose work is needed to keep Industrialization progressing.

Science is at growing risk of a major backlash stirred up by three largely distinct trends. We will look at the two more obvious causes for this potential backlash in the chapters on High-Tech Crises and Religion Crises. But less apparent to many people is the emerging risk to Science resulting from a long-standing and well-funded campaign that continues to be pursued by certain groups with oil and energy interests that wish to undermine the credibility of the science community on climate-change.

Combined with a largely-unintended distortion of how the scientific process is portrayed to the general public by the media, teachers and politicians, this apparently-narrow challenge to science is sufficiently prominent that it risks far more wide-reaching damage to public perception than is often assumed. To reveal how such misrepresentation is currently so very easy to achieve – and how the general public and politicians *ought* to view such complex scientific issues instead – it is necessary to examine the often-hidden reality of how science itself works.

## THE SCIENTIFIC PROCESS

Few people outside today's scientific community really understand the systems that drive the science industry. In reality, scientists tend to be extremely bright individuals who nevertheless sporadically make serious mistakes or (uncommonly) even conduct flagrantly bad science. A few so-called scientists – especially in the field of Nutrition – actually bought what effectively are fake PhDs and they are little more than con-artists with best-selling diet fads.

Sometimes, despite being above-average intelligence, true scientists – those with genuine PhDs from accredited universities – are nevertheless pretty dumb when it comes to interacting with the press, the public, or even each other. Occasionally they are petty, or selfishly ambitious, or arrogant. But what is not realized by the general public and nearly all politicians and journalists (a surprisingly small number of whom have scientific backgrounds) is that *none* of these failings ultimately matters. Uniquely – unlike any other profession – science in the long-run is immune to lying, cheating, stupidity and narrow-mindedness.

The reason is the Scientific Process. As we will examine in more depth in the subchapter on *The inexorable escalation of scientific revelation* (page 241), the underlying mechanism that drives science forward – only setting up hypotheses and theories that can potentially be disproved by those of a scientist's peers who truly understand the subject in great depth – results in a crucial set of behaviors across the scientific community.

The first group-behavior to understand is the way that good scientists may come up with well-considered suggestions that the scientific community as a whole accepts for a while but later rejects because new evidence comes along. For instance, when scientists observed the Gulf

Stream was slowing, it was good science to hypothesize this was caused by global warming causing Arctic ice to melt that in turn released cold fresh water that was disrupting the normal flow.

## THE ENGLISH RIVIERA

The Gulf Stream is like a giant conveyor belt across the ocean where warm water from the tropics flows on the surface, cools as it nears the Arctic, sinks to the bottom and flows back to the tropics again where it gets reheated and rises to the ocean surface once more.

The implication was that too much global warming might suddenly trigger the Gulf Stream to stop within only a few years (as it appeared to have done in earlier geological ages) and the UK, for instance, would then find itself suffering the cold winters of Canada. Hollywood and campaigners against global warming latched onto the idea – but it turned out to be wrong. It is now known that although there is dramatic short-term variability in the speed of the Gulf Stream, overall it does not appear to be slowing down. No one made any mistakes. It was good science at every step.

## SCIENTIFIC CONSENSUS

The second behavior that most people do not sufficiently understand is how 'scientific consensus' actually works. However much the scientific community as a whole appears to follow a particular science-fashion like sheep, treats a long-established hypothesis as 'fact' even though it is not fully proved, dismisses out of hand a new idea (especially from a non-scientist), or publically supports other scientists' work that they have not actually tested for themselves – nevertheless, some scientist somewhere will always eventually turn against the crowd and try to prove everyone else wrong. That is what science is all about. That is what gets someone a Nobel Prize.

When the highly-respected International Panel on Climate Change (IPCC) published a major report that included the warning that at current rates the Himalayan ice caps – which feed major rivers in Asia – might have melted by 2030, the worrying but authoritative claim was taken as

**97**

fact by politicians, climate-change activists, and indeed other climate scientists. Of course it was, because the source was the IPCC. Unfortunately (or perhaps 'fortunately' depending how you look at it) the claim was wildly inaccurate. It may even originally have been a typographical error.

## INTERNATIONAL PANEL ON CLIMATE CHANGE

The IPCC was established in 1988 through the mandate of the UN General Assembly to 'provide internationally coordinated scientific assessments of the magnitude, timing and potential environmental and socio-economic impact of climate change and realistic response strategies.' Its voting structure is designed to ensure that its assessment reports are fully bought-into by its 194 sponsoring governments around the world.

When the mistake was discovered, its fallout could probably have been handled with the press and the rest of the climate-change community far better than it was, but the fact remains that the claim was quickly denounced by those scientists that knew better. A few other scientists may have been left a bit bruised. But the scientific community as a whole acted exactly as it is supposed to do and quickly pulled things back on track.

An apparently more-worrying episode around the same time was the so-called 'ClimateGate' affair. However, despite the uproar stirred by the press over alleged conspiracies revealed by emails sent ten years earlier – in reality nothing dramatic was going on at all. The problem was that emails sent from the influential Climactic Research Unit at the University of East Anglia referred to a 'trick' in displaying temperature readings. In reality, this was merely referring to a graphical 'trick' for solving the problem of how simply to display a long period of historical temperatures.

Unfortunately, for those outside the scientific community who do not know how it actually operates, these sorts of episodes can be very disconcerting. Because politicians and the general public are typically unaware of the self-correcting mechanisms within the Scientific Process, those same corrections often come across to the outside-observer as mistakes that might not have been caught, U-turns, uncertainty or even signs of deliberate bias. When those incessant corrections relate to whether climate-change is indeed of vital importance, members of the public can rapidly become disenchanted. They conclude that there is no scientific consensus. And that is where other vested interests enter the story.

## THE CONSPIRACY THAT NEVER HAPPENED

The 'trick' mentioned in the ClimateGate emails was in fact referring to an existing chart that used tree-ring data as a proxy for temperature up until the 1960s and then tagged on thermometer readings from then on (because for reasons no one understands, tree rings stop being a good measure of temperature from that period). The originator of the chart was advised that including an explanation on the chart of the change in measuring device – from tree rings to thermometers – made the graph overly complicated for the general reader, so in the interests of simplicity it was left off from then on. Taken out of context and misinterpreting the usage of the word 'trick', this was then portrayed by the media as evidence of a conspiracy to defraud.

As already highlighted in *Rolling News and the unintended distortions it creates* (page 44), there are strong competitive pressures on today's media that can – sometimes completely unintentionally, though also sometimes less blamelessly – lead them to suggest that there is still serious doubt in the scientific community over whether global warming is manmade. There is not. If two competing views are reported it can appear far better radio or television, or seem a far more balance article, but that does *not* accurately represent the highly-consistent opinion across the scientific community that global warming is primarily a side-effect of Industrialization.

## PEER REVIEW

There is something very important here. Non-scientist politicians and journalists – however much they have deeply studied what scientists have said about global warming – are nevertheless *not* usually sufficiently competent climate-change experts credibly to take issue with genuine climate-scientists' conclusions. To be fair, neither even are other scientists *except in their particular areas of expertise.*

For climate-researchers to take that view is not scientific arrogance or elitism – although it is very easy for it to come across like that. Instead, their position reflects one of the irrevocable rules of the Scientific Process that specifies how the system of 'peer-review' must work: Only someone who is a comparable expert on a particular topic is competent enough to see the rights or wrongs of the science behind it. The reason is that PhD research programs are amongst the longest and most rigorous mental-training courses in the world. To earn the title Doctor by gaining a science PhD, it is not sufficient to demonstrate extreme knowledge of a particular subject – although a candidate also has to do that. Ultimately a contender for a PhD needs to demonstrate their mastery of the Scientific Process itself.

## GETTING PUBLISHED

In practice, Peer Review means that before you can publish your scientific work in a journal, the editor first sends your submission to one or more recognized experts on the topic you are writing about. Only if your 'peer reviewers' accept the quality of your science – even if they do not necessarily like all of your conclusions – will your article be published.

For a university graduate who has already received a top relevant degree, it typically takes a further three to eight years or even more to demonstrate mastery to the satisfaction of external examiners. Even after all that time, some post-graduate students nevertheless fail. Fundamentally, those several years of training are designed to instill a rigorous discipline into how researchers think about the world and interact with other scientists to tackle problems that are so new or difficult that no one has previously solved them.

The whole research-training builds to an ultimate test: The candidate must prepare a very-detailed written Thesis – and then defend it against experts in an oral examination – that demonstrates that the candidate has been able to push back the frontiers of knowledge and discover something that no one else knows. *But PhD students also need to be able to explain their logic in a way that allows fellow-experts independently to confirm or disprove the claims.*

To earn a PhD, coming up with new ideas alone is not sufficient. Being able to communicate and justify even supremely complex ideas in the precise shorthand of esoteric scientific jargon and previously-established scientific theory and laws is even more important. It can be an arduous training. Yet it inducts a researcher into a Scientific Process that is vastly more powerful than the intellects of even the greatest geniuses who have ever contributed to it. Moreover, it is a training whose impact never leaves somebody. In contrast, if someone does not go through that high level of prolonged initiation, then it is extremely difficult to pick up the skills by other means. And it is almost impossible to decode on-going scientific debate fully and correctly, let alone contribute to it.

Because climate change and global warming are such immensely complicated cross-disciplinary subjects, nearly all politicians, journalists and members of the general public – however bright and knowledgeable – are in practice largely excluded from contributing to a valid discussion on the rights or wrongs of the detailed science and its conclusion.

## ARE YOU A DOCTOR OR A DOCTOR?

Many people, of course, gain the title Doctor by studying medicine and becoming an MD. But that type of academic training is often very different to becoming a PhD because relatively few medical doctors specialize in conducting research that pushes back the frontiers of medicine – although there are a number of brilliant exceptions. In contrast to becoming a PhD, becoming an MD has historically demanded, amongst other things, a prodigious memory.

That is immensely frustrating to some people. But it is little different from someone without a Theoretical Physics PhD saying they do not agree with the implication of Einstein's Special Theory of Relativity that 'time dilates at velocities approaching the speed of light'. However passionately they may dissent, there contribution is not – to be really harsh about it – relevant.

Science is not quite like any other subject because of its unique internal ratchet-mechanism that over sufficient time keeps correcting errors and inexorably moving knowledge forward. And it is that Scientific Process – rather even than the complex ideas themselves – that it is very difficult for any other than scientists to access fully and to participate in credibly. Non-scientists (as well as scientists themselves) have a crucial role in debating the rights and wrongs of how science is applied. But – however hard it is for some people to accept – only those scientists who truly have depth in whatever subject they are talking about can fairly decide the rights and wrongs of the science behind it. And that necessarily excludes from the global-warming debate not just non-scientists but also a lot of non-climate scientists as well.

This is a difficult message for genuine experts to convey without it coming across as extremely insulting to everyone without the magic letters P, H and D after their names – and indeed even to many PhDs whose topic of expertise is not relevant to the debate. And such risk of offense is not helped by a small number of scientists who appear to revel in the intellectual elitism of their clique. But the fact remains, when it comes to modern science, most politicians and most of the general public just have to have faith *in the system.*

Everyone needs to trust – not individual scientists (who can be hopelessly wrong) but – the Scientific Method as a whole, which is built upon the healthy skepticism of peer-review applied to proposed explanations that fit all the evidence that has ever been gathered throughout the history of science. Peer-review is not the same as uncorroborated assertion on the internet. Healthy skepticism is utterly different to denial. Unpalatable as it may seem to those who feel their insights are as valid as anyone else's, Science is not a democracy. It is a search for the truth in which, unlike a political election, public opinion is irrelevant – because widespread public opinion, or long-accepted religious dogma, or commercial vested-interest does not change the truth.

## DISINFORMATION

Unfortunately, today's general misunderstanding of how the Scientific Method works makes it very easy for powerful lobbying groups to manipulate politicians and the public at large into questioning the validity of manmade climate change. All that lobbyists have to do is throw in a bit of plausible doubt. Some highly-skilled practitioners have tutored me in detail how to do it.

For a start you should point out that climate naturally changes anyway because of things like slow shifts in the Earth's angle and its orbit. You should then throw in concerns about accurately measuring temperature change given that modern cities act like massive storage radiators that distort readings. Follow up by explaining that, even though there was apparent global warming in the last quarter of the 20$^{th}$ century, some years this century have been unusually cool and no one predicted the fact. If the interviewer lives in an area that suffered a bad winter anytime in the last decade then, as a joke, use it as a local example of 'Evidence for Global Warming'. Throw in for good measure that, despite the alarmism of ecologists complaining about supposed Arctic ice loss, polar-bear populations have been increasing.

## SUNNY DISPOSITIONS

It has long been recognized that climate is impacted by astronomical factors. The precise timing of summer and winter varies on a roughly 26,000-year cycle, the tilting of the Earth's axis varies slightly according to a roughly 41,000-year cycle, and the shape of Earth's orbit relative to the sun squashes and stretches back again roughly every 100,000 years.

Before you can be pinned down, the trick is to keep changing direction. So add to the sense of confusion by pointing out that the latest research shows that warming in the Arctic increases evaporation from the Arctic Ocean and the resulting cloud cover reflects sunlight and so helps *counteract* any further warming. Suggest that there is a 'natural balance'. No need to interfere. Jump to the related statement that scientists accept that pollution actually causes 'global dimming' because it reflects sunlight, so if people are worried about global warming then the worst thing to do would be to reduce carbon emissions. This is probably a good time to throw in the phrase: 'In reality, the benefits of global warming may largely outweigh the negatives.' Follow this with the suggestion that it is far more cost-effective to *adapt* to any changes than give up the exceptional benefits of a relatively-cheap carbon-based economy.

If you are up against a real expert then throw in something esoteric to demonstrate your understanding of just how difficult climate-change prediction is. For instance, mention how climate models take account of the effects of 'sulfate aerosols' on temperature, and yet gases like carbon monoxide reduce the levels of sulfates – and that has not been built into the models. It really is extremely difficult (you should then sympathize) to get climate models to match what actually happens in the real world. Finally, subtly suggest – to get the maximum effect it is best hinted at rather than stated bluntly – that in the past there has been a deliberate political conspiracy to have the public focus on global Green issues rather than more-local concerns such as unemployment and public services.

By the time a journalist has ensured balanced coverage on the climate-change 'controversy' by including all those points, the TV interview or newspaper article will be over. It is all so easy. And nothing that has been said can actually be proved wrong. It is just that there has been a little economy with the truth. But what is the unbiased story that the public would hear if they could tap directly into the scientific consensus? What *are* the views of nearly all the relevant scientists with a deep knowledge of the subject? What is the truth, the whole truth and nothing but the truth about global warming – without the extras added by well-meaning journalists, politicians and celebrities and sometimes-less-innocent individuals who are lobbying for what (so they believe) are the best interests of oil and utility companies?

# THE REALITY BEHIND
# SCIENTIFIC CONSENSUS

The unbiased scientific consensus is there is an extremely high probability that manmade global warming is a genuine and serious threat to national security

THE INSIDE-STORY goes something like this. Changes in the Earth's average position relative to the sun (as well as changes in the sun itself) do indeed affect climate, but they do not explain present-day climate change. Neither does gas emission from volcanoes. By analyzing air trapped as bubbles in ice laid down in Antarctica and elsewhere, it has been possible to build a record of temperature and atmosphere stretching back over the last 800,000 years. This confirms that since the Industrial Revolution there has indeed been accelerated global warming, tightly matched by corresponding increases in $CO_2$ and methane. These measurements have nothing to do with historical temperature readings taken near cities – although they do corroborate them.

Since Industrialization began there has been about 1°C average global warming, $CO_2$-levels in the atmosphere have risen from 280 ppm (parts per million) to around 390 ppm, while concentrations of the far-more-potent but less common greenhouse-gas methane have grown from 700 ppb (parts per billion) to around 1750 ppb. 70% of all industrial emissions made since 1850 were made in the second half of the 20th century.

Average temperatures in any given year are influenced by a combination of largely-unpredictable factors. 2007, for instance, was an unusually cool year whereas 1998 was unusually warm. Despite this, January 2000 to December 2009 was the warmest global decade on record. 2010 was one of the hottest years on record. The last half of the 20th century was the hottest in a thousand years. The lion-share of that warming is attributed to human activity – mainly because we definitely know that average temperature is increasing very fast, we definitely know that we have been adding large amounts of $CO_2$ to the atmosphere over the same period, and linking those two facts by claiming that global warming is manmade is the *only* hypothesis that not only fits those facts but also centuries of scientific discovery as a whole.

In contrast, despite the claims of some climate-skeptics, something like 'solar activity' does not work as an explanation. Changes in the sun can indeed cause global warming – as is well researched. That makes it a good possible explanation to test out. But when we do, we find it does *not* correlate well enough with recent climate changes. That means that even though it was a good hypothesis, it is not consistent with all the evidence so is not a sufficient explanation.

## HOT OR COLD

Various factors affect a given year's average temperatures. For instance, sunspot activity primarily cycles every eleven years and impacts weather in highly-unpredictable ways. Recent research in fact suggests a slightly lower amount of overall solar radiation throughout the cycle than the historical norm, therefore if anything making *less* contribution to global temperatures than in the past. Another factor is the El Niño / La Niña cycle that repeats any time between three years up to seven years apart. 1998 was an El Niño year (when the sea-surface is warmer) whereas 2007 was at the opposite end of the cycle (when La Niña cools the sea-surface). If you only compare 1998 with 2007 it looks like the planet is getting cooler rather than warmer.

An important aspect of science is that it has to make sense in its entirety. Scientists cannot cherry-pick evidence to support their preferred explanation any more than different scientific disciplines are allowed to propose explanations that do not also fit every other discipline. Put at its most basic: Manmade global warming is the only explanation that not only fits all the evidence but also remains consistent with our wealth of understanding about how atmospheres and related phenomena work. Such climate models certainly are not perfect, but they are the best we have ever had, they are getting exceptionally sophisticated very quickly, and as a result they allow predictions to be made with far greater levels of comfort than were possible even just a few years ago.

Science is getting much better at modeling what is going to happen in the future, because of the exponential Simulation trend (referenced further in the subchapter relating to *High-Tech* that starts on page 298). It now allows us to take account of the complex interplay of things like the cooling effects of some forms of pollution combining with the impact of smoke clouds from forest fires – where the carbon particles *absorb* heat and so add to global warming. Similarly complex, as critics like to point out, is indeed the interaction of carbon monoxide from automobiles and power stations (as well as of methane) with sulfate aerosols.

## SULFATE SUBTLETIES

Sulfate aerosols – which have a cooling effect – are produced when sulfur dioxide ($SO_2$) oxidizes in the atmosphere. Methane and carbon monoxide (CO) have an indirect effect on sulfate production because they compete with $SO_2$ for oxidants such as hydroxyl, meaning that smaller quantities of $SO_2$ turn into sulfate. So, the more methane or CO in the atmosphere, the less cooling sulfates there are, and the warmer it potentially gets.

But the reality is in fact that these sulfates left alone have a cooling effect, so now taking account of the previously-unmodeled impact on them of gases like carbon monoxide only *increases* the predicted likelihood of global warming. In general, as we learn more, our original predictions – whether about average temperatures or sea-level rises – have turned out to be overly conservative and have eventually been upgraded into more severe forecasts. Unadulterated by the hysteria of Hollywood or the need for an alarmist headline, what the top scientists on climate change currently expect to happen over the next several decades is as follows.

### CLIMATE-CHANGE FORECASTS

Inevitably $CO_2$ will continue to build in the atmosphere because it will be a very slow process to reduce global-pollution rates – especially as the economies in China, India, Brazil, Vietnam and parts of sub-Saharan Africa take off. Plants absorb and process $CO_2$, so some will grow faster as a result. Unfortunately that includes weeds (including even things like poison-ivy, which also appears to grow more toxic). The oceans will fortunately absorb about half of the $CO_2$ made by industry. However that will make sea-water slightly more acidic, which in turn threatens species like Sea Butterflies because it makes it more difficult for them to manufacture their shells. Because these pea-sized animals are at the bottom of the marine food chain, reductions in their numbers are likely to ripple upwards to much larger species.

Despite the well-publicized proposals by numerous politicians, it now seems a major challenge to keep global warming down to only 2°C. Many scientists worry that there is a significant likelihood (specifically, about as likely that it happens as that it does not happen) that global temperatures rise by 5°C. If greenhouse-gas emissions continue at current rates then we should expect $CO_2$ concentrations to reach at least 560ppm by 2050 – which would be a *doubling* of $CO_2$ in the atmosphere since Industrialization began. By the end of the century it could be 800-900ppm.

Even just a 2°C increase is expected to bring major problems because it is estimated that around 20% of all plant and animal species would then be at increased risk of extinction. If the average global land temperature neared 5°C then that figure rises to around 40%. At the moment the consensus is that there is a 50/50 chance of 5°C warming by the end of this century. The last time the Earth saw those sorts of temperatures was 34-million years ago at the end of the Eocene period (which started around 56-million years ago).

There are many negative effects of rising temperatures. Milder winters are already risking explosions of malarial mosquitoes, cockroaches, tree-destroying beetles and disease-carrying rodents in areas that previously never suffered from them. However, it is important to qualify this point. As yet, it is unclear what the net effect of global warming in parallel with other changes will be. Measures for controlling a disease such as malaria, for instance, may have substantially more impact on its spread than climate change.

The impact of rising temperatures on agriculture seems clearer. Modern crops have been bred to grow best in the climates that farmers have become used to, and crop-yields typically drop dramatically as average temperatures increase. In addition, drier trees and plants lead to more and worse wildfires. There is also a more widespread effect. Global warming means there is more energy trapped in the atmosphere, so like a heated pot of water it becomes increasingly turbulent. Around the world, storms will be stronger and storm-surges will be more powerful. Everyone remembers how in 2005, Hurricane Katrina hit impoverished areas of New Orleans. But people tend to forget that in 1938 New York was also hit by a hurricane – as it had been a few times in the 19th century. In August 2011 more than 300,000 people were evacuated from low-lying areas of New York City prior to the arrival of Tropical Storm Irene. It will happen again and Wall Street will be brought to a standstill. Increasingly frequently.

## SEVERE WEATHER WARNINGS

A slight temperature increase can cause what feels like a disproportionate increase in severe weather. By definition, there are only a small number of extreme meteorological events that on average occur, say, each decade. If only a few extra are added as a result of temperature increases then the number of a given type of event (such as something previously designated as a 'once-a-decade hurricane') might double. Psychologically, it is the outlier events that increase far more noticeably than the bulk of far-more-common events.

Those who claim that 'the benefits of global warming largely outweigh the negatives' really do not understand – or they deliberately choose to ignore – that in many ways the threats are as much to do with *water* as with heat. For instance, loss of mountain snow and ice (because they have melted early) can lead to drought during summer months because mountain-fed rivers run dry. The major glaciers currently feeding the Indus, Ganges, Yellow and Yangtze rivers will probably last a long time. But smaller ones will not.

We simply do not know how high it is that sea-levels will rise by 2050 – let alone by the end of this century – but the trend is upward. Original estimates suggested that if we kept standing on the same spot on the seashore we would be up to our ankles or knees in water by the end of the century. Now some think we would be in way over our heads. Rising sea levels will impact the exclusive luxury resorts on the Florida Keys as well as the poverty-stricken homes of hundreds of millions of people in low-lying coastal regions of Asia. The rich can move.

But it is estimated that if the sea only rises to waist height it will cover about half of Bangladesh and leave tens of millions of its citizens with nowhere to go. Worse, as sea-levels rise, storm-surges travel further inland. Fundamental concerns about short-term rises in sea level have led the Association of Small Island States (AOSIS) – made up of low-lying countries like The Maldives, Palau and Grenada – to push for far lower $CO_2$ targets. Other countries that are richer or higher or both are currently unwilling to consider the notion.

Between 1920 and 2005 the snow cover in the northern hemisphere declined by 4%, which is an area significantly larger than the territories of Texas *and* France combined. And polar ice is in general melting faster than initially predicted. In recent decades the Arctic (a region the size of North America) has been warming at twice the rate of Earth as a whole – it has not been this warm for thousands of years. Indeed, since the 1980s there has been a 30% drop in the area covered by ice in the late Arctic summer.

As a result, in 2008 polar bears – which depend on broken sea ice for hunting – were officially declared a threatened species. In many areas, bears' condition has been deteriorating as the ice needed by them to hunt seals has reduced. And malnourished mothers give birth to cubs that are far less likely to survive to their first birthday. Early estimates of polar-bear populations were not very scientific (which is why it is easy for naysayers to claim that numbers have increased). However, under more stringent observation, it seems that at least eight out of nineteen recognized populations *are* decreasing, only one appears to be increasing, and for many of the other populations there is insufficient data to know.

Until recently, the more-pessimistic scientific forecasts suggested that the Arctic might see its first ice-free summer seas as early as 2030. But thanks to declassified data gathered by US, UK and Russian submarines since the 1950s, we now know that the thickness of Artic ice has almost halved since the 1980s. It is now understood that today's ice is thinner and has more gaps in it than had previously been appreciated. Reassessments of the Arctic ice now estimate that it is a *quarter* of the volume that it was in only 1979. As a result, in only a few decades (maybe even by 2020) the North Pole will be open water during the summer for the first time in recorded history. In addition, the mythical Northwest Passage sought for centuries by sailors as a trade route between the Atlantic and Pacific oceans, since 2007 has cleared of ice sufficiently for it to be navigable by commercial traffic for the first time.

## WHY MELTING ICEBERGS DON'T CHANGE SEA-LEVEL

Ice takes up more space than the water that makes it – which is why unlagged water pipes can burst if they freeze, and why icebergs float. However, anything that floats displaces its own weight, so an iceberg is displacing its own weight in seawater. When ice melts it contracts as it becomes water and exactly 'fills the gap' that was previously taken up by the part of the iceberg that was originally below the surface – so the overall sea level does not change at all.

When icebergs melt they do not increase sea level, but when glaciers break off from land and fall into the sea they do. Greenland is on average losing significantly more of its icecap than is being replaced by snow each year; its ice is flowing down to the sea twice as fast as two decades ago. In 2010, a single block of ice about a hundred square miles in area calved from the Petermann Glacier on the north-west coast of Greenland.

Antarctica has ten times the land ice of the Arctic, constituting about 70% of the world's fresh water. But it has also seen disproportionate warming each decade since the 1940s – a total of almost 3° Celsius – accelerated by changing wind patterns. That is about ten times the rate of warming for the rest of the planet. In 2002, an unusually large part of the Antarctic Larsen Ice Shelf broke up and disintegrated within a single season. The piece that was lost was the size of the US-state of Rhode Island. In 2008, the collapse and breakup began of the whole of the Antarctic Wilkins Ice Shelf. By 2012 its disintegration was well under way. It is roughly the size of Jamaica.

## POSITIVE FEEDBACK

All these examples of Industrialization backlash are important concerns. But scientists have even deeper worries. They relate to the concept of Positive Feedback. Most systems in nature achieve balance and stability by progressively slowing down as they near their goal. As a human being, you frequently adopt the same technique. For instance, you reach to pick up a fragile sliver of glass and as you get close to it you move your hand slower, then just your fingers, until you very slowly and gently touch it and stop. That is Negative Feedback. The deep worry about global warming is that it has the potential to do the exact opposite and run away with itself – like a growing snowball accelerating down a mountainside. The more that temperatures rise, the *faster* they may rise still more. That is Positive Feedback. It is the mechanism behind exponential trends. And climate change is full of these sorts of potential explosions.

The most common greenhouse gas on earth is not carbon dioxide as many people think. It is water vapor. In fact, water vapor has more impact than any of the others. The reason why it does not get much media attention is that unlike the other greenhouse gases the amount of gaseous water in the atmosphere is not directly impacted by human activity – however much greater the quantity of steam that pours out of power-station cooling towers. Instead, the concentration of water vapor is a function of air temperature.

The warmer the atmosphere, the more water vapor that it tends to hold. But that means that the more global warming there is, the more of the dominant greenhouse gas that there will be, so the more that global warming will accelerate. Positive feedback. We now realize that under those kinds of circumstances climate is potentially far more sensitive than we thought. Like that snowball on a mountainside, pushed too far it can run away with itself and change out of all recognition.

There are many other examples of Positive Feedback that could help trigger uncontrollable global warming. Some of them on their own are quite minor – but it is their collective effect that matters. For example, as temperatures on average get warmer, destructive beetles are not killed off in the winter so more trees are destroyed so less $CO_2$ is absorbed so temperatures rise further. At the same time, trees become drier, so they are more vulnerable to fire, which not only reduces their number (and so ability to absorb $CO_2$) but also adds to the black carbon in the atmosphere, which makes things still warmer.

Black carbon itself exacerbates some other examples of positive feedback. Clean ice reflects sunlight extremely well and bounces nearly all the energy back (technically called the 'albedo effect'). But when black carbon gets washed from the atmosphere it slightly darkens the ice, which absorbs more energy and melts more quickly. However, water reflects much less solar-energy than ice, so it heats up far more, which melts more ice even quicker – which is one of the reasons the Arctic has been warming twice as fast as the rest of the planet. Yes, cloud cover has indeed been increasing in proportion. And part of the impact of cloud cover is to reflect sunlight. However, it also acts like a blanket that traps heat. Despite the one-sided misdirection of certain warming-skeptics, we now know that except in summer, artic clouds appear to have an overall *warming* effect.

In addition, as the surface-ice on glaciers melts it collects into rivers that eventually cascade down through giant shafts (called moulins) that plumb the interior of the ice-sheet and as a result help to melt it from the inside. We have now found that some of the water makes its way to the bottom of the glacier where the ice-sheet is very slowly sliding across the land. The water acts as a lubricant, and so increases the speed at which the glacier heads for the sea, and so increases the calving of chunks of ice falling off into the ocean where they melt and raise sea-levels.

Yet another potential runaway effect is caused by 'gas hydrates'. These are ice-like deposits made of water and, most commonly, methane that are found underneath the oceans and in the permafrost regions of the world – typically near the poles. The best guess is that there is as much as ten trillion tons of carbon trapped in these gas-hydrate deposits. That is the equivalent of well over *ten times* the total amount of $CO_2$ currently in the atmosphere.

These deposits are stable if they are kept cold and under pressure. But global warming has the potential to change that. As temperatures rise, so more gas hydrates will release the methane trapped within them, which because it is more than twenty times more potent as a greenhouse gas than $CO_2$ will accelerate the warming still more, which will release even-more-disproportionate amounts of methane. That specific type of escalation is not unsubstantiated theory. It looks like it may be exactly what happened around 56-million years ago (during a period known as the Paleocene-Eocene Thermal Maximum).

## ADAPTING TO CLIMATE-CHANGE

These risks of runaway global-warming are all cumulative – any one of them can reinforce the likelihood of triggering the others. Yet, given the complex science and the deliberate disinformation, many people understandably nevertheless want to believe that changing the level of carbon-pollution is not necessary, or is not worth the cost, or can at least be postponed. Unfortunately, the combination of all these very-natural reactions are only in fact adding to the likelihood and the severity of an eventual backlash against those who are deemed to have 'confused the issue' of climate-change.

In the face of such confusion, the best hopes of most climate activists these days is to persuade countries to slow the increase of their global carbon emissions. Even that is proving incredibly difficult, so hardly anyone is suggesting actually trying to *reduce* the current $CO_2$-levels. And no oil or coal company or energy utility can currently be expected to take an active lead in warning the general public about Industrialization side-effects – quite to the contrary in fact.

As a result, during a decade in which the world is recovering from economic near-disaster, it can be very tempting for politicians to keep a little quieter than before on Green Issues – and as a result, indirectly pander to those who argue that we should eventually *adapt* to any changes brought by climate change rather than do anything now that could risk undermining the one-time opportunity that fossil fuels present. The trouble is that the alluring mirage of 'adapting to climate change' is itself a product of deliberate disinformation propagated by some of those I have worked with. In reality it is now generally accepted amongst scientists and economists that the eventual cost of adaptation would be unaffordable.

New research techniques have very recently allowed us to push back our knowledge of atmosphere to around 20-million years ago. As a result, we now know that the last period when $CO_2$-levels were sustained at concentrations close to where they are today – let alone the higher levels that many now think inevitable – there was no icecap on Antarctica and the sea had risen above today's levels by the height of an eight to twelve-story building.

## LONG, LONG AGO...

It has very recently proved possible to measure how much carbon dioxide there was in the atmosphere about 20-million years ago (at the start of the Miocene period). The new figures are derived from measuring ratios of boron and calcium in the ancient shells of tiny sea creatures called *foraminifera*. The ratio varies depending on the acidity of water, which in turn indicates $CO_2$-levels in the atmosphere.

# Climate-change misrepresentation

That does not necessarily imply cause and effect. Nor does it indicate how long such a transition might take. But it is a very serious warning to governments. That is not just because it is a relevant example of what potentially could happen. It is because such a development would currently be beyond the capacity of any economy on Earth to adapt to if it did.

## 6. HOW POLLUTION SIDE-EFFECTS IMPACT GLOBALLY

# FOSSIL–FUEL ADDICTION

Sustained Industrialization only possible because of once-only energy boost to world-economy from releasing trapped solar-energy in fossil fuels as well as using them to make organic chemicals such as plastics, fertilizers and pesticides

## POLLUTION SIDE-EFFECTS
### especially Manmade Global Warming

- Plastic (such as the huge floating Eastern Pacific garbage pack)
- Fertilizer into oceans killing fish (via deoxygenating algae blooms)
- Toxic mercury byproducts rising up food chain (to fish such as tuna)
- Black Carbon in atmosphere from incomplete burning of fossil fuels
- Methane (from landfill, natural-gas systems, cattle and rice paddies)
- Carbon dioxide (over 1/3 from burning coal, forests and vegetation, over 1/3 from burning oil, much of the rest from natural gas)
- Combined effects give a 50/50 likelihood of 5°C atmospheric warming
- Positive Feedback dynamics risk snowballing negative side-effects
  - Higher temperatures increase water-vapour that raises temperature
  - Water absorbs more heat than ice so melts the remaining ice faster
  - Thawed gas hydrates release gases that raise temperature still more

## *THREATS*

- Rising sea-level and storm surges will severely disrupt low-lying areas
- Extreme weather events will become more disruptive and frequent
- Temperature-sensitivities mean crop-yields risk dropping dramatically
- Loss of mountain snow and ice risks summer droughts
- Mild winters will not kill off agricultural pests and disease carriers

## DISINFORMATION

- 'There is still serious scientific debate over whether global warming is primarily manmade – despite what some say, the answer is unclear'
  *IN REALITY THERE IS EXTRAORDINARY SCIENTIFIC CONSENSUS*
- 'Just because there's broad consensus doesn't make it the correct explanation'
  *IT DOES MEAN IT IS FAR MORE LIKELY THAN ANY OTHER EXPLANATION*
- 'Scientists follow like sheep'
  *THEY THRIVE ON RADICAL THINKING*
- 'Climate-scientists with PhDs do not have a monopoly on deciding the rights and wrongs of global-warming claims'
  *ACTUALLY THEY DO*
- 'ClimateGate scientists deliberately falsified findings'
  *THEY DID NOT*
- 'The authoritative IPCC made false claims about glacial melting'
  *IT WAS AN ERROR IMMEDIATELY CAUGHT BY OTHER SCIENTISTS*
- 'The News-Media point out there is still controversy'
  *CONTROVERSY MAKES A STORY*
- 'Major oil-related organizations say there is no scientific proof of a problem'
  *PRIVATELY SOME SAY THEIR STRATEGY IS THE ONE TOBACCO FIRMS USED*

## *BROAD CONFUSION*

# WHY OIL AND ENERGY SUPPLIERS FEEL IT WRONG TO TELL THE TRUTH

## Energy producers feel unable to publicize that production of 'cheap' forms of crude oil is peaking and costs will on-balance escalate

WHAT ABOUT THE suggestion that Green issues are being used by some politicians around the globe as a bit of a diversion? As this subchapter highlights, to a limited degree that is true. But it is not a coordinated conspiracy – it is just state politics mixed with corporate politics. And it is the next strand of the hidden reality behind fossil-fuel.

Over the last few decades I have probably held more strictly-confidential, totally-off-the-record, multi-hour discussions with more senior members of oil and energy companies around the world than any of the top executives actually running those corporations. After all, it is not typically in the job-description of CEOs to spend their time in that way. I have heard the detailed private views of hundreds of key people across the industry, in many countries, fulfilling many different roles. And I have become aware that there are some broadly-consistent issues (not in any way specific to a given company) that raise severe concerns.

Recently, a few senior people in and around the oil industry have – typically for the best of intentions – begun breaking ranks in disregard of pressure from many of their colleagues. They have started to raise semi-publically the same anxieties that I know that many of their colleagues hold privately. So it is now doubly important to corroborate what they are saying by conveying the overall pattern of what many consider to be an open-secret within the industry.

## PROBLEMS WITH OIL

New crude-oil deposits are becoming increasingly difficult to find. Existing crude-oil deposits are becoming increasingly expensive and dangerous to extract. Future demand for crude oil is set to increase – whereas the rate at which crude oil can be economically extracted to satisfy that growing demand is set to *decrease* within this decade.

Put another way, after one-and-a-half centuries of drilling, readily-affordable crude-oil production is peaking. And yet, in public, the oil industry generally keeps quiet – or even denies – the very concerns about 'Peaking Oil' that many of their senior executives have held in private for several years. Some apparently-independent bodies maintain the same optimistic stance – at least in public. As do a few senior politicians – especially, it often appears, those with links to the oil industry. Consequently, most politicians along with the general public genuinely do not have a realistic view of what is about to happen.

All non-renewable resources – ranging from coal and corundum to diamonds and rubies – can theoretically be extracted and then used at almost-unlimited rates. But they remain non-renewable. It is not so much that they get completely used up, as that they eventually become too expensive to extract. However much prices go up and so justify ever-more-costly extraction methods, eventually the price becomes more than the market is willing to bear. Nations will never run out of oil – they eventually simply will not be able to afford it.

## SCARCITY AND VALUE

Carbon in the form of coal, and aluminum-oxide in the form of corundum, are relatively common. But exactly the same molecules structured differently become diamonds and rubies or sapphires – and they are rare. We value the largely-impractical forms of the identical chemical compositions as Gemstones and the other as Commodities.

That scenario is far more disruptive in the case of oil because the whole continued profitable growth of Industrialization remains strongly dependent on it. If oil production peaks in the near future, the global economy will still be geared to that peak-level of oil availability – and indeed to the expectation that production will continue to grow. If instead world production-levels drop then oil-shortages will mean prices inexorable edge up. So, asking when Peak Oil is likely to occur is a crucial question.

# Peaking affordable oil

The 'official' answer from the industry is that there is nothing to worry about because, very roughly, two-trillion barrels of oil have been found of which only one-trillion barrels have ever been extracted. We have only used up half the oil that we have so far discovered. And anyway there are alternatives. Where is the problem?

## ROLL OUT THE BARREL

For historical reasons a barrel of oil is defined as 42 US gallons (almost 159 liters) but does not actually correspond to any standard container used in the oil industry.

There are actually several. For a start, it is widely believed by those I discussed in detail with that even today the reserves are overinflated. Historically within the industry there has been a strong pressure to do this because showing high reserves helps market-confidence, boosts stock value and directly effects career prospects.

Following the fallout of scandals such as the disclosure in 2004 that Royal Dutch Shell had severely overstated its oil reserves, several Western-based corporations checked and quietly revised their estimates to be more conservative. However, many insiders still assume that OPEC-nation oil reserves remain systematically overstated because of an earlier agreement that specified that the amount of oil each member-state was allowed to sell depended on how large their reserves supposedly were.

## THE OIL CARTEL

Twelve nations make up the Organization of Petroleum Exporting Countries (OPEC) oil cartel: Algeria, Angola, Ecuador, Iran, Iraq, Kuwait, Libya, Nigeria, Qatar, Saudi Arabia, the United Arab Emirates and Venezuela.

The second problem about reserves is that nearly all of them have probably been found already. Over the last few decades the whole world has been seismically searched with immensely sophisticated equipment. For several years it has been a largely-secret but growing concern across the industry that all the major oil fields are already known about. For a long time even the best exploration divisions have been finding fewer new oil deposits. And those deposits have tended to be smaller than those of the past. Potentially-major economies such as China and India have rigorously searched their continents for oil to help fuel their Industrialization programs – and they have found little. In 2010, the global oil industry found the equivalent of only a fifth of the oil that it used.

The third reserves-problem relates to quality. It is true when oil-companies claim that there are still huge proved reserves that are yet to be extracted. But much of that oil is very poor quality when evaluated in terms of 'net energy' – in other words, the overall amount of energy that can be got from the oil once the amount of energy needed to extract it has been deducted. About sixteen tons of so-called oil-sands (also known as tar-sands) are needed to produce one ton of synthetic crude oil, and it requires huge amounts of energy to do so. As a result, far more greenhouse gases are released into the atmosphere.

In addition, the process of extracting synthetic crude from oil-sands uses large amounts of water that is left toxic. And because oil-sands are usually extracted by means of surface-mining there can also be major environmental concerns. Similarly, 'shale-oil' also currently needs high amounts of energy and water to extract. But unlike oil-sands – and despite what is often implied to the contrary – no one even yet knows how to extract oil from such deposits commercially.

## STICKY PROBLEM

'Tar Sands' do not actually contain tar – which typically is derived from pine resin. They are just very thick and sticky like tar. In fact, Tar Sands are a mixture of moist sand or clay and an extremely viscous form of crude oil called bitumen (also known as asphalt).

And the fourth problem concerning oil reserves is that nearly all the remaining reserves are far more difficult to extract than in the past. The one-trillion barrels the world population has already consumed was the *easy* oil. In the early days of the industry, crude oil could be found in-land rising to the surface on its own. Then by drilling down it could be found close to the surface. Then deeper. Then near the shoreline. But usually it was in large reservoirs, in relatively friendly and safe locations. Those days are largely already gone.

The technical complexity of some of the deep-water drilling in places like the Gulf of Mexico is almost incomprehensible. The most advanced rigs are designed to drop a drill on the end of a pipeline through a mile or more (a few kilometers) of water before then drilling down through rock to a total depth of up to five miles (almost ten kilometers). Even more impressive designs are being planned. But extracting ever-more inaccessible oil is not just progressively expensive. It takes longer. It is also increasingly dangerous – not least because any breach on the seafloor is so deep that pollution does not behave like a conventional single spill but instead spreads throughout a vast area, requiring huge resources to manage.

The unprecedented Deepwater Horizon disaster in 2010 was largely a reflection of the extremes to which oil companies are these days being forced to go to extract crude. If there were easier ways of getting large amounts of oil they would be using them. There are not. So the biggest companies are instead driven to risk financial and ecological disasters in Alaska or the Gulf of Mexico and fatal attacks on their personnel in unstable parts of Africa and the Middle East.

To put that in context, these are multinational corporations that are immensely wealthy, who spend on one production project more than many small countries spend on everything, who can have their own covert-operation forces to protect their interests in hostile territories, and who typically thrive when heroically overcoming apparently insurmountable technical challenges.

That is not to say that they are not fixated on safety – nearly all of them are to a far higher degree than the general public realizes. But all those traits mean that we should never rely on the major oil companies to apply the brakes. They are not just in it for the money. For many of them, pushing things – including themselves – to the limit so as to achieve the impossible against all odds is a way of life. They are the very last ones we should expect to chicken-out from extracting ever-more-inaccessible, ever-more-dangerous oil.

## PROBLEMS WITH TELLING THE WHOLE TRUTH

Those are some of the main issues about oil reserves that are not yet receiving enough government (let alone public) discussion. Instead, on the rare occasion when an oil company publishes a 'major new find' it is usually only an optimistic Discovery Estimate of what has been found without any detailed knowledge of size, quality or difficulty of extraction. And if someone – almost always from outside the industry – raises the issue of Peak Oil, they can often be pushed to become so strident and apocalyptic in their claims that it is all-too-easy calmly to dismiss them.

However, from my knowledge of what numerous industry insiders themselves privately believe, we should assume that globally the economy may be hitting peak crude-oil production around about now. *Readily-affordable* crude-oil production has almost certainly peaked already. Only because of reserves built up because of temporarily-reduced demand caused by the world economic recession may the side-effects of peaking production remain relatively hidden till the middle of this decade. The current unrest across Arab oil-producing nations adds an unknowable (but hopefully relatively short-term) perturbation to this overall long-term trend.

## SAUDI RESTRAINT

In 2009 and again in 2010, Saudi Arabia actually produced less oil than it did in 2003. Even in the few years before 2009, during which oil-prices at one point approached $150 per barrel, it still produced less than in its peak-production year of 2005 – which came in at a level about 13% higher than both 2009 and 2010.

A 2010 report by the International Energy Agency (IEA) suggested that Peak Oil had actually been reached in 2006. But in many ways, whether or not Peak Oil has indeed almost been reached or even passed already, the industry is *acting* as if it had. Many believe that increased prices and demand should have resulted in greater production than has occurred. For instance, in 2009 and 2010 total Middle-East production was lower than 2004 levels. Russia now produces more oil than Saudi Arabia – which had record production in 2005 and for whatever reasons has so far produced less ever since.

In 2009 there were anonymous accusations from two senior officials within the IEA that official figures had been deliberately and consistently underplaying a looming shortage for fear of triggering panic buying. And in 2010 the French oil company Total publically stated that it believed the global industry would struggle to produce even 10% more than current production levels – a figure far below (even the downwardly-revised) estimates then claimed by the IEA.

## INTERNATIONAL ENERGY AGENCY

The IEA is an autonomous intergovernmental organization that acts as a policy advisor to member states of the Organization for Economic Cooperation and Development (OECD) as well as to countries such as China, India and Russia.

This strand of the fossil-fuel hidden logic is itself incredibly entangled. The reality is that the IEA has a genuine responsibility to help maintain stability in its industry, and as a result it is bound sometimes to feel encouraged to present an optimistic portrayal of future developments. Privately-owned oil multinationals quite correctly feel their legal obligation is to maximize shareholder-value, and therefore they are in many ways *required* not to say things that might unnecessarily damage their stock price. State-owned oil companies are expected to act in the best interests of their country, and upon occasion that includes avoiding showing any form of perceived weakness such as diminishing oil-production capability.

Politicians caught in a major downturn already have their work cut out to regrow the shaky global economy, and shifting away from oil dependency is a costly process at the best of times. However, that is in fact one of the reasons why it *suits* many governments to continue to promote Green issues relatively strongly. It is not just that politicians who have been well briefed absolutely recognize the risks of $CO_2$ emissions (as many of them truly appear to do). It is not even because they think a Green philosophy is a potential vote-winner (though some of them probably do, despite it currently being a bit less fashionable than during the second half of the last decade).

It is because of twin political realities: It is risky to maintain oil-dependency on ideologically-differing nations, and oil is in danger of becoming prohibitively expensive as demand soars while production does not (or at least while timely, safe, energy-efficient oil production does not). Key statesmen already understand that a shift away from oil cannot be made without broad public support, so officially backing and reinforcing widespread concerns over $CO_2$ makes sense for reasons of both national and global security. In contrast, reducing levels of methane – despite its potential influence – hardly gets any attention.

It is largely unreasonable to claim that governments are playing games with the public just because politicians recognize that risks relating to climate change *and peak-oil-production* both imply the same need for the world-economy to face up to its fossil-fuel addiction. As alluded to earlier, Global Warming and Peak Oil are indeed two fundamentally different Industrialization side-effects that have recently started to combine to create exponentially-hazardous dangers. The reality is that when major politicians justify reducing oil dependency because of environmental benefits (but do not even mention the term Peak Oil) they are merely being pragmatic enough to push at a partially-open door. As you will next see though, unfortunately, that door appears to be stuck.

## 7. HOW DEPLETION SIDE-EFFECTS IMPACT GLOBALLY

# FOSSIL–FUEL ADDICTION

Sustained Industrialization only possible because of once-only energy boost to world-economy from releasing trapped solar-energy in fossil fuels as well as using them to make organic chemicals such as plastics, fertilizers and pesticides

## DEPLETION SIDE-EFFECTS
### especially **Peaking 'Cheap'-Oil Production**

- New crude oil deposits are becoming progressively difficult to find
- Existing deposits are increasingly expensive and dangerous to extract
- Future demand for crude oil is set to increase
- The rate at which crude oil can be economically extracted is expected to *decrease* this decade – but few in the oil industry admit it publically
- As oil prices increase so ever-more-costly extraction is possible but the net-benefits decrease

### *THREATS*

- Unprecedented challenges of techniques such as deep-water drilling will inevitably cause unconventional and potentially uncontrollable spills
- Disruptions in oil-rich nations (especially Africa and the Middle East) risk disproportionate impacts on the world-economy
- OPEC and other unofficial oil cartels risk disruption by individual members breaking unity in order to maximize self-interest
- Developing oil-exporting countries risk generating instability by keeping more oil for internal use and only offering the rest to preferred customers
- Major oil-price peaks will occur with each supply disruption, downward revision of reserve estimates or flexing of nationalist muscle
- Conflicts risk escalating into a world arena as oil-prices soar

## DISINFORMATION

- 'No problem – we've already found two-trillion barrels of oil and only one-trillion has ever been extracted.'
  *THOSE FIGURES ARE MISLEADING:*
  *- OPEC ESTIMATES OF RESERVES ARE LIKELY OVERINFLATED*
  *- NEARLY ALL FUTURE RESERVES HAVE ALREADY BEEN FOUND*
  *- MANY NEW RESERVES NEED A LOT OF ENERGY TO EXTRACT*
  *- ALL NEW RESERVES ARE DIFFICULT TO EXTRACT*
- 'We will not run out of oil'
  *WE WILL RUN OUT OF AFFORDABLE OIL*
- 'If oil companies thought they had a problem they'd be the first to say'
  *MANY FEEL LEGALLY OBLIGED TO PROTECT THEIR SHARE-PRICE*
- 'Major oil companies, leading politicians and industry-organizations all insist Peak Oil is irrelevant'
  *PRIVATELY SOME ADMITTED THAT THEY WERE BEING ECONOMIC WITH THE TRUTH*
- 'We can switch to Green energy'
  *THERE ARE NOT YET ENOUGH OPTIONS AND WE NEED OIL'S CHEMICALS AS WELL AS ENERGY*

# LACK OF AWARENESS

# Limited Alternatives for Alternative Energy

Despite numerous proposals to lower oil-dependency and carbon-emissions, there are in reality insufficient credible alternatives that can be implemented in time

YET ANOTHER STRAND of the largely-hidden reality behind fossil fuels, climate change, peak-oil production and their implications for a major backlash relates to the search for substitutes. After all, if the world economy is to wean itself off its energy-addiction to oil it obviously needs some other sources of energy as replacements. The last time human civilization thrived without fossil fuels there were only about a billion people on the planet. A population much larger than that needs more energy than burning renewable wood-supplies can provide, and global population is now about *seven times* that number – so nations definitely need to do more than just a 'return to basics'. But that is where the next problem in this complex system arises: Practical substitutes for oil are a lot more difficult to find than many had assumed.

## Coal

The Earth still holds large deposits of coal that look like they might remain economic for centuries, or at least far longer than oil. Even better, they tend to be found in relatively safe parts of the world. But burning coal releases far more pollution than oil, so there is a lot of talk at the moment about Carbon Capture and Storage (CCS) – in other words grabbing greenhouse gases like $CO_2$ before they are released into the atmosphere and then locking them away in porous rock underground.

The trouble is that it is still far from a reality. Coal-plants and energy utilities have a strong incentive to promote the idea as if it is just around the corner, but the fact remains that no one has yet built a commercial CCS system. No one yet even fully knows where or how to store the $CO_2$

from, say, a power station. What is more, it is expected that the energy needed to capture (and transport) the $CO_2$ for a CCS system would be around a *third* of the energy that the power station produced in the first place. So ironically, although the coal industry has every public-relations incentive to suggest that CSS is close, it currently has very little financial incentive eventually to adopt it – because it would risk making the cost of the power produced uncompetitive.

And there are other reasons coal is not an appealing substitute for oil. It is heavier, and more difficult to transport – rail travel is the only real option over long distances. And although it is possible to make synthetic fuel from coal (indeed, that is largely how Nazi Germany kept going for so long without access to alternatives), the process is extremely energy-intensive and therefore uneconomic unless at war. Despite the hype, Coal is not the New Oil.

## HYDRATES AND HYDROGEN

Neither are methane-hydrates, even though – as already explained – there are huge deposits trapped under the sea and in the permafrost. They are very expensive and dangerous to mine. And anyway, methane is itself a powerful greenhouse gas so any production leaks would be a major problem, and burning it produces the very $CO_2$ that countries are trying to cut down on. Just as unattractive is hydrogen. The much publicized Hydrogen Economy was based on the fallacy that the idea made sense. To be fair, the corporate politics certainly did. Automobiles and trucks (conveniently enough produced by existing manufacturers and requiring only minor modifications to current internal-combustion engines) would run on environmentally 'clean' hydrogen that only made water when it burned. People would all fill up their automobiles with hydrogen at gas stations (conveniently sited at the existing gasoline stations owned by oil companies).

The only problem is that it typically costs more energy to produce hydrogen than it eventually releases again when it burns. And the initial production process typically produces large amounts of pollution – even if eventually burning hydrogen does indeed only produce water vapor. On top of that, hydrogen is difficult and potentially dangerous to store and transport, it eventually leaks through almost anything, and anyway there is no existing distribution network and it would be prohibitively expensive to create one. Other than that, the Hydrogen Economy was a great idea.

# INDUSTRIALIZATION CRISES

## RECYCLED OIL AND BIOFUEL

Recycling vegetable oils for diesel also suffers from the laws of physics because it too is energy-expensive – although it is certainly better than simply throwing the oils away. Making oil from recycled plastic is also possible, but once again it uses lots of energy and it certainly is not sustainable because it still ultimately depends on oil (in the energy-expensive form of plastic) as its raw material.

The same problem of energy efficiency even hits the idea of growing biofuel. On the surface it seems extremely attractive to divert a proportion of everyday harvests of grain and other crops and use them to make ethanol – just as is done to make alcoholic drinks like beer – that can then be used as an additive to gasoline. However, once all the energy costs are taken into account, it turns out that biofuel ethanol (for instance, from US-grown corn) uses about as much energy to make as it releases. European sugar-beet appears slightly more attractive but this is confused by European farming subsidies and a tariff on ethanol imports, a form of protectionism the USA gave up at the start of 2012. Sugar-cane grown in countries like Brazil appears the most energy-efficient form of ethanol – but such biofuel then has to be transported, which lowers the benefits.

And biofuel has four other major shortcomings as well. Firstly, over its whole lifecycle it can release almost as much $CO_2$ as oil. Secondly, it uses up a lot of water, which is potentially a major downside (as covered in the subchapter on page 180 about *Why unsustainable water usage threatens food supplies*). Thirdly, it diverts farmland away from vital food production, so those in poorer countries can suffer food shortages as a result. And fourthly, because people are willing to pay more for fuel additives than for food, it rapidly inflates the price of staples like grain so that already-reduced supplies become even more expensive than they would anyway be because of shortages.

For many early-enthusiasts, first-generation biofuel has been a major disappointment – albeit that long-term research still looks promising. For the moment, however, even simply burning 'biomass' (that is, material that is grown in some way) in order directly to extract energy often is not particularly efficient overall because the original biomass tends to have already consumed a lot of oil-derived products in the form of pesticides and transport fuel.

# Problems with changing course

## Hydro, Tidal, Wind and Solar

The physics of hydroelectric plants, in contrast, is very attractive. But generating-stations have typically already been built on the best sites, so there often is not massive extra potential left. Countries like China are investing heavily in solar and wind power, and certainly these are also inherently attractive approaches. But they will only really come into their own when they are linked with new forms of electricity storage.

At the moment the only way to store large amounts of power – and a highly inefficient one at that – is to resort to something like using surplus electricity to pump water uphill into a reservoir and release it later to power a hydroelectric generator. Commercially-viable new-generation high-efficiency storage systems are probably a couple of decades away. In the meantime communities will have to rely on other forms of power generation overnight and when the wind drops. On top of all this, many countries simply do not have the geography or climate or even the spare space for current approaches to wave-power, wind-power or solar-power. Those technologies will evolve very fast. But they are currently expensive to build and maintain – even if the power-source is free and sustainable. New technologies are certainly not likely to be ready in time to take up more than a relatively small proportion of the role currently filled by oil.

In addition, despite the attraction of individual households being self-sufficient in energy – each with its own private generator using renewable power-sources – the reality is that small generators are typically inefficient generators. It is basic physics again. A large wind-turbine, for example, tends to be inherently far more efficient than a small one, even though it suffers from distribution losses if it has to feed households that are too far away. The idea that within decades the world will see a 'democratization of energy' as central generators disappear and everyone links onto an intelligent distributed-power network of individually-owned local generators is misleading. Such an approach may be useful in rural areas – especially in developing nations – but it will not be sufficient to supply areas of heavy population.

## Nuclear

The physics of nuclear power (combined with widespread electric land-transport) certainly makes far more sense than many of the alternatives. But there nevertheless remain major concerns over safety and waste-disposal – aggravated by the incidents in Japan caused by the March 2011 earthquake and tsunami. In addition, the cooling process in nuclear power stations typically uses large amounts of water that, although when it is returned to nature is perfectly safe, nevertheless ends up warmer than before so can disrupt things like fish stocks. It also means that a drought or other disruption to the water supply can potentially shut-down a power station (as happened at Fukushima).

However, there are other serious hidden problems with relying on nuclear power around the world to take over quickly from oil – and they have far more to do with corporate and state politics than with physics. For instance, although it is quite possible to work out ways for 'non-nuclear' countries to have nuclear power – by controlling and replacing the atomic fuel that they use – that level of dependency is understandably unattractive to many state-powers. And there are also many extremist groups that already have organized efforts to try to secure by whatever means any nuclear material that potentially could be used for weapons.

But the main problem with trying to adopt nuclear as a rapid replacement for oil is that in practice it is *very much slower* and more expensive to build nuclear power stations than it ought to be. The reason is a Legacy Effect left over from the 1960s. Early nuclear-generator designs were rather small, but it soon became clear that the claims suggesting 'nuclear-generated electricity will be so cheap it won't be worth charging for' were wildly off the mark. In order to improve cost-effectiveness, designers sought the well-established Industrialization benefits brought by economies of scale – they designed very much larger stations.

Unfortunately those designs proved dauntingly hard to build. Utility companies brought in contractors to help, but they often did not share a background in the earlier nuclear designs. Commissioning took so long that political attitudes changed as accidents elsewhere – often as a result of utterly different designs – raised public concerns. Updated state-regulations forced whole new safety-systems to be squeezed into partially-built stations delaying things further. And by then there was uncertainty over whether planned nuclear power-stations would even go ahead. Despite the 1973 oil crisis, Japan and France turned out to be amongst the only countries to invest heavily in commercial nuclear-power generation. As a result, worries about the long-term commercial prospects of the main contractors damaged their credit-rating and raised interest rates on the money they had to borrow to run their businesses. Time scales and costs escalated.

Just because many modern politicians suddenly now see nuclear power as an important component of energy security, does not overnight transform the dynamics of the nuclear industry. There is no 'standard' design of super-large nuclear power-station, so each proposal is one-off. On top of that, politicians in the past have proved fickle, not least because even when members of the public accept the idea of nuclear-generation in principle they still often do not want an atomic power station in their own neighborhood. So that means that investors are cautious.

## INSUFFICIENT ALTERNATIVES

- Coal is hard to transport and pollutes badly
- Carbon Capture and Storage is unproved
- The Hydrogen Economy was largely hype
- Biofuel shows promise but does not yet work
- The best hydroelectric sites are already in use
- Tidal / solar / wind need undevised storage systems
- Nuclear power is currently very slow to build

Which means that power-utility companies hold off placing guaranteed orders. Which means suppliers of costly components are reluctant to manufacture them. At every stage of building a new nuclear power-station, there are these kinds of bottle-necks. Nuclear power *could* relatively quickly take up much of the burden carried by oil. As things stand, it will not.

# ESCALATING ENERGY COSTS AND POWERLESSNESS

## Strongly-reinforced domestic and foreign policies keep the world-economy on a course of escalating energy costs and inadequate climate-change controls

AS LAID OUT in the previous subchapters, two-and-a-half centuries of Industrialization have left the world economy addicted to fossil fuels, but that addiction is bringing exponential problems that threaten a series of backlashes. The addiction risks indirectly contributing to a broad undermining of the scientific community. But far more severely its side-effects will build a major storm that initially will be dispersed across the general population but then will find the lightning conductor of the oil and energy suppliers and from then on its power will very largely be discharged through them.

The backlashes of High-Tech-Industrialization will come partly from growing pollution, which amongst other things risks catastrophic climate change. But it will also come from the depletion of one-time natural resources – most importantly oil – on which countries have been depending for 'extra' energy to fuel Industrialization. If, as now seems very likely, safe and cost-effective oil-production is currently peaking, then that risks destabilizing the whole global economy.

As a result, one might expect governments to be reducing society's addictive behavior. But that is easier said than done because there are not in reality any immediate substitutes for the amounts of fossil fuel being used – no combination of non-polluting alternatives looks to be ready in time to permit current lifestyles and global aspirations to continue at anything like the prices we are willing to pay for them today.

In addition, the huge investments needed to build as much alternative power-generation infrastructure as possible will necessarily end up reflected in still-further increases in energy prices. Indeed, such a Green Premium is already rippling through the world economy.

As this subchapter now highlights, the reality is that most governments are set to stay on course even though they *know* that to do so is inherently unsustainable. And that risks adding further to the growing backlash against Politics that has already been covered in the previous chapter on Capitalism Crises. This final strand of the hidden reality of today's High-Tech-Industrialization – the link to politics – is in many ways what ties all the other strands together because it reveals the overriding reason why governments risk being unable sufficiently to improve things: Society's addictive behavior is now entrenched so deeply into how the world economy operates that the rethinking of political assumptions that would be needed so as fundamentally to change course would be almost inconceivably complex and far-reaching.

## DOMESTIC POLICY

It starts with Domestic Policy. For the last sixty years in many Western countries – and these days increasingly even in nominally communist countries like China – politicians have aimed to sustain moderate growth by encouraging people to keep buying things. Consumerism, as a result, is now implicit throughout the global economy. It is as much built into the aspirations of youngsters striving for a better life in poverty-riddled African states as it is into those thriving on Wall Street. No one wants to lessen those hopes. In many ways, no one even has the right to try. Even as they warn individuals about the dangers of over-borrowing, governments are left with no choice but to endeavor to keep consumerism going strong.

Nor in practice do politicians have an option over many of the other biggest energy-drains in society. Huge cities are massively energy-intensive to run. It is not just the electricity they demand, but the energy needed to make and transport all the food, water and materials that flow into the city and to transport and process all the garbage and sewage that flows out again. The relatively-recent innovation of suburbia is even more costly per person in energy. Suburban buildings cost more to make and heat. The food, water, materials, garbage and sewage all tend to cost more to transport in and out to each individual home. And the average commute (whether to work or school) is profligate in its use of energy. Yet none of these infrastructural elements of society are capable of changing fast.

# INDUSTRIALIZATION CRISES

Land-usage is typically amongst the slowest evolving aspects of civilization. City layouts last for centuries, even millennia.

## WHY CITY LAYOUTS ARE SO SLOW TO CHANGE

In most long-established cities you can tell the direction of the prevailing wind by locating where historically the poor side of town was. It is all to do with pollution. If you are rich in the Middle Ages you do not want to smell tanneries and slaughterhouses. You make sure they are downwind. When the factories of the Industrial Revolution hit town, you place them on the sites of the tanneries and slaughterhouses. In the UK the prevailing winds blow from the west to the east. So in Victorian London they blew from Buckingham Palace in the West End toward the cockney slums in the East End. Only once the smellier occupations (and indeed occupants) had disappeared from the east of the city were warehouses converted into luxury accommodation for a new generation of traders – albeit City financiers.

Each city has its equivalent demarcation perpetuated maybe less by wind direction and more by the fact that people tend to want to be surrounded by like-minded neighbors. That is how neighborhoods develop – and remain. San Francisco is famous for both its long-standing China Town as well as its gay Castro district. In New York, Wall Street – which ran along the earthen wall built in 1653 by the Dutch to protect 'New Amsterdam' against the English – was recognized as the financial capital of the nation even before the American Civil War.

When I lived in Boston throughout the 1990s, the city was still neatly divided into the North End (Italian), the South End (bohemian), in the center the site of the original colonial city at Beacon Hill (conservative old money), just to the west the grand townhouses built in the 1860s as Back Bay (cosmopolitan newer money), and to the east was the poorer area that back then was unofficially known as The Combat Zone (because it became increasingly hazardous to your health as night fell and, so it was rumored, the police moved out). As in London, the prevailing wind in Boston blows from west to east.

# Problems with changing course

Cars may be made more fuel-efficient and shift to using electricity. Buildings that have not yet been properly insulated may be updated. Light-bulbs may be replaced with energy-efficient alternatives. But around the world there are politically expedient (and often economically vital) plans for far more – not fewer – automobiles and airlines and highways and suburbs and factories and processing plants. China necessarily constructs numerous new cities *each year.* At current rates it will add the equivalent of a new Chicago every year for the next two decades. It is these infrastructural trends that will utterly dominate the world-economy's collective energy-bill. While oil-companies continue to provide the most concentrated and convenient forms of trapped-energy, governments will largely feel obliged to protect them.

Few politicians or members of the general public before 2007 appreciated that some banks had become 'too big to fail'. Today, hardly anybody realizes that the largest oil multinationals and the state-owned energy companies have likewise become too big to fail. And yet, just like the banks, they *are* increasingly at risk of failing. As already shown, increased demand for oil combined with having largely used up any easily-accessed oil, means companies need to take greater and greater risks to get it. Sometimes, as with the 2010 BP catastrophe, things go wrong. The conditions governments are expecting oil companies to work in are technically as challenging as operating in deep space. Just as in space exploration, there will be accidents.

The difference is that, in addition to fatalities, there will be potentially unlimited cost-liabilities for environmental clean-up and compensation. Even the largest company could risk being brought down. But – just as with the banks – countries could not afford for that to happen. Every aspect of society needs the oil. On top of that, even if the public does not realize the fact, all citizens tend to carry a disproportionate percentage of oil-stock in their national or private pension funds.

The collapse of a major oil company would send shockwaves through the global economy that would impact everything from food prices in the developing world to availability of bank lending in the developed world. It would eventually have unforeseeable outcomes that in truth no one can even begin to estimate. Whatever the public rhetoric of politicians, behind the scenes governments will do everything they possibly can to avoid such a domino-effect. Even if they are still reeling from an earlier economic crisis. And even if, as a result of such a bailout – combined with growing outcries against 'profiteering' by oil and energy companies – the general public calls for the multinationals involved to be broken up and nationalized.

## CONFLICTING DOMESTIC COMMITMENTS

- Politicians feel obliged to maintain Consumerism
- Existing energy-drains are very slow to change
  - Huge cities are massively energy-intensive
  - Suburbia is even more profligate
- Much growth demands infrastructural expansion
- Oil-related stock dominates many pension funds
- Like Banks, many Oil firms are 'too large to fail'

## FOREIGN POLICY

Oil is also enshrined into Foreign Policy. Based on those I have met who were to varying degrees involved in decisions over the Iraq War, I have concluded that it is misleading to suggest that the invasion was 'only about oil'. It was just as much about getting some influence in the midst of an increasingly destabilizing Middle East. Iraq does indeed have substantial oil reserves. In fact, over the next twenty years Iraq is expected to represent 20% of the growth in global oil supply. So of course this was relevant. But to the degree that oil was a factor in US-UK political thinking at all, it appears to have been in consideration of avoiding terrorists being directly or indirectly funded by that oil rather than getting access to the oil for its own sake – however attractive that potentially was.

Nevertheless, the relatively fresh example of the Iraq War highlights the complex set of trade-offs within oil-politics. Saudi Arabia, for example, with its poor record on human rights is in many ways an unlikely 'friend' for the West to keep so close. But the oil-rich Saudis have very heavy investments in the West. Some estimates suggest they have three-quarters of a trillion dollars tied up in the USA alone. It would be devastating to financial markets if they suddenly pulled out their money and possibly triggered China – before the value of the dollar dropped too far – to do the same with their own even-larger investments.

# Problems with changing course

Anyway, despite the al-Saud infrastructure being inherently unstable, Western diplomatic services have tended to conclude that it is better that the well-understood Saudi royals be helped to stay securely in place – with all the implications that implies – than risk them being replaced, for instance, by Islamic radicals who might damage production facilities during an attempted uprising or else reduce oil production if they ever took power. At least, that was the gist of what seemed to be unassailable logic before the recent series of non-extremist uprisings in other Arab states (and the quickly suppressed attempt within Saudi Arabia itself) suggested that the Radical Threat might not be all it is cracked up to be.

The wave of protests in early 2011 across many of the Arab states reminded the general public of non-Arab countries that supporting autocratic regimes may bring stability for a few decades but not for the truly long-term. And it does come across as rather hypocritical when it is the policy of proudly democratic nations. But that high-art of 'political compromise behind closed door' is largely what foreign diplomacy has always been about. And it will increasingly typify explicit oil politics going forward.

The USA currently spends around half a trillion dollars a year on foreign oil. That potentially makes it vulnerable. Given that one of the primary roles of government is to protect its citizens – and for any country, foreign-oil dependency is these days a potential threat to stability – it is a clear obligation for the White House to pay attention to non-US oil-production and ultimately to protect its interests. The same increasingly applies for *every* nation.

As the stakes get higher, governments will make ever-stronger attempts at foreign influence in Saudi Arabia, Iran, Iraq, Kuwait, the United Arab Emirates, Venezuela, Russia, Kazakhstan, Libya and Nigeria – the countries with the largest proved oil reserves. Nearly always that involvement will be diplomatic. But if diplomacy fails, these countries – and the oil and energy suppliers holding interests within their borders – should not expect the rest of the world just to sit back passively and watch oil prices rise to unaffordable heights.

All too quickly the oil-insufficient nations (including the USA and the European Union) will justify defending themselves against those they consider to be making excessive profits from the undue suffering of others. Or, as with Libya, be quick to step in for humanitarian purposes.

## CONFLICTING FOREIGN-POLICY COMMITMENTS

- Oil has become enshrined in Foreign Policy
- Countries like Saudi-Arabia have such heavy investments in the West they 'must not pull out'
- Rather than risk losing oil, even liberal countries tend to support autocrats that promise stability
- Foreign-oil dependency is increasingly risky
- The only oil-rich nuclear-arms country is Russia

# LOCKED ON COURSE FOR A SLOW-MOTION ECONOMIC CRASH

Short-term local conflicting interests are currently set to undermine counter-strategies aimed at securing long-term collective national-economic benefits

THE EVOCATIVE PHRASE 'slow-motion train crash' could almost have been invented to describe the combined dynamics of the two most threatening trends within the High-Tech-Industrialization backlashes – global warming and peaking oil. It is increasingly clear to politicians what is coming and yet there appears to be little that in practical terms can be done to change course. So, if the metaphorical Industrialization train keeps on track and maintains its current acceleration then what is most likely to happen?

The probability-ranges of a variety of longer-term climate-change impacts have been widely debated in the public arena over the last few years – so there is relatively little new to be added. Certainly, some insurance companies have already explored the correlation between higher average temperatures and storm intensity, though it is proving difficult to calculate safe premiums because what has happened in the past is such a poor indicator of the future. Nevertheless, some regions should expect insurance premiums to rise inexorably.

Less talked about – at least in public – have been the implications that follow from the fact that readily-affordable world oil production is peaking (albeit confused because of wars and incompetence). Oil-rich countries will increasingly find themselves surrounded by a world that wants what they have and that is willing to be progressively persuasive to get it. OPEC and other more-unofficial cartels will find themselves under increasing internal competition as individual members break unity to maximize their self-interests. Developing countries that are also oil exporters will increasingly keep more oil for internal use and offer the rest to preferred customers. That is when decades of behind-the-scenes diplomacy is hoped to pay off. It is also when undeveloped countries without oil will potentially begin to suffer.

As oil prices on average drift upward because of scarcity, many 'oil' companies will increasingly shift their strategic focus toward natural gas – partly helped by technological advances that enable the economic extraction of natural gas from previously unexploited deposits in relatively stable regions such as Australia, China and the USA. Similarly, despite immediate local pollution problems caused by burning coal and despite its eventual impact on global climate (both of which concerns seem unlikely to be addressed in time by Carbon Capture and Storage proposals), for the next few decades the original Industrialization fossil fuel will once again be a mainstay for developing economies such as China and India.

## UNCONVENTIONALS

Over the last decade, shale gas and coal-bed methane (CBM) have become highly-touted 'unconventional' sources of natural gas. It is frequently suggested that they will contribute more than half of US gas production by 2030. Less publicized by supporters are the perceived problems. Natural gas trapped in shale is released by fracturing the rock using a technique called 'fracking'. That takes extra energy. But potentially far worse, it tends to release some of the highly-potent greenhouse gas methane directly into the atmosphere. As a result, although burning natural gas is very clean compared with using oil – let alone coal – the net impact on climate change of extracting natural gas in this way may be as bad as burning coal. There are also serious concerns about groundwater contamination. Environmental concerns over coal-bed methane relate to the impact of the numerous wells, pumps, pipelines and access roads that are needed. Economic concerns are that it is inherently costly and only justifiable with high natural-gas prices.

Although alternative technologies to fossil-fuels (nuclear as well as renewables) will continue to grow, as things stand one barrier after another will result in the growth being slower than politicians are relying on. And it is that gap between 'affordable oil' and 'affordable clean alternatives' needed for sustained economic growth that will fuel the worst Industrialization Crises.

Regardless of the upsurge in usage of natural gas and coal for power generation, there will continue to be major peaks in oil prices – just as in 2008 and again in 2011 – every time there is a supply disruption, a downward-revision of reserve estimates, or a flexing of nationalist muscle. Electricity prices will fluctuate accordingly as will food prices (which relate both to energy costs for irrigation and transport as well as the cost of oil-derived pesticides and fertilizers manufactured from natural gas).

## PARTLY-HIDDEN IMPACTS

There also risk being less-obvious side-effects of peaking affordable oil. For instance, asphalt prices for roads will go up, so the number of unfilled potholes risks increasing. Transport running-costs will increase even for vehicles that run on electricity, because one way or another the electricity still needs to be generated somewhere and for a long while low-pollution alternatives to oil will carry a significant premium. The price of vehicles will likewise increase because of the energy costs involved in their manufacture, and to an extent also because of the oil-based materials such as plastics used within them.

No one is proposing electric airplanes. Or even ones powered by natural gas. If, as currently seems to be a 'locked course', the rate at which the international community breaks its countries' addiction to oil is slower than the rate at which oil prices on average increase, then cheap airfares and package holidays will become progressively difficult to find. Increased airfares will impact not just airlines but also travel companies, holiday destinations and regional economies heavily dependent on tourism. If the trend continues then unseasonal fruit and vegetables will once more become luxury items and then potentially disappear from supermarket shelves altogether. Those nations that previously produced them will suffer as a result.

Distant communities like Hawaii that import almost everything they use would become steadily unviable. Globalization then risks slowing as conventional container-shipping becomes increasingly expensive. Under those circumstances, countries will gradually retreat and even split – just as the former Soviet Union did. The most powerful remaining countries will struggle to secure residual reserves. And at every step of the way along this increasingly uncontrolled disruption of the global economy, the general public will blame politicians – and in defense, governments will seek retribution from 'greedy oil and energy companies'.

As of today, the only truly oil-rich country with nuclear-weapon capability is Russia (which has well over double the proved reserves of somewhere like the USA). It will feel more secure than other nations. However, there will be Arab pressure on nuclear-capable Islamic Pakistan to help out if tensions rise. Anyway, Iran may have its own WMD by then, and the nuclear-capable rogue state of North Korea will likely do whatever it sees fit to add to its existing moderate oil reserves.

The means by which shrinking oil supplies are eventually shared out will shift from free-market forces to diplomatically-orchestrated international agreements. But if countries get desperate, global diplomacy will inevitably shift to conflict. And as covered in detail in the later chapter on Globalization Crises, there is in practice no existing mechanism in place by which an institution like the United Nations could stop it.

## PROGRESSIVE BACKLASHES

Those currently are by far the most severe backlashes being generated by Industrialization. The fossil-fuel addiction does indeed have potentially-fatal consequences. But that is not just for the reasons many Green activists have long been insisting. In reality, despite the eventual severe implications of manmade climate change, it is dangerous to portray that as the most important global threat. It may not even turn out to be the most threatening Industrialization crisis. Long before some of the more-ominous impacts of global warming have a chance to hit, governments may be past caring because increasingly-restricted production of cost-effective oil has choked-off the very industry that risked destabilizing the planet's atmosphere in the first place.

But that is just the Oil Tragedy currently set to play out over the next few decades. The same pattern – and similar backlashes – are also building in other commodities but delayed by a few more decades. There is certainly no depletion problem for coal, at least not for a century of so. However, at current production rates, important metals like tin and lead are predicted to run out around 2050 – though with even modest growths in demand it may be far sooner.

Copper is also expected to have become uneconomical to mine by then. And much less talked-about are apparently far-more-esoteric issues such as the availability of phosphorus - which is used in everything from fertilizers to matches. At current rates, phosphorus production is estimated to peak around 2050.

As far as manmade global warming is concerned, the timescale that politicians – and indeed all of us – should focus on for is *not* the second half of this century when many of the more harmful consequences are predicted. By far the most important period is the next three decades. The reason is because, as things stand, the world economy will stay on its existing Industrialization course for as long as it can, and worries about climate change will prove insufficient to wean countries off their oil addiction. Ironically, by 2040 future global warming may be the least of government worries concerning fossil fuels. Energy-availability is set to become the all-enveloping threat to national security.

## THE SHAME OF FAILING

Yet today, at only the start of the second decade of the 21$^{st}$ century, when there is still sufficient time to realign key components of the energy economy, many privately-owned oil corporations and nation states that equate their oil with power are set to continue to maintain an increasingly embarrassing pretense that all is well – not just for them (which, to be fair, it largely is) but for the oil-addicted world economy as a whole.

Having painted themselves into an oily corner, some of these powerful organizations now risk finding it very slippery to extricate themselves without looking absurd. As image is very important to some of the most senior of these individuals, the temptation is to refuse to back down and instead to fly in the face of an increasing onslaught of contrary evidence. This will only serve dangerously to hold up public debate and severely damage trust going forward. Oil and Energy companies risk – all too soon – suffering a progressive backlash as public sentiment (not just amongst younger generations) moves from its current lack of trust to active distrust and outraged anger as happened very quickly with Banking in 2007-8.

Given that governments and the news-media themselves are experiencing slower but inexorably-progressive deteriorations in public trust of their own, both institutions will rather side with the public and turn on Oil and Energy corporations than risk too much public scrutiny of their own respective roles in any oil crises. In the neat sound-bites of a time-constrained world of black-or-white contrasts it will be tempting for everyone who has ever felt fearful and powerless against escalating fuel and energy prices to unite in pushing the blame squarely (if not completely fairly) onto those 'bullies' most obviously directly involved. It will feel cathartic.

And the stereotypes will be so easy – especially given that those same huge faceless corporations and the oligarch empires with dubious backgrounds and the autocratic regimes with unpleasant human-rights are all so conspicuously and brashly (and enviably) wealthy. Clearly, it will appear, they are not just bullies, but greedy and selfish bullies. There will be so many scores to settle. It will be trivial to stir up resentment and justify righteous claims for retaliation and retribution – just as it currently is against Banking.

Yet, as with Banking, the very fact that such a backlash is allowed to happen brings tremendous shame – because, whoever actually is chosen to be punished, it is an indication that *many* components of the overall global system have in reality failed. And, with the Oil Tragedy, the shame goes further than that. In this of all sectors of the economy, for the greatest companies not publically to recognize and manage the risks of global crisis is beneath them.

The best oil and energy and mining corporations are amongst the most adept industrial organizations that have ever existed. Almost uniquely in today's world they maintain a long-term perspective that typically spans several decades. That is far better than most government departments achieve – let alone the politicians who nominally run them. The major budgets that these multinationals handle are comparable to those of whole countries. And their ability to organize vast numbers of exceptionally talented professionals so as to solve immensely complex and often dangerous problems is almost unprecedented. As is their ability to turn visionary but immensely-complicated plans into pragmatic reality.

What a shame, therefore, for them not to apply that great talent to working out how best to solve the integrated global problems of non-renewable resources. What a shame for them not to pull off what politicians could never possibly hope to achieve in isolation. And, for lack of refocusing their unique capabilities, what a shame for them not to avoid the growing backlash against their own industry.

# REDUCING THE THREATS:
# TRUE COSTING

Industrialization crises need *True Costing* – reflecting *all* the hidden costs and savings that different options *ever* bring

IF OIL COMPANY top-executives were running the world, they would not be behaving as they currently do. That is nobody's fault – but it is a wake-up call that their companies currently operate under a business model that assumes certain fundamental divergences between what is good for oil and energy producers (at least in the short-to-medium term) and what is good for the global economy as a whole (especially in the long-term).

Some of those oil executives have admitted to me that, as a result, they feel forced in public to be economic with the truth. Indeed. Less charitable commentators might accuse them of 'economizing' through their teeth. It is not a sustainable position. Some excellent people are setting up themselves and their industry for an irrecoverable backlash. There is a better way. Those in positions of greatest leadership can instead take the initiative – and forever change the unwritten rules of their industry.

In the previous chapter on Capitalism Crises I suggested that, in order to counter the types of systemic backlash to which they are particularly susceptible, sectors such as Banking and the News-Media need to extend the scope of their activities to include aspects of Unelected Responsibility. A major realignment is also needed by the oil industry, but in their case it is even more complex. Certainly they too – along with almost every other influential corporation – must accept Unelected Responsibility. But on top of that they must inject some realism and professionalism into the worldwide attempts to wean off fossil-fuel addiction without unacceptable withdrawal symptoms.

That level of realignment necessarily takes them into the heart of global politics. In the final chapter of this book we will examine the overall approach that they and other industries could use to achieve such radical realignment. But in the remainder of this chapter I will focus on the initiatives that are particularly relevant to avoiding Industrialization Crises.

Addressing pollution and depletion side-effects demands *True Costing,* that is, a full reflection of *all* the hidden costs and savings that different options bring throughout their *whole* life. But at the moment no one even agrees the basics. So, by one means or another (perhaps using a self-generated intermediary that acts as Trusted Observer, as explained on page 443) oil companies, energy companies and utilities must at last negotiate with governments – and with each other – in ways that they never could face-to-face. Those pioneers with the greatest influence must persuade the rest to transition away from the currently unstable situation in which it is in too many people's self-interest to maintain an unacceptably risky status quo.

They must agree how much economically-extractable oil there *really* is, and the true net-energy of that oil, and the hidden pollution costs and other risks of extracting it, and the equivalent True Costings of all the alternatives. And then, based on everything, they must work out how best to manage the strategic transition of the world's energy economy over the next several decades. Throughout all of this, oil companies must keep at the back of their minds the recognition that in the absence of such leadership many of their biggest national customers could, if they ended up feeling too powerless and too put upon, band together to do something like setting up a Buyer Consortium intended to discourage Oil Suppliers (including the OPEC cartel) from attempting to profiteer from the prolonged downward trend of oil production. And that could result in severe restrictions to *everyone's* strategic options.

In addition, oil and energy suppliers must help governments tie all plans relating to climate change into parallel plans that relate to an accurate reflection of peaking economic-oil. The full circumstances of the ease, efficiency and costs of extracting future fossil-fuels cannot simply remain somehow separate – let alone unacknowledged as they are in all the current negotiations (such as those in Durban 2011). It will continue to be impossible to harmonize global actions until these sorts of plans are coordinated.

The world's governments were unfairly and impossibly hampered in trying to address climate-change in Copenhagen and then in Cancún and then in Durban by the very fact that they were *only* addressing climate-change there. Delegates were, in effect, artificially butchering apart a highly-integrated system in which manmade-$CO_2$ is merely an unintended consequence of enmeshed strands of cause-and-effect that make little sense (or even appear to operate differently) when cut into pieces.

There can never be joined-up thinking about managing Industrialization backlashes while some important factors are denied even to exist. What is more, as addressed in the following chapter on Population Crises, any and all of those plans must likewise be tied into the additional – but interconnected – plans needed to tackle major issues such as food security.

## ADDING COSTS AND SAVINGS TO REFLECT HIDDEN REALITY

The metaphor of a 'slow-motion train crash' caused by the worst Industrialization side-effects – in particular peaking oil combined with pollution and global warming – is, more accurately, a train deliberately accelerating toward an avalanche of boulders that it set off earlier. The way out is to take two actions in parallel: decelerate the train and remove the largest of the boulders before the train reaches them.

The international community already fully-realizes that – in theory at least – that means all countries must in concert slowly wean themselves off oil, at the same time as reducing the damage they cause with greenhouse-gas pollution. Yet with today's absence of global governance (detailed in *The inevitable but fundamental inadequacies of the UN* starting on page 398), and without the most influential oil, energy and mining companies taking leadership, these sorts of problems are, in practice, impossible to solve. It is bad enough that each country is, in effect, forced to compete with each other to get the greatest one-time economic boost from fossil-fuels while they still can. But that is only part of the difficultly. The other part relates to hidden interconnections. Potential solutions to oil-dependency and climate change are so enmeshed but complex that, once again, we cannot see the forest for the trees. Joined-up thinking is very difficult.

For instance, some alternatives to oil – such as coal – risk polluting even worse. Saving rain-forests or growing biofuel impacts available agricultural land, which impacts long-term food-security. Officially admitting that economic-oil is peaking, risks damaging the share-price of multinationals that dominate the global economy and pension funds – risking panic buying, wild financial swings and (potentially) extreme hardship.

In order to help themselves at least compare like with like, key players in the potential Oil Tragedy need to be able to resort to a form of True Costing in which evaluations of different alternatives take into account not just those immediate costs and savings that are obvious, but also hidden costs and savings that may only occur very much later – for example, costs of cleaning-up pollution, or eventual savings in reduced healthcare. Such an approach is attractive not just at the level of individual technological options but also when a government considers its country's performance as well as when the international community evaluates the whole global economy. At the moment, governments typically measure the health of national economies, and by implication the overall global economy, in terms of Gross Domestic Product.

But GDP is in fact quite a recent invention. It was devised in the 1930s to try to get a handle on how effective interventions were for tackling the Great Depression. The trouble is that these days GDP is universally used to gauge how successful an economy is. Unfortunately, that is *not* what it was designed for, and it is not what it actually measures.

## THE GROSSNESS OF GROSS DOMESTIC PRODUCT

Officially, GDP corresponds to the market value of all the goods and services that a nation produces – though in reality it only corresponds to those things that people actually declare to their governments, so it does not include the large amount of unpaid work there is in any country, or the underground economy.

The almost-exclusive use of GDP as the indicator of national performance has become increasingly risky. For a start, it is very short-term. A country (or the global economy generally) can look good even though it is doing things that are destroying its long-term prospects – depleting unsustainable resources without planning sufficient alternatives for example.

Likewise, GDP does not reflect waste or efficiency. High-Tech, for instance, generally produces greater and greater benefits over time for the same cost. Yet as far as GDP is concerned, the benefits of a web-enabled laptop are no greater than those of an equivalently-priced mechanical adding-machine. And a gas-guzzling leviathan of a car is just as attractive as its highly-efficient hybrid rival.

## GROSS NATIONAL HAPPINESS

The former king of Bhutan famously proposed Gross National Happiness as an indicator for quality of life. In practice it is such a highly subjective measure that it can be misused by governments to justify actions or inactions that suit their politically-motivated goals. But the concept does raise the crucial question of whether increased GDP does in fact result in increased happiness.

It is broadly accepted amongst social scientists that above a certain threshold of comfort there is not a clear-cut link between happiness and money. And it is certainly true that many richer nations appear to be less happy than some of their poorer neighbors. However, despite some claims, it is actually extremely difficult to compare like with like and draw clear-cut conclusions. This is partly because people's expectations tend to rise as they earn more, so measuring 'happiness' becomes more subjective than ever. It is even more difficult to draw meaningful conclusions from claims such as: 'People were happier in the 1950s than they are today – even though today we are on average financially better off.'

In reality it is impossible to discount factors such as our greater exposure to 24/7 News telling us all the stressful things that are happening in the world and, worse, that might happen to us. That is potentially a negative side-effect of High-Tech, but it is not directly related to average wealth at all. To draw valid conclusions from the research we would need to know, for example, how happy (poorer) people in the 1950s would have been if they had been inundated then with the news coverage that we (richer) people have today.

Similarly, profits made by banks gambling on market fluctuations (but not in any direct way contributing to the success of a country) are viewed as just as valuable as the profits of an entrepreneurial inventor. But possibly most risky of all, GDP completely ignores hidden costs such as damage to the environment (technically referred to as macroeconomic 'externalities').

Often, something like air-pollution even shows up as extra *benefit* – because it results in more money being spent on healthcare.

All this needs to be enhanced. However, although at various times economists and others have proposed alternatives to GDP, it seems highly unlikely that within the timescales available any substitutes can be adopted broadly enough to be sufficiently useful over the next few decades. Far more pragmatic therefore is, when useful, to modify the detail of how GDP itself is measured by adding in otherwise-obscured costs and savings – so that it more accurately reflects hidden reality.

This approach has the advantage of being flexible enough to tie in large amounts of existing work (such as from climate-change advocates calculating the 'cost of carbon'), but not to exclude other efforts that come from very different disciplines (such as from economists trying to reflect the sustainability of economic growth, or from social scientists factoring-in education levels, wealth disparity, life expectancy and quality of life). Importantly, such an approach to True Costing also allows governments to keep nearly all the extraordinary number of processes that have grown up around GDP, but to maintain additional parallel sub-processes that make them far safer with regard how they impact government strategy.

## CARBON CAPTURE AND STORAGE WITH ENERGY-EFFICIENCY

Within this overall context, oil and energy companies must openly work with governments to evaluate a slew of specific initiatives relating to fossil-fuels and greenhouse gases. At a global level it is worth at least checking the True Costing of proposed 'geoengineering' approaches – such as ways of reflecting more light from Earth back into space for instance by releasing massive quantities of aerosols into the atmosphere or placing huge numbers of mirrors above the Earth. Both these proposals would merely mask the effects of increased greenhouse gases, whereas other suggestions attempt to lessen the trend – such as by absorbing $CO_2$ with huge numbers of artificial trees. On the surface, many geoengineering proposals appear extremely dubious – both in terms of success and unintended consequences – but they do nevertheless need to be evaluated properly.

Carbon Capture and Storage (CCS) systems likewise need True Costing. At the moment, power companies are promoting them as a solution, and they are certainly potentially very attractive. But in truth no one actually knows what their full economic reality will be. The various CCS demonstration-projects planned to come online over the next several years will be informative. But even then, the full True Costing of large-scale CCS will be unclear – not least because of the extreme difficulty of guaranteeing no significant leaks, for thousands of years, whatever else happens.

Of all of President Obama's various US energy-related policies announced in March 2011, energy-efficiency incentives may end up having more eventual impact than any of the more-publicized goals for energy security. That is because the rather lackluster approach of energy efficiency – which realistically can all-too-easily run counter to the self-interest of energy companies – tends to be by far the most cost-effective mechanism that there is to help economies wean off oil and reduce carbon emissions.

As a result, in addition to the obvious need for energy suppliers and governments to encourage businesses and the public to improve insulation, lights, heaters and appliances in their buildings – and for manufacturers to produce more fuel-efficient designs of cars, trucks, ships and airplanes – energy suppliers must also push for far-greater efficiency in how electricity is generated in the first place. Currently, a vast amount of useful energy at power stations is typically lost as heat – and, as usual, GDP does not notice. Similarly, suppliers must take the initiative for 'smart grids' that improve the efficiency of how electricity is distributed – for instance offering offices and households disproportionate savings if they allow something like their air-conditioning automatically to turn off for a few minutes during peak times.

## SHORT-TERM STOP-GAPS AND LONGER-TERM POTENTIAL

The next True Costings for oil and energy suppliers to take a lead on – so as to end up *pulling* governments rather than being 'encouraged' by them – are alternative energy-sources. Although wind-power and wave-power are attractive stop-gaps, their True Costings suffer because the cost of the primarily-mechanical technology that underpins them is largely fixed and can never dramatically drop in the same way that something that is essentially electronic can. Although wind farms and wave farms benefit from economies-of-scale, their cost of manufacture and maintenance can never fall exponentially over time. Solar technology, in contrast, has much greater long-term potential because it is linked to the exponential growth of the High-Tech supertrend (page 15) – primarily in the form of nanotech developments for solar cells and storage devices.

## GREEN MILITARY

For many governments there are direct military benefits from a widespread transition to alternative energy. For a start, a shift away from oil will reduce tensions caused by Middle-East dependency and so also reduce the military costs (not least in human life) of ensuring supply. But military and peacekeeping forces are in fact themselves major consumers of oil, with the result that during active service they lose significant numbers of personnel simply transporting their own fuel. In that context, fuel-efficiency and alternative energy *within* the armed forces is being actively pursued by top military organizations – including the US Department of Defense.

Similarly, although first-generation biofuels failed to live up to their hype, second-generation versions derived from waste products or grown on marginal land should have better True Costing. For example, biodiesel can be made from vegetable oil produced from the seeds of Jatropha – a plant that can be grown on marginal land. Current proposals for third-generation biofuels are based on the potential commercialization of lab experiments that farm algae and then turn the sludge into (biodegradable) fuel. That seems a great idea, but it still needs a lot more development. Fortunately, as with solar-research, biotech is on an exponential path. As a result, it is those two classes of long-term alternative-energy that should be prioritized both for private investment and as components of comprehensive government energy-security strategies.

## STANDARDIZING FISSION AND PRIORITIZING FUSION

None of the alternative-energy approaches will prove sufficient in the time that governments have. As a result, energy suppliers in general, and the nuclear-power industry in particular, must show far greater leadership. The public – and especially ecology activists – need to be better educated about modern versions of nuclear-power generation. This is more important than ever post-Fukushima.

The resistance from the most voluble groups tends to be a legacy of the anti-nuclear-weapons lobby of the 1960s. Many of those concerns have in reality now been addressed, though not all have (such as the problems of decommissioning), so the energy industry needs to lay out the full logic behind greater adoption of nuclear-fission generators not just in the context of energy-security but also in terms of the radical improvements there have been in designs. Yet that is not enough. The cost-effectiveness of current-generation nuclear-fission power-stations must be dramatically improved. To achieve this, the nuclear-power industry must urgently get its act together on reactor designs. Oil-rigs and commercial airliners all benefit from broadly-standardized global designs. Nuclear power-stations do not. That is no longer reasonable.

The current approach is not only unduly expensive but also dramatically increases delays, at a time when there is little wiggle-room in the global schedule. Coordinating nuclear-power design and development has truly become a matter of global security just as nuclear-weapons proliferation has been for six decades. So, governments as well need to get their acts together in order to support the necessary international agreements. Current designs of nuclear-power stations need to be rationalized and coordinated at a global level, with the added advantage that replaceable parts can then extend the operating life of the plants. All of these changes will not only substantially improve the True Costing of nuclear power-generation, but they will also strengthen the logic of pursuing nuclear as part of an overall energy-strategy.

As far as the general public is concerned, industry must take the lead in explaining why aggressively developing a nuclear-power option as one of the complementary components in a strategy of energy-security is more an issue of pragmatism, rather than a confrontation against idealism: Fossil fuels risk both global warming and economic-oil depletion, and the more-extreme Green proposals to reduce energy demand – for instance by huge changes to the Western lifestyle – would, in practice, never possibly be achieved in time.

Meanwhile, the public also needs to understand why populist 'solutions' – such as the 2011 decision by German politicians to curtail their country's nuclear-power program – often turn out not to be as clear-cut as they at first appear. For example, as a result of not being able to fill their energy gap with alternatives (as seems likely), Germany may eventually have to resort to buying electricity from neighboring countries – such as primarily-nuclear France.

In addition, the energy industry needs to explain far better to the general population the concept of risk-*management* – as opposed to risk-

*avoidance* (which in reality is impossible for many technologies). Statements by anti-nuclear lobbyists along the lines of 'You cannot guarantee that there is absolutely no possibility of a major catastrophe' are not easy to counter from scratch in a sound-bite. But then again, neither were the needs for major cuts in public spending that many governments have nevertheless endeavored to educate their electorates about.

Energy producers must also consider radically new designs of nuclear power-generators – for instance, sealed transportable stations that need no refueling and that at the end of their lives can be shipped back to the manufacturer for decommissioning. And they must also work with governments to devise at last a coordinated strategy for dealing with nuclear waste.

## THE NEXT GENERATION

There are six basic designs of far-safer reactor that are currently being evaluated in the search for $4^{th}$-generation nuclear-power (commonly referred to as 'Gen IV reactors'). Although the so-called 'pebble-bed' design is the one typically quoted by politicians and climate-change experts, that design is in fact only one of the alternative ways of solving just one of the six different approaches. It may not turn out to be the best route forward.

The nuclear-power industry must in addition take a far stronger lead in accelerating existing international research into the next-generation designs of nuclear-fission power stations expected to come on-line commercially around 2030. And – currently gaining far too little attention – in order to make any of these actions practical, they must also encourage and support governments around the world in urgently attracting and educating a sufficiently large new-generation of nuclear engineers and scientists.

Finally, it is vitally important that energy producers step up to the challenge of lobbying governments and the public to give far greater priority to ensuring that practical versions of nuclear-*fusion* power-generators become commercially viable by 2040. This fundamentally different approach (basically generating power by using the same physics as makes the sun shine) is immensely attractive – not least because it is very safe and clean and uses effectively-limitless resources.

What is more, its progress is so linked to the exponential growth of Simulation technologies that it now appears very much more likely to succeed than many have assumed until recently. It is utterly absurd that most politicians, members of the news-media, let alone members of the general public do not really even know what nuclear fusion is. They do not realize that the only thing it shares in common with what they think of as nuclear-power is the word 'nuclear'. And they know still less about the existing massive but anonymous international fusion-research programs on whose outcomes their very-long-term energy security may in reality depend.

## COST-OF-CARBON AND SHIFTS TO LOW-CARBON ECONOMIES

By definition, powerful multinationals exert their power across multiple nations. From the general public's point of view there is nothing inherently harmful about that, provided the goals of the multinationals are sufficiently aligned with the goals of the territories within which they operate. Consequently, as laid out already, the principle of Unelected Responsibility strongly applies to oil, energy and mining corporations (as a necessary counter to Capitalism Crises rather than Industrialization Crises).

In addition, as will be detailed on page 358 in the subchapter about *The unintended lack of control brought by multinationals*, the collective actions of numerous such self-serving corporations can bring unintended consequences that no one intends. As a result, in order to minimize the causes of such Globalization Crises oil, energy and mining corporations must adopt a far more Holistic Perspective (detailed in the chapter on Globalization) than otherwise might seem necessary.

However, for oil, energy and mining corporations the obligations – and opportunities – go further still. The main reason is that these businesses are already all heavily involved in global politics – albeit behind the scenes. And their actions or inactions sometimes impact whole nations. Such behavior is not necessarily any less democratic than, say, the machinations of the unelected representatives at the UN. But it does nevertheless carry clear risks of abuse that, if too much goes wrong as a result, threaten to create a coordinated retaliatory international backlash against the most obvious examples of 'over-powerful corporate interests'.

To defuse this escalating risk, it is time for at least some of the covert corporate influence of oil, energy and mining to move out of the shadows of political lobby chambers and sealed boardrooms and into the openness of full legitimacy. That means taking far more of an explicit and proud lead in ensuring globally-balanced implementation of transition-strategies to a low-carbon world economy – rather than maintaining what is often viewed both inside and outside these industries as a glorified Public Relations exercise.

The detailed political actions that associated multinationals will choose to advocate from the perspective of world-governance will necessarily be complex. But at the highest level, things like deforestation can probably only be substantially reduced by means of richer countries paying for the privilege. Ecological appeals alone simply will not work. Similarly, it is the developed countries that will have to demonstrate that low-carbon economies are possible. But before they do so, developing countries will first have to commit that, once the richer countries have shown the lead, they too will follow – albeit with further compensation in the form of overseas aid for any damage arising from climate change primarily caused by the prior industrialization of the developed world.

To assist in such a transition, energy industries – as part of their realigning – must change the endemic practices of their industry. Misleading advertising (for instance about 'clean coal') needs to be far more strongly self-regulated – before public distrust turns to anger and multi-nation politicians impose far-stronger regulation from the outside. Similarly, utility companies must get ahead of the curve in encouraging people to *reduce* their energy consumption, in contrast to now when they are principally rewarded for selling more power.

And finally, the oil, energy and mining industries must be seen to be grown-up enough to take responsibility for *all* of their constituent-organizations. Naturally they should publicize examples of what works well in their industries. But they should also actively Name And Shame those parts of their industries that, by association, risk damaging the whole and exacerbating the threat of backlash. For example, the worst polluters (as well as the most successful improvements) – at country level and company level – need to be broadcast worldwide. Just as politicians around the world are increasingly finding, however painful the process, it ultimately works out far better to be seen to take the actions needed to get your own house in order rather than be portrayed as being dragged kicking and screaming into an ethical makeover.

Over the next handful of years there is an extraordinary opportunity for the leaders of preeminent organizations at the very center of a few crucial industries that are themselves at the inner core of Industrialization. Oil and energy suppliers and mining corporations can realign themselves so as explicitly to take a leadership role in minimizing the worst backlashes within the global systems that they genuinely understand better than anyone else. In the past, oil, energy and mining have, between them, changed the world. It is now time for their executives once again to aspire to that same goal.

# INDUSTRIALIZATION CRISES

**Industrialization generates Pollution and Depletion side-effects that – starting with oil companies – are building major backlashes against those deemed responsible and require True Costing as a counter-measure**

The exceptional benefits of cheap sources of concentrated energy have left the world-economy addicted to fossil fuels

For convoluted and partially-obscured reasons the genuine threats from climate change are being heavily misrepresented
- *Although the damage of local pollution from Industrialization has been obvious for centuries, the effects of airborne pollution remain far less clear-cut*
- *Politics, self-interest, complex science and unintentional media distortion are complicating interpretation of the manmade contributions to climate-change*
- *However, the unbiased scientific consensus is that there is an extremely high probability that manmade global warming is a genuine and serious threat to national security*

Energy producers feel unable to publicize that production of 'cheap' forms of crude oil is peaking and costs will on-balance escalate

Governments know the economic threats from climate-change and peaking oil-production but find it close-to-impossible to change course
- *Despite numerous proposals to lower oil-dependency and carbon-emissions, there are in reality insufficient credible alternatives that can be implemented in time*
- *Strongly-reinforced domestic and foreign policies keep the world-economy on a course of escalating energy costs and inadequate climate-change controls*
- *Short-term local conflicting interests are currently set to undermine counter-strategies aimed at securing long-term collective national-economic benefits*

# Chapter summary

Industrialization crises need TRUE COSTING – reflecting *all* the hidden costs and savings that technological options *ever* bring

- *Break the 'code of silence' within the oil industry and debate True Costings of oil reserves and help tie plans on climate-change into parallel plans relating to peaking economic-oil*
- *Create a GDP+ measure that modifies the detail of how GDP is calculated by adding in otherwise-obscured costs and savings so it better reflects hidden reality*
- *Evaluate the True Costing of proposals such as Carbon Capture and Storage over very-long timescales while pushing energy-efficiency in buildings and energy grids*
- *While using mechanically-based alternative-energy sources as stop-gaps prioritize exponentially-improving developments in solar and $3^{rd}$-generation biofuels*
- *Globally coordinate broadly-standardized nuclear power-station designs while accelerating international next-generation development and prioritizing fusion research*
- *Enhance existing moves to reflect 'cost of carbon' in international agreements that lay out how the global community should transition toward low-carbon economies*

## 8. HOW HIGH-TECH INDUSTRIALIZATION RISKS SYSTEMIC CRISES

# FOSSIL–FUEL ADDICTION

Sustained Industrialization only possible because of once-only energy boost to world-economy from releasing trapped solar-energy in fossil fuels as well as using them to make organic chemicals such as plastics, fertilizers and pesticides

## POLLUTION EFFECTS
### especially Manmade Global Warming

- Plastic (such as the huge floating Eastern Pacific garbage pack)
- Fertilizer into oceans killing fish (via deoxygenating algae blooms)
- Toxic mercury byproducts rising up food chain (to fish such as tuna)
- Black Carbon in atmosphere from incomplete burning of fossil fuels
- Methane (from landfill, natural-gas systems, cattle and rice paddies)
- Carbon dioxide (over 1/3 from burning coal, forests and vegetation, over 1/3 from burning oil, much of the rest from natural gas)
- Combined effects give a 50-50 likelihood of 5°C atmospheric warming
- Positive Feedback dynamics risk snowballing negative side-effects
  - Higher temperatures increase water-vapor that raises temperature
  - Water absorbs more heat than ice so melts the remaining ice faster
  - Thawed gas hydrates release gases that raise temperature still more

### THREATS

- Rising sea-level and storm surges will severely disrupt low-lying areas
- Extreme weather events will become more disruptive and frequent
- Temperature-sensitivities mean crop-yields risk dropping dramatically
- Loss of mountain snow and ice risks summer droughts
- Mild winters will not kill off agricultural pests and disease carriers

## DEPLETION EFFECTS
### especially Peaking 'Cheap'-Oil Production

- New crude oil deposits are becoming increasingly difficult to find
- Existing deposits are increasingly expensive and dangerous to extract
- Future demand for crude oil is set to increase
- The rate at which crude oil can be economically extracted is expected to decrease this decade – but few in the oil industry admit it publically
- As oil prices increase so ever-more-costly extraction is possible but the net-benefits decrease

### THREATS

- Unprecedented challenges of techniques such as deep-water drilling will inevitably cause unconventional and potentially uncontrollable spills
- Disruptions in oil-rich nations (especially Africa and the Middle East) risk disproportionate impacts on the world-economy
- OPEC and other unofficial oil cartels risk disruption by individual members breaking unity in order to maximize self-interest
- Developing oil-exporting countries risk generating instability by keeping more oil for internal use and only offering the rest to preferred customers
- Major oil-price peaks will occur with each supply disruption, downward-revision of reserve estimates or flexing of nationalist muscle
- Conflicts risk escalating into a world arena as oil-prices soar

## DISINFORMATION

- 'There is still serious scientific debate over whether global warming is primarily manmade – despite what some say, the answer is unclear' IN REALITY THERE IS EXTRAORDINARY SCIENTIFIC CONSENSUS
- 'Just because there's broad consensus doesn't make it right' IT DOES MEAN IT IS FAR MORE LIKELY THAN ANY OTHER EXPLANATION
- 'Scientists follow like sheep' THEY THRIVE ON RADICAL THINKING
- 'Climate-scientists with PhDs do not have a monopoly on deciding the rights and wrongs of global-warming claims' ACTUALLY THEY DO
- 'ClimateGate scientists deliberately falsified findings' THEY DID NOT
- 'The authoritative IPCC made false claims about glacial melting' IT WAS AN ERROR IMMEDIATELY CAUGHT BY OTHER SCIENTISTS
- 'The Media point out there is still controversy' IT MAKES A STORY
- 'Major organizations say there is not a problem' PRIVATELY SOME ADMIT THEIR STRATEGY IS THE ONE TOBACCO FIRMS ADOPTED

## LACK OF AWARENESS

- 'No problem – we've already found two-trillion barrels of oil and only one-trillion has been extracted.' THOSE FIGURES ARE MISLEADING:
  - OPEC ESTIMATES OF RESERVES ARE LIKELY OVERINFLATED
  - NEARLY ALL REMAINING RESERVES HAVE NOW BEEN FOUND
  - MANY NEW RESERVES NEED A LOT OF ENERGY TO EXTRACT
  - ALL REMAINING RESERVES ARE VERY DIFFICULT TO EXTRACT
- 'We will not run out of oil' WE WILL RUN OUT OF AFFORDABLE OIL
- 'If oil companies thought they had a problem they'd be the first to say' MANY FEEL LEGALLY OBLIGED TO PROTECT THEIR SHAREPRICE
- 'Major oil companies, leading politicians and industry-organizations all insist Peak Oil is irrelevant' PRIVATELY SOME ADMITTED TO THE REVIEW THAT THEY WERE BEING ECONOMIC WITH THE TRUTH
- 'We can switch to Green energy' THERE ARE NOT YET ENOUGH OPTIONS AND WE NEED OIL'S CHEMICALS AS WELL AS ENERGY

*BROAD CONFUSION*

## HEAVY-RESTRICTIONS ON COUNTER-MEASURES

| Insufficient Alternatives | Conflicting Domestic Commitments | Conflicting Foreign-Policy Commitments |
| --- | --- | --- |
| Coal is hard to transport and pollutes badly | Politicians feel obliged to maintain Consumerism | Oil has become enshrined into Foreign Policy |
| Carbon Capture and Sequestration is unproven | Society's energy-drains are very slow to change | Countries like Saudi-Arabia have such heavy investments in the West they 'must not pull out' |
| The Hydrogen Economy was largely hype | - Huge cities are massively energy-intensive | Rather than risk losing oil, even liberal countries tend to support autocrats that promise stability |
| Biofuel shows promise but does not yet work | - Suburbia is even more profligate | Foreign-oil dependency is increasingly risky |
| The best hydroelectric sites are already in use | Much growth demands infrastructural expansion | The only oil-rich nuclear-arms country is Russia |
| Solar / wind need undevised storage systems | Oil-related stock dominates many pension funds | |
| Nuclear power is currently very slow to build | Like Banks, many Oil firms are 'too large to fail' | |

# POPULATION CRISES overview

Population backlashes threaten extensive destabilization resulting from Competitive Overuse of resources crucial to the world economy and require Collective Sustainability as a counter-measure

- Overpopulation has triggered a systemic pattern of Competitive Overuse that has led to chronic overexploitation of natural resources

- Competitive Overuse is depleting even readily-visible resources but is building especially-threatening backlashes in systems that are largely obscured

- Developing nations – including major countries like China and India – are at severe risk of medium-term Population-driven disruptions

- Even well-developed nations risk catastrophic destabilization long-term as a result of systems collapsing from Competitive Overuse

- Population crises need COLLECTIVE SUSTAINABILITY – countering the risk that Competitive Overuse leads to system-collapses

*Threats of backlashes to: FISHING, AGRICULTURE, RETAILING and ASIA*

*OVERFISHING...*

*...DROUGHT...*

*...ECOSYSTEM FAILURE...*

*...SOCIETAL COLLAPSE...*

# POPULATION

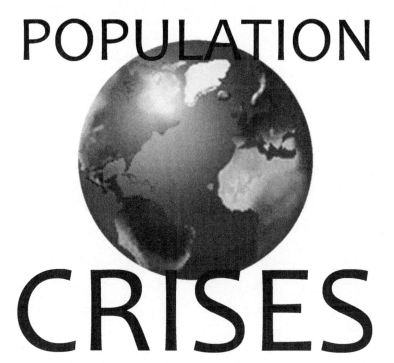

# CRISES

# COMPETITIVE OVERUSE

## Overpopulation has triggered a systemic pattern of Competitive Overuse that has led to chronic overexploitation of natural resources

MODERN HUMANS FIRST emerged in Africa around 200,000 years ago. Yet of all the humans who have ever lived, 7% are alive today. In any year there are almost 2½ times the number of births as deaths, so the overall size of global civilization is growing by around two-hundred thousand people – *each day*. That is equivalent to the population of Manhattan being added to the planet every week.

In truth, global population has been growing exponentially for several centuries. From around 70,000 years ago until agriculture began about 10,000 years ago, world population stayed at around 1-million people. Only then did it begin to grow. By the end of the Roman Empire it had topped 50-million. By the early 19$^{th}$ century, humanity had for the first time reached 1-billion. More than a century later (around 1927) it reached 2-billion. 33 years later is was 3-billion. 14 years later, 4-billion. Another 13 years, 5-billion. Add 12 years, it was 6-billion. A bit over a decade later, and today the global population is approaching 7-billion. During the 20$^{th}$ century the number of people each demanding their 'fair share' of the planet grew four-times larger.

## HOW MANY PEOPLE HAVE EVER LIVED?

For a very long time, human populations were extremely small compared with today. Even after humans neared extinction around 70,000 years ago, it is believed that global numbers only rose to around one-million and stuck there until the introduction of agriculture about 10,000 years ago. These assumptions, combined with a low average life-expectancy suggests that the total number of humans who have ever lived is very roughly 100-billion.

**164**

# Chronic overexploitation

The momentum built into this growth will take a long time to slow because there are currently so many people around the world who are in their twenties or younger. In fact, there are twice as many fertile women on the planet as in 1970. So, although birth-rates overall are now expected slowly to fall (each woman on average will have slightly fewer children), for a long time the world will continue to see the repercussion of the high birth-rates throughout the last few decades – because those offspring will mature into child-bearing adults who have babies themselves.

What is more, dramatic improvements in medical science mean that many of those new babies, even in far-flung parts of the world, will on average live much longer. As a result, despite dropping birth-rates, overall global population is set to keep growing. Forecasts estimate that it could well reach 8-billion people by around 2025 and 9 billion by 2050. But those figures on their own are misleading. In reality, the population of today's most-developed countries will be largely unchanged in 2050. It is the less-developed nations that will see their populations grow by a couple of billion, with the poorest states expected to triple in size within only four decades.

That in turn masks a radical shift in the dynamics of world population. As overall birth-rates peak, there are never again as many babies being born. But population keeps growing – because more babies survive and grown-ups live longer – so the average age of the global population will gradually get older. The number of people aged 60 or over is expected to almost *triple* by 2050.

## CONTINUING TO AVOID MALTHUSIAN COLLAPSE

On the surface at least everything seems manageable. Humanity has, after all, demonstrated an extraordinary ability to keep growing in numbers. Around the time that the global population was reaching one-billion, the Reverend Thomas Malthus promoted the idea that overpopulation was inevitably kept in check by the famine and disease that it eventually created. Published across six increasingly-sophisticated editions from 1798 to 1826, *An Essay on the Principle of Population* ran counter to the then-popular view that on average societies grow ever-better.

But overall, Malthus's hypothesis does not appear to match what has actually happened. On the contrary, despite frequent warnings of an imminent 'Malthusian Collapse' of civilization because of too many people on the planet, such a catastrophe demonstrably has not yet happened – even though there are now seven times more of us than Malthus was worried about. Clearly, or so many argue, mankind's ingenuity – first as Industrialization then as High-Tech – always comes to the rescue. It has done throughout the last few centuries. What is suddenly going to change? The simple answer is: Almost everything.

Since the start of the Industrial Revolution countries have in many ways been cheating. As pointed out in the subchapter on *How one-time energy got the world-economy addicted* (page 86), it has been artificially easy to thrive since 1750 because people have been clever enough to exploit massive reserves of fossil fuels. That one-time-boost of cheap energy led to steadily-improving technology and better medicine and increased life-expectancy. Population increased not because people were having more babies but because more children survived eventually to have families of their own.

The spurt in world population from the 1950s was not really any different. Contrary to what Malthus had predicted, famine did not stop the exponential growth because ever-cleverer technology meant fossil-fuels again came to the rescue. Oil-derived pesticides, synthetic fertilizers from natural gas, gasoline-run machinery and transport, carbon-based energy for irrigation and refrigeration and home-cooking, all led to a Green Revolution during which agricultural yields shot up and fed far more people than previously had been possible.

But as already highlighted in the last chapter, in the 21st century High-Tech-Industrialization backlashes resulting from imminent peaking oil and longer-term climate change for the first time raise serious concerns about the continued validity of the argument that 'more people results in cleverer technology that can support more people'. By 2030, demand for food and energy is projected to rise by a half, and for water by a third. Already, many scientists are warning that population-growth is going too far.

## SHIFTS IN TASTE AND LIFESTYLE

The risks are far more complicated than just numbers of people. The reality is that even if the population was *not* growing, there would still be the likelihood of growing crises because what the average person wants is rapidly changing. And those new demands – even just as they relate to food – are far more energy-intensive than in the past.

# Chronic overexploitation

In general, people around the world are moving to a more 'Western' diet. In India, for instance, since the 1970s there has been a six-fold increase in milk consumption. But that has not just been caused by population growth. It actually corresponds to a doubling in milk-consumption per person. That trend is expected to continue. Similarly, world meat production is forecast to double by 2050 – driven particularly by demand from China and India. Already, the global population of cattle is approaching 1.5-billion, around one cow for every five people. By 2050 the population is predicted to be closer to 3-billion cattle, representing roughly one cow for every three people. In reality, that is a highly-wasteful shift.

Depending on the way it is produced, meat can be a very inefficient use of resources in comparison with growing grain – although this can vary substantially depending on rearing practices. In the UK, for instance, cows tend to be fed on grassland unsuited for crops, whereas in the USA they are often fed on grain for their final six months to double their weight before they are slaughtered. Under those circumstances, the amount of land needed to produce 1 kilogram of beef could maybe produce 15 kilograms of grain instead. Rearing meat also uses very much more water than the equivalent amount of grain. As will be addressed in the subchapter on *Why unsustainable water usage threatens food supplies* (page 180), for some farmers that will rapidly become a major problem.

Taste in food, however, is only one important transformation within developing nations. There are also changing uses of land. New roads are vital in emerging economies for transporting food and other products around – as well as providing access to international markets. New buildings are crucial for housing the growing population. But as more roads and cities get built, they not only use up fossil fuels but also some of the agricultural land needed to feed people.

Overall lifestyle is another critical shift. More than ever – not least because of the internet – people in developing countries see how those in successful economies get to live. And they want some of the same. As an example: Except for oil, China already consumes more than the USA. Yet even with today's populations, if average Chinese citizens lived like their US counterparts, and so did Indians and Brazilians and Russians and Mexicans, and indeed much of the rest of the developing world, where exactly would all the wood, paper, plastic – let alone energy, water, food, tin, lead, copper and phosphorus – actually come from? Even as things stand, the garbage from throwaway societies means cities such as New York are running out of suitable landfill sites nearby. Where would all the rubbish actually go if everybody threw away the same amount as someone in the Big Apple?

If developing countries continue growing even only at the rate that they have maintained during the global economic-downturn, as early as 2030 the aspirations of their people may be utterly unsustainable – simply because it is not at all clear where all the raw materials they will want will come from (let alone all the refuse they produce go to). Even an abundantly occurring substance such as potash, which is an important fertilizer, nevertheless needs to be mined and distributed to increasingly demanding rival nations. That has already resulted in soaring prices and concerns about shortages.

The forecasts for any individual country – such as China – seem demanding enough. But when all the main countries' forecasts are added together, they come up with consumption levels that are multiples of today's total global production levels. Yet it is in no country's interest unilaterally to hold back. And *that* is the first symptom of a partially-hidden set of looming crises rapidly developing as a result of High-Tech-Population.

## COMPETITIVE OVERUSE

Despite the well-publicized concerns that relate to High-Tech-Industrialization crises, even the major dangers of peaking oil and global warming may turn out to be far less-immediate than those caused by Population. The reason is because of a classic pattern of 'Competitive Overuse' that occurs when lots of people all use the same apparently-renewable resource. For instance, if one shepherd grazes his flock on his own pasture, everything tends to remain in balance because the shepherd maintains the appropriate size of flock for the amount of grass he has available. Also, any early signs of overgrazing take long enough to develop that there is plenty of time to move the sheep if necessary – which the shepherd has every incentive to do.

But if many rival shepherds let their flocks graze together on an area of commonly-owned land, there is a tendency for each shepherd to graze a larger number of sheep than (in combination with all the other flocks) the land can actually sustain long-term. Worse, because of the inbuilt competition between the shepherds to maximize their share of the common-land, overgrazing when it inevitably occurs can happen so quickly that early-warning signs are not apparent in time even to realize what is happening.

Anyway, it would require all the shepherds to agree to take their flocks off the land for it to have time to recover – so even if someone did recognize what was happening, it might still in reality be too late to get everyone to take corrective action. After all, one shepherd alone is unlikely to take his flock off the deteriorating land while the other shepherds are still exploiting it and 'unfairly' gaining an advantage as a result.

## TRAGEDY OF THE COMMONS

In the early 1990s I was lucky enough to work with many of the world-experts in the field of Systems Thinking (in a company co-founded by the leading authority Peter Senge, author of the highly-influential book *The Fifth Discipline*). For those of us who studied the behavior of complex systems, the pattern of Competitive Overuse was sufficiently recognizable that amongst fellow-academics we usually referred to it using a rather-poetic name – even though to the general public the term was, and remains, almost completely unknown. Based on the maybe historically-inaccurate metaphor of shepherds overgrazing common-land, systems-thinkers refer to the pattern as The Tragedy of the Commons, a term first coined in 1968 by the ecologist Garrett Hardin. The combination of characteristics associated with the phenomenon is considered to be such an important pattern that it is referred to as one of the key archetypes within system-dynamics theory. Unfortunately, I have never found anyone who lives in the real world that intuitively understands what the term 'Tragedy of the Commons' actually means. So instead I came up with the term 'Competitive Overuse' to try to make the idea a bit clearer. It refers to exactly the same dynamic as Garret Hardin first highlighted.

The typical symptoms of this complex (but very common) group-behavior is that overall activity keeps increasing, even though after a while the individual gain that each person receives starts to diminish. Then suddenly everything crashes. That is what happens every time a community –

typically quite unintentionally – gets locked into Competitive Overuse. For the most part unrecognized, that largely-hidden pattern of Competitive Overuse is currently dominating the way that High-Tech-Population crises are forming. It is strongly reinforced by the High-Tech-Capitalism side-effect of heightened competition that I detailed in the first chapter of this book. But it is also strengthened by Industrialization and, at least historically, also even by Religion.

One of the unintentionally more-damaging of the Religion side-effects turns out to have been the belief of many major faiths that mankind had the God-given right of Dominion over the Earth and everything within it. As a result, until relatively recently, no one really even questioned the validity of exploiting natural resources to the absolute maximum. As soon as the ability to act according to that historical assumption was amplified by High-Tech, the series of growing backlashes that we will examine throughout the rest of this chapter became inevitable.

# Chronic overexploitation

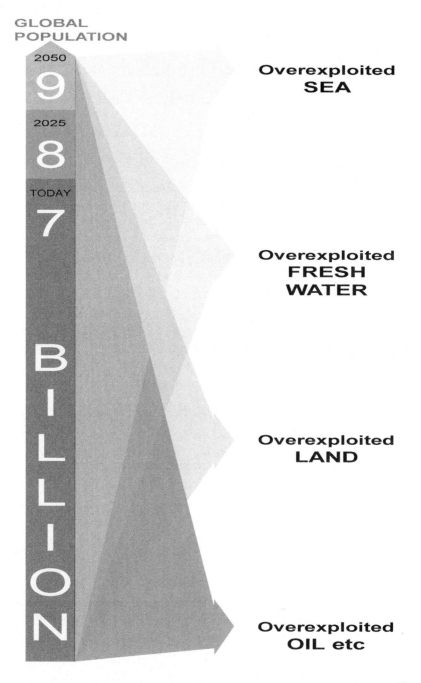

GLOBAL
POPULATION

2050
**9**

2025
**8**

TODAY
**7**

**B
I
L
L
I
O
N**

**Overexploited
SEA**

**Overexploited
FRESH
WATER**

**Overexploited
LAND**

**Overexploited
OIL etc**

# DEPLETING FORESTS AND DEPLETING TOP-SOIL

Vast areas of forest and productive land are being depleted despite being highly visible forms of Competitive Overuse

## DEPLETING FORESTS

These days, in contrast to the past, campaigns to Save the Rainforest are so widespread that the public almost takes them for granted. Yet in rapidly developing countries such as Brazil there are strong financial incentives (often these days stimulated by Chinese investment) for locals to cut down their forests. Despite increased efforts by the Brazilian government to protect the rainforest in the last few years, deforestation is exacerbated by illegal logging of exotic hardwoods such as jatoba, the need to clear farming land so as to cultivate crops such as soybeans, and the insatiable demand for charcoal to smelt nationally-mined iron ore into pig iron.

### MEASURING DEFORESTATION

It is actually incredibly difficult to be accurate about rates of deforestation. For a start it depends on what is defined as forest. An often-quoted statistic about annual losses the size of Greece (about 13-million hectares, or 32-million acres) is taken from a 2005 UN report that it now seems might actually have been understated. However, almost half of that loss may in fact be offset by new growth and organized replanting. The analogy with Greece seems to have taken on a life of its own. Two of the most popular books on dealing with climate change each quote the statistic, but one claims it as the losses per year and the other as the losses *per decade.* It is the book written by a former Vice President that correctly claims it as an annual loss.

# Depleting resources

No one could complain that society-at-large no longer recognizes the benefits that such forests bring – whether in terms of locking away $CO_2$ or in hosting an extraordinary diversity of life, including possible cures for diseases no one is even aware of yet. No one can suggest that we 'cannot see the forest for the trees' when it comes to somewhere like the Amazon rainforest. Nevertheless, every year, humanity clears an area of rainforest the size of Greece – probably more.

In the last sixty years maybe half of the Earth's mature rainforests have been destroyed. Some estimates predict that by 2030 there will only be 10% left – although it is important to realize that there will also be new plantings that partially offset that loss. Burning forests is the second-largest source of $CO_2$ after burning fossil-fuels for electricity and heat – which is one of the reasons why, after the USA and China, the largest contributors to global warming are Indonesia and Brazil.

Even when the forest is replaced with oil-palms, however, it does not end up storing anything like the same amounts of $CO_2$ as the original forest – and the initial burning, of course, releases massive quantities of black carbon into the atmosphere. Studies also indicate that only more-mature trees capture large amounts of $CO_2$, so early foresting of any replanted trees loses out on the potential benefits of a mature forest.

## HOW TREES EVAPORATE WATER

More correctly, the tree process is called 'transpiration' – the minute pore-like openings (stomata) on leaves and elsewhere are opened to let in $CO_2$ from the atmosphere to be used for photosynthesis, which makes energy for the tree and creates oxygen as a by-product, but in the process they release as water-vapor a large proportion of the water drawn up from the ground by the root-system.

Logging also causes far more problems than just the loss of forest. Rainfall-patterns, for instance, can change because the woodland is no longer evaporating water-vapour into the atmosphere. And even partial-logging lets the sun reach the forest floor, which dries it, making it more prone to fires. A dry forest-floor also loses much of its ability to absorb water – so heavy rain tends to run over it instead of soaking in. In some cases the eventual cost of flood-damage may be higher than the price gained for the lumber. As water flows over the exposed land it erodes gullies that rapidly wash away soil and nutrients. The land can soon become useless.

## DEPLETING TOPSOIL

It is a similar story to the general loss of topsoil around the world. Fertile soil forms very slowly over eons. Yet today, deforestation and overgrazing mean that much of it is eroding away far faster than it can naturally form. Huge areas in Western and Northern China, Africa, Iran and India are turning into deserts as the damaged topsoil disappears. The same process turned the Great Plains in the USA into Dust Bowls in the 1930s and did the same to the Soviet Virgin Lands Project in Kazakhstan during the late 1950s. The soil blows away leaving coarser sand that can then stir up into fierce sandstorms and be transported far distances. Each year, clouds of sand from the newly-forming deserts of China blow from once-fertile plains over to South Korea.

All these instances of Competitive Overuse – just as with rival shepherds on common-land – follow the pattern of collective overexploitation of apparently resilient land ultimately resulting in desert. But they are actually relatively-mild examples because at least when side-effects like these occur, they are visible and so future behavior can potentially alter as a result. There is a chance to learn from mistakes.

But when the damage happens out of sight – so no one really knows what is happening, let alone is constantly reminded of what is going on – then far more dramatic versions of Competitive Overuse occur. For the remainder of this chapter I will work through the main interrelated patterns of severe overexploitation, followed by rapid collapse, that are set to play-out in everything from fish-stocks to available water. High-Tech-Population backlashes even risk destabilizing the whole complex web of life across our planet – including human societies. All those dangers risk reinforcing each other. But even without combining together, any one of them on its own represents a severe global crisis in its own right.

# THE IMMINENT COLLAPSE OF WORLD FISH STOCKS

World fish stocks across numerous previously-common species are at risk of imminent collapse from unintended Competitive Overuse

TO MOST ADULTS the sea looks very similar today to how we remember it as children. But it is actually a very different place. Like some of the land above it, below the waves the oceans are themselves on course to becoming a desert. The reason is that as global population has been growing faster than ever before, so global fishing power has been exploding exponentially. From the 1950s, rising demand for seafood – combined with new High-Tech designs of sonar and refrigerated factory-ships – led to unparalleled levels of fishing. By the turn of the new millennium fishing fleets were extracting each year five times the annual catch of half a century before.

The warning signal should have been that about 90% of the large fish that had been in the oceans fifty years earlier – were now gone. Only smaller fish tended to remain. That made fishing even more of a challenge. But the latest massive nets were capable of encircling a whole shoal, closing the net so the fish could not escape, and hauling in over 100-tons of fish in one go.

## BAGS OF MARINE GOLD

The most common example of high-capacity fishing net is the Purse Seine. Similar to the old-fashioned 'bag of gold' beloved of pirates in swashbuckling films, the huge net has a drawstring that closes the net to trap an entire school of fish such as tuna, salmon, mackerel or herring.

Mankind had easily become the top predator of the oceans. No species that we wanted stood a chance. So our fishing fleets kept going. And the general public remained largely unaware of what was happening. It still is. The average Atlantic cod that is caught today is about a third the size it was when the catches were fully sustainable. The largest cod used to be longer than the fisherman catching it was tall. Now it is typically less than the length of his arm. The fish caught often are not even sexually mature.

## DEPLETING FISH STOCKS

Indeed, these days, fish are often not even where they are supposed to be. Canadian fishing fleets in Newfoundland used to haul in massive catches of cod. When the annual catch peaked in the late 1960s the fishing fleets did not ease up. Instead, they became even more competitive in their search for cod. In the classic Competitive-Overuse pattern, the overfishing continued even though the catches (and indeed the fish themselves) became ever-smaller.

Then in the early 1990s the Newfoundland fish stocks collapsed completely. There were not any Atlantic cod left. Tens of thousands of people lost their jobs. A moratorium on all cod-fishing was declared so as finally to give the oceans a chance to replenish. The stocks never recovered. Almost twenty years later it is estimated that the stocks of cod around Newfoundland are about 1% of what they were in the late 1970s. Exactly the same pattern has been played out by European fishing fleets. In the 1950s and 1960s the quotas for Norwegian herring were set far higher than experts recommended, but for short-term political reasons the general public was reassured that everything would be alright. The overfishing that resulted was almost disastrous.

In the 1970s and 1980s almost exactly the same thing happened again, and for the same reasons, only this time it was the cod supplies that were devastated. The fish stocks partially recovered. Overfishing of cod – at levels far above those of scientific recommendations – resumed. And now there are severe concerns in the scientific and conservation communities that other important fish such as haddock and Atlantic salmon are also being fished into collapse.

A less-talked-about example is the Giant Bluefin Tuna. It is a magnificent fish. It can live for thirty years and grow to more than four meters (thirteen feet) long and weigh over half a ton. It is also called the

# Depleting resources

Atlantic Bluefin tuna or Northern Bluefin tuna – correctly it is only examples weighing more than 150 kg that earn the title Giant Bluefin.

This is the fish seen in the pictures of Ernest Hemingway proudly standing beside his enormous suspended catch on a long-forgotten quayside. It is not the tuna that comes in tins and gets put into sandwiches – that is typically the smaller and far-more sustainable Skipjack. But there is nothing like the Bluefin. Sports fishermen love it. Marine divers love it. Fish-eaters love it so much it may soon be extinct. It is severely overfished because it is a sushi delicacy. But as its rarity increases, so does its price. It can be so hard to find in the open ocean that under normal circumstances it would not be commercially viable to fish for it. But a single Giant Bluefin at auction has already reached prices as high as $100,000. At those margins, it remains lucrative to be a marine bounty hunter.

Unfortunately the more mature fish – those that could produce offspring – are the more valuable to catch, and market forces will ensure that the reward for capturing them will rise as and when needed. Worse, many of the tuna are caught even before they are mature enough to have bred at all. Theoretically it would be extremely easy to break this cycle and save the Giant Bluefin – all it would take is for sushi lovers around the world to eat something else. In practice, the Giant Bluefin is set for extinction.

Other tuna are also increasingly in danger. Yellowfin catches have been dropping since the 1990s and show signs of severe overfishing. Even the resilient Skipjack tuna now seems at risk. Many species of sturgeon – famous for their caviar – have already collapsed. And, practically unnoticed, around half of the top predators in the oceans seem to have disappeared. Populations of Whitetip sharks – whose fleshy fins are highly valued in Chinese cuisine for shark-fin soup – have dropped precariously.

In areas like the Gulf of Mexico, Whitetip numbers have sunk to 1% of what they were fifty years ago. Such extreme disruption to the balance of predators in the oceans is itself likely to result in major unintended and unanticipated backlashes throughout the food-chain. That damage has now been done. It may be irreparable. So too may be the damage to fish stocks overall. The point is that there are now far too many hugely-advanced High-Tech factory ships chasing far too few fish. As a result, about three-quarters of ocean fish-stocks appear at risk of a Competitive-Overuse collapse.

## DAMAGE TO MARINE ENVIRONMENTS

It is not just overfishing that is threatening the health of the seas. As already mentioned in the subchapter called *Clouded interpretations of pollution* (starting on page 90), pollution is killing fish. For instance, the artificial fertilizers and sewage carried by the Mississippi flow into the Gulf of Mexico and every summer create enormous algal blooms that kill fish. The same occurs to varying degrees around the world. In 2010 a vast algal bloom spread in the Baltic Sea from Finland in the north to parts of Germany and Poland in the south. It was the largest bloom since 2005, primarily because of prolonged warm weather and lack of wind.

Loss of mangrove swamps, coastal wetlands and coral reefs needed for fish-spawning is also a problem. It is thought that around a third of marine fish live at some stage on coral reefs – but a quarter of all reefs are at risk of significant loss. Even fish farms are causing problems. Fish escape and can dilute the diversity of wild stocks. But also, the cultivated fish need food and they are often fed with wild fish such as anchovies. Under those circumstances, fish farmers are rather inefficiently converting one edible species into another at a time when there are decreasing numbers of fish available for the escalating human population to eat. And – because of habits formed when fish were plentiful – land farmers still feed fish to agricultural livestock and use it as organic fertilizer.

For people living in developing countries such as Bangladesh, Cambodia and Ghana, fish represent a major source of animal-protein. Yet, although those populations will suffer first, it is not those countries that are systematically pushing the oceans into catastrophic collapse. It is in fact the relatively-rich nations that are exploiting wild fish in ways that are unsustainable. Such well-resourced countries are, largely unintentionally, squandering the world's greatest natural food resource. However, just like the shepherds refusing to 'lose out on a fair share' of the common grazing, each fishing fleet continues to catch as much as it can, wherever it can. This situation will not last. Across the community of marine-scientists, ecologists and conservationists, there is a very-serious concern that if the global community sticks on its current course then within a few decades all major world fish-stocks will – probably irretrievably – have collapsed.

## 10. HIGH-TECH POPULATION BACKLASHES: SEA

## Overexploited SEA

Weak regulation
Wrong quotas
Subsidies
Factory ships
Massive nets
Refrigeration
Sonar

## ESCALATING THREAT:
## Global collapse of fish stocks

• After 20-year moratorium on Newfoundland cod-fishing, collapsed stocks have *not* recovered – still only 1% of levels in late-1970s
• Quotas for global fishing are far higher than experts recommend
• Government subsidy is encouraging uneconomic overexploitation
• Cod, haddock, Atlantic salmon, Yellowfin tuna severely overfished
• A single Giant Bluefin – a sushi delicacy – can auction for $100,000 and consequently the species is being hunted to extinction
• Demand for sharkfin soup has devastated some shark populations leading to severe and unpredictable disruption of marine food-chains
• Weak regulation results in illegal – and cruel – 'finning' of sharks
• Fish-farms use up edible wild fish (eg, anchovies) to feed fish stock
• Land-farms use up fish to feed livestock and as organic fertilizer
• Countries such as Bangladesh, Cambodia and Ghana – where fish is a major source of animal protein – are vulnerable to stock collapse
• Accidentally-released toxic aquarium seaweed is now spreading uncontrollably through the Mediterranean crowding out other species
• Run-off of fertilizers is creating huge algal blooms that also kill fish

# WHY UNSUSTAINABLE WATER USAGE THREATENS FOOD SUPPLIES

## Unsustainable use of water is leading to unprecedented risks of drought and an associated curtailment of food supplies

MOST PEOPLE IN developed countries think that if there is a sustained drought in an isolated community and water-supplies run low then there is a risk that people will die of thirst. There is not. Long before that point, they will starve. The point is that communities do not actually drink much of the water they use. The vast majority of it is needed for irrigation. That is true even in developed countries – where the remaining water is taken up by industry and by homes (for things like baths and flushing toilets). So, to understand how water-stocks risk collapse, it is also necessary to understand agriculture.

### HOW LAND-USE DETERMINES WATER-USE

The world grain harvest is now four times larger than it was at the start of the $20^{th}$ century. But it does not take four times the area of farmland to grow. Instead, thanks to High-Tech, productivity has been improved to about three times what it once was as a result of planting new high-yield plant-hybrids as well as taking advantage of an unsustainable boost from fossil fuels in the form of artificial fertilizers and mechanization. What many forget though is that, just as important as these changes has been *widespread irrigation*. That amount of irrigation has demanded a lot of water. And even after the agricultural needs, there remained the lesser (but still substantial) requirements of industry and cities and homes. All that water has had to come from somewhere.

These days the Colorado River in the USA rarely makes it all the way to the sea. Hydroelectricity generators take out some of its energy, and reservoirs evaporate some its water, but most of the river is now simply diverted and used as irrigation. The same is increasingly true of the Yellow

# Depleting resources

River in China and the Ganges in India. As a result of these sorts of developments, when a major river runs through more than one country, water politics is gradually taking on an importance all of its own. Much of the Nile starts in Ethiopia, then flows through Sudan, and only finally reaches the sea by flowing through Egypt. Each country is making increasing demands on the Nile in order to feed expanding populations. How long the existing water-rights agreements will survive is unclear. Equally uncertain is how peaceful any renegotiation process will be.

The same is true of the waters of the Tigris and Euphrates that flow through Turkey, Syria and Iraq. The land between the two rivers is often thought of as the Cradle of Civilization. It was here that the first cities grew up around five-thousand years ago in the ancient area known as Mesopotamia – from the Ancient Greek for 'between the rivers'. Water grievances are now set to aggravate still further what have *long* been territorial animosities.

## LAKE CHAD

Although Lake Chad in Africa is typically quoted by conservationists as a prime example of catastrophic water depletion, it is often not appreciated that historically the lake has in fact varied in size tremendously anyway – even before substantial irrigation. The statistic normally quoted is that at the end of the 20th century Lake Chad had reduced in size by 95% in only thirty-five years. Less-often added is that it has grown significantly since then. Nevertheless, however you look at it, a combination of climate and over-irrigation is clearly causing very severe problems.

The impact of extracting too much water can sometimes look worrying. Lake Chad, the Sea of Galilee and the Dead Sea have all shrunk dramatically. However, sometimes the effects are horrific. In the 1960s the Soviet Union set up a major irrigation project that diverted water from rivers feeding the inland Aral Sea (one of the largest lakes in the world, situated between Kazakhstan and Uzbekistan). It was home to a large and prosperous fishing industry. Today that is all gone.

The lake has become an environmental disaster. It has lost as much water as the whole volume of Lake Erie and Lake Ontario combined. It only covers a tenth of the area that it occupied decades ago, and the remaining water is three times saltier than the sea. The fishing industry that once employed 40,000 people has disappeared, its deserted fleets stranded miles from the largely-dead lake. The receding water has revealed huge areas of salty earth that blows onto agricultural land and makes it infertile. The dust storms are also toxic because of pollution that previously had been washed into the lake.

## INVISIBLE WATER DEPLETION

At least the damage to the Aral Sea is visible. As with fish-stocks, the greatest dangers of backlashes from water-depletion develop out of sight. Water-demand has tripled over the last fifty years, and diverting rivers is not sufficient to satisfy modern needs. So in much the same way as societies drill for oil, they drill for water. It is found trapped in subterranean layers of porous rock or gravel called 'aquifers'. Often these aquifers are slowly refilled naturally – usually as a result of it raining somewhere, although possibly a very long way away. Some aquifers, however, contain 'fossil water' that has been trapped underground for eons and (like oil) once used up can never be replaced.

Around the globe the human population uses a vast amount of subterranean water. About half the world's inhabitants now depend on it. 80% of the irrigated lands in China, 60% in India, and 20% in the USA all rely on aquifers. The trouble is that the level of the water in each of those aquifers – the 'water-table' – is typically going down. The same is true in Mexico, Iran, Israel, Pakistan and Yemen. As a water-table lowers, it is necessary to drill deeper. But at lower levels the water is often saltier, so it increasingly damages the land that it irrigates.

In the Punjab – the 'Breadbasket of India' – intensive farming using artificial fertilizers and pesticides demands so much irrigation that in some places the water-table is dropping by waist-height every year, and so much salt is building up in the top-soil that it is becoming infertile. What is more, the deeper a well the more electricity needed to pump water to the surface. Millions of shallow wells have already dried up. Some newer wells are now up to a kilometer (over half a mile) deep, and keeping the pumps going can account for around half of a rural community's electricity. When there is a blackout – which is quite common in rural India – all irrigation stops.

The Punjab's dropping water-tables and increasing energy demands are ultimately unsustainable. At some point a village's economics just do not make sense any more. The wells run dry. The agricultural land turns to dust. People are forced to migrate. The soil erodes. And once again, a Competitive-Overuse collapse leaves nothing but dust bowls. Around the world, subterranean-water is not being replenished as fast as it is being extracted. The wells are being seriously over-pumped. However, the situation is even direr when the wells are using up fossil water. Much of Northern China, Saudi Arabia and several states in the USA are heavily dependent on fossil water aquifers that are estimated to be within a decade or so of being depleted beyond economic use.

Yet, largely because of population growth, global water consumption is predicted to double every twenty years. And most of the population-growth is in countries where water-tables are dropping. Already-strained rivers cannot make up the difference. As a result, Northern China, Northwest India, Pakistan, Mexico, nearly all of the Middle East, Northern Africa and the Southwest of the USA risk acute water shortages within a couple of decades. Some of these areas are feeding their populations with food that is *doubly* unsustainable – both the fossil fuel and the fossil water risk becoming uneconomic. All of these areas are unknowingly living beyond their means. And inevitable crises are building

## HOW THE WATER-DEPLETION BACKLASH WILL PLAY OUT

Desalination plants are not an obvious answer – at least not for a few decades. Current designs are expensive, use a lot of energy, and are particularly uneconomic for those living a long way from the sea or at high altitudes. And anyway, many countries do not even have access to seawater they can desalinate. Once again, the global community seems locked on a heading toward resource-scarcity – this time of water.

Just as with oil, the politics of who gets what water will become increasingly contentious. But although several commentators have suggested that, as with oil, there will be wars fought over water, many of these people misunderstand how very different water is. Although there may indeed be conflicts over water-rights for rivers such as the Nile or the Tigris and Euphrates, in reality, despite what people say, very few countries are likely to fight over water itself. That is because there is a far more concentrated form of water that makes much more sense to worry about. Food.

What will happen is that countries will increasingly divert scarce water away from agriculture and into cities. And with the money their populations make in their cities, they will import grain. After all, it takes roughly a thousand tons of water to produce just one ton of grain. So importing grain is actually a very space-efficient way of importing water. Meat is even better because a ton of beef or lamb represents maybe ten thousand or more tons of water. If a country is running out of water then, rather than using most of that water to make food, it makes far more economic sense – if there is the choice – to use it in the manufacture of something like steel or electronics or for air-conditioning in an office, and then add to the value of those components and services by turning them into, say, an automobile that can be sold abroad and the profit used to buy food.

That is why in California many cities buy up water-rights from farmers – who get far more for them than if they were selling water to each other. Similarly, it is the reason why in Chennai (formerly Madras), during water shortages entrepreneurial Indian farmers sacrifice some of their crops and instead store the water they would have used for irrigation and take it into the city where they sell it to the inhabitants for more than they would have got for the crops. That is a microcosm of the way the next decade or so will play out around the globe.

When it comes to water, cities will win out over farmland. And it is the richest countries – with their access to international distributors – that will then use the proxy of food as a way to import water and export drought. They will swap with each other certain foods that one rich country makes better, or at different times of year. But overall they will all be net-importers of food, and they will not initially worry too much about running low on water. Other than between rival countries sharing a single major river, no wars will be fought over something as far down the food-chain as water. At the bottom of that food-chain, though, will be the poorest countries that nevertheless for the moment have sufficient water. They will be the ones that produce and export far more food than they buy-in.

However, that strategy is just the setup for a truly-global backlash from Competitive Overuse. Today's worldwide pattern of water use is inherently unsustainable. In China, falling water tables, combined with agricultural

# Depleting resources

land being used for other purposes, and farm-labor moving into industry, all mean that the annual grain harvest is already shrinking. That is not a problem. China is rich so it can import grain from elsewhere to feed its growing population. India's population is set to grow so fast that it will soon overtake China in numbers. The struggling Punjab will not be able to cope. But that is not a problem either. India is at the forefront of many areas of High-Tech and will earn more than enough to import whatever food it needs. As will Europe. As will the USA. As will Russia and Brazil and South Korea. As will all the oil-rich countries in the Middle East. As will those oil or mineral-rich countries in Africa.

That is how water ultimately risks triggering a progressive global famine. In the short-term the increasing problem of water-scarcity for many rich countries will relatively-easily be addressed by using imported-food as a substitute. Every successful nation will start using the same quick-fix. Yet there is still too little water for the number of people on the planet and for the type of (water-intensive) food that people increasingly want to eat.

That remains true however much countries are willing to pay for the water-proxy of food. The global crisis from water depletion will not ultimately be caused by lack of water but by lack of what the water is used for. Even in a couple of decades, many city-dwellers in poorer countries may still believe as they do today that if water-supplies run low there is a risk that people die of thirst. But it will then not be long before they find that in reality people starve.

## 11. HIGH-TECH POPULATION BACKLASHES: FRESH WATER

## Overexploited
# FRESH WATER

Agriculture
Hydroelectricity
Reservoirs
Deepening wells
-Rainfilled aquifers
-Fossil water
Food as 'proxy'

## ESCALATING THREAT:
## Widespread irrigation failures

• Water-demand tripled over last fifty years and is now expected to double every twenty years – about four times today's usage by 2050

• Major waterways such as the Colorado, Ganges and Yellow River are largely used up for irrigation (plus hydroelectricity and reservoirs)

• About half the world's population depends on subterranean water (80% irrigated lands in China, 60% in India, 20% in USA)

• Insufficient replenishment of water in overpumped subterranean aquifers means the water-table is typically going down in China, India, Iran, Israel, Mexico, Pakistan, USA and Yemen

• Deeper wells are typically saltier (causing progressive damage to irrigated land) and it also costs more to pump up the water

• The water-table of the Punjab 'Breadbasket of India' drops by waist height each year, land is becoming infertile and being vacated

• Northern China, Saudi Arabia and several US states are heavily dependent on irreplaceable 'fossil water' that is rapidly depleting

• Limited water will be used for profit-generating cities and factories rather than agriculture – passing the water-burden to poor countries

# CURRENT EARLY-STAGE FAILURE
# OF CRUCIAL ECOSYSTEMS

## There are clear symptoms of early-stage failure of destabilized ecosystems crucial to many national economies

THE MOST COMPREHENSIVE studies on extinction rates have been conducted by the United Nations – although they appear to be confirmed by numerous more-local studies of particular environments such as select rainforest. The overall conclusion: Before Industrialization and Population first began to impact the planet significantly, each year about one species in every million went extinct. Today, in a world of High-Tech-Industrialization and High-Tech-Population that figure seems closer to one in a thousand.

Primarily because of changes we make to habitat or because of non-local species that we introduce (by accident and by deliberate intent), extinctions appear to be running around a thousand times higher than historical background rates. As the human species exerts its 'dominion' over the $21^{st}$ century, almost fifty-thousand species are now listed as threatened. Of those, over a third are deemed at serious risk. That is one-in-eight species of bird, one-in-five species of all known mammals, four-out-of-ten species of primate. The global population of the Bonobo ape – possibly our closest living relative – was already down to around 100,000 in 1980. It now may be as low as 5,000.

What is being observed is actually a highly-complex example of Competitive Overuse. And it is that inherent complexity that makes it especially hard to deal with. Global warming, for example, is already changing the timing of breeding seasons, the flowering of plants, the dates that given animals migrate, and the geographic ranges of different species. But those changes can trigger completely-unexpected consequences.

## BONOBO SEX

The Bonobo apes are amazing creatures that, together with the Chimpanzee, are our closest cousins. Some of their behavior is extraordinarily human – including their habit of frequent social-sex that is commonly face to face and surprisingly often with same-sex partners. Until recently this was portrayed by many primatologists as being a reaction to captivity. As a result of detailed field-studies, however, it now appears that exactly the same behavior occurs just as frequently and quite naturally in the wild.

Pollination patterns, seed dispersal, insect numbers, predatory behavior and nutrient cycling all get modified. As a result, maybe migrating birds miss out on the emergence of insect larvae needed to feed their newly-hatched offspring, and their species dies out as a result. These are convoluted and complex chains of cause and effect whose outcomes are often impossible to foresee. What is more, it will always be like that – however sophisticated we become. The reason is: Complexity.

An important finding of Complexity Theory is that even for a simple system in which we can fully-describe the relationship between all its components – it may nevertheless be absolutely impossible to predict how it will end up, however advanced our analysis. Nature is vastly more complex than a simple system like that. Indeed, for now, we hardly understand the detailed interactions of components within ecosystems at all. As a result, there is no possible way of predicting all the unintended consequences of destabilizing parts of an ecosystem.

## BACKLASHES TO ECOSYSTEM-DISRUPTIONS

Early studies evaluating the impact of climate change on biodiversity (for instance as a result of destruction of coral reefs) may have overstated the losses. Local variations of geography, and the microclimates they create, can allow species to survive even though the average changes suggest they cannot. However, the extinction-forecasts remain extremely bleak owing to the destruction of habitat that is going on.

# Depleting resources

## CORAL GRIEFS

Coral seems particularly sensitive to the effects of global warming – which makes it a good early-warning system. Coral bleaching (where the coral whitens because it loses vital symbiotic single-celled organisms that normally live in its tissue) occurs because of environmental stresses such as raised water-temperature or a change in water-acidity caused by increased $CO_2$ absorbed from the atmosphere.

Rainforests now only cover a few per cent of the Earth's surface, but they contain somewhere between half and three-quarters of all species, including millions of insects, plants and microorganisms thought to be as yet undiscovered. However, it is not just the overall loss of rich environments such as rainforests that makes the difference. Fragmentation of rich environments can make it far harder for species to maintain long-lasting populations. And even huge nature reserves do not solve the problem if, as a result of climate change, species move.

Wherever mankind is active, it tends to disrupt the often-delicate balance of nature around it. Communities modify land use, protect themselves and their livestock, and as a result big predators often die out. That is exactly what happened across Europe and parts of the USA, and consequently other species were left uncontrolled and eventually caused problems in their own right. As part of a trend toward 're-wilding', wolves and bears are now being reintroduced in some areas – for instance, most successfully, wolves into Yellowstone National Park to control over-populous elk that were destroying aspen forests.

Even when they are not a direct threat to people, large animals tend to suffer as their natural habitat is reduced. Compared with smaller species, they usually live longer, have fewer offspring and need lower population-densities in order to find enough food. All those factors place them at risk when things change too much, which is why tigers, pandas and polar bears are so close to extinction.

On some occasions people make mistakes and introduce species, such as rabbits into Australia, that become uncontrollable pests that go on to destroy the natural environment around them. Similarly, domestic cats can go feral and eradicate whole bird populations. Other times, snakes, rats, plants and insects come as stowaways on people's transported goods. House mice accidentally introduced into Australia have intermittently exploded in number and resulted in major losses to grain crops – 2011 saw the worst mouse plague ever.

For similar reasons, and despite heavy controls, the tropical paradise of Hawaii is also one of the extinction capitals of the world. Meanwhile, Europe has more than 10,000 alien species, about a tenth of which are having an impact. Recent research estimates that around 1,300 alien species are influencing the European environment, economy and human health – with a probable cost of tens of billions of Euros.

## INVASION OF THE KILLER SEAWEED

Although it has always officially denied any culpability, the source of the toxic *Caulerpa taxifolia* currently spreading across the Mediterranean was almost certainly the Monaco Oceanographic Museum. Its former director, the famous Jacques-Yves Cousteau, certainly considered that this was the only believable explanation. Unfortunately, because no one took responsibility, protracted debates over possible causes meant that the spread of the highly-invasive weed was uncontrollable by the time anyone actually got around to doing anything sufficiently practical.

Even the Mediterranean seems at risk in this way. In the early 1980s, a very-hardy seaweed specially bred for use in domestic cold-water fish tanks was accidentally released into the sea. Because it was toxic to anything trying to eat it, the aquarium-weed spread uncontrollably, crowding out native species and changing the balance of life on the seafloor. It is still spreading.

## THE BIRDS AND THE BEES OF DESTABILIZED ECOSYSTEMS

Although human hunting of land species such as the American Plains bison can bring them close to extinction, societies typically pull back when they see they have gone too far. But, as described earlier, when it comes to marine hunting people appear to have less control over how far they go.

# Depleting resources

Irrespective of the eventual outcome for the species that is overfished, by disrupting the balance of marine-life in order to feed the growing human population, all kinds of unexpected mini-backlashes are triggered.

In some places, as cod levels go down so lobsters seem to increase, as shark populations drop like a stone so ray populations explode, as overall fish numbers decrease so prawn and shrimp and jellyfish and worms and algae all increase. The whole balance shifts. And once it is shifted it can be an ecological one-way street. Upstart species that opportunistically take advantage of a recently-vacated niche do not necessarily just give it back again simply because humanity reduces its hunting of the species that originally occupied the slot. That is one of the reasons why endangered species may sometimes never recover.

This is also at the heart of why the current manmade disruption to the world's web of species has become so dangerous. Even specialized scientists have absolutely no idea why some things are happening. By 2010 the eel population in the River Thames had fallen by 98% in only five years. No one fully understands why. Neither does anyone know what the knock-on effects will be for other species.

The London sparrow population has dropped by 70% in the last fifteen years. It is assumed that this may relate to some combination of heavier traffic, people paving their gardens, removing trees, or building new houses on suburban plots that used to be back gardens – all of which perhaps reduce available seeds and insects. But is that the same reason that British songbird populations as a whole have been crashing over the last thirty years? Is it maybe also something to do with different sorts of pesticides? Or new types of crops? Or changing methods of agriculture?

Over the same period that the Thames' eel population was collapsing, so was the US bee population. In late 2006, many US beekeepers noticed that their beehives were largely empty. There were no signs of poisoning. No dead bodies. The queen and sometimes a very few bees were still there. The honey was always present. But the colony as a whole was simply missing. What is more, highly-unusually, other bees did not immediately move into the empty hives to steal the honey.

Nobody understood what was going on. And it was a serious concern because commercial beekeeping is these days of great importance not so much because of the honey produced but because many agricultural crops now depend on bees to pollinate them. All crops – including things like fruit trees and almonds – used to be naturally pollinated. But the long-term adoption of pesticides and huge fields means that there are not enough wild bees and insects nearby to do the job.

Consequently, vast numbers of hives of European honey-bees are trucked around the USA. They are used to pollinate about ninety different types of crop, from Florida oranges to Californian almonds to Maine blueberries. It is a big industry. In the USA alone about $15-billion of crops are pollinated by honeybees in this way. Yet by early spring 2007, some beekeepers had lost 90% of their bees. Since then, many have lost about a third of their bees – every year. European beekeepers also began reporting major losses. Experts were brought in. They still struggle to explain – and prevent – what has become known as Colony Collapse Disorder (CCD).

## COLONY COLLAPSE DISORDER

The latest research suggests that the widespread devastation of pollinating-bee colonies may be caused by a particular combination of infection by fungus and virus that pulls a bee colony down. But other researchers propose that the logic might be exactly the other way around and in fact bees only get infected because their immune system is already weakened by something else. The fungus *Nosema cerenae* is often found in higher quantities than normal in hives suffering from CCD, which is why the first set of researchers think that – when the fungus is combined with a particular family of viruses – a colony is predisposed to collapse. An obvious transmitter for the virus would be the *Varroa destructor* mite.

However, the contrary argument is that it is something else that first depresses the bees' immune systems – and in that condition the bees are more susceptible to infection, whether by mites or another cause. For example, it could be the bees' immune system is weak because they are stressed from being constantly moved about the countryside. But that raises the issue of why the stress is affecting them now, after the industry has been operating this way for forty years. Other hypotheses are that bees are perhaps susceptible to a cocktail of pesticides that are not even realized to be dangerous. That raises further concerns about whether a similar cocktail might ultimately prove dangerous to other species, including humans.

# Depleting resources

No one yet has the answer. The net result is that already in parts of China and the USA so many pollinators have been lost that crops require manual pollination – which is understandably expensive (especially in the USA where labor costs are relatively high). That raises several questions. Will whatever combination triggers CCD also set off something similar in another species? If experts could not predict CCD, and six years later still cannot explain it, how can something worse in the future be avoided? After bees, eels, and birds, how many unexpected collapses will there be?

The painful truth is that none of us – in science or elsewhere – has the slightest idea which species will collapse next, or what the knock-on effects will be. What we are observing are the classic symptoms of a system running out of control. In many ways that is even more worrying than the threats of famine and drought that we have already examined. Fish-stocks are collapsing, but governments know that is largely because of sustained overfishing. Water-tables are dropping, but that is mainly caused by unrelenting over-pumping. However, when things start happening that even experts did not predict, cannot explain, cannot stop and do not know the full implications of – that is a very-serious warning. We are not so much playing with fire. We are playing with the health of our planet.

Many scientists now worry that in total between one quarter and a half of all terrestrial species are set to become extinct *within the next few decades.* That is comparable to the highest levels of species-collapse the world has ever suffered – the rare so-called 'mass-extinction events'. The most-recent equivalent loss occurred 65.5-million years ago during what is known as the 'Cretaceous-Tertiary extinction event' – now believed almost certainly to have been triggered by a massive asteroid striking the Earth at a point known as the Chicxulub crater, just off the coast of Mexico. It is that same level of crisis that we may be facing today.

When too many species near extinction, it becomes impossible to maintain stability within the complex interplay of those species that remain. Last time something comparable happened, mammals took over from dinosaurs as the dominant species. Humanity is now in the midst of a similarly uncontrolled and escalating set of extinctions and repercussions whose hidden domino-effect it cannot begin to fathom. The eventual cumulative backlashes are completely unknowable. Even as far as predicting the backlashes in only 2050 on our agriculture, our surroundings and our lifestyle – already, all bets are off.

## 12. HIGH-TECH POPULATION BACKLASHES: LAND

Overexploited
LAND

### ESCALATING THREAT:
Uncontrolled agricultural loss

Garbage disposal
'Western' diet
Farm subsidies
Slash-and-burn
Overlogging
Loss of habitat
Unknown impacts

• World meat-production is expected to double by 2050 as more people eat a 'Western' diet (lowering land productivity because an area producing 1kg of meat could potentially produce 15kg of grain)

• Deforestation and overgrazing and sustained irrigation with salty subterranean water is turning fertile land into dust bowls

• Garbage landfill close to major cities is all becoming used up

• Rainforests contain between ½ and ¾ of all the Earth's species, but around 50% of the Earth's mature rainforests have been lost since 1950 – forecasts suggest only 10% may be left by 2030

• Forest burning is the second largest source of $CO_2$

• Today about one-in-a-thousand species goes extinct each year – up from one-in-a-million species prior to the Industrial Revolution

• About fifty-thousand species are now listed as threatened and more than *half of all land species* may be extinct within decades

• Interconnected impacts of changes in land-use, pesticides, new crops, mechanized agriculture and other unknown factors is causing population collapses of everything from commercial bees to eels to songbirds, but even after intense study the process remains unclear

# CHINA AND INDIA – AND SO US ALL – AT SEVERE MEDIUM-TERM RISK

## Developing nations – including major countries like China and India – are at severe risk of medium-term Population-driven disruptions

MANY PEOPLE TAKE food for granted. But in living memory, somewhere between fifteen- and thirty-million people died during the Chinese famine of 1959-61. Even as recently as 1995-99, an estimated two-and-a-half million people died from the famine in North Korea. And in 2008, there were food riots on three continents. Throughout all those events, there was plenty of food on the planet. That reveals something very important. Even if it did turn out to be possible – using solutions no one has yet been able to propose – that enough food could be grown for around 9-billion people in 2050, that of itself would not necessarily solve very much. Famine is as much to do with *distribution* as it is with availability.

Even today there are about 1-billion people who are permanently undernourished. There are also approaching 1-billion people who are obese. Ballooning world-population over the next few decades will do nothing to change that societal disconnect. Those who claim that 'population growth is not a problem because innovation will allow the world to grow enough food' rather miss the point. Even if technology does improve food production – as it is very likely to – there will *still* be a major lag in the global system before these innovations translate into anything approximating 'fair' distribution. During the transition, as now, the richest will tend to be fat and the poorest will often starve to death.

### DESTABILIZED HUMAN SYSTEMS

In reality, it is extremely difficult for a developing nation to grow rapidly in population while constantly maintaining its ability to feed that population by farming (or importing) enough food and distributing it effectively. It requires an increasingly-sophisticated infrastructure. It is difficult to do if there is corruption at any level of the government. And it is extraordinarily difficult – even for those who have experienced it before – to decide how best to handle the inevitable hiccups that occur. If there is a drought, for instance, and food prices go up, should the government ban exports of food? If it does, then foreign markets may get used to buying food elsewhere. And should the government attempt to stop people profiteering from high food prices during a famine? If it does, it risks cutting the flow of food to those most in need, and then the Haves and Have-Nots are more likely to start fighting

All these sorts of dynamics mean that developing nations are typically far less stable than developed nations. Even when they seem set on a productive course, they are often still living on the edge of chaos. And if they slip it can get nasty very quickly – as happened in Rwanda during the 1990s when, during an awful period of about 100 days, what is now known as the Rwandan Genocide saw the best part of one-million Tutsis and Hutu-moderates systematically murdered. The impact of those sorts of state-failures can then spread to surrounding nations – not least because of mass exodus – and that risks destabilizing those countries as well. State-officials in the USA, which has the longest shared-border in the world between a fully-developed and still-developing nation, are well aware of the inherent risks that major instability in Mexico could bring in terms of potentially-uncontrollable immigration.

One of the big problems, not just with relatively-advanced nations like Mexico, is that widespread small-arms combined with the High-Tech of distributed communication mean that under the right conditions even impoverished groups can these days hold their own against the military-might of far richer countries – as has been seen in Afghanistan. However, armed conflict is itself a major cause of famine that leads to a spiral of further conflict. Crops may initially get destroyed. Far more likely is that distribution networks are disrupted. That cuts others off from food so they get desperate and fight for their survival. What starts as a local skirmish in a developing nation can rapidly deteriorate into country-wide civil-war.

Famine can also be triggered by market forces that disrupt distribution even though the physical distribution-systems remain intact. A common example is when wages stagnate during a time of inflation so only the rich can afford food. So-called 'stagflation' is unpleasant in rich countries, but potentially fatal in poor ones. Far less obviously, however, even foreign-aid programs intended to alleviate famine can disrupt distribution and actually make the suffering worse. For instance, if food-aid arrives at harvest time then it drives food prices down so local farmers cannot even earn the reduced money from their meager harvest that they were depending on, their crops remain unsold and then spoil, and the farmers can eventually starve because they cannot afford food or seeds to grow more food.

These are some of the reasons why it is so easy for a developing nation to fail. Ultimately they all relate to mismatched distribution of food and population-size leading to famine. But, as we will now examine, the chief cause of death from famine tends not to be starvation itself but disease, which usually carries on long after the original causes of the food-shortage itself.

## POPULATION-CRISES IN FAILING STATES

At the moment, around one-billion people do not have access to clean drinking water. When combined with famine, this easily leads to major bouts of dysentery, cholera, malaria and smallpox. And as will be covered in the subchapter on *Unmanageable pandemics* (page 362), new strains of disease can also develop – strains that even fully-developed nations initially find difficult or impossible to treat if they get introduced from abroad and turn into a pandemic.

With so much disease around, parents in failing nations usually want to have as many babies as possible – often up to around seven per mother – so that enough children may survive to look after the parents in old age when otherwise they would likely starve. That is why a failing state tends to have rapid population growth. It is also why perhaps 40% of its population may be under 15-years old. However, as soon as survival-rates improve, that baby-boom works its way through the population, which overall needs more food, resulting in deforestation or deterioration of farmland, which all-too-easily can lead to a bad harvest, which causes disruption, with deepens the famine, which leads to disease, so more children die, so mothers want to have as many babies as possible. It is a tragic cycle for a country to get out of. And then to stay out of.

Struggling countries are not helped in dealing with these sorts of Population side-effects by the fact that population-growth leading to deteriorating environments and widespread poverty also risks complete societal collapse. What begins as progressive instability makes the country less attractive to outside investors. And as law and order breaks down and local warlords take over it becomes impossible for the government to collect taxes. As a result, the country cannot pay off its international debt. Foreign governments stop offering support, any efforts to control international terrorism break down, illegal drug-trafficking and weapons-trading increase. Once even foreign-aid workers become threatened, the country risks being left completely alone.

Today there are already numerous states at risk of failing, including Iraq, Afghanistan, Sudan, Somalia, Chad, the Democratic Republic of Congo, and Haiti. They are the usual suspects at the weak-end of the global-spectrum of economic activity. Some of them are already so far gone that they are rarely mentioned in the news because journalists are in genuine peril if they try to report from inside their borders.

Nevertheless, although there are a few potentially-serious risks to the developed world if any of these precarious states do collapse – such as them acting as centers for terrorism or spreading-diseases that turn into pandemics – their failure would not (at least not directly and immediately) noticeably damage the global economy. At completely the opposite end of the spectrum of developing nations, however, there are two countries whose failure would be extremely destabilizing to all nations. And they are both at risk of severe crises.

## POPULATION-CRISES IN MASSIVELY-DEVELOPING STATES

Those two apparently-impossible candidates to add to the list of countries in potential danger of catastrophic Population Crises are: India and China. They are currently so successful and are growing so fast that no one even considers them at risk – any more than the Global Banks were considered at risk. But in reality, both nations are performing utterly amazing balancing acts. Using very different political systems, they are attempting to coordinate the actions of over a billion people each.

In terms of population sizes they are in a completely different league to the other so-called BRIC nations Brazil and Russia, or to other emerging economies such as South Korea or Mexico. Yet even a far-smaller country like Brazil is already struggling because its road infrastructure is insufficient to transport its growing population's vast natural wealth efficiently. In both China and India, huge (but poor) rural communities are doing what they can to feed an insatiable population. Relatively well-off (but relatively few) politicians are doing what they can to ensure that their country's vast infrastructure can grow and adapt fast enough to distribute food effectively. Of course both groups achieve many other important things as well, but in the harsh analysis of what fundamentally stops even major developing-nations from imploding, it is keeping those two roles in synch that ultimately will decide the fate of both extraordinary economies. What each country is attempting has simply never been successfully demonstrated before. There have never been so many people endeavoring to change so fast in such an integrated way.

## THE BRIC ECONOMIES

Although there is currently a fashion for lumping the BRIC economies (Brazil, Russia, India and China) together, in reality the first two are very different to the last two. For a start they are about a fifth the population and, unlike India and China whose economies are based on manufacturing, Brazil and Russia currently depend on raw materials that in the long-term will run out. Just because all four are major growing economies is not really sufficient justification to select them and yet, for example, exclude South Korea or Mexico or even some of the oil-based Arab economies. Moreover, the different political systems play crucial roles in determining how fast each country can respond to global changes. China is the only BRIC nation *without* a meaningful electoral system (though Russia's democratic process recently became a bit dubious) yet *with* massive overall political clout on the world stage. And for the moment, it is China that completely outperforms the other three BRIC nations it is corralled with.

As China found out fifty years ago, despite the tremendous benefits of strongly-centralized control, there can also be major disadvantages to rigorously top-down management and it is worryingly easy for unanticipated backlashes to cause problems – which in that case led to widespread famine. Since that time, Chinese political leaders have built up a list of increasingly widely-publicized human-rights violations that mean that in the future their population may be unforgiving of those in authority if things ever go dramatically wrong and even-localized famine ever returns. India, likewise, has an in-built potentially-unsustainable strain of intense rural poverty misaligned with fabulous urban wealth that could easily degrade into conflict and so translate into famine. And India also has deep-set conflicts with Pakistan that could readily bubble over and cause sufficient disruption to distribution channels to cause localized famine.

In either society, if the unprecedented growth of infrastructure ever falls significantly out of step with the astonishing size of population, for instance because of inexorably-dropping water-tables, tens of millions of people will go hungry. Many of the hungriest will fearlessly and implacably rebel – despite even the most draconian state responses – long before starvation and disease threaten to kill them anyway.

# ONCE AGAIN LOCKED ON COURSE

Global overpopulation is increasingly locking the world economy into multiple patterns of Competitive Overuse

EVEN THOUGH MANY politicians are well-aware of the eventual problems that will arise, in the short-term it is almost impossible for a government to lower its country's overall population: individual people want to have babies, individual doctors are dedicated to extending people's lives, and often individual business-owners want immigration to remain high so labor-rates stay low. It is in each individual's immediate interest to do things that keep population growing, even though it is in everyone's collective interest for it to slow.

India and China are the world's only population billionaires. But India's population increase has exceeded China's for each of the last thirty years – because it is largely uncontrolled. That carries obvious risks. China, in contrast, is the only major power to force population cuts. Since 1979 it has applied its One Child Policy, which in principle restricts married urban couples to having a single baby. On the one hand this approach may have saved possibly hundreds of millions of people from starving as a result of famine caused by overpopulation. On the other hand, to ensure compliance the Chinese authorities have sometimes had to resort to measures that would be unacceptable in most other countries. And that has caused resentment even within China.

What is more, there is already an imbalance of the ratio of males to females in Chinese cities (partially because, it is assumed, more female than male foetuses have been aborted by their parents) making it increasingly competitive for young men to attract a wife. And in any country, deliberate intervention on who gets to conceive babies is always open to abuse – not least to attempts to stop particular categories of people from breeding at all (in other words 'Eugenics' as notoriously applied, amongst others, by the Nazis).

A far more generally-acceptable approach to lowering population turns out to be Female Education. The reasons this seems to work are actually quite complex because they require numerous conditions to be in place. In essence though, it appears that if women in a developing society gain better education then they rapidly tend to aspire to greater freedom – not least from male domination. As female education improves, child survival also usually increases. Women realize they want to achieve more with their lives, and have their children achieve more too. As a result they take greater control over family planning, typically choosing to have fewer children, later in life.

It is estimated that around the world approximately 80-million unplanned babies are born each year. Coincidentally, that is almost exactly the same number as the global annual increase in population. So it might be thought that it would be relatively easy to nudge that figure down. One of the problems with managing population, however, is that at multiple points the beneficial-cycle of better education ultimately leading to reduced birth-rates is very easily broken. For example, as highlighted in the next chapter, fundamentalist Moslem communities forbid female emancipation, fundamentalist Roman Catholicism condemns contraception, and the fundamentalist Religious Right is rigidly anti-abortion. Ironically, all three groups also strenuously fight gay lifestyles – despite (or, historically, probably because of) the undeniable fact that same-sex acts are unlikely to produce many offspring.

There is another problem with breaking out of the poverty-trap of overpopulation. The unwritten rules of family planning mean that – as highlighted in the last subchapter – few women are going to choose to reduce the number of babies they have until they feel secure that enough of their children will survive to look after them in old age. That means there is always a long lag between child mortality-rates dropping in a particular community and birth-rates eventually also falling. It typically takes half a generation or more for the change to ripple through the community.

Consequently, many countries that recently have economically developed enough so as dramatically to improve public health (and so significantly reduce child-mortality) nevertheless have women giving birth to as many babies as ever. Unlike in the past, however, thanks to High-Tech developments – especially in medicine – several of those babies now survive. Unfortunately, as a result, yet another population-based poverty trap can be sprung: Rapid continued population growth breeds greater poverty because of scarce local resources, which increases local famine and disease, which raises child-mortality again, which encourages mothers to keep having as many babies as they have the strength for.

Foreign-aid and charity funding of massive vaccination programs save lives in the short-term. And such initiatives appear self-evidently beneficial to all the well-meaning contributors. But such programs do not of themselves necessarily reduce overall misery and pain. Indeed, in isolation they risk merely increasing the overall suffering. Certainly at the local level, the cycle of population-growth followed by Malthusian Collapse really can all too easily still occur today.

## INTERCONNECTED BACKLASHES

There is a deeply-engrained reason why, even at the global level, extreme Population Crises now seem inevitable: Those instabilities are themselves being strongly exacerbated by other deeply-embedded trends within the world economy. For instance, as already highlighted in the chapter on Industrialization, modern agriculture depends on fossil fuels for distribution, processing, packaging and refrigeration, to run tractors and irrigation pumps, to warm hothouses, and to provide fertilizers and pesticides. The huge fluctuations in crude-oil prices directly or indirectly affect all these things. So the cost of farming is unpredictable – which adds to any incipient instability in a community.

Also, as will be covered in the sixth chapter of this book, Globalization has an impact because the prices of commodities such as grain these days depend on global market-forces. So, in addition to fluctuations in the costs of farming, the prices that crops can then be sold for is also unpredictable – again adding to local instability. All these uncertainties mean that it is increasingly difficult for farmers to decide what to grow. That leaves the global economy at risk from yet another Competitive-Overuse effect – when too many farmers, by making the 'right' economic choice for themselves, nevertheless make the 'wrong' choice for feeding the global economy as a whole.

An obvious recent example of this has been biofuels. In the last few years, the produce of so many sugarcane plantations was diverted to make ethanol (as a fuel-additive) that it pushed sugar prices up. Similarly, diversion of grain for biofuel-production did the same. For individual farmers it made perfect sense. The global market pays more for fossil-fuel substitutes than it does for food. So, at the local level it is more attractive to grow fuel for automobiles rather than food for people. That means there is less food available, so prices go up. Even though there may actually be enough food globally to feed everybody sufficiently well, in reality the food then gets distributed to those who can best afford it – even if they do not actually intend to 'waste' it as food at all.

The interconnections are even more convoluted than that. At a time when economically-extractable oil-reserves are diminishing, the Biofuel Solution results in communities draining still faster those aquifers with rapidly-dropping water-tables that are already stretched too far to produce sufficient food. And the international community tries to top up its escalating global food requirements by stepping-up overfishing of oceans in which some stocks have already collapsed as a result. Meanwhile, completely-obscure processes affect bees and birds and – almost certainly – cycles of life that no one yet even realizes are collapsing.

As ever, it is the obscured interconnections across Population Crises that make the risks so threatening. And as ever, the main challenge for governments and others that attempt to avoid the worst backlashes – is the problem of seeing the forest for the trees.

# NATIONAL SELF-INTEREST AND POLITICAL SHORT-SIGHTEDNESS

National self-interest and political short-sightedness are maintaining many of the most threatening examples of Competitive Overuse by the global community

ALL POPULATION-RELATED examples of the Competitive-Overuse pattern are closely coupled. They each exacerbate each other – just like each shepherd seeing his counterparts grazing their flocks and wanting his individual flock at least to get its fair share of the grass (and ideally a bit more). Governments are supposed to act as referees in these sorts of games and, knowing what could go wrong, regulate activities to avoid the worst outcomes. However, when it comes to Population Crises, the track-record of national governments being able to regulate for the global good is, at best, confused.

## STABILIZING THE POPULATION

Although it is easy to assume that if on average every woman had two children then population levels would stabilize, in fact they would go down. Not everyone lives to adulthood and not everyone has children. In most developed countries the more accurate 'replacement' figure is an average of around 2.1 babies per female in the population. In developing nations the balancing birth-rate can sometimes be higher even than three babies per female – primarily because more children die before they themselves reach child-bearing age.

Even in highly-developed countries that are worried by overpopulation, many governments nevertheless continue to provide child-subsidies or tax-breaks for couples having more than the two babies needed largely to stabilize the population. There have even been occasions where unmarried mothers on unemployment-benefit have been offered state-funded fertility treatment.

Agricultural subsidies encourage overproduction so food prices are low and exports high, but those same subsidies can also encourage wasteful production-techniques that use far more fossil-fuels and water than necessary. Developed-nations provide foreign-aid to food-producing emerging-nations at the same time as potentially undercutting them by subsidizing local farmers. As a result, the average cow in the European Union is subsidized more than the individual earnings on which almost half of the global human-population each survives. In the Punjab, biodiversity has gone, the water is going, the fields are salting up, but fear of famine means Indian politicians continue to push their own Green Revolution.

In consequence of all this, some rich countries are already worrying about 'food security' and are responding by buying up agricultural land abroad. But although emerging superpowers like China are buying extra land in Africa and Brazil, and former superpowers like the UK are picking up parts of Angola, Malawi and the Ukraine, it will never turn into a land-rush. There is simply not enough land for that strategy to be sustainable for everybody else to adopt. Any more than there is enough oil for current aspirations to be sustainable for everybody to adopt. Or enough fresh water. Or fish.

When it comes to overfishing, governments did not even realize until 2002 that the world fish catch was going down – even though it had probably actually peaked around ten years earlier – because Chinese bureaucrats had apparently been inflating reported catches in order to look good to their superiors. How did politicians respond? They subsidized fishing at levels that made even diminishing catches attractive to the fishing fleets involved. Financial estimates suggest that if all the full costs of fishing were reflected, many of today's fleets would no longer be economically justifiable. But as it is, in many well-subsidized fishing communities, a life as sea is seen as a particularly well-paid job. And fishing fleets can afford to apply increasingly sophisticated techniques to hunt down ever-diminishing fish-stocks. The heavily-subsidized European fleets now fish as far afield as Africa. Closer to home they still heavily-overfish cod. Even though European officials know perfectly well that the

# Well-developed nations

Newfoundland cod have not recovered despite a total ban – still they consistently refuse to cut cod-quotas to the levels that experts insist on. For some of those EU officials, it might be political-suicide back home if they ever did.

Today, around half the world's fish catch – around $100-billion worth – is traded internationally. Despite often being fished in far-away waters, most is sold to North America, Europe, China and Japan. But it is estimated that around one sixth of the catches come from so-called 'pirate fishing' – in other words, they are illegal catches. Official estimates suggest that one in two cod caught in the North Sea are illegal. For sharks, the figures are probably far worse. Species like Hammerheads are subject to 'finning' – they are caught, have their valuable fins cut off from their less-valuable torso, and then they are thrown back into the sea to drown or more likely be eaten alive by other fish. In practice, protections against finning and discarding are very weak. In many countries, for instance, fins sold must weigh no more than 5% of the body weight of shark-meat that is also brought ashore. But that allows significant levels of abuse. It is estimated that between two and three sharks are illegally finned and discarded for every one that is brought back and accounted for.

And as already highlighted in the subchapter about *The imminent collapse of world fish stocks* (page 175), a small minority of the world's dining elite are encouraging hunting the Giant Bluefin into extinction. Politically-justified quotas by fishery managers for the Bluefin are three times as large as the levels that experts told them were needed for recovery. In practice, even those quotas are too easy for fishermen to cheat. It appears that fleets are in fact currently killing *six times* more Giant Bluefin than the catch that would allow stocks to recover. Governments are just not very good at handling these sorts of problems.

The history of whaling probably most-accurately sums up humanity's collective inability to respond appropriately to Competitive Overuse. It is a sadly-typical example of successive depletion – and sometimes extinction – of economically-valuable natural resources. To start with it seemed obvious to whaling fleets that the right whales to kill were the ones that were easiest to hunt, floated when they were slaughtered, and were most profitable. However, when (what even today we call) 'Right Whales' were increasingly hunted almost to extinction, whalers moved onto the next-easiest species, and so on, working through one variety after another.

# POPULATION CRISES

## THE RIGHT STUFF

'Right whales' actually comprise four species of *baleen* whale – in other words whales that do not have teeth but instead filter food through baleen plates made of flexible keratin (which was famously used by Victorian society to make so-called 'whale-bone' corsets – even though baleen is not in fact bone but is instead the same material as nail or horn).

Even though it was always in everyone's collective self-interest to hunt sustainably – to let stocks of the most valuable species recover – people never did. Whaling fleets always inexorably kept going until the next species collapsed. Even when there were clear warnings that whale numbers were dropping, and even when some local communities responded accordingly, in practice the global community as a whole still found it impossible to slow down. It still does. Some countries always claim special privilege and continue the slaughter – if necessary asserting that they are conducting 'scientific research'. Despite major opposition motivated by everything from ecological to ethical concerns, despite official bans, despite collapsed whaling populations, nevertheless unsustainable commercial whale-hunting continues. That is how clever national governments are at collectively managing shared global resources.

The magnificent Blue Whale is, as far as we know, the biggest animal ever to have lived on Earth at any time throughout the history of our planet. Abundant at the beginning of the 20th century, it has now been hunted close to extinction. In addition, as with all other marine mammals that use sound to communicate and echolocate, it is increasingly being drowned out by noise pollution from shipping. Less than 1% of its original population survives. As the following subchapter now explains, the same hidden human dynamics that threaten to exterminate our world's largest-ever species are at risk of taking effect across the whole of our planet.

# NEARING AN END-STAGE OF CATASTROPHIC COLLAPSE

## Increasing numbers of those systems that underpin the world economy are nearing an end-stage of catastrophic collapse

MANY ASSUME THAT modern society is highly resilient. But in the last few decades, it has actually become incredibly dependent upon nearly every aspect of the complex system we call the World Economy all interacting properly. When something out-of-the-ordinary happens – such as volcano-ash from a distant country disrupting international aircraft traffic – everyone is surprised. Yet that high level of interconnectivity and sensitivity is the context in which the fully-global examples of Competitive Overuse are set to play out.

People are already well-familiar with some of the relatively-minor backlashes that are building. As population levels increase and congregate, traffic in cities and on connecting roads will continue to clog worse than ever. Tokyo and Los Angeles are already nightmares to commute, but so too will be many cities in emerging superpowers like China. No city planner and no congestion-charge can avoid the tendency toward progressive gridlock once a city becomes too large. It is the same classic pattern of Competitive-Overuse symptoms again – individual commuters put in more and more effort despite diminishing satisfaction until eventually the traffic jams.

The aging populations in many developed nations are another well-recognized problem that has nevertheless been left in many of them far too long now to avoid crises. For purely-political reasons, retirement ages have been allowed to remain far too low. Despite gender equality, women's retirement-ages have typically taken much too long to adjust to match men's. Public-sector workers have tended to be granted gold-plated final-salary pensions. Healthcare funding has not sufficiently taken account of enhanced medical treatments combining with aging populations that are suffering progressive obesity.

# POPULATION CRISES

As the global economic downturn first began to bite in 2008, all these fudged issues began to become unavoidable. Yet by that time, in many developed nations, political targeting had gradually shifted toward older members of society (there were more of them, and they tended to vote more than youngsters), so there was no question of politicians biting the hand that put a cross next to their name in the polling station. As a result, Healthcare became a major issue – it would have to be paid for by cuts elsewhere. National pension schemes would have to be paid for by the young who were in work, even if there were proportionally fewer than ever of them to pay for those who had retired and who were now living longer. For similar reasons, those same young could not have the unaffordable pensions that their parents would benefit from. Over the next two decades, emerging Population Crises will grow to dominate government policy in the West. But even in the short-term there will be crises.

For a country such as Greece, a sustained unwillingness to address such looming social issues (exacerbated by widespread political-corruption) forced them into an inescapable endgame that, sooner or later, required them effectively to default on their international debts. Yet the political reality of the hidden interconnections across the Eurozone meant that national leaders became almost paralyzed because of concerns about triggering a further backlash. To protect the political ideal of a united Europe, leaders refused (at least in public) to consider the 'unthinkable' option of Greece leaving the Euro. But the risk of contagion had been built into the one-size-fits-all design to which politicians had warped member-economies when the Euro was first formed. It was only ever a matter of time before other countries such as Portugal, Ireland, Italy, and even Spain (all of which had structural problems in their own economies) came under extra pressure. In each case, their past always risked catching up with them. It is about to catch up with many other countries as well.

## POPULATION BUBBLES

Most people in the Arab world, for instance, are under thirty years old. That is one of the main reasons why so much is likely to change over the next decade as the newly-dominant generation flexes its muscles – continuing the rebellious spirit exhibited in the 2011 Arab Spring Revolutions. In reality there are likely to be successive waves of Arab Spring (just as historically the French and Russian Revolutions came in waves) as the population-bubble of youngsters grows older and more confident.

Moreover, the 'Arab' Spring is also likely to spread South into sub-Saharan Africa – as the bubbles of relative-youngsters there also take on some of the old potentates that seek to rule them unopposèd. What they will all do is directly equivalent to what the Baby Boomers did in the West from the late 1950s onward as first they created the concept of 'teenagers' and then went on to change their whole society.

## THE BOOM OF THE BABIES

The original period referred to as the Baby Boom saw a dramatic surge in pregnancies following the end of World War II. The resulting 'baby-boomers' are generally viewed as anyone born from around 1946 up until the early 1960s.

The temporary baby-boom in the West is like all other baby-booms. It created a long-lasting bubble in population levels. And its full effects are even now still drifting their way through many economically-sound nations. One looming backlash relates to finding sufficient numbers of future workers. Although the USA will benefit from the fact that it had another mini-baby-boom that started in the mid-1980s (especially amongst its Latin population), many other developed nations, such as Japan and Germany, are forecast to see the proportion of their population that is of working age drop by around a third by 2050.

That of itself may not be the problem it appears. I have worked with many major organizations as they plan their strategies to outsource work over the next several decades to other countries, and there is a common pattern amongst them. In general, the expectation across US and European businesses is that their current trend of outsourcing operations like customer-service Help Lines to India and East Asia will (with a few corrections) be followed by also outsourcing a large proportion of office-based jobs like general admin, IT and accounting. At first glance, that seems like a workable long-term solution to maintaining a sufficient workforce.

# POPULATION CRISES

The largely-undiscussed problem that will arise, however, is that although successful (if aging) major economies may have sufficient people of working-age to fill all available local jobs, misalignment in their education systems and problems with social mobility will mean that they simply do not have the right number of people *with the right sorts of backgrounds*. Just as famine is often a problem of distribution rather than availability, so is structural unemployment (in other words, a fundamental mismatch between available skills and available jobs).

Over the next two decades the developed world is headed for major disconnects between employment vacancies and suitable local candidates. And despite the fact that the USA will have a good proportion of its population at working age – which in theory would seem to solve the problem of paying for healthcare and pensions – in reality it too is threatened by major mismatches in quality and type of education that risk leading to even greater rates of unemployment than in those countries that did not have a second baby boom in the 1980s at all.

## THE END-OF-THE-WORLD-AS-WE-KNOW-IT SCENARIO

Such forthcoming crises relating to 'fair' job-distribution around the world will coincide with crises relating to 'fair' food distribution, which will themselves be exacerbated by collapsing fish-stocks and growing depletion of sufficiently-extractable water and oil. In numerous nations, previously-agricultural land will become increasingly infertile – initially as a result of salts from deep-aquifer water, then from lack of irrigation either because the water-table has dropped too far or energy costs for irrigation-pumps have become too high. And that threatens a very nasty scenario indeed.

Even before their land turns to sand, refugees will migrate. Within China and India this risks major internal disruption. However, mass exoduses from Mexico and Africa threaten the USA and Europe. And within the already-unstable Middle East they could be a collective-disruption too far. Any early symptoms of global-warming are likely only to make the repercussions of insufficient irrigation even worse. And the net effect of any disruptions in the developing world will rapidly also translate to the developed world. Half the world's population lives in cities. But high-rise offices require high energy. In addition to escalating costs for cooling and heating the buildings, traffic-clogged commutes to and from the offices will also be increasingly expensive. For their continued survival, cities like Las Vegas – until recently one of the fastest-growing cities in the

# Well-developed nations

USA – currently depend on shipped-in water and power (not least for air-conditioning). Beyond a certain cost, such cities become unviable.

As infrastructures get strained so they increasingly break down. Power outages caused by electricity rationing – common in cities throughout developing countries – risk appearing in developed countries as well. But in modern society, losing electricity cuts people off. It is not just that they get trapped in elevators or on the upper floors of skyscrapers, but they cannot use their cordless phones. They cannot watch the television or access the internet through their PC. Then their mobile runs out and they cannot recharge it. They cannot get money out of the automated-teller at the bank or access their funds on-line. Traffic does not flow because the lights at junctions do not work and the subway is not operating. Gas pressure drops so boilers automatically shut off. If that occurs during winter, people and pipes freeze. If the power goes off in summer, so does the air-conditioning. And modern high-rise buildings do not have windows that open.

Even apart from power outages, the combined effects of higher fuel prices and food prices mean that cities risk becoming dangerous and suburbia risks becoming an expensive luxury. Superstore retail chains based around cheap manufactured goods risk one after another going out of business as running costs and distribution costs go up at the same time as customer-visits go down (because people cannot justify the transport-cost of the trip). Maintenance costs of roads will potentially escalate, so long-distance travel will become both difficult and expensive. The 'Hollywood-blockbuster' consensus suggests that under these circumstances, more-rural areas that can become relatively self-sufficient by drawing on the resources of only a small geographic area will survive reasonably well – withdrawing into local communities living a simpler life, with farming taking over from High-Tech. But that populist consensus is completely wrong.

## NOT BEING ABLE TO COPE

Maybe even forty years ago that is indeed what could have happened. But even though it remains the standard 'Post-Apocalypse' scenario – small centers of semi-rural civilization surrounded by dangerous marauding gangs of outlaws, a bit like a cross between Robin Hood and the Wild West – it can never happen now. Unlike the peasants of the Dark Ages hardly anyone today has any experience of surviving. Unlike the pioneers on the

American Prairies, no one today can repair everything they use. Until only a few decades ago, many people knew enough about their tractor, their radio, their vacuum cleaner that if it went wrong they had a good chance of repairing it or at least finding a friend who could.

Then, around 1970 that changed for good. It became impossible. The technology was too complex. And people changed too. They took for granted that when someone was giving birth they had access to a hospital operating-room in case of emergency. The mother was more worried by the thought of pain than the risk that she would die of complications. By that time the general public had already stopped living beside death. People hardly ever saw a dead body and rarely even watched someone dying. Now, in the early-21$^{st}$ century, old age is something to be held off, and most youngsters do not even understand issues of incontinence – any more than they expect to die from appendicitis, or an unknown fever, or an infected cut.

These days, with most people around the world living in towns and cities, the general population is totally unprepared to cope with a 'simple rural life' that is unsupported by the massive High-Tech infrastructure that actually underpins even the most idyllic 21$^{st}$-centurty country village. It is not just the lack of access to the internet or the telephone network or television or radio. It is not our total ineptitude when it comes to making or repairing nearly everything that a traditional cowboy would take in his stride. It is not even our exceptional ignorance about the very basics of simple living that an 'uneducated' young child a century ago would have known – such as being able to tell from the shape of the moon whether it will get bigger (and so brighter) over the next few nights. It is our attitude.

As an example, my grandmother – brought up as she was to be an elegant Victorian lady – once rode her pony and trap to a rural dentist. He diagnosed gum disease and said she should have all her teeth out. She checked the time and decided to go ahead there and then. Without any anesthetic the dentist pulled every one of her teeth. She then quickly rode herself back home so as to be in time to supervise the maid cooking dinner. Back then she thought little of it. Few of us today might take the same view. The world has changed – and so have we.

## THE FINAL ACT

The evocative and emotive images of threatened whales, polar bears, tigers and pandas are what they are because of the way that humans collectively

# Well-developed nations

behave when faced with an apparent bargain. Up to now, the international community has not been very good at stopping its individual members all chasing after the same Free Giveaway. If global society proves as incapable of avoiding the cumulative tragedy threatened by peaking oil, global warming, collapsing fish-stocks, depleting aquifers and uncontrolled species extinctions – then it will have left it too late. Modern society no longer knows *how* to retreat into a simpler existence. However heroically we would like to see ourselves, and however much we would like to believe that we could handle the excruciating pain and confusion and powerlessness, the sad reality is that if it comes to that, the vast majority of us will be completely unable to cope.

When stated baldly like that, such a scenario can appear absurdly alarmist. I nevertheless have to conclude from all the data that I have been granted access to that the cumulative effects of High-Tech-Population Crises – especially given their tight coupling with Industrialization Crises – present a genuine and potentially-extreme threat to the world economy and indeed even local communities. This is made far-more-threatening because (as is covered in detail in the chapter on Globalization Crises) there is little evidence that nations are able to implement effective counter-strategies *even when they attempt to work together.* The ironic implication is that, ridiculous as it may sound, like all those it has almost destroyed – humanity itself now potentially risks becoming a threatened species.

At best, pre-industrial global civilization was only able to sustain itself at about one tenth of the number of people that is likely to have been reached when all the cumulative components of the Population side-effects take a grip. If the world economy breaks down because it just cannot stop itself chasing after a series of one-off bargains, then at least initially – until communities relearn many of the skills and attitudes of their ancestors – it will be unable to support even the global population-levels of three-hundred years ago. At the end of the final Act of our international-community's self-written Tragedy, it is not yet-another unsustainable resource that risks suddenly becoming depleted. It is the human population itself that could collapse.

# POPULATION CRISES

## 13. THE CUMULATIVE EFFECTS OF HIGH-TECH POPULATION

World stocks of cod, haddock, Atlantic salmon and some tuna risk collapse – irreplaceably losing the world-economy's greatest natural food resource

Fish-dependent developing countries such as Bangladesh, Cambodia, Ghana risk famine if stocks collapse – leading to unending drains on relief budgets

Water-right conflicts over use of the Nile (running through Ethiopia, Sudan, Egypt) and the Tigris and Euphrates (Turkey, Syria, Iraq) risk destabilizing the region

Within decades Northern China, Northwest India, Pakistan, Mexico, nearly all the Middle East, North Africa and Southwest USA risk acute water shortages at the same time as oil scarcity – leading to potential major civil unrest

Attempts by rich countries to compensate for lack of water by buying food as a proxy risk rapidly being unsustainable – causing escalating international conflict justified by claims of national profiteering

Unanticipated and unexplained phenomena (similar to Colony Collapse Disorder in commercially-pollinating bees) risk severely disrupting animal husbandry and cultivation – further destabilizing commodities markets

Developing nations (including China and India) carry increasing risks that whole regions suffer uncontrolled agricultural loss – from depleting economic water, soil damage or other factors – leading to uncontrolled migration and/or rebellion that severely disrupts the world economy

Population backlashes risk sustaining failing-states in countries such as Iraq, Afghanistan, Sudan, Somalia, Chad, DRC and Haiti – leading to increasing drains on aid funds, more potential for the growth of terrorist groups, more frequent pandemics and international conflicts

Costs of oil-based products (eg, plastics, pesticides), tin, lead and copper all risk soaring – severely aggravated by commodity speculation

Demographic 'bubbles' risk major unrest (as with Middle East youth) or extreme financial drains (as with Western old age)

***Combined these present the realistic threat of a domino-like collapse of one overextended nation after another developing into global near-chaos***

# REDUCING THE THREATS:
# COLLECTIVE SUSTAINABILITY

## Population crises need *Collective Sustainability* – countering the risk that Competitive Overuse leads to system-collapses

AVOIDING POPULATION CRISES is a deeply-systemic challenge. In a failing country, for example, aid-workers may focus on healthcare to reduce mortality, and vaccination programs may seem the most cost-effective form of positive intervention. But, as explained earlier, without also addressing the complex system that determines birth rates (including female education-levels) a resultant population explosion can later lead to widespread famine. At the global level, addressing Population Crises is even harder. Direct actions such as education programs on birth-control, or governments no longer 'subsidizing' more than two children per family, may certainly be necessary and valuable but realistically they only tackle the visible portion of the Population iceberg. Far more difficult are the more-hidden side-effects. Overfishing of international waters, over-depletion of communal water-tables, shifting to an unsustainable Western lifestyle, all occur – just as population explosions in failing countries do – because the behaviour that leads to the sudden collapse that follows Competitive Overuse nevertheless at the individual level makes perfect sense to each of the people involved.

Despite what many have suggested, these are problems that could not even be solved by a fully-democratic World Government with everyone on Earth voting on referenda for what they wanted to happen. Most individuals would *still* tend to vote for more food, more water, more consumer products in the near-term – even though everyone's collective demands were in the long-run unsustainable. This aspect of world-governance requires a far more sophisticated solution than merely 'better representation'. To address these sorts of problems, those industries most tightly involved (especially Fishing and Agriculture but also Retail generally) must reframe their strategies so as to sponsor a principle of

*Collective Sustainability* that counteracts the system-dynamics of Competitive Overuse that otherwise risk eventual catastrophic collapse. All the guidelines for fulfilling Collective Sustainability are based on the fact that, at the level of a village all the way up to the whole Earth, there are basically only four approaches that potential-rivals can jointly adopt to overcome issues relating to Competitive Overuse. And often, success requires a combination of all four approaches.

The first approach is to 'hold a mirror up' and bring the unintended side-effects of the collective behavior to everyone's attention – which is an important role for Fishing, Agriculture and Retail if they are not to become the lightning conductor of a popular backlash against the industries deemed responsible for unnecessary destruction of the ecosystem. The second approach is to reduce the risk of a crash by regulating depletion rates or even blocking access completely in order to give time for the resource to replenish – such as by setting appropriate fishing quotas or creating a marine reserve. The third approach is to replenish a resource directly – say, by reintroducing endangered species back into the wild. And the fourth approach is to use High-Tech (or some other innovative means) to increase the tolerance of the resource being overexploited – for instance by using new strains of crops that need less water or provide greater yields.

It is by using a combination of all these approaches that in the past it has often proved quite possible to avoid the Malthusian Collapse that can otherwise occur if a population grows too large to sustain. More precisely, it has proved possible provided that everything remains well managed. The problem is that failing countries are often *not* well managed. And, in the absence of effective world-governance, neither is the complex collection of around two-hundred states that have recently coalesced to form a tightly-integrated global economy. It is for that reason that encouraging nations nevertheless to live up to a shared standard of Collective Sustainability is so crucial. Here are some specifics.

## AVOIDING WASTE AND UNNECESSARY CONGESTION

As with energy-efficiency, the most effective way of mitigating overexploitation is to help people avoid wasting food and materials or causing unnecessary congestion. Many households in developed countries throw away around a third of their food – much of which ends up in landfill and releases the powerful greenhouse-gas methane. Recycling paper, aluminum, plastic and glass not only saves raw materials but potentially also energy (depending on issues such as how far the materials travel). Given that waste disposal is a growing issue in cities, it is especially important for governments to encourage urban recycling.

Likewise, to reduce congestion, public transport must not only be made highly efficient, but also more attractive. People drive their own cars to work not just because of the convenience, but often because they find public transport unpleasant. The alternative experience needs to feel far more sophisticated and stylish (terms not often associated with public transport) if it is to attract-over those who can afford cars, fuel, congestion charges and parking-costs. And to avoid city-gridlock, governments and automotive manufacturers need to take actions that accelerate the long-term development of partially-autonomous vehicles – especially taxis and minivans that can operate robotically in their own lanes, far faster and more tightly-packed than human-driven vehicles.

## REALIGNING AGRICULTURAL AND FISHERY SUBSIDIES

Agricultural and fishery subsidies are currently a major cause of Competitive Overuse. Their failings must be widely publicized and the subsidies themselves must urgently be realigned on a fully-scientific basis. Farm subsidies help trap poor countries in poverty. Fishery subsidies are leading to a collapse of fish stocks and driving some species to extinction.

Governments need to shift from encouraging overproduction to encouraging Collective Sustainability. In terms of fishing – in addition to vastly expanding no-fishing zones and marine reserves – scientifically (not politically) determined caps on production should translate into permits for fishing quotas that are then auctioned off, an approach commonly referred to as 'Cap and Trade'. The potentially-disastrous side-effects of the current subsidies also need to be far better communicated around the world – another useful role for coalitions of the media, retailers, governments and suppliers. And the political leaders of those countries locked into Competitive Overuse need to be helped to restore this aspect of sustainability – and as a result improve everyone else's as well – rather than continue to undermine it as they currently feel forced to do.

## SPECIES AWARENESS PLUS PIRATE-FISHING AND FINNING

Public awareness of popular fish-stocks at risk of collapse must be heightened – at the same time as concerted action is taken to stop pirate-fishing and finning abuses. Importantly, the media can play a crucial role in fully-informing public opinion in those countries that eat types of fish whose stocks are at risk of collapse. Without that, no government will take extreme action – and no fishing fleet can be expected to support it. In contrast, if consumers stop buying increasingly-endangered species, then there will simply no longer be an economic reason to overfish them. Given the growing international emotions around things like finning sharks and slaughtering whales and Giant Bluefin – corporations within major economies like Japan and China have an important role to play in encouraging transitions within their countries that avoid what otherwise risks turning into an international backlash against them.

In addition, the media and retail outlets have a powerful influence over educating the public about alternatives to species like cod, tuna and salmon. Trying other tasty types of fish such as mackerel, gurnard, pouting and dab relieves the pressure on the 'bulk standard' species that most of us otherwise buy without thinking. But broadening our tastes also takes advantage of the huge proportion of a fishing-fleet's catch (sometimes more than half) that is thrown back into the sea – already dead – because there is no market for it. Even more absurd is when popular fish are caught, killed and then discarded because quotas prevent them being landed. That is the most wasteful situation of all.

Advances in fishing techniques can also have a major impact. Nets that maintain a mesh of square holes rather than distorting into diamonds make it easier for smaller species and immature fish to escape – although even now some fisherman use tricks to lessen the escape of fish from 'regulation' nets, so in parallel that sort of abuse needs to be made harder to get away with. In addition, some designs of trawler net are more selective of the species they capture – leading to reductions in the 'by-catch' that is then discarded. Such designs need to be improved and standardized. Similarly, public pressure is already forcing a rethink of how tuna are caught. Previously, fishermen used a combination of FADs (floating platforms called Fish Aggregation Devices that attract the smaller fish that tuna like to eat) and huge purse-seine nets. But that approach can also catch lots of turtles and sharks and sometimes even dolphins. Ultimately, if things get too bad, rod and line fishing may become the only sustainable approach to commercial fishing of tuna.

Finally, pirate-fishing that abuses quotas needs to be aggressively clamped down on at a global level. For instance, every commercial vessel can be granted a unique ID – similar to the number on the engine-block of an automobile – so that it cannot change identity just by changing name or flag. Then, every vessel convicted of pirate-fishing or finning or any other abuse of Collective Sustainability, can be black-listed and refused unloading access at commercial ports. If necessary, systems can be created so that factory-ships illegally operating in protected waters are monitored by satellite.

## IMPROVING FARMING AND PROTECTING THE FUTURE

Agricultural policy must improve water and oil efficiency in farming, reduce topsoil erosion, extend seed-bank archives, and urgently research ecosystem-failures. In terms of farming, governments should encourage far-greater water productivity – if necessary by charging for extraction of water from aquifers – and incentives should be offered to biotech corporations to fast-track cost-effective alternatives to the current oil-based products used for everything from powering farm machinery to making pesticides.

Agriculture itself must be streamlined to reduce inefficient use of such oil-derived products. And topsoil must be protected from erosion – for instance by using 'no till' approaches that do not require farmers to plough their land or irrigate as much. This is an emerging form of agriculture that allows farmers to grow crops without disturbing the soil – and so reduces topsoil erosion. The land also tends to need less water. In contrast, advanced techniques such as hydroponics require very little water and no soil – but need a higher level of skill and discipline.

As a protection against the extinction of plant species, especially those from rainforests, the international community must continue to fund and extend comprehensive seed-banks. It now appears that most seeds stored in carefully-controlled refrigeration facilities can be kept alive for maybe a thousand years. A few plants that have what are known as 'recalcitrant' seeds (such as avocado, cocoa, lychee, mango and rubber) cannot be protected in this way because the seeds do not survive long-term storage. But for these species, the plants themselves can be constantly recultivated.

Finally, urgent analyses of systemic ecosystem failures (whether of bees or rainforests) must reflect their full economic impacts so that – linking back to the chapter on Industrialization Crises – the True Costing of activities such as hand-pollination or maintaining hedgerows can be built into policy making.

## Maximizing Sustainable Food-Security

Overall international food-security seems best served if countries do not overreact to concerns of *national* food-security by falling into the trap of trying to produce everything that they need themselves. Instead, everyone benefits if countries produce those things that they are best at and then export any overproduction while importing everything else that still adheres to the principle of Collective Sustainability.

For instance, it creates a smaller carbon footprint for the UK to import lamb from New Zealand than to rear it domestically. But for reasons of health as well as for land and water efficiency, it is even more attractive if many Western populations simply eat a bit less meat. Rather than, as some have suggested, governments encouraging people to become vegetarian, it is far more practical simply to encourage them to have slightly smaller portions of meat on their plate. If, for example, people on average have servings 80% the size – maybe compensating for volume by having extra vegetables – that is equivalent to one-in-five of the meat-eating population becoming completely vegetarian. And many people would probably hardly notice the change in their diet. That sort of transition is at least realistic for a government to attempt.

It only makes sense for a country to be self-sufficient (if that is even possible) on its most critical foods. But it is not attractive to be *completely* self-sufficient, because then the country would suffer far more from a crop failure caused by disease or bad weather. It is far safer – in terms of both national security and global security – to maintain strong domestic food production as well as contribute to a global market where countries can buy food from each other. Even flying in some foods may make sense if the alternative is to use more energy growing them in a heated greenhouse – though once again, it is even more preferable that, just as in the past, rich populations get reacquainted with more seasonality in fruit and vegetables. To encourage such behavior, governments can, for instance, offer tax breaks on food that is produced, packaged and distributed locally.

Even more importantly, to help consumers make their own decisions, all food can be clearly labeled with the amount of carbon and the amount of water it took to produce it and get it to the shelf. That sort of solution typifies how retailers and others can most-effectively encourage governments to approach Collective Sustainability. At the core of how such an approach works is the principle of creating the circumstances and providing the information that makes it easier for people to make individual decisions that collectively have the clout to force a change of the status-quo. In effect, rather than trying to force through change, the skill is to *create the conditions for change.*

It is a deceptively powerful technique. It is, after all, a means of triggering the unlimited influence of Boundaryless People-Power. And, as we will now see in the next chapter, it is maybe the only approach powerful enough to counter the backlashes of one of the most ancient and potent and creative and destructive forces in humanity: Religion.

# POPULATION CRISES

**Population backlashes threaten extensive destabilization resulting from Competitive Overuse of resources crucial to the world economy and require Collective Sustainability as a counter-measure**

Overpopulation has triggered a systemic pattern of Competitive Overuse that has led to chronic overexploitation of natural resources

Competitive Overuse is depleting even readily-visible resources but is building especially-threatening backlashes in systems that are largely obscured
- *Vast areas of forest and productive land are being depleted despite being highly visible forms of Competitive Overuse*
- *World fish stocks across numerous previously-common species are at risk of imminent collapse from unintended Competitive Overuse*
- *Unsustainable use of water is leading to unprecedented risks of drought and an associated curtailment of food supplies*
- *There are clear symptoms of early-stage failure of destabilized ecosystems crucial to many national economies*

Developing nations – including major countries like China and India – are at severe risk of medium-term Population-driven disruptions

Even well-developed nations risk catastrophic destabilization long-term as a result of systems collapsing from Competitive Overuse
- *Global overpopulation is increasingly locking the world economy into multiple patterns of Competitive Overuse*
- *National self-interest and political short-sightedness are maintaining many of the most threatening examples of Competitive Overuse by the global community*
- *Increasing numbers of those systems that underpin the world economy are nearing an end-stage of catastrophic collapse*

# Chapter summary

Population crises need COLLECTIVE SUSTAINABILITY – countering the risk that Competitive Overuse leads to system-collapses

- *Overpopulation side-effects such as overfishing and water-depletion cannot be solved even by full representation of those involved – but systems reinforcing such actions can be changed*
- *As with energy-efficiency the most effective way of mitigating overexploitation is to help people avoid wasting food and materials or causing unnecessary congestion*
- *Agricultural and fishery subsidies are currently a major cause of Competitive Overuse that must be widely publicized and urgently realigned on a fully-scientific basis*
- *Public awareness of popular fish-stocks at risk of collapse must be heightened – at the same time as concerted action is taken to stop pirate-fishing and finning abuses*
- *Agricultural policy must improve water and oil efficiency in farming, reduce topsoil erosion, extend seed-bank archives, and urgently research ecosystem-failures*
- *Food-security should be maximized by countries producing what they are best at, exporting overproduction, and importing foods that satisfy Collective Sustainability*

## 14. HOW HIGH-TECH POPULATION RISKS SYSTEMIC CRISES

**GLOBAL POPULATION**

- 2050 — 9
- 2025 — 8
- TODAY — 7

### Overexploiting SEA

Weak regulation
Wrong quotas
Subsidies
Factory ships
Massive nets
Refrigeration
Sonar

**ESCALATING THREAT: Global collapse of fish stocks**

- After 20-year moratorium on Newfoundland cod-fishing, collapsed stocks have *not* recovered – still only 1% of levels in late-1970s
- Quotas for global fishing are far higher than experts recommend
- Government subsidy is encouraging uneconomic overexploitation
- Cod, haddock, Atlantic salmon, Yellowfin tuna severely overfished
- A single Giant Bluefin – a sushi delicacy – can auction for $100,000 and consequently the species is being hunted to extinction
- Demand for sharkfin soup has devastated some shark populations leading to severe and unpredictable disruption of marine food-chains
- Weak regulation results in illegal – and cruel – 'finning' of sharks
- Fish-farms use up edible wild fish (eg, anchovies) to feed fish stock
- Land-farms use up fish to feed livestock and as organic fertilizer
- Countries such as Bangladesh, Cambodia and Ghana – where fish is a major source of animal protein – are vulnerable to stock collapse
- Accidentally-released toxic aquarium seaweed is now spreading uncontrollably through the Mediterranean crowding out other species
- Run-off of fertilizers is creating huge algal blooms that also kill fish

### Overexploiting FRESH WATER

Agriculture
Hydroelectricity
Reservoirs

**ESCALATING THREAT: Widespread irrigation failures**

- Water-demand tripled over last fifty years and is now expected to double every twenty years – about four times today's usage by 2050
- Major waterways such as the Colorado, Ganges and Yellow River are largely used up for irrigation (plus hydroelectricity and reservoirs)
- About half the world's population depends on subterranean water (80% irrigated lands in China, 60% in India, 20% in USA)
- Insufficient replenishment of water in overpumped subterranean aquifers means the water-table is typically going down in China, India, Iran, Israel, Mexico, Pakistan, USA and Yemen

### COMBINED POPULATION THREATS TO NATIONAL SECURITY

- World stocks of cod, haddock, Atlantic salmon and some tuna risk collapse – irreplaceably losing the world-economy's greatest natural food resource
- Fish-dependent developing countries such as Bangladesh, Cambodia, Ghana risk famine if stocks collapse – leading to unending drains on relief budgets
- Water-right conflicts over use of the Nile (running through Ethiopia, Sudan, Egypt) and the Tigris and Euphrates (Turkey, Syria, Iraq) risk destabilizing the region
- Within decades Northern China, Northwest India, Pakistan, Mexico, nearly all the Middle East, North Africa and Southwest USA risk acute water shortages at the same time as oil scarcity – leading to potential major civil unrest
- Attempts by rich countries to compensate for lack of water by buying food as a proxy risk rapidly being unsustainable – causing escalating international conflict justified by claims of national profiteering

226

## B I L L I O N

### Deepening wells
- Rainfilled aquifers
- Fossil water
- Food as 'proxy'

- Deeper wells are typically saltier (causing progressive damage to irrigated land) and it also costs more to pump up the water
- The water-table of the Punjab 'Breadbasket of India' drops by waist-height each year. land is becoming infertile and being vacated
- Northern China, Saudi Arabia and several US states are heavily dependent on irreplaceable 'fossil water' that is rapidly depleting
- Limited water will be used for profit-generating cities and factories rather than agriculture – passing the water-burden to poor countries

### ESCALATING THREAT: Uncontrolled agricultural loss

### Overexploiting LAND

Garbage disposal
'Western' diet
Farm subsidies
Slash-and-burn
Overlogging
Loss of habitat
Unknown impacts

- World meat-production is expected to double by 2050 as more people eat a 'Western' diet (lowering land productivity because an area producing 1kg of meat could potentially produce 15kg of grain)
- Deforestation and overgrazing and sustained irrigation with salty subterranean water is turning fertile land into dust bowls
- Garbage landfill close to major cities is all becoming used up
- Rainforests contain between ½ and ¾ of all the Earth's species, but around 50% of the Earth's mature rainforests have been lost since 1950 – forecasts suggest only 10% may be left by 2030
- Forest burning is the second largest source of $CO_2$
- Today about one-in-a-thousand species goes extinct each year – up from one-in-a-million species prior to the Industrial Revolution
- About fifty-thousand species are now listed as threatened and more than *half of all land species* may be extinct within decades
- Interconnected impacts of changes in land-use, pesticides, new crops, mechanized agriculture and other unknown factors is causing population collapses of everything from commercial bees to eels to songbirds, but even after intense study the process remains unclear

### ESCALATING THREAT: Unaffordable energy/materials

### Overexploiting OIL etc

See Chapter 2
- Oil production is currently peaking – most 'cheap' oil is already gone
- At current rates tin, lead and copper will largely be depleted by 2050

---

Unanticipated and unexplained phenomena (similar to Colony Collapse Disorder in commercially-pollinating bees) risk severely disrupting animal husbandry and cultivation – further destabilizing commodities markets

Developing nations (including China and India) carry increasing risks that whole regions suffer uncontrolled agricultural loss – from depleting economic water, soil damage or other factors – leading to uncontrolled migration and/or rebellion that severely disrupts the world economy

Population side-effects risk sustaining failing-states in countries such as Iraq, Afghanistan, Sudan, Somalia, Chad, DRC and Haiti – leading to increasing drains on aid funds, more potential for the growth of terrorist groups, more frequent pandemics and international conflicts

Costs of oil-based products (eg, plastics, pesticides), tin, lead and copper all risk soaring – severely aggravated by commodity speculation

Demographic 'bubbles' risk major unrest (as with Middle East youth) or extreme financial drains (as with Western old age)

***Combined these present the realistic threat of a domino-like collapse of one overextended nation after another developing into global near-chaos***

# RELIGION CRISES overview

Inevitably-escalating instabilities within some world faiths are generating Religion backlashes that further destabilize the religions as well as whole economies and require Mirrored Tolerance as a counter-measure

- Rigidity is deeply-embedded into the structure of successful world religions – making them both resilient and very hard to change

- Social changes, scientific discoveries, failings in faith leadership, and access to conflicting insights are rapidly destabilizing religions

- Actions by some sects to bolster rigidity through intolerance and dogmatism are polarizing – and so further destabilizing – their religions

- Growing polarization in (especially) Islam and Christianity is now causing extreme reactions that threaten the economic stability of many states

- Religion crises need MIRRORED TOLERANCE – members of a community can expect only as much tolerance as they grant others

*Threats of backlashes to: CHRISTIANITY, ISLAM and SCIENCE*

*DESTABILIZATION OF RELIGIONS...*
*...POLARIZATION...*
*...POLITICIZATION...*
*...SOCIAL BACKLASH...*

# RELIGION

# CRISES

# THE BLESSING AND THE CURSE OF LONG-ESTABLISHED RELIGIONS

## Rigidity is deeply-embedded into the structure of successful world religions – making them both resilient and very hard to change

THE COMBINED POWER of five names has irrevocably changed the course of history. There have been many remarkable religious founders throughout antiquity, but it is irrefutable that just a handful of them, for some reason all men, have between them dominated, and continue to dominate, how the global community interacts. Even just five names – Buddha, Confucius (although in many ways he was a philosopher), Jesus, Mohamed and Moses – denote the religions of billions of people across millennia.

The exceptionally far-reaching influences on civilization of those and other religious inspirations have shown themselves in terms of the tremendous bedrock they provided to so many, the moral codes they taught, the passion and fervor they generated, the supremely beautiful buildings, art and music they inspired, and the tremendous acts of intellect, love, kindness and self-sacrifice enacted in their names. Yet, as we have already seen throughout this book, powerful trends inevitably cause backlashes.

However overwhelmingly positive the benefits from any complex trend may be, there are *always* unintended consequences that are far less beneficial. Religion is no different in that respect to, say, High-Tech – other than that any perceived negatives can be uniquely sensitive. Indeed, out of respect these days, most politicians and religious leaders play safe and choose not to risk upsetting people with any implied criticism of their Faith. The trouble is though that this same well-intentioned courtesy is now masking an unprecedented set of risks that are building within various religions (and often being misrepresented as race issues).

Similarly, economists, scientists and futurologists universally tend to avoid including religion in their analyses of the world economy – let alone any unpleasant religious side-effects. After all, it is a very easy omission to choose to make. It avoids any risk of upsetting people. And anyway, what really have spiritual matters to do with the robustly-material world of Capitalism and Industrialization?

Once again, such an attitude completely misses the forest for the trees. Like everything else we have examined, Religion deeply intertwines with every other powerful trend. And it does so whatever your faith or lack of interest and whether you are a fervent believer or an ardent non-believer. Moreover, just like all the other major trends, Religion's interactions with High-Tech are stirring up potentially-devastating global crises.

## RELIGION AND POLITICAL-CORRECTNESS

The attitude of modern politicians to want to avoid public criticism of any aspect of religious faith is very understandable, and certainly well-intentioned. After all, a whole spectrum of people become very passionate on the topic of Religion – whether they are advocating their particular faith, denouncing other faiths or warning against all faiths. What is more, because religions such as Buddhism, Islam, Judaism and Shinto are often seen as primarily associated with particular ethnic groups (Asians, Arabs, Jews, Japanese), highlighting any unintended repercussions of a particular faith can risk being misinterpreted not just as a criticism of that religion but also as thinly-disguised racism. Partly as a result, politicians and the media have for a long time tended to defuse their language slightly by referring to religiously-inflamed conflicts in non-religious terms – such as the 'Arab-Israeli conflict' or the 'Troubles in Ireland'. And especially today, world religious leaders and public officials far prefer to make pronouncements about tolerance and multiculturalism than suggest there are any growing problems relating to faiths themselves.

Some of those crises are to the religions themselves – although many of the crises also include substantial threats to social stability more broadly. What is more, certain religions and certain sects within particular religions are at far greater risk of backlash than others.

## MAINTAINING STABILITY

To understand what is going on – and understand why the risk of religion-driven global crises is suddenly escalating – we need to examine how, for at least five millennia, organized faiths have worked below the surface. Historically, religions have been all about Stability. Even before Stonehenge was begun over five-thousand years ago, communities around the world were held together by a type of authority figure that is not recognized today – state leaders who were also viewed as living gods.

The examples most people know about are the pharaohs of Egypt, but God-Kings also sprang up everywhere from Mesopotamia to China and from the Indus Valley to South America. Those early combinations of formalized religion and state-authority were internally very logical: Only the God-King had sufficient power to gain access to the gods who in turn granted him the divine right to rule. Whichever way you came at it, a God-King's authority was unassailable.

## STABILITY OF THE PHARAOHS

4500 years ago, at the time of building the Great Egyptian Pyramids, the concept of Stability Through Religion was already deeply encapsulated in the concept of Ma'at (pronounced muh-art). Sometimes personified as a goddess, Ma'at was the divine order of a universe in balance. Each new pharaoh reaffirmed his role as the living representation of the Sun God Ra – the god with the closest links to Ma'at. In that role, the pharaoh had a divine responsibility for maintaining truth, balance, order, law, morality and justice. Without the pharaoh fulfilling that role the whole universe would decay into chaos. Maintaining the law of Ma'at meant maintaining tradition rather than adopting change. Indeed, any new discovery was viewed as just a re-discovery of the original ideal form of the universe. The whole of Egypt and all the individuals within it were components of a natural order maintained by Ma'at. Anything or anyone who risked disrupting that order risked disrupting the universe and pulling everyone down with them. And as representative of the gods on earth, the pharaoh was the only one to know just which form of stability it was that people needed to follow.

# Resilience to disruption

The assumption that the central role of religion was to hold a community together and fight the forces of chaos was already inextricably ingrained into society as each of the 'big' religions that people recognize today became popular. So although the concept of God-Kings now no longer exists – the closest examples today are the Roman Catholic popes – the major faiths nevertheless still carry deeply-entrenched legacies based on the original assumption that a given religion is tied into every aspect of its community and its role is to provide continuity and stability. But to fulfill that purpose, *the religion itself must remain stable.*

It is not a new problem. As a result, organized religions have extraordinarily well-evolved mechanisms for self-perpetuating themselves without significant change – far better than any other type of organization or institution. For a start, the basic assumptions of true Faith are immune to being dominated by mere Power or the logic of Reason. So they are inherently resilient to change. In addition, the ideas of the founders and early leaders of formalized religions get written down – and once documented they can only ever be commented on and interpreted but never updated. On top of that, throughout the centuries those ideas have typically been exposed to children by their parents and extended family and by the religious leaders who many times offered the only access to free education (even today, many parents opt for a faith-subsidized school in the hope of gaining their child a better overall education).

That form of early exposure to religion is crucial because it appears to be a survival trait that young children are predisposed to believe unquestioningly what authority figures tell them. As a result, later in life even some of the stranger ideas can remain unchallenged. For instance, in parallel trenches during the First World War when German and English chaplains of the same faith and same denomination prayed to the same Christian god each pleading for victory when their lads went 'over the top' the next morning, despite the impossibility of both sets of prayers being answered the process nevertheless no doubt brought great comfort to both sides. No corporate chief executives could dream of commanding levels of unquestioning loyalty in their employees comparable to the troops' blind faith wielded by those humble army chaplains.

Religious stability like that is itself reinforced simply by people of a certain faith being surrounded by fellow-believers – even if their chosen religious label is the only means of them distinguishing themselves from otherwise very-similar people. In the company of other devotees, the more unwavering that someone's faith is seen to be then often the greater the respect of their fellows.

Indeed, many religious leaders (and their more ardent followers) have tended to reinforce this further by appearing to equate 'level of faith' with 'level of unquestioning faith' with the implication that if someone does not blindly agree with them then that person is not really a 'good Christian' or 'good Moslem' or 'good Jew'. In a related way, even in quite secular societies religious leaders by tradition are still granted respect by those who are members of other faiths or those who are not themselves particularly religious.

## HIGH-TECH AND RELIGION

All these deeply-established ways of operating – common to all the main religions – have kept them amazingly stable and resilient throughout their very long histories. And that has remained true even when they have come into violent contact with each other. Given how strongly immunized against fundamental change all successful religions are, there is nothing inherently surprising in the faith-based conflicts that continue to be seen today.

The self-same traits of unquestioning faith, immunity to change, and resistance to conflicting logic that have helped ancient religions to last to the present day have also regrettably led to the extreme levels of human suffering inflicted in the name of one faith on another – with possibly more unquestioning cruelty than for any other causes. However, despite the fact that all major religions are susceptible to slipping into conflict, two are particularly at risk: Christianity and Islam. There are many complex causes for this that have far more to do with history than anything that Jesus or Mohamed were ever recorded as saying.

At their most basic, the reasons are that although (or maybe because) both religions share a broadly-common heritage, both state that *only* their faith is the correct one and – because fulfilling that faith is the sole purpose of human existence – many more-fervent believers feel a moral obligation to convert others to their way of thinking (in a way that Judaism, for example, despite sharing many similar foundations, does not). That, if the dogma is taken at face value, is a recipe for conflict. Indeed, Christians and Moslems have been fighting for more than a millennium, even prior to the First Crusade.

# Resilience to disruption

But over the last several decades something new has progressively been added to this ages-old Religion side-effect – High-Tech and everything that it has stirred up (not least the emergence of Boundaryless People-Power). For the last twenty-five years I have been analyzing these impacts across several continents, and my conclusion is that the interaction of High-Tech with Religion risks breaking the relative equilibrium of the past. The disruption to religions, and the broader backlashes that follow, have the potential to get significantly worse over the next twenty years. It is not so much that what we will see will be *new* Religion Crises so much as far-more volatile, fast-acting and uncontrollable versions of the old ones.

The basic reason is that religions worldwide are being inexorably destabilized in at least four distinct ways, yet the rigidity of the most dogmatic faiths means they cannot adapt. And when intolerant religious factions feel threatened, they tend to consider it to be their sacred duty to push back. The combination of all four forms of destabilization has now formed a trend that is already building serious stresses around the globe. And, fed by High-Tech, that trend is exponential.

## 15. RELIGION BEFORE EXPONENTIAL DESTABILIZING INFLUENCES

*BEFORE* DESTABILIZATION

## SUCCESSFUL WORLD RELIGIONS
Very resilient BUT very hard to change

- Faith immune to domination by Power or Reason
- Founder's ideas can only be interpreted but never changed
- Ideas are passed onto children by their authority figures
- Members of a given sect prefer being surrounded by fellow-members
- The greater someone's perceived faith the more others respect them

# ALTERNATIVES THAT PEOPLE WERE NEVER EXPOSED TO BEFORE

Well-communicated social changes across the globe increasingly are raising alternatives that people previously were never exposed to

FOR A START, the slew of social changes ultimately triggered by High-Tech, everything from The Pill and porn on the internet to vaccines and mobile phones, is a potentially destabilizing influence on religions for reasons that stretch back to the formation of early communities. When the major religions were founded, as part of their stabilizing role they tended to claim a monopoly over not just morals but also many quite specific rules of behavior (relating for instance to things like acceptable foods or hairstyles) that were far less obviously moral issues.

In nearly all countries – other than those run solely on religious dogma, like Saudi Arabia and Iran – the State these days has its own set of laws. But very importantly, unlike religions themselves, State Laws keep evolving because they largely have to reflect what the general public considers reasonable. Otherwise, in a democracy (where the police can only operate with the broad consent of the public) law breaks down. What is often missed, however, is that many religiously-inspired ideas *are* nevertheless *included* in State Laws. In the background, over centuries, carefully selected portions of religious teaching have got written into countries' laws and, as necessary, have then been continually adapted. What were perceived as the best religious ethics became encoded into constitutions.

Concepts about fairness and protection of basic human rights became part of the mainstream legal system. But unlike the rules specified in the various religions, these concepts were in many places later updated to protect slaves and then women and then blacks and then gays. Where previously only religion could offer structure and support to people, now the State offered the same – with the added attraction that it included what to many were crucial updates.

236

# Destabilizing effects

Another important social change is simply the standard of living people now have thanks to trends like High-Tech-Industrialization. Historically, religions offered solace to individuals often living under awful conditions – even the richest suffered levels of pain and uncertainty that these days most people would consider intolerable. But for many successful parts of the world today, that is simply no longer true.

For some, that has made it feel much less of a sacrifice to 'break free' from the security offered by religion. They no longer feel the pressure to believe that can come from being scared of *not* believing. This has, in turn, combined with a general trend away from automatic deference to authority. Even back in the 1960s there was a growing rebellion against the Establishment. These days, fuelled by free-speech and the internet, there is often an active skepticism about the claims of religious authority-figures. In the not-too-distant past, those same attitudes could have led to prison, torture or death.

## FORCED COMPARISONS

To the surprise of many, the trend in some parts of the world toward an increasingly secular society does not appear to have caused a resulting slide into lawlessness – quite to the contrary in fact. Despite the claims of many religious leaders that 'Faith is an absolutely necessary foundation for a healthy and moral society', recent evidence does not appear to support that assertion. Over the last few decades, the majority of the USA has remained staunchly devout while in the UK church attendance has dropped substantially. Yet comparable statistics relating to violent crime, murder, suicide, abortion, and sexual promiscuity seem worse in the USA. And the same remains true when the USA is contrasted with countries such as Japan, France and Scandinavia that are even more non-religious than the UK.

Although few members of the general public ever study the academic research into such topics, they do nevertheless have an intuitive sense of how it feels to live in their country. And nothing that they have experienced – for good or for bad – seems to have stemmed the growing tide of non-believers in those countries that are steadily giving up their faith. Nor, to be fair, has it stopped the growth of Islam in some European countries or the spread of Christianity in Africa. The best that can be said is that the true role of religion in maintaining morals in the modern world is no longer as obvious as was once assumed.

# RELIGION CRISES

In some ways, the social changes of the last several decades have been even more confusing for those who maintain their faith. Global trade, widespread immigration and international travel have forced together not just the major religions but also all the different factions within those religions. Naturally that has sometimes inflamed the in-built tensions between different faiths, but for those who believe in a single god it has also raised a far-less-traditional problem.

It has for some become increasingly difficult to persuade themselves that it is 'obvious' that their god, and their god alone, is the right one to worship. After all, about *five billion* people are utterly convinced that the Christian Trinity is a superstition. Closer to six billion people think that Mohamed was wrong and that Allah is not great. And despite the visibility of Israel on the world stage and the disproportion of Jews in the USA compared with other countries, almost seven billion people disagree with them that their interpretation of Yahweh even exists.

In the past it was much easier for individuals to feel it was self-evident that their own god was the right one – and that pagans, heathens and infidels had what was coming to them. Today's in-your-face global world offers little escape from the recognition of just how far in the minority *any* religion is. For some at least that is a humbling realization. As is the appreciation of just how many 'heavily-worshiped gods' have to be denied by someone who only believes in a single god – indeed, they must disbelieve in only one less god than is required to become a full atheist.

## UNRELENTING WORLD NEWS

And there is a final social change that also appears to be destabilizing religion – the 24/7 News cycle triggered by High-Tech Capitalism. When there is a major natural disaster, whether it is another huge earthquake or another devastating tsunami, the pictures of the associated human heartbreak are relentless. And they are in color. And they are in high definition. And the clips are deliberately selected to convey just how great the unwarranted suffering is.

In the past, perhaps, it was more comfortable just to read about disasters. But these days, no compassionate believer in an all-good, all-knowing, all-powerful god can avoid the soul-wrenching question of why does such a god allow the horror to occur at all. Modern believers are persistently forced to question the cruelty and enormity of suffering in the world. These days, there is very little escape.

238

# Destabilizing effects

Even if there is some lesson in the tragedy, they ask themselves, or there is a deserved punishment in it, surely at the very least innocent youngsters do not deserve such agony. And those who survive a disaster and are filmed thanking their god and saying it was a miracle that He answered their prayers and saved them (or their house, or their pet) – surely the desperate pleadings of those who were not saved were equally valid. Were those people not as religious? Were their desperate prayers not as fervent? And anyway – the deepest soul-searchers question themselves – why are only the good things attributed to god's intervention but not the bad? Who caused the tragedy if not god himself?

These are not new questions. Centuries before Christianity, the Greek philosopher Epicurus posed an often-referenced riddle. It may actually be a later encapsulation of the spirit of his thinking rather his actual words, but above all else it epitomizes what – uniquely in Greece at that time – had become a fundamental rift with the God-Kings of the past:

> *Are the gods willing to prevent bad things, but not able to?*
> *Then they are not all-powerful.*
> *Are they able, but not willing? Then they are cruel.*
> *Are they both willing and able? Then why is there so much suffering?*
> *Are they neither willing nor able? Then why worship them?*

In different forms and across three millennia the Riddle of Epicurus has tested the most intelligent of devout believers. The modern High-Tech reincarnation of Epicurus is in many ways – the World News.

## 16. Destabilizing influences on religion  — 1

# Social Changes

Historical religious monopoly on morals and behavior no longer exists

Moral attitudes and State laws have transformed since 1960s
(e.g., sex, women, blacks, gays, pornography)

Improved living standards mean less perceived sacrifice to 'break free'
from the security of religion

Diminished automatic deference to authority

Lack of correlation between lawlessness and increasing secularization

Increasing contact with other religions (including rival monotheisms)

Detailed media exposure to the intense suffering from
natural catastrophes 'allowed by god'

# THE INEXORABLE ESCALATION OF SCIENTIFIC REVELATION

## Exponentially-growing scientific revelation has now encroached on every area (including morals) that previously was the province of religions

AROUND 2600 YEARS ago, before even Epicurus, the Greek philosopher Thales is accredited with being the first person seriously to ask the awesomely courageous question: Is it possible to explain natural phenomena in terms of matter and physical forces rather than the actions of the gods? That is a staggering leap of intellect when you consider that elsewhere in the world at that time the same question did not even make sense to people. His student, a brilliant man called Anaximander, went on to propose an origin of the cosmos without reference to supernatural forces. Religion and Science have had an uneasy relationship ever since.

When today's major faiths first grew up, religious doctrine was still by far the most satisfactory way of explaining creation and human existence, and early science was if anything expected to confirm and strengthen these divine revelations. Moslem scholars built on the relatively few ideas that survived after the collapse of the Roman Empire, and thanks to them Christian scholars much later were themselves able to take that research even further, albeit with the understanding that their role was to illuminate still more the majesty of god – not in any way to undermine the authority of religion.

However, by four hundred years ago the relationship between Faith and Reason was becoming strained because for the first time science claimed to disprove the religious orthodoxy that the earth was at the center of the universe. This was a double 'heresy' because it not just flaunted religious teaching (which was also backed up by some Ancient Greek scholars) but also weakened the logic that man – not yet 'woman' in those days – could do whatever he liked to the Earth as well as to everything and everyone on it that was not of the same religion.

When Galileo as an old man was threatened with torture by the Roman Catholic Church unless he denied the facts he had observed through his telescope, for a while scientific progress was stifled and the earth remained at the center of the universe. But the infallibility of faith-based explanations had in reality been seriously undermined. In 1992 pope John Paul formally admitted that the church's 'infallible' denunciation of Galileo's work had been a tragic error. But centuries earlier, many scientists had already known that – because, unlike any of their religious tormentors, they could *prove* it.

## AT THE CENTRE OF GOD'S UNIVERSE

Almost eighteen-hundred years before Copernicus revived the idea that the earth went around the sun, a brilliant astronomer and mathematician called Aristarchus from the Greek island of Samos had not only suggested that the sun was at the center of things but had also accurately described the correct sequence of planets in the solar system. Unfortunately, about four centuries later when the astronomer Ptolemy wrote about the universe in his *Almagest* he sided with the earlier astronomer Hipparchus who had decided that Aristarchus had been wrong after all to claim the Earth went around the Sun. The dogma of an Earth-centered universe then became sacrosanct as it was passed down through first Moslem and then Christian scholars.

Analyses of the religious beliefs of modern scientists suggest that the vast majority are atheists, but those that I have spoken with who *do* believe in a god typically say that they view their two belief systems as complementing one another rather than conflicting. However, some of them also privately acknowledge that it is feeling increasingly difficult to avoid a head-on rivalry.

The reason is that the two systems are increasingly heavily overlapping – and it is Science that is 'encroaching' on what by ancient historical agreement was Religion's turf. That is why further major destabilization is occurring. To understand what is really going on it helps to think of Science in terms of the *way* it works rather than (as most non-scientists do) *what* it produces. The Scientific Method is at its most basic merely a way of structuring a researcher's thinking. Instead of only relying on a stream of intuitive assumptions – which is the way that everybody, including scientists, very successfully gets through much of their lives – scientists train themselves to build models in their heads of how the universe may work.

But whenever they do this, they force themselves to follow a number of unbreakable rules, one of which is that they can only come up with models that are sufficiently specific that they *can potentially be proved to be wrong*. When a scientist comes up with a 'hypothesis', it is not allowed just to be an interesting or clever idea. It *has* to be an idea that is testable to prove whether it is right or wrong – in principle by anyone anywhere. And when a scientist (in practice quite rarely) comes up with a new 'theory' that neatly ties together various hypotheses that no one has yet been able to disprove, that theory – however respected it is – can at any time in the future be undermined by a junior researcher if something the theory predicts is shown not to correspond with how the universe actually works. If others also confirm that flaw, then the long-established theory will need to be replaced by a theory that – at least for a while – works even better.

That is how Science gets more and more powerful. In reality, the best scientists are not those who claim that Science is right but those who prove that part of their previous understanding of existence was wrong – and who also propose an alternative (testable) explanation. The very best scientists are perhaps those who later go on to disprove even their own cherished improvements.

## INTELLIGENT DESIGN

That is an utterly different approach to religion – which is why, despite what some have suggested, in practice it is *impossible* to compare like with like. The suggestion that any evolution of species is best explained by assuming the intervention of a higher intelligence – rather than by an undirected process such as natural selection – does not actually move the debate along at all. It is not that the god-based explanation is inherently 'wrong' in any way, so much as 'a totally different category of thinking to a scientific explanation'.

Whatever passionate and well-intentioned people may claim, it is completely meaningless to suggest that biblically-derived Intelligent

Design is an 'alternative theory' to Darwin's Theory of Evolution by Natural Selection. They are utterly different at a very fundamental level.

If people believe in the literal interpretation of the Christian Bible, then Intelligent Design is an explanation of evolution that is perfectly consistent with their faith. But it can never legitimately be called an alternative 'theory' to Evolution because, *by definition*, a theory can potentially be disproved by subjecting to Peer Review the findings from a reproducible experiment (as earlier explained in the context of *Climate-change and confusion* – starting on page 95).

The guidance of evolution by a higher intelligence may be a perfectly valid idea, but it can no more be called a valid *theory* than the idea that nothing physical exists at all and god is projecting all our experiences into our disembodied souls. Claiming that Darwinism and Creationism are alternatives is not even like comparing apples with oranges. It is like comparing apple-picking instructions with the name of the orchard-owner.

## WHY FUNDAMENTALIST SECTS ARE MORE AT RISK

The example of Intelligent Design is an important one because it illustrates how – unlike with the disruptions caused by social change – different religious denominations are not equally destabilized by scientific progress. More moderate and adaptive forms of religion are nothing like so directly at risk as are fundamentalist sects that maintain literal interpretations of faith-texts sometimes written thousands of years ago. Because those texts are unchangeable, but scientific knowledge is growing exponentially, it becomes increasingly difficult for more-fundamentalist religious leaders to keep up with the full details of the perceived conflict.

When Darwin proposed evolution by natural selection, some viewed it as a body-blow to religion because it provided an explanation for what previously to many people had been the most powerful 'proof' of the existence of god – namely the extraordinary sophistication of nature. But there was still plenty of room for religious counter-argument. Creationism suggested that fossils represented those animals killed by Noah's Flood and that huge gaps in the fossil record showed that evolution had not actually occurred as Darwin claimed.

But the gaps in the fossil record were steadily filled. They fitted with the theory of evolution. Quite separately, overwhelming numbers of examples of natural selection occurring in the modern world (in everything from moths to birds) also fitted. Intelligent Design countered that any good scientist should choose the simplest explanation to fit the facts, and it made far more sense to assume a divine designer behind the miracles of nature than that such incomprehensible order spontaneously arose from chaos by accident.

Science responded that if god was the explanation, then who had designed god? And anyway, given that 'survival of the fittest' had accurately predicted what had subsequently been found to be true in both primeval and more-recent times, it was a far simpler explanation than resorting to divine creation. For a while each explanation had such vocal support that many schools were persuaded to teach Intelligent Design alongside Darwinism.

Then DNA evidence began to explode. And its insights were in no way dependent upon either fossils *or* natural history. With unprecedented acceleration the building blocks of nature were progressively analyzed in a way that meant the evolution of nature from one species to another could be followed precisely. Once again, it fitted Darwin. But this time it revealed something new. The code of life was full of evolutionary cul-de-sacs, mistakes. Hardly the signature – many scientists suggested – of a hands-on all-knowing divine designer.

The literalists have not yet come up with a particularly strong rebuttal, though they are certainly trying. But the real point is that they will never again be able to keep up with the scientific explosion. As they are the first to tell me, that of itself does not in any way undermine their religious faith – it merely shows to them that science cannot reveal the hidden truth. But each time they feel the need to respond to a progressively-detailed scientific discovery that apparently conflicts with divine revelation, it *does* destabilize how their religion ties into society as a whole.

## EXPONENTIAL DESTABILIZATION

In a lesser way, the same is true even for more moderate religions. Physics proposes increasingly sophisticated yet testable theories to explain the start of the universe. Biology steadily progresses in being able to create artificial life. Computing-science is moving ever-closer to human-level intelligence in machines. Anthropology is even beginning to explain in terms of genetics everything from celebrity-culture and generosity to altruism and self-sacrifice. As a simple example, it is now recognized that there would be mutual survival benefits for early-humans living in tribes who were genetically predisposed to be generous to those who were generous back to them.

Those discoveries – relating as they do to morals and ethics – probably represent the very last encroachment onto areas previously thought the sole province of religion. There is nothing else left for which science does not offer an explanation that excludes dependency on the existence of a god. Of the numerous scientists that I talk with, the overwhelming majority claim they would be perfectly willing to believe in a god if there were sufficient justification. But, they tend quickly to add: 'Extraordinary claims demand extraordinary evidence.'

There *might* be a magic pink elephant that lives on Mars. But by the rules of the Scientific Method, that idea runs so contrary to current understanding that the burden of proof lies on those who say they are sure the Pink Elephant exists – not on those who say that it is wishful thinking. In that spirit, a few of the more-conciliatory scientists and religious leaders continue to propose that there still is not really an inherent conflict between Faith and Reason. But even that comfortable accommodation may in practice by now be invalid.

There are no longer any types of question about creation, existence, life or morals for which Science is not exponentially preparing detailed answers – backed up with proof. Even the spontaneous initial emergence of the universe from nothing at the time of the Big Bang is viewed by modern physicists as a potentially fully-explicable (and indeed, inevitable) consequence of the law of gravity. By their very nature, those sorts of answers simply do not *need* faith. And even though Religious and Scientific enlightenment are utterly different approaches, they *are* now addressing all the same issues. As a result, a 'real-world alternative' to faith-based explanations is inherently destabilizing to *all* religions – although especially so to the more dogmatic ones.

It is unthinkable to many that Religion will ever back down – that is what faith is all about. But then neither will Science conceivably back down from applying the rules of the Scientific Method to provide increasingly unassailable explanations for everything without need of reference to a supreme being. Science will not give up on its destabilizing rules of thinking because those rules have stood the test of time. They have proved to be one of the most important inventions of human civilization. And today those same rules are continuing to accelerate human knowledge faster than ever before. There is a very important implication to

# Destabilizing effects

that trend: Any current destabilizing effect on Religion from Science – and consequent push-back on Science from Religion – will not stop soon. It is only just getting going.

## 17. DESTABILIZING INFLUENCES ON RELIGION – 2

## SCIENTIFIC REVELATIONS

The 'Scientific Method' requires testable hypotheses in a way Faith never can

Religious dogma on the centrality of the Earth (or at least mankind) overwhelmingly disproved

Science is now 'encroaching' on every explanation of creation, existence, life and even morals

Faith-dependent explanations of 'inconsistent' scientific observations are exponentially difficult to maintain:

e.g.,
'God created all life at once' BUT fossils reveal other life
'Some species died in Noah's Flood' BUT evolution explains life changing
'Evolution shows Intelligent Design' BUT evolution is full of cul-de-sacs
and absurdly-inefficient designs and DNA confirms this

# 24/7 ON HOW RELIGIOUS LEADERS BEHAVE AND THE ADVICE THEY GIVE

## Proliferating communication media have enabled fundamental critiquing of how religious leaders behave

THE EXPONENTIAL RISE of the internet, citizen journalism and the voracious hunger of around-the-clock News coverage have fuelled yet another importantly different form of destabilization to religions – fundamental critiquing of how religious leaders behave and of the advice they give. Whereas the causes of the destabilizing effects on organized religions of social changes and scientific discoveries largely come from outside, the root causes of this third set of effects is primarily internal to organized religions.

As an example, the various independent reports on allegations of child-abuse by Roman Catholic priests around the world were shocking at many levels. To several of the people I talked with in affected communities, one of their most confused reactions is that it was *possible* for 'men of god' to get away for so long with acts such as severely beating boys in their care, forcing them to have sex, and then beating them again as punishment. For some loyal Catholics, the apparent inability of the Vatican to prevent such widespread behavior seems a fundamental breach of trust. But the reality appears to have been far more complex than merely 'poor management from the top'.

Whenever any national institution – in this case it was the Roman Catholic Church, but during the same period it could have been Royalty, or Parliament, or the Office of the President – is held in awe, and granted extreme respect, all kinds of unwritten rules in the general community appear as a result. Many of those 'rules' relate to the fact that it feels very important to those associated with the institution not to allow anything to tarnish its reputation.

So – as with many forms of abuse – it can seem fully-justified to keep any problems 'in the family'. Even external authority figures (such as the police, politicians or, until recently, media chiefs) often also feel that it is appropriate to hush-up issues that might otherwise cause the institution damage. What is more, they rationalize their actions as being 'in the greater public interest'. After all, imagine the tremendous harm that could follow from undermining such an important body.

With these unwritten rules prevalent, even if a victim of the institution has the courage to complain (as some of the abused Roman Catholic boys did), and even if anyone believes their accusation against such a respected authority, still nothing may happen. Or worse, by one means or another the whistle-blower may be silenced or discredited. Over the years, I have analyzed a wide-ranging group of communities that all exhibited this pattern. And whenever it occurs, a widespread 'conspiracy of silence' tends to build up that often *no one is centrally controlling.*

Put another way, just because a large number of people collude to varying degrees in keeping secret something like child-abuse (or indeed any other form of criminal activity) does not of itself mean that anyone at the top of the organization even knows what is going on – let alone authorized the cover-up. Indeed, when this pattern of unwritten rules is prevalent it is often the person at the top that will be the very last to find out what is actually going on. This sort of setup, however, is inherently unstable – if it ever starts to erode then things tend to go bad very quickly. Over the last few decades, as society has become increasingly 'connected', the likelihood of things falling apart has become dramatically higher than in the past. Presidents have been threatened with impeachment. There have been numerous 'royal scandals'. Politicians have been accused of fraud and corruption. The Press themselves have been called to account.

Many religious institutions are strongly predisposed to inducing these sorts of conspiracies of silence. Consequently, like a dam starting to break, there has been first a trickle and then a rapidly growing deluge of allegations of physical and sexual abuse by religious authority-figures. These have not been confined to priests. Having personally interviewed a large number of people who were educated in Ireland, some of the god-fearing nuns a few decades ago could purportedly be pretty cruel too. Allegations of physical and sexual abuse have dogged even the strictly religious and highly-internally-focused Amish Mennonite groups in Pennsylvania, USA. To put this in context, in Amish communities a child even pulling faces can result in corporal punishment. The accusations of Amish abuse have been in a far more severe league than that.

## DIVINE JUSTICE

Religious authority-figures administering savage cruelty to children in the $20^{th}$ century was in no way restricted to Roman Catholicism – it had a long history in Protestant England as well. Even a former archbishop of Canterbury (head of the Church of England) who is now immortalized on film and TV crowning Queen Elizabeth II was previously the priest at a public school where he reportedly beat boys so severely that he required someone to stand by with a bowl of water to clean off the blood afterwards.

The trouble with all these sorts of examples is that they are so emotive that they risk giving *all* religion a bad name. Just as politicians in many parts of the world have lost the full trust of the public – which can be tempted to lump the whole political-class together with the phrase 'They are all as bad as each other' – so there is an increasing danger that unrelenting media coverage of one allegation after another of abuse by religious authority figures, and one supposed cover-up after another, slowly undermines public trust in *all* religious institutions and their leaders.

After all, spiritual guides claim a higher path. If they are no better than the general public (indeed, if some of them are far worse) then to many of that public it seriously challenges their religious authority. Moreover, as we will see in the next subchapter, the impact of ready-access to information about religions stretches far further than just criticisms of faith-leadership.

## 18. DESTABILIZING INFLUENCES ON RELIGION – 3

## FAILURES IN FAITH-LEADERSHIP

Dominant religions were historically respected because of
their key role in the greater community

It seems 'in the greater public interest' that no one tarnishes
the reputation of a crucial institution

External authority figures (police, politicians, media chiefs)
may choose to 'hush up' damaging stories

If victims of abuse come forward they may not be believed,
may be discredited or may be silenced

'Conspiracies of Silence' can emerge that *no central leader controls*
(or may even be aware of)

Interconnected modern society makes it increasingly likely that
institutional malpractice will be exposed chaotically

# UNPRECEDENTED ACCESS TO CONFUSION

## Well-educated believers with unprecedented informal access to historical and other evaluations of religion are increasingly confused

THE EXAMPLES OF 'self-induced' religious destabilization just considered are increasingly being made worse for believers by a drip-drip feed – from all different technology-enabled directions – of perceived errors of judgment by supposedly infallible faith leaders, as well as 'new' insights that lead to general confusion about important aspects of religions. These are instances of the fourth source of destabilization to organized faiths.

### THE POLIO FATWA

Smallpox is the only disease ever to have been completely eradicated from the world. Thanks to a massive immunization program begun in 1988 by the World Health Organization and others, polio was also set to be consigned to history by now. It almost was. However in 2005, just as this cause of lifelong paralysis in children was about to be eliminated, a spiritual ruling by Islamic leaders in Nigeria blocked further immunization. Polio spread far out of Nigeria again – setting back decades of work.

Maybe an article on immunization explains how in 2005 some Islamic Nigerian spiritual leaders issued a fatwa (a ruling) that polio vaccine was a conspiracy against the Muslim faith and would sterilize true believers – and as a result these clerics prevented the eradication of polio. Or perhaps a documentary about poverty in Africa tells how Roman Catholic priests, once again seemingly beyond the control of Rome, have been incriminated

# Destabilizing effects

in the hugely-publicized Rwanda massacres of Tutsi schoolchildren. And then an even-handed history program on World War II mentions how the Vatican kept a low profile as millions of Jews were sent to the Nazi gas chambers. At the same time as Buddhist and Shinto priests recruited and trained kamikaze suicide bombers.

Part of the undermining effect of these sorts of examples is that believers (as well as non-believers) come across them unexpectedly in contexts that are typically not even religious – let alone anti-religious. However, the main damage comes because the examples are all actions taken by spiritual leaders claiming divine guidance. Their particular faith can sometimes almost seem of secondary importance because the examples would be bad enough if they were the actions of executives in an oil multinational or pharmaceutical conglomerate claiming the authority of their CEO. But all Religion bases its authority on the divine.

The cumulative destabilization effect goes far further because the same 24/7 free-flow of multimedia information that is increasingly bombarding everybody, also encourages an unprecedented number of ideas to be compared, tested and questioned. In most communities that leads to enhanced creativity. But, as already stated, age-old religions are structured for rigidity and resilience not creativity and innovation. Faith (in all its forms) has *never* previously been so publically exposed to such a stark spotlight as the modern information age provides. How well the pillars of organized religions will stand up to decades of such unrelenting exposure is unclear. But the additional destabilization that it brings is already apparent. The soul-searching it sets off can affect anyone.

I have had senior members of religious organizations tell me they question the basic moral logic implied by 'old fashioned' religion, namely that people should be good because then they will be rewarded in the afterlife but otherwise they will be punished. It seems, so these faith-leaders worry, a little primitive. After all, they confide to me, if the reason 'religious' people are moral is because they are being self-serving (hungry for Heaven and scared of Hell) then below the surface maybe they are not really very moral individuals after all. And those atheists who live good lives even though they do not believe in an afterlife are perhaps the most morally pure of all. Indeed – some of the religious leaders uncomfortably conclude – if god truly were such a 'manipulative tyrant', he would not *deserve* to be supported even if people did believe in him. The courageous stance would not be that of the atheist so much as the 'antitheist'.

## Casual Destabilization

In my interviews regarding this fourth form of destabilization, the most common point made to me is that the triggers for such forced-contemplation are now everywhere. For instance, it is increasingly a topic of TV documentaries that there are elements of many stories that act as a common foundation to the Talmud, Old Testament and the Koran that in fact also appear in far earlier religions – such as the story of the Great Flood. So how, even the most passive viewers find themselves asking, can the later slightly-different versions (making reference to a very-different divinity than the multiple-gods of the originals) be included in a book claiming to be written by *their* One God?

## THE ORIGINAL COMMANDMENTS AND GREAT FLOOD

More than four-thousand years ago in ancient Egypt, the rules of Ma'at were increasingly reflected in the Book of the Dead inscribed on tomb walls. They were written as negative confessions, some of which are hauntingly familiar, such as: *I have not despised god, I have not killed, I have not committed adultery, I have not stolen, I have not borne false witness...* and so on. They vary in detail from tomb to tomb, although one of the cutest that for some reason was never picked up by any of the future Abrahamic religions was: *I have not harmed cats.*

Around the same time, people in the city of Ur in Mesopotamia (modern-day Iraq plus areas of Syria, Turkey and Iran) claimed that their recently deceased God-King Sargon had – just as in the much later story of Moses – been found as a baby in a basket floating down the river. They also told the tale of the Great Flood: The gods decided to destroy all life on earth, but one god choose to warn a man about the forthcoming deluge and instructed him to build an ark big enough to save his family and cattle (the man's name was actually Utnapishtim, not Noah). After the waters retreated, the gods felt so bad about all the mess that they gave Utnapishtim and his wife eternal life in compensation.

Even religious festivals can be fraught with destabilizing influences. Around Christmas there are a slew of programs and articles discussing the inconsistencies in the Christian New Testament in general and the story of the nativity in particular. Maybe in one program a respected historian points out that scholars now recognize that early church leaders did not know their Roman history well enough, and in consequence Jesus was definitely *not* born in 0 A.D. but probably about six years earlier, though no one is quite sure within a couple of years. As a result, the global dating system – created by Christians and then imposed on everybody else – in reality celebrates that a very important child was maybe six and a bit years old. Maybe in another program a trusted celebrity casually mentions that Jesus' birth was certainly not at Christmas time – which is simply a popular Roman festival that Christians commandeered hundreds of years later.

## SPIRIT OF CHRISTMAS

No one actually selected December 25$^{th}$ as being a good date to celebrate Jesus' birth until almost two hundred years after his death. However, since before the building of Stonehenge the winter solstice, the shortest day of the year after which every day gets longer again, had carried tremendous significance as symbolizing the rebirth of spring and summer. In the Roman Empire it was a popular holiday known as *Dies Solis Invicti Nati* ('the day of the birth of the unconquered sun').

The holiday eventually adopted by Christians blended elements of both the feast of the Saturnalia – which ran to December 24$^{th}$ – and the birthday of Mithra, the extremely popular Iranian god of light, that was held on the 25$^{th}$, a day dedicated to the invincibility of the sun. Those who bemoan the way 'Christmas has turned into a time of wild merrymaking and revelry' maybe underestimate the strength with which some legacies of our past become embedded. For more than 5000 years that holiday has been a time of wild merrymaking and revelry. Frustratingly for some perhaps, and despite numerous short-lived attempts toward seriousness, the spirit of the season has simply never changed.

'And by the way,' a still-more erudite academic adds, 'we are not quite sure that religious texts claim that Mary was a virgin at all. The word in the original Hebrew text is *almah* – which translates either as *virgin* or simply *young woman*.' The progressively widespread airing of these sorts of textual inconsistencies and factual inaccuracies is causing a build-up of destabilizing backlashes within not just Christian sects like the Pentecostals and Fundamentalists (who believe in the literal meaning of the Bible) but also within the more conservative branches of the Roman Catholic church such as Opus Dei and the Vatican, as well as the strictly conservative form of Wahhabi Islam sponsored by Saudi royals.

Each sect is storing up problems for itself in the future, because they are largely sweeping the issue of alternative interpretations under their faith-based carpet. I have myself heard some say words to the effect of: 'We know there are issues, but we shouldn't allow academics or the media to spoil things for the devoted.' Unfortunately that is another version of the conspiracy-of-silence dynamic that *inevitably* sets up a major backlash in the future. If only these leaders studied the religious and spiritual and humanist blogs and discussion pages and articles mushrooming all over the internet and covering every faith from Cao Dai (a relatively modern monotheistic religion adopted by millions in Vietnam) to Wicca, they would see just how academically well-informed – and increasingly confused – some of their devout followers already are.

## EDUCATED INQUIRY

There are numerous unresolved questions that believers are asking. Now that stylistic experts have demonstrated that some 'divinely-dictated' texts have multiple authors, how is that possible? Given that after Jesus' execution his own family steadfastly held out that he was a truly wonderful man, why did the early Church instead insist that the claim of Paul – who had never actually met Jesus – was correct and that Jesus was in fact divine and that the views of his own family were heretical? Now that the Dead Sea Scrolls have been analyzed, why are they so different to the version of the Hebrew Bible everyone uses? Why does the Christian church skirt around the issue that Jesus spent most of his adult life trying to improve the Jewish faith – not create a new one – and that when he was baptized it was *as a Jew* (and therefore he must have been circumcised)?

In that context, some ancient religious rituals themselves raise difficult questions in modern society. It worries some parents that in the 21$^{st}$ century, in civilized countries where people pride themselves on their sophistication and modernity, where in some places it is illegal even to dock a dog's tail, it is nevertheless still legal to ritually mutilate children's genitals. Of course as soon as it is described as 'circumcision' it seems less contentious. Unless someone adds the word 'female'. Modern medical consensus – many parents point out – no longer claims overall health benefits from male circumcision, and there are concerns that it reduces sexual pleasure (indeed for a long time it was seen as a 'cure' for masturbation in adolescent boys). There is no doubt whatever that female circumcision *does* dramatically reduce sexual pleasure – though notably only for the woman.

## ROMAN DIVINITY

Jesus' own family viewed him as a human prophet – as did Mohamed over five centuries later. But the influential Paul, who had never even seen Jesus, nevertheless proclaimed him as the 'son of god' and it is that view that eventually won out within Christianity. The conflicting beliefs regarding the divinity of Jesus are interesting for a variety of reasons – not least that Paul lived at a time when even Roman Emperors were gods. In addition to any other more important justifications, it is easy to see why for a Roman like Paul it would feel utterly wrong that Jesus was not recognized as being at least comparable to the likes of Emperors Nero and Caligula. This was a time when the currency of being deified had become seriously devalued.

And while on the apparent preoccupation with sex of many (male) religious leaders, there are growing schisms over what to many seems an unclear – others would say 'biased' – selection of certain religious passages over others. Anti-gay Christian, Islamic, and Judaic rulings are predicated on shared ancient passages that, for instance, declare male same-sex acts to be an 'abomination'. But then, as many different interpreters point out, there are other passages that declare eating shellfish to be an abomination too. And none of the rulings seem explicitly to prohibit lesbianism. Perhaps – some more-flippant gay-rights campaigners point out – that is why, despite the Christian Fundamentalist claims in the 1980s that AIDS was a 'gay plague', to this day lesbians are one of the groups *least* affected by AIDS (or indeed any other STDs).

Anyway, other more-serious commentators add, how can modern religious leaders – including the pope – continue to claim that homosexual behavior is 'against Natural Law' (in the sense of 'unnatural') when scientists now know that it commonly occurs in many species across Nature? What is more, although few literalists seem to stress the fact, many religious scholars point out that there are equally clear directives about stoning people to death for all sorts of 'crimes' (children being disobedient, for example) that are these days completely out of alignment with what is considered civilized.

Many of the other 'morals' illustrated by God, Allah and Yahweh in these same ancient texts also, moderates add, seem totally unacceptable today. Abraham is encouraged by the Almighty to kill his son so as to show his devotion. Slavery is valued whereas women, typically, are not – although, on at least one occasion (as recorded in Numbers 31:18), divine instructions are given for Moses' army to kill all civilian boys yet *not* to kill virgin girls, who were to be kept alive for the soldiers. Attempts by even the most moderate faith-leaders to explain such apparent problems in religious texts all hit a difficulty: Any justification is not obvious, otherwise fellow-believers would not have concerns in the first place, so any ruling about modern-day relevance is necessarily seen as an *interpretation*.

That means that the religious text requires an external standard to judge it against – it is no longer self-standing. But if part of the modern interpretation is that some of the more extreme stories and miracles are 'meant to be symbolic' then where does that end? How does a believer know when to stop cherry-picking examples? Is *everything* in the religious texts actually symbolic in the modern world? Some clergy are certainly heading that way. Indeed, a recent study by the Free University of Amsterdam found that one-in-six clergy in the Dutch Protestant Church were either agnostic or fully-atheist.

## THE SPIRIT NOT THE LETTER OF THE LAW

This sort of selective interpretation has been going on a long time. The acts committed in the names of various Faiths have often been dictated not so much by the words of the founders of those religions as by the 'clarification' of those words by leaders promoting either their religion's best interests, their own inspired ideas, or both. The definition of a Holy War is a history-changing example. But it can also be see today in relatively minor everyday actions.

258

# Destabilizing effects

Some Orthodox Jews feel that although they cannot work on the Sabbath it is only practical to pay someone else to do the work for them. Some Shia Muslims rigorously adhere to Sharia law by visiting establishments that marry them to a prostitute before divorcing them again a few hours later. Some US Christian Fundamentalists try to impose the Ten Commandments (including 'not coveting your neighbor's goods') but also staunchly advocate Consumerism. And all the major organized religions preach giving to the poor – from within some of the most opulent buildings on the planet. It is understandable why some believers end up bemused as a result.

The destabilizing effect of conflicts between the dogma of ancient religions and the increasingly informed attitudes of modern populations is growing inexorably. Backlashes are building around an unstoppable and ever-more-unrelenting series of questions – difficult and soul-wrenching queries to which few members of the general population have sufficient answers. Yet at the same time as billions wrestle with their faith in the light of cruel natural disasters, comprehensive scientific explanations, widespread abusive behavior by religious authority figures, and inconsistencies in texts meant to have been dictated by god, the most powerful faith-leaders in the world warn against condoms and gay sex, claim their divine-right to populate a strip of land, and argue whether there are heavenly rewards for suicide bombers.

Only those same faith-leaders can judge how their current performance might be rated by the original founders of their respective religions, if those founders were preaching amongst today's populations. But that is an important test that well-educated believers increasingly find themselves applying to today's religious authority figures. It is a variation on the sense-check that over the years I have encouraged the heads of all types of organization to apply in order to test whether 'untouchable dogma' genuinely reflects core ideology or whether it is merely long-established habit. It is a thought-experiment that helps highlight the higher-purpose behind strategies, rules and processes set up by founders – the 'spirit of the law' as opposed to the pedantic rules.

As an example, long after the death of Walt Disney top executives of The Walt Disney Company he co-founded were always tempted to make business decisions based on the answer to the question: 'What would Walt have done?' For almost two decades this risked trapping the corporation in the past. The Disney of today only emerged once executives realized that the amazingly-creative Walt would almost certainly have kept *updating* his views if he had lived. By implication, the test question that many devout believers are implicitly asking is: If Moses, Mohamed, Jesus, Buddha and the others were completely up-to-date with the full complexity of the modern world, how would they feel about the current focus of the religious leaders that today act in their names? Would they be immensely proud?

# CONFUSING INSIGHTS

Believers suffer a drip-drip feed of reported errors of judgment
by supposedly infallible faith-leaders

Negative facts are particularly undermining when in contexts
that are not even religious (let alone anti-religious)

Believers interested in adding to their religious knowledge end up confused:

e.g.,
- Elements of sacred texts appear in earlier very-different religions
- Jesus was not born in 0 AD or at Christmas
and the word 'virgin' may be a mistranslation
- Textual analysis reveals some 'divinely-dictated' texts have multiple authors
- Passages declaring male same-sex acts as 'abominations' say the
same about eating shellfish – but lesbianism does *not* seem excluded

# HOW INTOLERANCE AND DOGMATISM LEAD TO POLARIZATION

## Actions by some sects to bolster rigidity through intolerance and dogmatism are polarizing and politicizing whole communities

THOSE THEN ARE the four distinct ways in which ancient religions are at progressive risk of destabilization from the escalating impact of High-Tech on everything from social mores, 24/7 news, scientific understanding and readily-accessible details on the web. But not every type of religion is being affected in anything like the same way. Indeed, some types appear to be flourishing.

There is strong evidence that in the USA – unlike much of the rest of the developed world – some new styles of organized Christianity are thriving as a direct result of how well they are *adapting* to change rather than attempting to negate it. Drawing heavily on High-Tech developments, huge new forums for worship directly apply the technology and skills of the entertainment industry. They offer to their massive congregations levels of convenience typical of an attractive shopping mall. Moreover, they actively welcome, rather than just tolerate, a far broader range of beliefs than other churches accept. This may seem 'inappropriate' to more-traditional sects. But these new styles of religion are proving extremely attractive to many believers, not least to younger generations.

However, more generally such flexibility is uncommon. That is primarily because, as stated earlier, long-established sects carry strongly-reinforced ways of thinking and doing things that are heavily intertwined with everything around them – simultaneously making those religions highly resilient to disruption, as well as extremely difficult to adapt. As a result, most examples of formalized religion *do not* significantly respond to change. On the contrary, they often feel that the greatest test of their faith is to withstand the onslaught of the modern world and remain solid in their unshakable belief that divine revelations made millennia ago hold an unchanged relevance today.

## HOW INSTITUTIONS GET STUCK IN THEIR WAYS

Any community when it first starts up usually has only a few formal or informal rules holding it together. Indeed, there is often so much freedom that getting everyone to pursue a single chosen future can feel like herding cats. But as the community gets established, the leaders tend to formalize progressively more-codified ways of doing things. Meanwhile, as individuals start giving their close friends advice on how to survive and thrive in the community, informal guidelines turn into deeply-embedded 'unwritten rules' on how to behave. The more all these formal and informal rules link into each other, the more difficult it is to change any one of them. In fact, the same social glue that holds people together can also gum up the works when it comes to changes they really want – sometimes even sticking them to a course they are desperately trying to escape.

After centuries, many of the community's ways of working get inextricably tied into those of the other old establishments, institutions and organizations it interacts with. Once that happens, whole sections of the wider-society become set like concrete. For a 1600-year-old body like the Roman Catholic Church, that is a blessing and a curse. It means that as an institution it is very resilient – it will not declare bankruptcy during a credit crunch. But it also means that when it ever does want to change, it can be really tough.

It is this 'inherent-stability' that ironically is now placing many religions (and the communities they are within) at risk of catastrophic destabilization. It is a similar situation to trees in a major storm: a huge solid oak will hardly seem to move until suddenly it uproots and falls, whereas a flexible willow may bend almost in half yet survive the tempest unscathed. The 'storm' in this case is the exponentially circulating concerns, uncertainties and apparent inconsistencies to which those with Faith are being exposed. So far, the response of the majority of formalized religions has tended to be to mimic the oak. From everything I have analyzed, that strategy is not sustainable. The implications for the religions themselves are substantial. But the progressive backlashes that they risk will not only affect them. They will affect everybody else as well.

## CHOOSING IDENTITY

In Cairo during the 1970s, for many young women removing head scarves felt like joining the modern age. Yet long before the resurgence of Islamist propaganda brought by the Arab Spring of 2011, many Liberated Mothers could not understand why their daughters wanted to cover their heads again. In my trips to Egypt over the last decade it has become increasingly uncommon to see young women who do *not* these days 'wear the scarf'. And the same is just as true within some city-neighborhoods in the UK. Yet almost universally all those women will explain that wearing the scarf is their choice, and their choice alone. No one is putting them under pressure. However, despite the apparent lack of duress, the trend has been very strong. Understanding why such social transitions come about is a crucial insight.

Educated Moslem women wearing headscarves or even full veils in Cairo or Western inner-cities is an indication of identity – and an indication that an important part of how that person identifies herself is as part of the Islamic faith. Within that context, covering up often makes the wearers feel they are demonstrating their piety to the world – even though, importantly, their uncovered mother may in reality also feel (and be) just as pious. The fact that in predominantly non-Moslem countries wearing a veil can these days sometimes also be interpreted as provocatively symbolic of both female subjugation as well as of an 'intolerant' and 'increasingly threatening' religion is usually totally irrelevant to why it is in fact being worn in the first place.

But importantly, the contrasting emotions in multicultural communities relating to headscarves and veils – 'I am proud to belong and show my piety' versus 'Why are you being so provocative and not integrating with the wider community?' – are mild versions of the same tensions that can polarize into terrorism and corrosive social backlash. In both cases, an initial desire simply to belong to one group rather than another can escalate and polarize. And that is true whether the differences are between communities of Moslems and Christians, Moslems and Jews, Shia and Sunni, Roman Catholics and Protestants, or any other combination of long-standing religious rivalries. As I will now explain though, some combinations escalate into extremes that others never reach. And very importantly, for that to happen does not just require one group to be rigid and intolerant. For the worst backlashes, it requires the other group initially to be unduly flexible and over-tolerant.

# Counter-reactions

## INTOLERANCE TAKING ADVANTAGE OF TOLERANCE

The reason for this only becomes clear once you examine the dynamics of intolerance within an otherwise-tolerant society. There is in reality a whole spectrum of responses by faith leaders to the universal destabilization of organized religions. These range from the fluid tolerance and open-mindedness of mainstream Hinduism and Buddhism, Liberal Islam in Turkey and the new-style Christian faith-centers in the USA to the strident intolerance and dogmatism of fundamentalist religious sects of every faith.

At first glance this seems a broadly stable situation. After all, the majority of people along the spectrum have attitudes that can be summed up by varying degrees of 'live and let live' – only at one end are there voluble groups that seem ready for a fight. But that is only the current snapshot of the types of people involved. Below the surface, there are hidden forces at work that are changing the balance of those participants. The point is that, in any community, *professionally-organized intolerance and dogmatism gradually tends to **dominate** over a hands-off approach of tolerance and open-mindedness*. To many, that dynamic seems counterintuitive. After all, is not the lesson of history that societies inevitably become increasingly tolerant and liberal over time? The simple answer is: No. Nazi Germany is a classic example.

A partial explanation is that, as examined in the subchapter about *Rolling News and the unintended distortions it creates* (page 44), a side-effect of the competitive pressures on modern media is that the more extreme religious views in society are often granted the greatest visibility – and with it the greatest potential to influence others. The average, although more representative views, are considered relatively 'boring' and therefore much less newsworthy. It makes more arresting news to show a church leader saying that a natural catastrophe is god's punishment for a society that tolerates gay lifestyles than to interview another who is quietly working for a relief charity. As a result, extreme views tend to receive disproportionate publicity. Similarly, the internet makes it increasingly natural for those holding unrepresentative views nevertheless to avoid much exposure to ideas other than those similar to their own.

However, there is a very important but even-less-visible dynamic that is also at work in polarizing communities. The more dedicated that extremists in any religion are, the more fervent their pronouncements are likely to be, and the more they are likely to be willing to sacrifice. They will typically want to interact (either in person or via the internet) primarily with those sharing broadly the same views. And that type of self-imposed segregation is very easily institutionalized. Hard-line faith schools, for instance, end up segregating impressionable children from their wider community and encouraging them to cherish and maintain their differences. Insularity then becomes a badge of honor and piety. Children are warned not to make friends outside their immediate community, not to watch 'offensive' television, dress in the wrong way or listen to the wrong types of music.

That dynamic rapidly creates a form of voluntary religious apartheid. And everyone who is a non-believer (or who is deemed to be an insufficiently pious believer or a member of the 'wrong' sect) is normally lumped together with some convenient form of pejorative name that reinforces the sense of belonging for those on the inside. This is similar to the dynamics of inner-city gangs. Indeed, under these circumstances religious sects can become surprisingly gang-like. When children and adults only tend to hear the (typically hardline) ideas of others within their segregated community, those ideas appear validated – not least to those growing up in or considering joining the sect but who initially perhaps hold less-extreme views. Indeed, there can be a great feeling of belonging and fellowship for those who 'come in from the outside' and maybe for the first time feel a sense of genuine purpose in their lives.

When the mass-media then publicize those extreme views, even if it is a negative portrayal, not only does it help more potential recruits to hear about the ideas but it also reinforces the camaraderie of those who are already banded together to 'fight the good fight' – in an increasingly political way. When this kind of intolerant faction is surrounded by people who broadly tolerate it (either because they do not realize how extreme the group is or because they feel obliged to uphold free-speech and freedom of religion), the faction's goals tend to ratchet-up because in a tolerant society there is little to constrain it.

## ESCALATION

Over time, the rights of the few can end up overriding the rights of the many. Intelligent Design *must* be taught in schools because that is only balanced science, but any stem-cell research must be *banned* even if most scientists do not agree that it is murder. Anti-Western clerics *should* be allowed to preach whatever they like within Western Mosques because that is the law, whereas non-Muslim cartoonists in the West *cannot* represent Mohammed because that is insulting. The Ten Commandments or Sharia are *more important* than mere human regulations because they come from a higher authority, so they *overrule* any conflicting democratically-elected Laws of the State.

## DANISH HUMOR

I have studied the twelve Danish cartoons published in 2005 that caused a furor by depicting Mohammed's face (which, irrespective of content, is considered by Moslems to be an insult to Islam). Some of the cartoons no doubt made far more sense if you lived in Denmark. Others – such as the image of a bearded-man in Paradise halting a group of approaching young terrorists with the words: 'Stop, stop, we've run out of virgins…' – were more explicit. If the subject-matter had been about anything other than religion, the discussion on all sides would have been utterly different and it is unlikely that both the pope and the archbishop of Canterbury would have considered it worthy to condemn satirical humor. Nor would the usually fearless media afterwards have – as some of them explained to me – simply been *too scared for their physical safety* to dare republish the cartoons even within liberal democracies built on the promise of free speech.

Yet as the goals become more extreme, so too do the valid means of achieving them. And the more that a religious faction feels under attack – from state-intervention, secularism, the 'lowering' of moral standards, or from being labeled as 'extremists' or even 'potential terrorists' – so the faction feels the necessity to push even harder, and actively try to convince more-moderate believers of the need to support the extremist cause. Whatever the rights or wrongs of the Iraq War, the decision triggered a cascade of implications for how Islamic extremists were perceived by far-more-moderate Moslems. For a start, the absence of WMD confirmed in many minds the accusation that the USA and UK had been unfairly aggressive and that the war maybe indeed was (in the minds of the unusually-devout Christian President and Prime Minister) a Crusade against Islam.

# RELIGION CRISES

The temporarily patriotic renaming of French Fries in the USA as Freedom Fries, because France had been an outspoken critic of the invasion, seemed to many to be a little hollow after the subsequent Presidential order denying detainees at Guantanamo Bay even the most basic rights of freedom offered by the Geneva Convention. This together with pictures of abuses by the US-military at Abu Ghraib inevitably gave pause for thought to everybody, not least moderate Moslems around the world. Of course it fuelled feelings of justification in the more extreme elements of society. But more worryingly, it made it very-much-easier to encourage moderates to become more radical. Meanwhile, throughout that time, attention had been diverted from Afghanistan during the very period that Pakistan attempted a ten-year appeasement of the Taliban that eventually backfired on everybody.

## INHERENT FAILINGS IN MULTICULTURALISM

In any community that is broadly-tolerant of intolerant behavior, there is an inherent instability that means that the situation cannot remain static. From all the analyses I have conducted, what appears to happen is that the more that the tolerant and open-minded 'permit' the intolerance and dogmatism, so the more that those closer to the faction feel that their extreme position is being tacitly condoned. It becomes still more politicized.

A policy of multiculturalism (that is, deliberately taking efforts to preserve cultural diversity within a community rather than aiming for full assimilation and integration of minorities) can substantially enrich a community made up of individually *tolerant* and *inclusive* cultures. It is an exciting and stimulating rejuvenation. But pursuing multiculturalism where one or more factions are inherently *intolerant* and *exclusive* inevitably leads to instability. Many European countries are only now discovering this. As things stand, the risk of escalating backlashes across many of their less-integrated multicultural communities is substantial.

All of this dynamic is itself overlaid by a 'stretching' of society between parts that change very fast and parts that adapt much more slowly – similar to the dynamic that also occurs as a result of High-Tech changing some jobs (say, in the office) far more than others (such as managing livestock on a farm). While much of society is rapidly evolving, the more-deeply religious sects – with all their in-build stabilization – tend to resist those changes more strongly than any other parts of society, creating a clear gap. The faster the general pace of change across the global community, the greater the gap grows.

For instance, whereas younger generations in many Western (more secular) societies are growing more egalitarian, that is far less obvious in many strongly-Moslem countries where teenage attitudes to sexual-orientation, women's rights, public displays of affection, alcohol, abortion and divorce remain similar to those of their parents. Only in a city such as Istanbul – in rigorously secular Turkey – can you begin to see young Moslem men holding hands with their girl-friends as they drink beer at a café. After the declaration of the Turkish republic in 1923 by Mustafa Kemal Atatürk, public displays of Islamic piety were strongly discouraged. Almost ninety years later, the trend is slowly in the opposite direction as the country adopts a more overtly Islamic identity. There is a potential Religion Crisis building even in Turkey. But the main crises will be far more widespread. Here is why.

## 20. RELIGION AFTER EXPONENTIAL DESTABILIZING INFLUENCES

DESTABLIZING INFLUENCES

RESPONSE DEPENDS UPON THE INHERENT PHILOSOPHY OF A RELIGIOUS SECT

**AFTER**

Inherently *tolerant* and *inclusive* sects **ADAPT**

• Liberal Islam, e.g., Turkey
• Liberal Christianity, e.g., Church of England
• Mainstream Buddhism
• Mainstream Hinduism

Inherently *intolerant* and *exclusive* sects **TRY TO DOMINATE**

CAUSING

**POLARIZATION** AND **POLITICIZATION**

# WHY 'WESTERN DEPRAVITY' INSULTS ISLAMIC FUNDAMENTALISTS

## Some Moslem authority figures are revolted by 'Western-style depravity' that they view as an attack on Islam that must be repulsed

AFTER THE JEWS and then the Christians, the Arabs were the last group to have a prophet reveal the 'true nature' of the Abrahamic god to them. From that time they demanded deference and respect from nonbelievers, and there were many claimed rights to extend their religion by war. Of course, the Christians had the same idea and their pope even promised soldiers forgiveness of all sins provided they went on a Crusade and killed Moslems. Both sides performed atrocities in the name of their god – although modern Arab children tend to be encouraged to study the details far more than their Western counterparts do.

Just as every other religion, almost from its start Islam split into different sects. However, about 270-years ago a scholar called Muhammad ibn Abd-al-Wahhab began preaching a particularly puritanical version. He sought to purge Islam of all innovations and return to basics. It might have remained a minor sect, except that the al-Saud family formed an alliance with him: They would enforce his ideas and he would confirm their God-given right to rule. The deal remains intact in the form of Saudi Arabia – along with Iran the world's only Islam-run state – funded by oil and ruled by the strictest Sharia law

In reality, although it is often spoken about as if it was devised by Mohammed himself, Sharia law was only detailed a couple of centuries after he died. As a result, it encapsulates the judicial-thinking of 9th-century Arab society. And it has not changed. Flogging and amputation are common punishments and, even with the number of cars in modern Saudi Arabia, women are not allowed to drive in public. Some sharia punishments can in practice be crueler than many outside the communities tend to realize. For instance, cutting off a hand for theft in a culture where people eat food from a shared bowl effectively means that the amputee can no longer eat with others because their only remaining hand now has to be used both for eating and for performing unsanitary tasks – and no one wants eat with someone who risks contaminating the communal food. Whatever your views on the matter, the fact remains that this is the judicial system of one of the world's largest oil exporters. As oil-wealth has increasingly dominated the history of the last several decades, so the flavor of Islam worldwide has progressively been influenced by the interpretation rigorously promoted by Saudi clerics.

To better understand how it is possible for such a major religion to be so open to interpretation, you must realize that in the earliest authorized versions of the Koran there are many vowels missing in the original Arabic, so some words can mean different things. On top of that, the Koran is written like highly-sophisticated poetry (which is why it is potentially impossible to understand fully in translation). Those two factors alone mean that a devout Moslem typically has to depend on the interpretations of others to get accurate guidance from the Koran.

But it gets more complicated even than that. In addition to the Koran, there are orally-generated texts called the Hadith describing what Mohamed did throughout his life. The Shia and Sunni sects (the main split in Islam) have different versions. What is more, a useful copy of the Koran has many annotations designed to help the reader interpret it in the 'right' way. But those annotations necessarily reflect *the interpreter* as well as the teachings of Mohamed. And there are an extremely large number of mass-produced editions of the Koran in circulation that originated from Saudi Arabia and reflect the views of Saudi clerics – which can only enhance any gradual shift of moderate-Islam toward puritanical-Islam.

## HIDDEN-LOGIC OF SUICIDE BOMBING

Even that in no way explains the upsurge of Suicide Bombers who believe they will be rewarded in heaven for killing civilians (even if the deaths include Moslem children). Islamic terrorists in general certainly preach an extreme form of Islam, as did the late Bin Laden. But in many ways that should make them the least likely people to advocate the atrocities that they perpetrate. At every level suicide-bombing appears prohibited by the Koran. Suicide is forbidden, as is the murder of civilian non-believers, and children, and especially fellow Moslems. Although Mohammed certainly on occasion fought wars and exacted retribution from those who proved disloyal, his general life-message was overwhelmingly one of striving for peace and reconciliation. So how can suicide bombers square their actions with the overall message of their prophet? The answer shows how far the polarized destabilization of Islam has already escalated. The hidden logic of suicide bombers goes something like this:

'The global economy means that the logic of war has changed. Armed conflict is not now usually for territory or resources it is for ideology – and since fascism and communism have fallen the only ideology that matters is religion. Western-style depravity (allowing women to act like prostitutes and treating homosexuals as if they have rights) is an affront to Islam. And it is our children and wives that are at risk of being polluted by the filth spewed out by Hollywood and the like.

'The USA and the UK, headed then by a President and Prime Minister that were both extremist Christians, illegally invaded Iraq and Afghanistan and even publically called it a Crusade – a thinly-disguised religious motivation for a head-on attack by Christian forces trying to subjugate Islam. In addition, the US government supports Israel in its fight against Palestine. But that too is an explicit fight against Islam.

'US and UK citizens elect and pay those officials, and in doing so they too choose to attack Islam. They are guilty because they pay the salaries of those who act in their name. Those infidels who are citizens of democracies are not innocent bystanders, they have chosen to fight Moslems. They are ultimately responsible. As are the citizens of any country that associates with them.

'The USA and its allies are too powerful to fight head-on, so guerrilla-tactics and terrorism are the only valid options. But our religious war is even harder than that. Christianity is very strong in the USA and is even growing. Worse, women and homosexuals flaunting themselves, pornography and abortion everywhere, it's spreading like a disease. With the uncontrollable reach of the internet it risks infecting the morals of true-believers everywhere. There is no greater goal than that the world should be purged – and Allah would rightly punish us if we did not try.

'Although fellow-Muslims and innocent children may be killed in the process, Islam is facing exceptional danger against an all-powerful enemy. Under those circumstances, martyrdom is better than capitulation – as has been recognized throughout Islamic history. And there is no greater religious sacrifice, no more sacred act, than giving your own life to further the ultimate triumph of The Prophet's mission.'

# Growing polarization

## ABSENCE OF COUNTER-LOGIC

Although some mainstream clerics have denounced this sort of logic, the clerics themselves are viewed with suspicion by Islamic extremists. After all, those same 'authorities' are considered to be tools of either oppressive or perverted state regimes – and therefore already suspect. Anyway, although some fatwa undermine al-Qaeda, others do not. And because Islam in inherently decentralized, there is no final arbiter. In addition, very-deep suspicions about the 'thinly-disguised religious motivation' of the USA can apparently easily be justified merely by reference to media reports of statements made by top officials at the time. President Bush himself regularly used the term 'Axis of Evil' (which, unpublicized at the time, he in fact changed from his speechwriter's original wording of 'Axis of Hatred').

And only days after the 9/11 attack, in an unscripted remark, the President did indeed describe the War on Terrorism as a 'Crusade' – a deeply provocative association for Moslems brought up with vivid accounts of Christian atrocities committed during the historical Crusades. There are innumerable other examples. For instance, for several years General William G Boykin (a Christian Fundamentalist and one of President Bush's top generals in charge of war policy) made several comments that were easily interpreted as framing the War on Terror as a religious war. On one occasion the press reported that, whilst he was dressed in full military uniform, he told a church congregation that the USA invading Iraq was a 'Christian nation battling Satan.'

A decade later, all these dynamics continue to exacerbate the cumulative risk of backlashes relating to Islam. The global pressures on Islam's multiple forms are reinforcing an overall trend that risks sliding Moslem interpretations of Mohamed's words toward the fundamentalist end of the spectrum. Whatever the relative merits or otherwise of those versions of Islam, the reality is that they are inherently and deeply divisive and intolerant in comparison with the interpretations of more-moderate Moslems. That trend on its own dramatically increases the danger of backlashes between countries – and within them. However, the outcome is made all-the-more likely because the high-risk trend toward progressive extremism in Islam is in fact being mirrored by an equally dangerous equivalent trend in Christianity.

# WHY THE RELIGIOUS RIGHT FEELS IT HAS TO TAKE OVER THE WORLD

Well-organized and well-financed fundamentalist Christians are attempting to realign foreign and domestic policies around only their beliefs

THE RELIGIOUS RIGHT fundamentalists in the USA are reacting to the destabilization of religion in much the same way as the Islamic fundamentalists – they too are waging what some of them have told me they sincerely believe is a Holy War. What few people even within the USA fully appreciate is that these US Christian extremists are extremely well organized. Managerially they are a highly impressive body that in many ways is easier to understand if it is viewed as a large and radical political faction driven by religious dogma – rather than considered to be a religious sect alone.

From everything they have indicated to me, it appears that now 'godless communism' is no longer a threat, many of the leaders of this political movement want to break down the separation of church and state on which the US Constitution is based and instead forge what, when their goals are analyzed coldly, would effectively be a Christian version of Saudi Arabia. Based on their most voluble lobbying to US government, their key Domestic Policies can most easily be summarized as being Anti-Abortion, Anti-Gay and (with respect to things like stem-cell research and evolution) Anti-Science. Far less visible – more-moderate Christians point out – are the very issues that such a Jesus-led movement might have been expected to promote, such as helping the poor, curing the sick or protecting the most vulnerable.

But it is their Foreign Policy that is most relevant in terms of backlashes to the world economy. To put this in context, President Reagan as well as both President Bush Senior and Junior were all evangelical Protestants. Many of their close advisors and senior military personnel were also. This sect is not the most extremist interpretation of Christianity, but in company with Pentecostals and Fundamentalists it does believe in the Second Coming of Jesus. The detailed interpretations of how this will happen vary, but many literalists that I have spoken with believe that the Christian bible indicates that the Second Coming will involve a major war between Jews and Arabs first. Several of these literalists also interpret their Bible to mean that Israel has a divine right to Palestine. These same people have had – and continue to have – significant influence on US Middle-East foreign strategy.

Some of them sincerely believe that prior to the Second Coming they will experience the 'Rapture' during which (because they have been good Christians) they will be transported to heaven from where they will have a bandstand view of Armageddon as world-war brings the End of Days. They *look forward* to this time as the glorious vindication of their Faith. These beliefs are represented by officials at many levels of the US military and government. I have met some of them. As with extremist Islam, whatever the relative merits of such Christian fundamentalism, the views are deeply inflammatory when compared with the views of moderate Christians. Yet throughout the USA (and especially in Washington, DC) the Religious Right is campaigning and lobbying with a zeal and coordination and relentlessness that is currently unmatched by its more-tolerant critics. And – just like fundamentalist Islam – it is very well-funded.

But there is more than just US Protestant fundamentalism that is increasingly putting Christianity at risk of undermining itself – and with it, global stability. There is also pressure from other quarters. Pentecostalism is growing rapidly in developing countries although (as with Protestant fundamentalism) it is as far as I can see in fact primarily led and internationally-organized from within the USA. With its beliefs in the infallibility of the Bible, as well as modern-day 'speaking in tongues' and prophesy, it is becoming a potent adversary for both Protestantism and Catholicism. Indeed, many Pentecostals believe it is their evangelical destiny to 're-convert' more-moderate Christians in Europe and the USA back to the true faith. It is an inherently confrontational stance. It also risks being the genesis of a series of backlashes that rebound back and forth throughout the Christian world. Moreover, that dynamic will itself be exacerbated by yet another set of repercussions that are currently set to erupt within Christendom.

# WHY THE VATICAN HAS TO BE SO CONSERVATIVE IT RISKS SCHISM

## Roman Catholicism risks internal schisms that could escalate into widespread social disruption comparable to the Reformation

THE OPUS DEI group described by Dan Brown in *The Da Vinci Code* certainly exists, but in reality it is different in important respects to how it is portrayed in the book – not least in its relationship with the current pope, who is a strong supporter. However, although such highly-conservative branches of the Roman Catholic Church have come in for criticism, by far the greatest risks of global crises relating to 'extremist' Roman Catholicism unintentionally come from the Vatican itself.

As the oldest continually-operating major organization on the planet, the Holy See – or central government – carries Legacy Effects that for good and for bad are immensely hard to change. In many ways, that is the reason Roman Catholicism has remained so strong. But the institutions within Vatican City (the state, officially only set up in 1929, from which the ancient Holy See operates) are coming under unprecedented strains. The infallibility of the current pope Benedict XVI is being questioned not just on his handling of the international child-abuse scandals, but on fundamental issues such as women priests, abortion, gay-rights and contraception.

Recent criticisms have increasingly been encapsulated in deliberately-emotive language such as: 'The pope rules that no woman on earth is suitable to be a priest, all gay people are inherently sinners, a raped teenage girl cannot have an abortion, and a husband with HIV cannot wear a condom to save his wife from the disease.' Partly as a result, it seemed, in 2010 the pope apparently softened his views on the use of condoms – using in an interview the example that a gay male prostitute with HIV might use a condom to protect his client.

However, in November of the same year the Vatican clarified that although the interview had been reported accurately, nevertheless the pope's comments on the use of condoms were in reality his private views and not official teaching. Other aspects of the pope's interview confirmed that his overall attitudes to homosexuality and contraception were unchanged. This example symbolizes the extraordinary difficulty that the Vatican faces in shifting its orthodoxy. *Whatever* it says risks destabilizing things still further.

In consequence, albeit quietly, many of the pope's flock are simply ignoring him, as they did his predecessor. Even within Italy itself the birth-rate has dropped dramatically – which suggests either increased use of contraception or a major fertility problem. Other critics are not so quiet, and denounce the pope's official ruling against condoms as effectively condemning millions in the developing world to contracting HIV and AIDS, and they point out that condoms no more 'kill unborn babies' than abstinence does. As a result of issues like these, there is a growing chasm between what the pope says, and what many in his church actually do. That of itself is not a problem in terms of global disruption. The risk of backlash comes from how the Holy See, the pope and his immediate successors are most likely to respond to the growing challenge of papal authority.

## POWER OF THE VATICAN

The Vatican is inherently (and probably necessarily) extremely staid. It is in every way a truly awesome organization. It has survived for sixteen-hundred years. It is steeped in extraordinary history. It is permeated with magnificent treasures. And it has evolved in a way that makes it staunchly resilient to forced change. The hidden dynamics by which a new pope is elected by the Cardinals are very similar to how a partnership of attorneys selects its Managing Director or the UN elects the Secretary General. The winning candidate tends to be the one that most people can best live with – not necessarily the one most likely to shake things up. Even if – as with the current pope's predecessor John Paul II – the elected candidate has a prior reputation for progressive views, once within the orthodoxy of the Vatican he will have almost no further contact with reality other than as filtered and interpreted by the establishment that makes up the Vatican itself. Just like any new CEO of a huge corporation, a new pope finds himself severely isolated and dependent upon 'soundings' of those few granted an audience. Progressive thinking tends rapidly to become heavily regulated.

# RELIGION CRISES

The most likely response to threatened papal authority is therefore for the Vatican to respond as it often has – an appeal to the faithful to withstand the temptations of the modern world and hold true to the existing ineffable dogma of the one true church. Or risk eternal damnation. Yet given the inexorable and accelerating destabilization to the Catholic Church caused by social change, science, internal failings and well-informed questioning, this classic response will almost certainly fail.

Far more likely is that instead the existing cracks will broaden. Internal critics will argue that this indicates the need for radical reform. The response will be that it demands the exact opposite – unwavering resolve, unbending steadfastness, and above all unconditional Faith. Meanwhile, external critics will seek to leverage the cracks open still wider. The upper levels of the church risk slipping toward confusion, internal rebuke and schism (just as the Anglican church even today has begun to do). But the inner-workings of the Roman Catholic establishment are very much more deeply entrenched than those of Protestantism or Pentecostalism. And the preeminent roles of the Vatican and pope have no equivalent in the highly-decentralized organization structure of Islam.

As a result, if there is a fundamental schism in Roman Catholicism, it is potentially far more disruptive. The last time something comparable happened was during the 16th-century Reformation when self-described Reformers protested against the dogma of the Vatican and split off as the Protestant branch of Christianity. Today's growing backlash has the same potential for disruption. Without full alignment to its pope and Vatican dogma, the Roman Catholic Church risks anarchy. With full alignment, the Church risks perceived irrelevance. Either way, a crisis is forming that risks destabilizing Catholic communities across the world.

# END OF DAYS

The cumulative impact of a wide range of increasingly-desperate religious conflicts deeply threatens the world economy

FAITH-INFLAMED CONFLICTS have the potential to become bitter and corrosive struggles that affect many billions of people over the next several decades. The scenario is as follows. In the more 'Western' Islamic countries like Turkey, secular progressives will increasingly battle religious conservatives as individuals throughout the community develop a self-image that is confidently more Arab and more Moslem than before. As the repercussions of the Arab Spring Revolutions work their ways through the region, previously moderate countries such as Egypt will strain under similar tensions – as the well-organized Moslem Brotherhood gains new freedom to express itself. In strongly Christian countries such as the USA, exactly the same pattern of secular and moderate views straining against radical literalist (Jesus-based) dogma will play out as well. And as the spirit of the Arab Spring spreads south into sub-Saharan Africa, newly-liberated Christian states will suffer the same wrenching instability themselves.

As ever-more-extreme views become seeded in the mainstream, so widespread polarized-intolerance will become the norm as those holding different religious ideologies become inescapably entrenched into sectarian opposition. Israel will increasingly feel the stakes becoming higher and – despite pressures from the USA – will be tempted to move its strategy into an end-game and finally consolidate those territories it believes are its promised destiny. US hawks in the Religious Right may see this as the sign that something wonderful is about to happen, and depending on who then is the US President, they may even achieve some influence with the Commander in Chief. Arab nations are all-too-likely to interpret such developments as a real and present danger to Islam. As will those non-Arab converts – once perhaps relatively moderate but then persuaded to a more radical path.

Extremists will be willing to pay the ultimate sacrifice by martyring themselves if only they can detonate a back-pack 'dirty' nuclear device or biological weapon in the center of a major city. In many places, the War on Terror will then justify Martial Law – and in leading democracies, long-established human rights risk being waived in the name of national security. If Religion backlashes escalate much further, cities with significant Moslem, Christian or Jewish minorities will be vulnerable to a slew of violent riots and sectarian killings comparable to those that until recently continued for decades in Ireland. In some countries the religious conflicts would then deteriorate into civil wars.

Whole sub-continents such as India will potentially be torn apart as, despite the original intent behind splitting-off Pakistan, Muslim increasingly battles Hindu. China will simply not tolerate such internal religious disruption, but it will nevertheless suffer if its external markets are progressively lost to religious conflict. And throughout all of this, there will be the ever-present danger that a nuclear-capable regime (such as Pakistan) is pushed too far. And that the rest of the world is then forced to choose sides.

None of these globally-defined threats to economic security are made inevitable by the words attributed to a few extraordinary men millennia ago. The risks of escalation are nearly all being determined by individuals alive today. There are two groups, above all others, who are holding the international community to an increasingly dangerous path. Yet both groups are, in their own minds, well-intentioned. And neither group can be categorized according to its particular religion.

The first group is immensely influential. It is made up of charismatic, zealous, deeply-religious authority figures who interpret the words of the founders of their Faith in ways that are inescapably divisive. The second group is even more powerful, but does not realize the fact. This is the larger group of more-tolerant believers who, because they value free-speech and multiculturalism and religious tolerance (or sometimes because they value their own prosperity or position or physical security) *allow* their more-extreme fellow-believers to prosper amongst them – largely unchallenged.

# Growing polarization

## 21. BACKLASHES OF POLARIZED AND POLITICIZED RELIGIONS

**PRIORITY EXAMPLES OF WELL-ORGANIZED ATTEMPTS TO DOMINATE** — each risking an increasingly heightened threat of civil instability as well as backlash against the sect itself

HARD-LINE ISLAMISTS
*'Purge the world of Western-style depravity before it pollutes our women and children'*

RELIGIOUS RIGHT
*'Realign the foreign and domestic policy of Western nations around a literal reading of the Christian Bible'*

PENTACOSTALS
*'Actively re-convert more-moderate Christians in Europe and the USA back to the true faith'*

VATICAN ORTHODOXY
*'Resolutely oppose any tolerance of abortion, gay-rights or contraception in any society whatever its situation'*

# REDUCING THE THREATS:
# MIRRORED TOLERANCE

Religion crises need *Mirrored Tolerance* – members of a community can expect only as much tolerance as they grant others

MINIMIZING THE WORST unintended Religion backlashes has nothing to do with undermining religious faith and everything to do with modifying interpretation. From everything I can analyze, the best way to achieve this is to counter the dynamics that reinforce polarization and politicization. Global economic performance is under grave threat from the current destabilization of religions that in various countries is progressively leading to terrorism, perversion of political decision-making, social breakdown and war. But as I have highlighted, those dangers come from the more-fundamentalist and extremist interpretations of religions – especially those within Christianity and Islam. They are not inherently driven by the religions themselves.

In reality, all the major faiths (and a large number of minor ones as well) are broadly tolerant of people from other religions or those with no religion at all. That is certainly true of Islam, which tends to be far less tolerant of Moslems who convert to another religion than it generally is of the members of that rival religion as a whole. Indeed, despite the exclusionist way the term is often used today, Mohammed's original 'Islamic Community' *included* Christians, Jews and Pagans.

Christianity has a built-in tendency actively to try to convert people, which necessarily brings risks of disruption. But primarily, the risks of Religion Crises that constitute threats to the world economy come from *human interpretation* of the words attributed to religious founders not so often from what those religious founders explicitly said. That is very helpful. It means that in principle the threats to the religions – and to the international community as a whole – can be managed. Although, from my analysis, I find that relatively little can be done from the outside, multiple threats can largely be averted by those *within* the religions themselves.

# Growing polarization

To do so, the more-moderate members of religious communities (in alignment with society as a whole) must adopt the guiding principle of *Mirrored Tolerance* – members of a community can expect only as much tolerance of their ideas as they themselves offer others. In other words, rather than all-or-nothing approaches (tolerating any religious interpretations that are within a threshold of acceptability), communities should use graduated responses to dampen growing extremism far earlier.

## AVOIDING AN ALL-OR-NOTHING APPROACH

The reasons for adopting such an approach relate to the system-dynamics detailed in the subchapter explaining *How intolerance and dogmatism lead to polarization* (page 262). Specifically, although there is a widespread belief that communities thrive better if they always remain tolerant, that is not what I repeatedly found in my investigations. Instead, as already explained, what actually happens is that if an overall community remains consistently tolerant – even of members of the community who are *intolerant* – then the intolerant faction begins to bully those around it.

It grows. It increasingly tramples over more-tolerant members of the society that it does not agree with and that it considers weak. It threatens and cajoles people not to get in its way, not to get involved, to stick with a habitual response of 'tolerance'. And after a while, the more-tolerant members of the community find they are no longer in a position to take a stand even though by then they want to. Adopting a classic all-or-nothing approach to tolerance along the lines of 'Whatever people say or do is OK provided it is not utterly extreme,' tends to mean that a relatively-liberal community leaves it too late to protect itself against extremist elements. By the time the intolerance becomes intolerable to enough people, it may also be unstoppable. That is what happened in Berlin in the 1930s.

Mirrored Tolerance breaks that cycle. It offers a far-more-graduated response that pushes back against localized intolerance in a highly focused way – a bit like immediately damping down flying embers from an open-fire rather than waiting to see if they catch the hearth-rug alight. What is more, if previously-extreme behavior becomes more tolerant, those who have changed are automatically 'rewarded' by their community by being given greater license. If they revert, so does the broader community. Developing the community-wide habit of consistent application of Mirrored Tolerance in effect immunizes a society against extremism.

## INTOLERANCE OF INTOLERANCE

It is worth noting that the concept of 'intolerance of intolerance' is not in any way a paradox. In the English language the word 'intolerance' has two meanings, and a different meaning is in fact used for each of the occurrences in the phrase. The first meaning (always followed by the word 'of') is an *unwillingness to endure something*. The second meaning is a *lack of respect for practices and beliefs other than the person's own*. So in reality the phrase 'intolerance of intolerance' is shorthand for *unwillingness to endure a lack of respect from someone for practices and beliefs other than their own* – which is not paradoxical whatsoever. Those who claim otherwise are merely playing word-games.

## EMBOLDENING MODERATE-FAITH MEMBERS TO PUSH BACK

When it comes to religious extremism, Mirrored Tolerance works far more effectively from *within* a religion. Those outside a given faith-community certainly have a need to express their views. But they risk being portrayed by those they are holding to account as arrogant, racist or as attacking religious freedom. Only more-moderate members within the religion itself are immune to being rendered powerless in this way – because they alone can in effect ask fellow-believers the test-question of page 259: 'Would our founder be proud of us if he were still alive today?' It is progressive and liberal members of religions (who by inclination are typically *tolerant*) that importantly need to stand up and push back against intolerance.

By doing so, they will not only save their religion from greater internal disruption and damage, but they will also diminish the risk of broader damage to the wider international community and of a resultant backlash against their given sect or their overall faith or even a backlash against formal religion as a whole. In the spirit of Mirrored Tolerance, moderate Islamic clerics must be encouraged to issue provocative fatwa vociferously condemning suicide bombing and terrorism. Progressive Roman Catholics must continue to wrestle with two-millennia of dogma and encourage the Vatican to listen to them afresh. Liberal Anglicans must continue to attack Religious-Right hatred and denounce fundamentalist bigotry.

## FATWA FOR PEACE

Ever since 1989, when Ayatollah Khomeini (the Supreme Leader of Iran) issued a fatwa against the author Salman Rushdie for his fourth novel *The Satanic Verses*, many people in the West consider that 'a fatwa' is something akin to an Islamic death-sentence. But it is in fact merely a religious ruling. Some fatwa are exactly what the West, and everywhere else, needs to secure peace and an end to religious conflict. As an example, in 2010 the authoritative Islamic scholar Dr. Muhammad Tahir ul-Qadri issued a 600-page religious ruling (in other words, a fatwa) that came down unequivocally against extremism and terrorism. Born in Pakistan, Dr. Qadri also strongly argues for integration of Islamic communities into foreign cultures.

More generally, moderate religious leaders worldwide must – to a far greater extent than till now – choose to stand up against the demands of their more-extreme colleagues. And they must find the courage to withstand any threats by those colleagues that they will split away (or force the moderates to split away) if their demands are not met or if progressive measures are adopted that they do not like. Under such circumstances, if those with intolerant views refuse to moderate them then despite all the disruption to the religious community it is nevertheless better that a religion splits *in a relatively controlled way* than that its more-liberal leaders – by giving into blackmail – demonstrate that they have lost faith even in their own beliefs. That route does not even lead to the lowest common denominator of attitudes. It leads to domination by the most fanatical. Appeasement of intolerance risks being no more spiritual or harmonious than actively condoning bullying.

## TAKING THE INITIATIVE IN COUNTERING INTOLERANCE

Despite the disproportionate impact of those within a given religion exercising Mirrored Tolerance, there is also an important role for politicians and legislators. Governments need to be proactive in countering religiously-fuelled intolerance, for instance by adopting policies to integrate self-isolating communities into broader society.

Governments have a *responsibility* progressively to intervene in religions, with greater intervention reserved for those sects whose intolerance poses a greater risk of social disruption. Even fully-secular governments with legislative responsibilities to protect freedom-of-religion can no longer fulfill their primary obligation of national security without proactively getting involved.

Religious leaders must help governments do whatever they can to support those within religions who are exercising Mirrored Tolerance. But it is also crucial that governments themselves extend the principle of Mirrored Tolerance to encompass policies relating to integration of religious communities into broader society. This is especially important for immigrant populations. Without, for example, being able to speak the language of their adopted country, it is extremely difficult for immigrants to integrate with a broader group. But almost as important as accepting the language of their new home is that immigrants also accept its broad values – including, for instance, the equality of women and gays.

These are in no way irreligious values. But they are values that are incompatible with various intolerant interpretations of religion. If immigrants, whatever their ethnicity or nationality, cannot accept the basic values of the country that they elect to move to, then the State has an obligation to evaluate the potential long-term escalating impact of their presence – especially if they are likely to remain unintegrated other than with those who think at they do.

## DISTINGUISHING ATTACKS *ON* RELIGION AND *BY* RELIGION

In order to facilitate Mirrored Tolerance, legislation must be flexible enough to interpret 'attacks against religion or race' quite differently to situations where society-at-large (or maybe a subset within that society) seeks protection against increasingly-threatening human interpretations of religious faith or against deliberately politicized faith. In any community, basic rights often conflict. Agreeing to be a member of a given community means accepting a trade-off between personal rights and the rights of the community as a whole. It means accepting that your individual actions may have wider consequences for which you are still responsible – and will be held accountable.

Religions are no different in this. For example, the right of individuals to believe or not believe in one or more supernatural beings does not imply the right to impose those beliefs on others. Freedom of Religion is not Freedom of Imposition. And even Religious Freedom in practice must these days reflect both civil liberty *and* social stability. When it comes down to it, to maintain overall stability in a multicultural community, the laws of the State must always dominate over potentially-conflicting religious rulings – whether on rights to family planning, abortion, female equality, gay equality or the acceptance of scientific proof. Even the rights of parents to bring their children up as they see fit do not automatically supersede the rights of children to expect that society will protect them from intellectual, just as much as physical, abuse.

It only exacerbates threats to economic and social stability if governments attempt to duck these sorts of issues. In the modern world, many politicians try extremely hard to avoid suggesting that there even are any downsides to Religion – at least in their own country. For instance, in some European cities with unintegrated Moslem populations, concerns about social unrest are usually positioned in terms of racism or nationalism. That is potentially misleading. In those cases, the root-cause of any social misalignment often rests less in race as in religion and the associated stereotypes that each community holds of the other. Indeed, as indicated by the nationality of recent suicide bombers, it was their religious convictions not their ethnicity that drove them (at least to try) to detonate themselves.

## ENCOURAGING SCIENCE TO COUNTER NARROW-MINDEDNESS

The scientific establishment must itself use Mirrored Tolerance when dealing with religiously-based attacks against facts-based evidence or potentially-vital research. There are growing numbers of situations – such as teaching Evolution (and science-education generally), genetic research, embryonic stem-cell research – where it is increasingly critical that Science pushes back against religious dogma.

To do so, scientists must stand up to be counted, and themselves adhere to the principle of Mirrored Tolerance in their attitude to religious claims. Yet despite what many faith-leaders sometimes suggest, scientists taking a tough stance on some issues will not only minimize backlashes against Science but in the long run actually *help* religions minimize potential backlashes against themselves. As an example, teaching thinly-disguised Creationism in schools as a legitimate alternative to Evolution is unsustainable – not to Science but to Religion. In the short-term, faith-schools that nominally teach Evolution but persist in trying to persuade children that there is actually a better explanation in an ancient holy text, on the surface appear only to undermine the Scientific Method (and maybe risk stifling the healthy skepticism that should be encouraged in any child – or adult – when someone in authority tells them something is true without offering analyzable evidence).

## BAD DESIGN

The light receptors in the eyes of all vertebrates are in effect the 'wrong way around'. As a result, the optic nerve carrying their signals has to pass through the array of light receptors to get to the brain – causing a blind spot. In contrast, the apparently similar eye of an invertebrate such as an octopus has no blind spot because the nerves (far more 'sensibly') approach the light receptors from behind. Similarly, the laryngeal nerve in mammals runs from the brain to the nearby larynx (the voice-box). However, the route of half of this particular nerve happens to take it the 'wrong' side of a ligament next to the heart. In early stages of evolution that made little difference because without a neck it is still an almost-direct route for both halves of the nerve. However, because evolution cannot retrace its steps and correct 'mistakes', as necks got longer so did the circuitous route of the part of the laryngeal nerve that was caught around the heart. In a giraffe, that part of the nerve runs from the brain, all the way down the extremely-long neck, wraps around the heart-ligament, and then climbs all the way back up the extremely-long neck to finally join its other half – a hand's-breadth from where they both started. There is absolutely no 'intelligence' in *that* design. Quite the opposite.

But in the long-term, that stance will ultimately prove damaging not to Science but to Religion – as well as to Education and to those governments that permit, let alone fund, children to be indoctrinated with dogma that is in reality fully discredited. Whatever science teachers in faith-schools suggest, in truth there is now completely-overwhelming proof for Evolution by natural selection. As scientific discovery exponentially advances, to claim that some of the irreversible 'mistakes' that have resulted over eons – such as the vestigial limbs inside snakes, the completely unnecessary blind-spot in the eyes of vertebrates, and the absurd route of the laryngeal-nerve in giraffes – are nevertheless a function of Intelligent Design risks being seen as increasingly untenable.

Although faith-leaders will continue to provide divine explanations for whatever they consider appropriate, the reality is that when those answers deeply conflict with well-established science then the credibility of those faith-leaders, and their religions themselves, become increasingly vulnerable to instability. The longer such a situation continues the more that all parties will suffer, and the more that children caught in the middle will be poorly served and potentially will become disillusioned with their religion.

## WATCHING THOSE WITH POTENTIAL CONFLICTS OF INTEREST

Finally, it is very important that governments – and the media and the general public – pay extreme attention to potential conflicts of interest for those more powerful members of the Establishment in influential countries who hold fundamentalist religious beliefs. Government (and society as a whole) must apply Mirrored Tolerance to deeply-religious politicians, military leaders and other important members of the Establishment such as the judiciary. In an increasingly multi-faith, scientific and secular world, Spirituality is different from Faith. And ethics is not the sole province of religion.

## IMPROVING ON THE GOLDEN RULE

A surprising amount of ethics actually distils from the so-called Golden Rule reflected in many religions (such as Christianity, Islam and Judaism) of only doing to other people what you would want them to do to you. An even better formulation of this idea though comes in Confucianism, which counsels not forcing on other people what you would not desire for yourself. This improves on the Golden Rule by incorporating the more-sophisticated concept that others may not want what you want.

The more that any faction preaches something different to that, the greater the risk to collective social order. Politicians, the military and the legal system are not immune to the undue influence of a particular religion or of religion as a whole. And politics linked with law combined with religion and couched in terms of patriotism is a corrosive combination. These days, the nationalist fervor it stirs can all-too-easily lead a country, and then the world, into danger – ironically, in direct contravention to the primary obligation of the State. The government, and the public, needs to hold such members of the Establishment in check.

A still-stronger reaction is needed against those officials of key nations who actually view international politics as an opportunity for 'their' religion to win over others. On the surface, their attitude merely appears a rather naive and arrogant assumption. But for two reasons, it is more dangerous than that. Firstly, trying to get one religion to win-out against rival religions (or, against the 'ungodly') completely misses the reality of current circumstances. Given the exponential trends impacting developments in artificial-intelligence, nanotechnology and life-sciences, the international community has about thirty years before, one way or another, things change out of all recognition. *No religion has time to 'win' in only thirty years.* But they – and everyone else – could all lose if religious fanaticism ultimately led, as an extreme example, to nuclear war.

The second reason that some fundamentalist officials are a threat is more worrying. As for example highlighted in the subchapter on page 274 about *Why the Religious Right feels it has to take over the world*, there are some senior figures of some very-powerful bodies (including, in my own experience, certain individuals in upper-echelons of the Pentagon) for whom winning the religious battle does not mean that their religion dominates over the others because everyone converts. Winning to them means worshiping, in this case, the Christian god at the time of the Rapture, when because of their piety they get transported to heaven before everyone else and get to watch all those who backed the 'wrong' religions being destroyed.

The signal that this great event is imminent is, so some of them insist to me, growing global chaos leading to war in the Middle East. Unfortunately for those pursuing a more-diplomatic solution, international unrest to such believers is not necessarily something to avoid. Those religious fundamentalists (certainly including Christian fundamentalists) that hold positions of military or government authority – especially those who, for instance, openly look forward to the End of Days – need to be recognized as having conflicts of interest that pose direct potential threats to national (and global) security. They need to be tightly monitored.

Ironically, right at the opposite end of the spectrum of Beliefs About Existence, other developments also need to be tightly monitored. Here there are threats of equally-devastating backlashes as there are from Religion. Part of the irony in this is that those backlashes are building as a result of the very same supertrend that is destabilizing Religion and escalating the risks of its backlashes in the first place. I am referring, of course, to High-Tech itself.

# CHAPTER SUMMARY
# RELIGION CRISES

**Inevitably-escalating instabilities within some world faiths are generating Religion backlashes that further destabilize the religions as well as whole economies and require Mirrored Tolerance as a counter-measure**

Rigidity is deeply-embedded into the structure of successful world religions – making them both resilient and very hard to change

Social changes, scientific discoveries, failings in faith leadership, and access to conflicting insights are rapidly destabilizing religions
- *Well-communicated social changes across the globe increasingly are raising alternatives that people previously were never exposed to*
- *Exponentially-growing scientific revelation has now encroached on every area (including morals) that previously was the province of religions*
- *Proliferating communication media have enabled fundamental critiquing of how religious leaders behave and of the advice they give*
- *Well-educated believers with unprecedented informal access to historical and other academic evaluations of religion are increasingly confused*

Actions by some sects to bolster rigidity through intolerance and dogmatism are polarizing – and so further destabilizing – their religions

Growing polarization in (especially) Islam and Christianity is now causing extreme reactions that threaten the economic stability of many states
- *Some Moslem authority figures are revolted by 'Western-style depravity' that they view as an attack on Islam that must be repulsed*
- *Well-organized and well-financed fundamentalist Christians are attempting to realign foreign and domestic policies around only their beliefs*
- *Roman Catholicism risks internal schisms that could escalate into widespread social disruption comparable to the Reformation*
- *The cumulative impact of a wide range of increasingly-desperate religious conflicts deeply threatens the world economy*

# Chapter summary

Religion crises need MIRRORED TOLERANCE – members of a community can expect only as much tolerance as they grant others

- *Rather than all-or-nothing approaches (tolerating any religious interpretations that are within a threshold of acceptability) use graduated responses to dampen growing extremism far earlier*
- *Above all other groups embolden moderate members of faith communities to apply Mirrored Tolerance in standing up to more-extreme members of their own faith*
- *Ensure governments are proactive in countering religiously-fuelled intolerance – such as adopting policies to integrate self-isolating communities into broader society*
- *Refine legislation so that it is flexible enough to distinguish between attacks on religious-freedom and society protecting itself from dangerous religious politicization*
- *Encourage the scientific establishment to use Mirrored Tolerance when dealing with religiously-based attacks against facts-based evidence or potentially-vital research*
- *Pay extreme attention to potential conflicts of interest within key nations of those more powerful members of the Establishment who hold fundamentalist religious beliefs*

## 22. HOW HIGH-TECH RELIGION RISKS SYSTEMIC CRISES

# BEFORE

## SUCCESSFUL WORLD RELIGIONS
### Very resilient BUT very hard to change

- Faith immune to domination by Power or Reason
- Founder's ideas can only be interpreted but never changed
- Ideas are passed on to children by their authority figures
- Members of a given sect prefer being surrounded by fellow-members
- The greater someone's perceived faith the more others respect them

## DESTABILIZING INFLUENCES

| SOCIAL CHANGES | SCIENTIFIC REVELATIONS | FAILURES IN FAITH-LEADERSHIP | CONFUSING INSIGHTS |
|---|---|---|---|
| Historical religious monopoly on morals and behavior no longer | The 'Scientific Method' requires testable hypotheses in a way Faith never can | Dominant religions were historically respected because of their key role in the greater community | Believers suffer a drip-drip feed of reported errors of judgment by supposedly infallible faith-leaders |
| Moral attitudes and State laws have transformed since 1960s (e.g., sex, women, blacks, gays, pornography) | Religious dogma on the centrality of the Earth (or at least mankind) overwhelmingly disproved | It seems 'in the greater public interest' that no one tarnishes the reputation of a crucial institution | Negative facts are particularly undermining when in contexts that are not even religious (let alone anti-religious) |
| Improved living standards mean less perceived sacrifice to 'break free' from the security of religion | Science is now 'encroaching' on every explanation of creation, existence, life and even morals | External authority figures (police, politicians, media chiefs) may choose to 'hush up' damaging stories | Believers interested in adding to their religious knowledge end up confused: e.g., |
| Diminished automatic deference to authority | Faith-dependent explanations of 'inconsistent' scientific observations are exponentially difficult to maintain: e.g., | If victims of abuse come forward they may not be believed, may be discredited or may be silenced | • Elements of sacred texts appear in earlier very-different religions |
| Lack of correlation between lawlessness and increasing secularization | | | • Jesus was not born in 0 AD or at Christmas and the word 'virgin' may be a mistranslation |

- Increasing contact with other religions (including rival monotheisms)

- Detailed media exposure to the intense suffering from natural catastrophes 'allowed by god'

'God created all life at once'
BUT fossils reveal other life
'Some species died in Noah's Flood'
BUT evolution explains life changing
'Evolution shows Intelligent Design'
BUT evolution is full of cul-de-sacs and absurdly-inefficient designs and DNA is full of junk

'Conspiracies of Silence' can emerge that *no central leader controls* (or may even be aware of)

Interconnected modern society makes it increasingly likely that institutional malpractice will be exposed chaotically

- Textual analysis reveals some 'divinely-dictated' texts have multiple authors
- Passages declaring male same-sex acts as 'abominations' say the same about eating shellfish – but lesbianism does *not* seem excluded

## RESPONSE DEPENDS UPON THE INHERENT PHILOSOPHY OF A RELIGIOUS SECT

### *AFTER*

Inherently *tolerant and inclusive* sects **ADAPT**

- Liberal Islam, e.g., Turkey
- Liberal Christianity, e.g., Church of England
- Mainstream Buddhism
- Mainstream Hinduism

Inherently *intolerant and exclusive* sects **TRY TO DOMINATE**

CAUSING

**POLARIZATION AND POLITICIZATION**

## PRIORITY EXAMPLES OF WELL-ORGANIZED ATTEMPTS TO DOMINATE
## — each risking an increasingly heightened threat risk of civil instability

HARD-LINE ISLAMISTS
'Purge the world of Western-style depravity before it pollutes our women and children'

RELIGIOUS RIGHT
'Realign the foreign and domestic policy of Western nations around a literal reading of the Christian Bible'

PENTACOSTALS
'Actively re-convert more-moderate Christians in Europe and the USA back to the true faith'

VATICAN ORTHODOXY
'Resolutely oppose any tolerance of abortion, gay-rights or contraception in any society whatever its situation'

# HIGH-TECH CRISES overview

In addition to triggering crises in otherwise-benign global trends the four established exponential trends in High-Tech generate crises directly and require Pre-emptive Recovery as a counter-measure

- The combined dominance of the four established High-Tech trends makes the global economy vulnerable to any disruption to them

- Each of the four established High-Tech trends carries major risks to economic stability in its own right

- The riskiest High-Tech crises arise from unintended consequences throughout the world economy escalating too fast and being too interconnected for conventional responses to work

- High-Tech crises need PRE-EMPTIVE RECOVERY – devising responses to risks as part of the overall development-process

*Threats of backlashes to: I T, TELECOMS and PHARMACEUTICALS*

*VULNERABILITY...*

*... CYBERATTACK...*

*... BIOTERRORISM...*

*... ESCALATING UNINTENDED CONSEQUENCES...*

# HIGH-TECH

# CRISES

# GLOBAL VULNERABILITY TO DISRUPTIONS IN HIGH-TECH

The combined dominance of the four established High-Tech trends makes the global economy vulnerable to any disruption to them

UP TILL NOW this global story of hidden consequences has focused on how High-Tech, and all the wealth of by-products and services that it stimulates, is interacting with the other four giants of our world civilization: Capitalism, Industrialization, Population and Religion. As you have seen, even just those camouflaged interconnections risk stirring up unintended backlashes that are deeply destabilizing. But, inevitably, in the intertwined global-forest of modern civilization, nothing is in isolation. The backlashes themselves interact. Over the next two main chapters we will explore what happens when those turbulences come together and reinforce each other. And we will start at the very heart of the vortex – High-Tech itself.

## DISRUPTION BUT NOT ECONOMIC DESTABILIZATION

On the surface, the High-Tech supertrend seems very-largely beneficial. Even when you consider those of its largely-hidden components that have become deeply established – Digitization, Networking, Miniaturization and Simulation – they each seem broadly benign. There are certainly likely to be many side-effects, ranging across everything from a Surveillance Society (largely operated by the general public, not government) all the way to some people becoming addicted to virtual reality. Many of these risks are well documented. But none of them seems a major threat to the world economy.

Even when broader implications of the overall supertrend are considered, the risks still do not seem unduly alarming. Certainly, there will be substantial social strains caused by the amount of change. And politicians, planners, indeed nearly all of the population, are likely massively to underestimate just how fast those changes will come – after all, human intuition just does not seem to be able to grasp the reality of sustained exponential acceleration. Indeed, there may well be too few people in politics and the media that have sufficient scientific backgrounds even to grasp the detail of what is fundamentally going on anyway.

However, although stresses in society may cause real suffering for some, in reality the disruption will probably be no more radical that when at various times over the last few centuries peasants around the world have migrated from their farms to newly-forming cities at the start of an Industrial Revolution. Historically, as pointed out in the chapter on Capitalism Crises, whole rural communities sometimes collapsed as a result. Yet despite such local devastation, overall the march of progress has tended to be welcomed by all levels of society.

## WHEN 'HIGH-TECH' WAS STEAM

The disruption of the shift in working practices caused by the Industrial Revolution in England during the second half of the 18th-century is well documented and makes disconcerting reading. Imagine what it felt like for teenagers and younger, brought up to help wherever they could on their parents' remote farms, instead to be told to stand in one place in an unbelievably noisy production shop and repeat the same simple action every few seconds for up to fourteen hours a day, seven days a week, for almost fifty-two full weeks a year.

High-Tech will similarly favor some national economies over others. But that of itself does not threaten the world economy as a whole – quite to the contrary. In harsh economic terms it is merely an example of market forces optimizing production (albeit in an inherently short-term fashion). It is only when we examine the hidden process that sustains the underlying exponential growth of High-Tech that the first severe globally-defined threat to economic stability becomes clear.

## RUNNING UP A DOWN ESCALATOR THAT IS ACCELERATING

Since integrated circuits were first commercialized in the 1960s, their complexity for the same price has grown exponentially. For many decades the self-fulfilling prophesy of Moore's Law (the number of transistors on a chip doubles every two years) has become embedded into how the whole global economy operates. What is more, High-Tech is also driven by other largely-unrelated explosive trends relating to everything from the capacity of hard-disk drives to the size of flat-screen monitors. Throughout the world economy, expectations of new games, new computers, new business services, new industrial processes – all depend on the continued growth of these other exponential trends as much as on Moore's Law. The whole of modern civilization is geared to each of these High-Tech trends continuing. Many, many business strategies depend on it. As a result, reinforced by all their shared incentives and the global momentum that has built across five decades, it is a very good bet that High-Tech's exponential trends will almost certainly continue throughout the next thirty years. Almost certainly. But not definitely.

The High-Tech supertrend carries a truly unpleasant sting in its tail. The fact is that although any really deeply-embedded aspect of society is very difficult to change, if it ever *does* change then most times that results in widespread trauma and disruption – simply because it is so interconnected with the rest of civilization. High-Tech is an extreme example. If for any reason the world economy *cannot* keep the supertrend on a fundamentally exponential trajectory for the next few decades, then there will be dire consequences. This supertrend is no longer just a 'nice to have'. It has become the essential heartbeat of the world's infrastructure; if it falters over the next thirty years, then our whole global economy risks going into cardiac arrest. Even if Moore's Law alone stops its explosive growth, every other associated explosion risks shutting down. All the global industries whose business plans depend on the continued escalation of High-Tech will become extremely vulnerable. Yet no one will know the full extent of the crisis.

Pension funds will not know which of their shareholdings are at highest risk. Bankers will not know which of their business-loans are in greatest danger of default. Global infrastructure will degrade immeasurably because existing financial systems will simply implode. The loss of confidence caused by concern over sub-prime loans – which kicked off the economic collapse of 2008-9 – is a minor trigger in comparison. Credit crunches (in other words, lending institutions making borrowing far harder or even impossible) typically result from a sustained period of overenthusiastic lending related to a growing bubble that eventually bursts resulting in far too many unanticipated bad debts. However, the High-Tech supertrend is a 'bubble' that has been growing for so many decades that most bankers have never experienced life without it.

For them, lending based on the implicit assumption of High-Tech's continued growth is simply business as usual – and there is hardly any loan made throughout their career that could be guaranteed immune from going toxic if that growth ended. Even without any other contributing factors, a radical failure in just Moore's Law (not to mention the other interconnected exponential explosions) could directly lead to extremely serious consequences. The unpalatable reality is that even though it is a progressively insurmountable challenge to sustain the High-Tech supertrend, it has become vital to keep doing so. As explained in the subchapter about *Changing faster than the competition* (page 34), we are running up a Down escalator. But it is worse than that. The escalator is *accelerating*.

## No choice but to keep running

As already explored in the chapter on Population Crises, there are several billion too many people on Earth to be able to survive without a properly functioning global economy. For the next several decades at least, there is no longer an option to 'live the simple life' and nevertheless sustain a massive global population without the benefits of accelerating High-Tech and all the industries now dependent upon its exponential progress.

In the medium-term, countries simply could not survive trying to Stop the escalator – even if it were *possible* to stop it within a reasonable time without devastating repercussions. And it is not. Fortunately, the global economy has a little slack built in. Most people will hardly notice if Moore's Law slows slightly from Intel's current commitment of every two years. It would be a bit unpleasant, but certainly not catastrophic, if it slowed by as much as 50% and only doubled every three years (more likely may be that the growth trend continues much as at present, but there is a longer wait between each new design). And it will not cause too much disruption if the other associated exponential explosions also slow a bit.

The reason is that 'slightly-slower exponential' is still exponential. The progression still keeps doubling. Ten doublings bring more than a thousand-fold increase. Another ten doublings makes it over a million-fold increase. That sort of progress will always race ahead of everything else that merely progresses in a linear fashion. That is what makes the High-

Tech supertrend unique and so dominant. There are simply no other major influences that can keep up.

With that said, rather than accept the traumatic consequences of the supertrend-escalator even slowing a bit too rapidly, governments are far more likely to commit unprecedented funding simply to keep it moving. After all, the benefits of the High-Tech supertrend over the next thirty years are so exceptional that no informed governments will risk losing them. But that means governments will in reality have to keep their checkbooks permanently open. The harsh truth is that the global economy is now utterly dependent upon keeping the High-Tech supertrend exploding. Almost whatever its continued success costs the international community, the cost of it failing would be even higher.

Conceptually the logic that politicians will quite-correctly follow is straightforward: If for whatever reason the international community is unable to maintain a fundamentally-exponential growth of factors such as computer complexity, internet size, miniaturization capability and high-capacity data-storage, then the global economy risks collapsing under a flurry of backlashes. Not only will every electronics-related business suffer, so too will every form of modern manufacturing, every trade that depends on customers buying 'the latest model', every branch of science, technology and medicine, and every institution, shareholder and pensioner that is in any way financially involved with any of those organizations.

Despite the solely-optimistic light in which it is tempting to portray it, there is a shadow-side to High-Tech that is progressively High-Risk just as much as it is High-Return. And as we will now examine, in addition to the threat of massive indirect crises if High-Tech ever failed, it also enhances the threat of *direct* crises the longer that it succeeds.

## 23. HOW DISRUPTIONS TO HIGH-TECH RISK CRISES

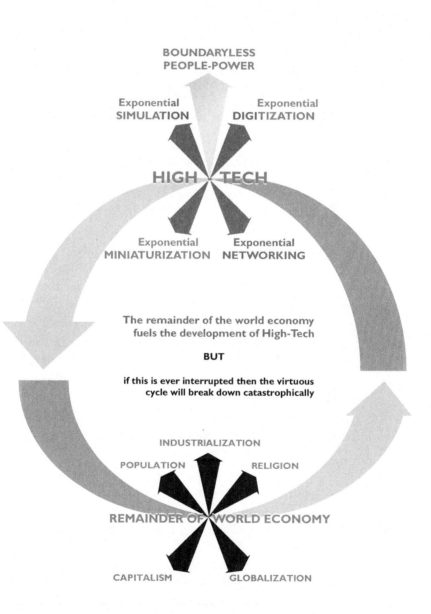

BOUNDARYLESS
PEOPLE-POWER

Exponential
SIMULATION

Exponential
DIGITIZATION

HIGH-TECH

Exponential
MINIATURIZATION

Exponential
NETWORKING

The remainder of the world economy
fuels the development of High-Tech

**BUT**

**if this is ever interrupted then the virtuous
cycle will break down catastrophically**

INDUSTRIALIZATION

POPULATION

RELIGION

REMAINDER OF WORLD ECONOMY

CAPITALISM

GLOBALIZATION

# THE NEAR-TOTAL DEFENSELESSNESS OF MODERN SOCIETY

## Although many perceived risks of overdependence on Digitization are unfounded there is a severe vulnerability to technologies such as Pulse Bombs

THE MAJORITY OF negative side-effects caused by the Digitization of society are unpleasant rather than dangerous. For example, people will understandably feel exposed and largely defenseless against an environment where everything is potentially 'on the record'. Even today, politicians and police are increasingly commonly being caught unawares by mobile phones used as video and audio recorders. Soon most people, most of the time, will learn to be far more guarded in what they say to whom. On balance that is probably a shame, but it is not disastrous.

Similarly, although High-Tech is likely to minimize some social divides it will exaggerate others. But it is not obvious why this will be any more or less acceptable than at present. Some members of society will continue to labor rather-mindlessly in relatively-disordered factories that do not justify heavy robotization, while other people who may be no more intelligent (but, for instance, got more qualifications at school) will work with computerized systems that greatly amplify their intellectual capabilities and earning potential.

Equally divisive will be robotic agricultural equipment that suits arable-farming but not the relative disorder of livestock. These types of changes will represent deep shifts in how society formally and informally values people's contributions. Many of the inequalities that result will not feel fair. But then again, for a lot of people today, neither is the fact that many city bankers earn a hundred times the salary of a typically-far-more-valued hospital nurse (as indeed, to be fair, also do many sports stars, pop stars and film stars, none of which may work as long hours as the star bankers). In the future, as now, social divides will not of themselves pull social-order down, although they may be painfully visible.

# Risks to economic stability

However, there is a far-more-hidden side-effect of the Digitization trend that has the potential to bring whole nations to their knees in a number of quite different ways: The more a country electronically digitizes, the more unintentionally vulnerable it becomes to crises that result from deliberate attack.

## ELECTROMAGNETIC PULSES

A major vulnerability is caused by dependence on microchips. When an artificial satellite is launched into space it is typically placed in a Low Earth Orbit only a few hundred miles (or kilometers) above the Earth. There are currently hundreds of active satellites – and thousands of inactive ones – all now circulating at this sort of distance above the globe. Most are communication, observation or navigation satellites, but the payload of some of them is completely classified. What is more, no single country knows what all of the classified satellites passing overhead contain. That is particularly relevant because of an experiment that the USA conducted half a century ago.

On 9th July 1962, the 'Starfish Prime' test involved the launch of a rocket into space carrying as its payload a 1.4 megaton thermonuclear hydrogen-bomb that was detonated 400 kilometers (250 miles) above the mid-Pacific. That is the height of many modern day satellites. Like all thermonuclear bombs, as a by-product of the explosion, it created a strong electromagnetic pulse. Fifty years ago, that pulse took out about thirty strings of street lights in Hawaii – around a thousand miles away.

The modern digitized circuits in everything from surgical operating theatres, automobiles and power-grids, to communication devices, computers and commercial-aircraft flight systems are far more susceptible to electromagnetic pulses that the old-style lighting controls in Hawaii were. And it is now recognized that a strong pulse generated by a satellite as it passed over the USA, or Europe, or China, or India, would be sufficient to create a power surge in every unprotected digital circuit across the whole continent. It is impractical to protect even all military equipment sufficiently to avoid damage. Yet in a fraction of a second, every unshielded digital circuit in line of sight of the pulse-generator would permanently stop working. For practical reasons, almost *all* existing commercial and privately-owned electronic circuits are completely unshielded from major electromagnetic pulses. The reality is that there are no plans for them to be suitably shielded in the future either.

These days there are also ways of generating a powerful electromagnetic pulse without detonating a nuclear device – indeed one may have been used above Baghdad during the 2003 invasion of Iraq. They are much less powerful pulses than from thermonuclear weapons – but these new devices can be made far smaller and lighter. In due course they will be accessible to rogue states and well-funded terrorist groups. Consider the eventual impact of destroying every electronic circuit in every automobile, subway train, phone, power-supply, building and electrical device in downtown Manhattan, or the City of London, or the financial district in Tokyo. Defense Departments and Security Services are well aware of the increasing digital vulnerability of their civilian hardware-infrastructure. Few medium-level politicians (let alone the general public) are even aware that there is an issue

# IT AND TELECOM NETWORKS UNDER GROWING CYBERATTACK

Many risks from Networking are already well-addressed but Cyberattack remains a major threat because of acute vulnerabilities in civilian targets

WITH CIVILIZATION BECOMING increasingly dependent on GPS navigation, for everything from Sat Nav systems to social-networking devices, some worry that the global economy is overly-dependent on the US-controlled network of satellites that makes it all possible – not least because that system was designed so that service can selectively be turned off or distorted in any chosen territory.

## HOW SAT NAV REVEALS THE LEADERS IN HIGH-TECH

In many ways, the six socio-political zones (China, Europe, India, Japan, Russia, USA) that are developing independent satellite navigation systems reveal the *true* leaders in High-Tech – and therefore those who will have an increasingly dominant role in the global economy. The list makes an interesting contrast to the largely historically-determined members of the group of industrialized nations represented by their heads of government at the important G8 Summits – Canada, France, Germany, Italy, Japan, Russia, UK, USA.

But for most countries this is a diminishing risk. Few members of the general public realize that there are soon likely to be around six independent satellite navigation systems. Russia (with a bit of help from India) has already reinstated its own 'GLONASS' system. Europe will soon have 'Galileo'. China, Japan and India (this time independent of Russia) are each on course to have their own separate systems. Collapse or deliberate corruption of the satellite-navigation network is therefore a lessening potential source of global crises going forward. In contrast, the other world network that everyone uses is *highly* vulnerable.

## TOO MANY EGGS IN ONE BASKET?

Global communications are at risk. To a very limited extent this is because of the vulnerability of communications satellites to deliberate attack. However, satellites are in fact far more likely to be made inoperative simply because these days there are hundreds of thousands of destructive pieces of space junk whizzing around in uncharted orbits. In 2007 a Chinese weapons-test blasted a decommissioned weather satellite into around 150,000 uncontrolled missiles each larger than a pebble. In 2009 a working satellite crashed into a derelict satellite and the two of them continued their respective journeys in vastly more smithereens than before. Between them, just these two events doubled the number of potentially-destructive fragments randomly firing through Earth orbit. Like a swarm of Evil Supermen, any one of these shards can be travelling up to twenty-five times faster than a speeding bullet. Any single one could destroy a key component of a satellite – or indeed depressurize the International Space Station.

As it is, there are over twenty-thousand items of space debris that are large enough to be monitored from Earth. Yet there are more than ten times that number of smaller projectiles in unknown orbits, each capable of destroying a working satellite. Even more likely, however, is that old boosters and defunct satellites and derelict space flotsam will smash into *each other* and create innumerably more chaotic missiles. If something is not done soon, this risks triggering a chain-reaction of collisions of an increasing number of increasingly small pieces of destructive debris – seeding the narrow band of orbits used for communication satellites as a No-Go-Zone of unintended cluster bombs. At the moment, there are no funded missions to reverse this escalating risk of communication-satellite failure.

Meanwhile, back on Earth, there are far-greater dangers to global communication. For a start, there are physical problems with the fiber-optic network – primarily under the oceans. Ninety per cent of internet traffic passes through submarine cables that are vulnerable to damage from earthquakes or even deep-water trawler fishing. Worse, around the globe there are various choke-points where numerous cables come together and so risk all being taken out by the same event. Fortunately, the paramount design criterion of the original ARPANET that evolved into the internet was for it to be intrinsically robust against physical damage. As a result, if one node of today's global network goes down then the system just routes around it.

Apparently more worrying is that there are only a very small number of key hubs that keep the complete worldwide internet going. These so-called Root Name Servers are effectively where the internet first starts to 'look up' an internet address. As a result, every bit of internet traffic has to pass through one. Limits dictated by the original design of the internet's addressing system currently restrict the total number of Root Name Servers for the whole world to be only thirteen.

However, despite scare-stories to the contrary, in practice most of these hubs are clusters of computers in different physical locations. And to speed things up, there are also duplicates across many continents – which make the overall system still more resilient. As a result, whatever the apparent threat, Root Name Servers are sufficiently distributed that they do not represent the Achilles' heel that many have assumed. Despite this, nearly the entire internet (and certainly the worldwide web) is nevertheless under extreme threat.

## THE 'POTATO-BLIGHT' OF THE INTERNET

By far the greatest risk to the internet arises for similar reasons to why so many starved during the Great Irish Famine in the middle of the 19th century. In that case, although the Irish population had many different types of job and lived all over the country in a variety of homes, about a third of them were completely dependent for their food on only one type of crop – the potato. When that single species got infected by potato-blight, whole communities died of starvation or had to emigrate to survive.

The modern internet has very many different types of computer connected to it – there is a tremendous diversity of hardware. But they all run extremely similar software. Most personal computers run on Microsoft operating systems. Most of those that do not, run on Apple software instead. For personal computers, that is effectively about it. Computer games now almost all use variants of Windows. And applications for mobile phones and other handheld devices are typically designed to spread around as many different models as possible. As a direct result of this aspect of the Networking trend, the global community is pretty much as vulnerable to infected software as the Irish were to blighted potato crops.

Most private individuals already take for granted that they need to be careful of computer viruses, and they typically use a software equivalent to vaccination that regularly updates their computer to recognize and block those viruses that have newly been discovered. It is far less obvious to most people that devices such as mobile phones or BlackBerries are potentially just as vulnerable to cyberattack. What is more, automobiles typically now use on-board integrated computer software to control everything from engine performance to in-built Sat Navs, and the trend is toward automatic wireless software-updates covering everything from traffic congestion to new road layouts to operating-system improvements. So, even potentially-lethal consumer devices are increasingly vulnerable.

A few governments are now worried about viruses getting into systems that control things like water-distribution systems and power grids – which if disrupted would cause disproportionate backlashes – but that is about as far as politicians tend publicly to voice their concerns on computer viruses. However, behind the scenes there is a war being waged between writers of malicious software ('malware') that can spread across the whole internet or mobile communications network and with those who are trying to stop them. Even now, it is not at all clear which side is winning. And in the future, things are set to get worse.

## MALWARE

As everyone in cybersecurity is well aware, the fact is that there are many types of malware that are far more sinister than the computer-viruses the public is familiar with. Technically, a computer 'virus' can only be spread by a user deliberately opening an attachment or running some software, whereas 'worms' can make their own way between computers, and 'Trojan horses' quietly hide within apparently innocent software. Each type of delivery-system can be made to run computer software that the user does not want – whether an 'innocent' pop-up, or a program to delete what is on the hard-drive. The reason why in the last few years governments have suddenly become very attentive to malware is that the latest dangerous software is being coded for very different purposes than in the past.

Early malware tended to be written by (often rather bright) computer students as something of a prank. That still continues, and the sophistication of some of their programming is extraordinary. But in general, although these 'amateur' projects can be very disruptive, they are not written for commercial or political gain. The new types are. In the last ten years, malware has become the tool of organized crime and political activism. And it has gone undercover. Earlier malware tended to advertise its success by acts of vandalism – 'professional' malware hides.

Sometimes it merely spies on what people are doing and relays to its controller what their passwords and security codes are when they contact their bank or access their company's secure intranet. Sometimes it spreads around an otherwise-secure corporate network (maybe infecting it via a USB memory stick) and seeks out a specific configuration of industrial-control software in order to give the machinery new instructions – as the 'Stuxnet' attacks on Iran's uranium enrichment centrifuges in 2009-10 were designed to do.

## STUXNET

There were repeated cyberattacks on five targeted industrial processing organizations in Iran between June 2009 and April 2010. Although, for security reasons, the facilities' networks were not normally connected to the internet, it is assumed that the Stuxnet worm used for the attacks was introduced either intentionally or accidentally. Despite media reports to the contrary, the malware itself was not exceptionally sophisticated. However, the overall operation that was needed to introduce that specific software by infiltrating targeted facilities via external contractors was operationally highly advanced – suggesting the involvement of one or more government-sponsored agencies with skills far broader than just malware development.

Other times it secretly takes over someone's computer and joins it to a 'botnet'. In essence, what happens is that one way or another a special type of malware infects a computer – not necessarily via the internet, maybe simply by plugging in an infected memory-stick. Computer users do not know that the malware is there. Their anti-virus software does not detect it. But from that moment on, their computers are like zombies. Each zombie can be directed by some central authority to send a message to wherever it is told. And that sort of zombie-army can be very dangerous. Botnets are typically rented out to criminal groups who want to avoid any risk of detection. Spam mail and pop-up advertising are the most visible consequences – and sometimes those two irritations are secretly connected because the pop-up advertises software to block the spam that the self-same botnet is producing.

Many of today's botnets are made up of *hundreds of thousands* of compromised computers and each of those botnets has the capacity to spew out tens of billions of spam messages a day – which all help to clog up the internet. It is generally estimated that there are a few thousand botnets running at the moment. But it is not even known how many computers are compromised by the largest ones, though at their peak some have been able to control at least *ten million* different machines.

As an example, a computer worm variously referred to as Conficker or Downadup initially spread in late 2008 primarily through file sharing. Months later it had infected around ten million machines. Each became part of a massive externally-controlled botnet. Despite a major subsequent eradication program, machines continued to be reinfected via USB devices such as memory-sticks. In February 2010, the Greater Manchester Police in the UK had to be cut off from the Police National Computer while the force's infected computers were cleaned to avoid the worm spreading onto the central system.

Prior to removal, covert software of the largest botnets has been found to be secretly controlling important computer-systems in government, police and the military as well as commercial and private computers across approximately two-hundred countries throughout the world. That is a lot of spam and pop-up advertising. But it is not junk email that is the worry.

## BOTNET ATTACK

The most disruptive use of botnets is, as many governments are well aware, to attack major computer systems. In its simplest form this merely involves telling each zombie-computer to send a message to the system that is being attacked – all at the same time – so as to swamp it. In the jargon of cybersecurity this is referred to as a 'distributed denial-of-service attack' or DDoS.

Alternatively, if the attackers have done their homework, maybe they try to log-in to every user account, deliberately using the wrong password several times in succession so that the system under attack automatically blocks those accounts. As a result, none of the genuine users are able to get access to their own accounts. If the botnet is big enough, it can slow the response of even the largest system.

Although a few organizations – such as WikiLeaks – can try to stay one step ahead of such blocks by 'mirroring' (in effect, copying) their site to numerous unrelated on-line addresses and then alerting people to where they have moved, that is an option unavailable to most organizations. Access to bank-servers, government networks and global chat-rooms can all effectively be blocked, and on-line companies can be forced to cease trading. In what can appear to be an explicit example of Boundaryless People-Power, individual corporations and agencies can be singled-out for 'punishment' – supposedly by vast numbers of individuals who do not like what the organization is doing. But in these cases the deluge of on-line attacks may in reality be triggered by only a handful of individuals with access to a sufficiently large botnet.

That is what occurred to WikiLeaks in late 2010 just as it was about to leak US diplomatic cables, and then a few days later as occurred to Visa, Mastercard and others (orchestrated by so-called 'hacktivists' from the online group Anonymous) in retaliation for the companies having blocked payments to WikiLeaks. Similarly, in support of anti-government protests in early 2011, members of Anonymous became involved in cyberattacks on various Middle-East targets including websites of Egypt's ruling party and ministry of information.

Whether they are motivated by political or financial gains, these types of cyberattack are, in reality, increasingly easy to set up, extremely difficult to prevent, and their perpetrators are very hard to track down unless they make a mistake. As an example, in March 2010 Spanish police arrested three men responsible for the so-called Mariposa botnet that had taken control of nearly 13,000,000 computers across 190 countries. The perpetrators lived off their earnings from renting out parts of the botnet to other cybercriminals as well as using banking information stolen from the compromised computers.

Most worryingly, none of the arrested men had particularly advanced computing skills – indicating just how accessible this form of cyberattack has already become. The only reason they were caught was that one of them made the mistake of logging-in directly rather than via a system that disguised his whereabouts. The FBI monitored his log-in and determined from the IP address of his computer that he was in Spain. However, if he had been living in a country that had not had treaty arrangements with the USA then that is as far as the trail would have led.

As a result of their ease of use and yet difficulty to defend against, botnets are increasingly the weapon of choice for hostile governments, organized crime and terrorist groups. What is more, because the whereabouts of the ultimate puppet-masters behind botnet attacks is usually completely disguisable, most rogue states would feel that as far as the international community was concerned they were fully protected by the old concept of 'plausible deniability'. Organized crime and terrorist networks no doubt think the same.

## DOUBLE-EDGED SWORD

Cyberattack is already considered a real and present danger to the national security of many advanced countries – especially since botnets have become readily available for purchase on the internet. For instance, in late October 2010 the 'Iranian Cyber Army' (which had previously attacked Twitter as well as the Chinese version of Google called Baidu) announced that fellow hacktivists would be able to buy access to its botnets for a few hundred dollars.

But equally worrying to many governments is the relatively-unchecked power of those using the universality of the internet and mobile-communication networks to try to circumvent the historical top-down control of governments. When that form of Boundaryless People-Power is used in the service of rebellion against autocratic regimes, the international community tends to be supportive. Journalists praise the positive impacts of secure instant-messaging systems such as BlackBerry Messenger in helping a new generation of rebels to coordinate in previously impossible ways. That misses an important point.

Exactly the same technologies are also used to coordinate a new generation of thuggish riots and looting. In August 2011, as the world looked on with reactions ranging from horror and disbelief to self-congratulation and ideological one-upmanship, London burned. The next night other major English cities joined it. Until a few days later when they sent unprecedented numbers of officers onto the streets, the police were largely unable to stop widespread criminality. For a short while, inner-city communities lived in fear. Shops were broken into. Landmarks were destroyed. People died.

# Risks to economic stability

One of the main problems was policing rioters and looters who were going on the rampage at multiple different locations all at the same time. Some of the criminals belonged to street gangs used to coordinating themselves via social networking. Others were opportunists that nevertheless – just as part of their everyday means of interacting with the world – used electronic communication to inform their actions.

As a result of all these sorts of painful lessons, top government agencies around the world are actively working on cybersecurity both for defense and offence. Just as with espionage and counter-espionage, nation-states feel they must focus not only on defenses to combat malware of all forms, but also on devising suitable malware of their own so they can as needed go on the offensive and cyberattack those who threaten their national security. Leading governments have concluded that they must simultaneously help protect the internet as a whole at the same time as devising techniques of bringing parts of it down. They must maintain the freedoms of mobile communication and social networking – but also get on top of how to protect their citizens against the Enemy Within who use those same systems not just to break the law but also to tip social stability into anarchy.

## FIGHTING FIRE WITH FIRE

That, of necessity, is forcing ideologically-open societies to consider whether government agencies should routinely intercept and block Instant Messaging and other forms of social networking during extreme circumstances, such as looting and rioting, albeit those governments are well aware just how close that brings them to exactly the behaviors they denounce in autocratic regimes. Debates around these issues will necessarily become increasingly frequent and public – after all, such highly-visible state sanctions cannot survive in a democracy without the broad acceptance of its citizens. However, what will remain far less visible is the escalating arms war that is already well-underway in cyberspace.

For a long time, a few major government and security-service departments have been in the vanguard. They examine new releases of software to try to understand what security breaches the programs may open up, and they have a quiet word, as appropriate, with software producers and anti-virus services to let them know of any dangerous flaws that they discover.

# HIGH-TECH CRISES

## INTERCEPTING BLACKBERRY TRAFFIC

The National Security Agency (NSA) in the USA and the Government Communications Headquarters (GCHQ) in the UK are generally recognized by rival states as the leading intelligence agencies responsible for monitoring communications and other electronic signals, as well as assuring the security of their own governments' communications. Both services use the most advanced computers in the world and can access many important servers that route through their territories. This brings many security advantages. For example, the UK government can encourage civil servants to use smartphones such as BlackBerries for information classified up to Restricted levels because the data is sufficiently encrypted that probably only organizations like GCHQ could decode it in a reasonable time. In contrast, the United Arab Emirates, Saudi Arabia and India felt the need to threaten to ban BlackBerries because of national-security concerns. They did not have access to such advanced computers as had NSA and GCHQ. Nor did they have access to the foreign servers that route the BlackBerry data traffic. A work-around was agreed 'in the strict context of lawful access and national security'.

But across the global community, there appear to be far fewer software engineers working on cybersecurity than there are those trying to devise ways of getting around it. As a result, many countries are experiencing a broadly exponential increase in malware attacks. In response, and despite general cutbacks, most governments have if anything supplemented their funding of efforts to counter malware attacks. However, as thing stand, those responsible for protecting against clandestine attacks by a hostile-state, an organized crime syndicate or a terrorist group are increasingly finding the odds building against them.

## EASY TARGETS

Computers belonging to members of the general public tend to be easy targets for recruitment into botnets. And civil companies other than those at obvious risk (such as banks) find it extremely hard to justify the expense and hassle of securing their operations against all forms of cyberattack.

# Risks to economic stability

Most do not even consider it a high priority and they are largely unaware of how sophisticated some industrial espionage has become. In addition, many companies are moving toward outsourcing their IT requirements to 'cloud-computing' services run by other people. Cloud-computing in effect offers companies a virtual IT system accessed over the internet (historically IT engineers have represented the internet on information diagrams as a cloud). As a result of the way that cloud-computing operates, no one typically knows where the physical equipment they are accessing actually is.

This allows tremendous flexibility for a company to grow and change its IT system. In addition, corporate planners can take advantage of the fact that many aspects of most companies' IT-needs are very similar, and so there are financial savings from adopting relatively standard approaches rather than creating a system from scratch. But cloud-computing also concentrates the corporate risk of many companies onto one system. That system usually has far higher physical and cyber security than most independent companies do, but for some people – just like an art gallery or jewellery store – its content makes it especially attractive to break into.

Quite separately to any potential concerns raised by cloud-computing, there is another reason that organizations in the private sector can be at risk – the employees of most companies simply do not tend to view their day-to-day access to the internet as a potential security threat. That is especially true if they view their job as completely 'innocent'. Schools, for instance, rarely consider that their computers are potentially only one or two steps away from infecting crucially important installations: A computer-generated birthday card lovingly emailed by a child from the classroom to a home computer from where a parent pops it onto a memory-stick in order later to display it proudly to colleagues on an office computer – risks infecting an apparently-secure network.

Perhaps even more concerning is that it is not the more-obvious targets of malware that cyberterrorists will necessarily target. Breaking any crucial thread in the complex web of modern society can throw a nation's infrastructure into trauma. Disruptions to supermarkets, healthcare, travel and communication potentially create a far more immediate and painful backlash against the general public than disruptions to (far better protected) international funds-transfers or military databases.

## TOO LITTLE TOO LATE

In May 2011 the US government announced a bill aimed at protecting domestic businesses from cybercrime by providing incentives from the federal government for companies that enhance and test their security systems. Although a step in the right direction, the absence of any mandated actions is likely to result in too little change in behaviour that is anyway potentially too late.

Already, defenses are constantly being tested by newer, cleverer forms of attack. In May 2011, the major defense contractor Lockheed Martin came under significant cyberattack, as it had done before. At the same time, Woodside Petroleum (Australia's largest oil company) was under concerted attack – apparently from Eastern Europe and Russia. At the start of 2012, hackers managed to steal $1.8-million from a South African bank – only three years after the bank had installed a computer-fraud detection system. The war is escalating. And the nature of malware is rapidly evolving.

A form of survival-of-the-fittest keeps adapting the software-approaches that attackers use so as to take best advantage of what at any time are the web's weakest defenses. Yet the more complex the internet grows as it expands over the next few decades into a 'supernet' (that by 2040 is set to be a *billion* times more powerful than today's internet), so the more dependent on it the smooth-running of the global economy will become. Although the internet's structure is inherently resilient, the near-total lack of diversity in its software is not. A malicious prankster just conceivably might cause sufficient disruption to trigger, for instance, an economic crash. Very much more likely is that the major global crisis caused by such an internet-driven crash, if it happens, will be engineered deliberately.

# HOW PHARMACEUTICALS RISK BEING OVERWHELMED BY BACTERIA

## Miniaturization crises primarily relate to healthcare – especially if advances in antibiotics and other treatments do not keep pace with emerging risks

ALARMIST REPORTS ABOUT extreme crises caused by Miniaturization (such as the whole world being turned to 'grey goo' by self-replicating nanobots) are unfounded given current research routes. In contrast, there are legitimate nanotechnology health-issues that relate to the unknown impact of incredibly small particles entering the bloodstream, and therefore getting to organs such as the brain. But such concerns are pretty easily researched, and protocols can readily be devised to protect us all. In reality, health-related problems are more likely to arise as a result of High-Tech research opening up more healthcare opportunities than can in general be afforded. Developed nations are already becoming familiar with discussions about Healthcare Rationing, and sophisticated new approaches involving nanomaterial coatings on medical inserts, special drug-delivery systems and lab-on-a-chip analyses will only add to the repertoire of potentially-unaffordable treatments going forward.

Although some of these alternatives will prove more cost-effective than existing treatments, overall the pressure is for average healthcare costs per person to increase – because there are more and more options becoming available to save and improve people's lives. Anticipating all this, responsible politicians are alerting their populations to the looming crises in medical treatment. In addition, given the spending constraints in many countries that are demanded by the current economic difficulties, governments are more than ever seeking greater efficiencies in how healthcare operates. However, no government feels able publicly to discuss the fact that none of these proposals may be sufficient to keep up with what, largely out of sight, is actually going on.

# HIGH-TECH CRISES

## SUPERBUGS

The unvoiced problem is that strategists do not in reality know how big a hurdle medical treatment is going to have to overcome. Even the most alarmed governments take as a basic assumption that, thanks to the developments brought by High-Tech, medicine will at least become increasingly effective at managing diseases. But that may be totally wrong. It could well be that nasty healthcare side-effects from High-Tech grow even faster than the ability to treat them. Far from steadily winning battle after battle against disease, the medical profession may soon find itself being beaten back, finding itself defeated in areas in which it long-thought it had triumphed, and eventually losing the Healthcare war completely.

Antibiotics are a simple example. Ever since they were first used successfully during World War II, their ability to kill bacteria has delivered incalculable benefits. But their widespread use has created a serious backlash. Like the DNA in any other living organism, as bacteria multiply their genes sometimes randomly mutate. Very rarely that mutation helps a strain of bacteria to resist antibiotics better than the unmutated version. When that happens, 'survival of the fittest' means that only the more-resistant strain endures. Over time, increasingly resistant strains have evolved. That process has now been going on for seventy years.

It has been made worse by ignorance (patients wrongly assuming antibiotics can help viral infections like a cold, or thinking it is safe to stop taking a full-course of antibiotics because they are feeling better) as well as by lack of professionalism (doctors in some countries even now handing out antibiotics indiscriminately). And in many countries, including the USA, antibiotics are widely used in standard animal feeds – even when there is no illness at all – which has been associated with the emergence of antibiotic-resistant strains of bacteria like salmonella. In essence, the more that the international community uses antibiotics, the more it unintentionally creates bacteria that do not respond to those antibiotics.

It first happened back in 1947 when, only four years after penicillin was mass-produced, 'Staph infection' became resistant to it. These days Staph has evolved into the well-publicized superbug MRSA, which is increasingly difficult to control in hospitals because it has become resistant to a number of important antibiotics. Less generally well known is the discovery in 2010 of an equally-resistant superbug NDM-1 in the USA, Canada, UK, Japan, Brazil, India and Pakistan.

## MISLED BY A PRESS BARON

Most people are taught that the undisputed hero of antibiotics is Alexander Fleming – but that is not really true. The media baron Max Aitken (made Lord Beaverbrook) was a sponsor of the teaching hospital where Fleming worked and apparently felt it was his duty to promote the idea that it was Fleming who primarily was responsible for the 'miracle drug' penicillin – even though in reality Fleming quickly abandoned it as being unsuitable for humans. It was an Oxford-based team under Prof Howard Florey that really deserves nearly all the credit of taking Fleming's discarded findings, eventually extracting penicillin against incredible odds, and then *refusing to patent it for commercial gain.* We also now know that a Costa Rican scientist noticed the antibiotic effect of the Penicillium mold even earlier than Fleming, but he reported it to a French institute and the discovery was disregarded – just as Fleming's most likely would have been had it not been for Florey's team. Rather unfairly, it was Fleming's name that went down in history and whose face was put onto postage stamps and banknotes.

The so-called 'New Delhi Metallo-beta-lactamase' enzyme makes bacteria resistant even to the *Carbapenem* group of antibiotics that are the usual fallback doctors resort to for treating antibiotic-resistant bacteria. As a result, only a small range of antibiotics remain as possible treatments, and there are serious concerns that NDM-1 could soon jump to other strains of bacteria that are already antibiotic-resistant. NDM-1 probably emerged from the Indian subcontinent but it is feared to be spreading worldwide. Similarly, in countries such as Russia and China it has been recognized for some time that there are strains of tuberculosis that are resistant to many types of antibiotics. But then, in 2012, Indian doctors reported that they were struggling with new strains of TB that appeared totally resistant to *all* antibiotics. Amongst infectious diseases, TB has the dubious honor of already being second only to HIV in killing most people around the world.

Unfortunately, pharmaceutical companies have often not prioritized development of new antibiotics – historically there have been bigger profits elsewhere – so there are growing concerns in the medical profession that there will soon be previously-treatable infectious diseases for which there are no longer any effective antibiotics. Consequently, many medical experts have warned me, patients who previously would have shrugged off illness – will die instead. But escalating resistance to antibiotics is just the tip of the backlash. It is just one example of the crucial lesson that complex systems typically create hidden-but-growing crises through a chain of cause and effect that is itself so complex that people often completely miss what is going on. As a result, the overall link between action and eventual crisis ends up being completely unexpected.

For instance, indiscriminate spraying of the insecticide DDT not only eventually led to the emergence of DDT-resistant mosquitoes (which was the first surprise) but it also had totally unexpected impacts on birdlife that led to concerns about consequences for human health (which was all so unexpected that it helped kick off the environmental movement in the 1960s). Although DDT was largely banned in the 1970s, the sorts of questions that it raised are, as we will now explore, even more important today.

## ESCALATING HEALTH CRISES

The point is that the success of High-Tech has changed everyone's lives. But some of those changes, often for very complex reasons, seem to be damaging people's health. For instance, at a time when a billion people on the planet are starving, escalating obesity is already a major contributor to bad health in richer countries. Across the world, diabetes is rapidly increasing – in China it has recently reached epidemic proportions. Recent studies suggest that almost 10% of the adult Chinese population have diabetes (nearly all Type Two diabetes), with the majority of cases undiagnosed or untreated. The equivalent figure in the USA is around 8%. Yet until the 21$^{st}$ century, diabetes was relatively uncommon in China. The assumption is that changes in levels of physical activity, unhealthy diet and pollution are contributing factors – especially as obesity is strongly correlated with Type Two diabetes. China has now moved ahead of India as the country with the most diabetics in the world.

Similarly, many countries are facing growing public-health problems from substance-abuse – not just of traditional alcohol and cigarettes but also far-more-modern drugs. Much more confusingly, over the last fifty years there has been a dramatic and growing increase in allergies, some of them very severe. The reason? The truth is that absolutely nobody really knows. It may be something to do with how clean home environments impact children's immune systems. It may be something to do with how we no longer tend to be infested with parasites or eat dirty food so maybe our bodies are looking for something else to 'protect' us against, which is really what an allergic reaction is. The point is, science just does not know. And that is what is particularly worrying.

In the same way, science does not actually know the very-long-term *combined* impacts of all the food preservatives and artificial additives and vitamin supplements and over-the-counter medications and changes in diet and new forms of pollution and high-stress jobs and breakdown of family-structure and sedentary occupations and changes in how people interact and socialize. And science certainly does not know the eventual backlashes that might follow from the fact that over the last few centuries many children – who in earlier days would not have been strong enough to survive – were, as a result of medical knowledge, kept alive long enough to grow up and have children (who themselves might have died in earlier times).

On top of that, the physical and other traits that couples find attractive in each other – some of which they potentially pass onto their children – are sometimes very different to those that were typically selected in the past. By one means or another, humanity is significantly changing its unofficial 'selective breeding' program. The eventual effect of all these sorts of changes is unknowable. But what *is* already known is that some factors somehow, whether they are environmental or genetic or a combination of both, are escalating human health problems. And these are backlashes that may soon escalate out of control.

## UNABLE TO KEEP UP

When High-Tech medical research took off in the 1950s, many assumed that by the early 21st-century doctors would feel far more in control of healthcare than they do. To be fair, part of the problem is caused by the apparently-positive result that better medical treatment means that more patients are surviving long enough to suffer from the diseases of old age (with all the well-recognized huge healthcare costs that result). But it is also because of unrecognized medical backlashes from all the changes in lifestyle that High-Tech has enabled, the hidden global backlashes that follow from High-Tech developments like mass-production of antibiotics, and possibly even from the cumulative backlashes of one generation after another being kept alive long enough to have children, when previously they would not even have made it to puberty.

Whatever the combination of reasons, the fact remains that many contributors to ill health are *accelerating*. Medical ability is also, of course, accelerating. But given the glacial rate at which a new generation of scientists and medical practitioners can be educated, it is not at all clear that there will even be sufficient healthcare researchers to benefit from the explosion of scientific data that will become available, or that they will then be able to make an adequate number of breakthroughs rapidly enough, or that the medical profession and hospitals will then be able to absorb all the new ideas. Moreover, changes in healthcare are actually far more difficult to implement than those looking from outside the profession expect. Apart from the tensions sometimes created by pharmaceutical corporations and governments, there are also deeply ingrained rivalries between three major factions: Doctors, Nurses and Administrators. It is a historical legacy that still carries major implications for modern medicine.

The overall impact of all these factors combined is that there is absolutely no guarantee that science will be able to keep pace with – let alone overtake – escalating health problems. What is more, the general public is unlikely to realize what is going on until it has become such a major crisis it can no longer be camouflaged. After all, a government's first responsibility is to protect its citizens. But no government is ever going to volunteer that this may not in reality be possible.

# DELIBERATE BIOTERRORISM OR A SILLY MISTAKE

## The Simulation trend brings major risks of crisis from deliberate bioterrorism and organized crime (such as super-addictive drugs) or accidental release of pathogens

BASED ON THE results of a long-running worldwide 'experiment' of some nations (such as the USA) wholeheartedly adopting GM-crops and others (such as Japan and countries across Europe) steadfastly avoiding them, it increasingly appears that many of the concerns about GM-crops were unfounded. Many, but not necessarily all. Unexpected consequences from unintentionally disrupting complex interconnected ecosystems – for instance, indirectly affecting population-sizes of a particular insect because of the introduction of a GM strain – are, by definition, unknowable in advance. What is more, often the tangled chains of cause and effect cannot fully be unraveled even *after* the event. If there are problems with GM crops, they will most likely be of this sort.

As a result, even if severe backlashes eventually emerge, they may not be traceable back to GM-crops at all. Little is therefore likely to change. Anyway, the extraordinary near-term potential for GM-crops to reduce global starvation and suffering seems likely to outweigh concerns about such long-term probably-unprovable issues. So, in practice, it is likely to be only a matter of time before most of the world follows the lead of the USA.

In other areas, our exploding ability to simulate the behavior of bacteria and viruses is set to transform not just medicine but also biotech-production of all kinds of useful substances. These High-Tech versions of the Master Brewer's technology have already become extremely sophisticated – so sophisticated in fact that someone does not have to be a top scientist to use them. These days, almost anyone with enough money can run a biotech factory. One can even be set up by a well-funded terrorist group.

# HIGH-TECH CRISES

## GERMS AS WEAPONS

Germ warfare is not new. The Ancient Greeks poisoned wells, and medieval armies catapulted corpses that had died of the Black Death over the walls of castles they were besieging. But it has long been understood by modern military leaders that biological weapons can be more trouble than they are worth. Unlike explosive devices or even chemical weapons, germs (more technically, pathogens) take time to have an effect, and casualties may later infect a commander's own troops. On balance, biological warfare is too uncontrollable to be attractive for conventional military strategists. But those self-same attributes are ideal for a terrorist group whose primary goal is to induce widespread panic into a civilian population.

Although governments appropriately keep relatively quiet about it so as to avoid undue alarm, bioterrorism is today recognized as one of the major attack-threats to industrialized populations. Media in some countries that complain that there was an apparent overreaction by government health-officials to the 2009 swine-flu epidemic fail to understand that it rather conveniently provided an opportunity to test out many of the recently prepared procedures for dealing with a biological attack of a more malicious sort.

## STOCKPILES OF SMALLPOX

Because smallpox is the only killer-disease to have been officially eradicated worldwide (the WHO declared victory in December 1979) there is a whole generation that has never been vaccinated against it. What is more, even vaccinated people lose their immunity over time. It is now known that stockpiles of smallpox were maintained in the former Soviet Union – and some have suggested that the strains may have been modified to resist vaccines. With the breakup of the USSR, no one knows where all the stockpiles or the related specialist expertise ended up.

The trouble is though, preparing for rapid response is one of the few measures that nations can take. One of the problems of defending against bioterrorism is that in reality it is practically impossible to avoid. In the extreme, suicide-terrorists can simply infect themselves with something equivalent to smallpox – a highly contagious and often fatal disease – and get into close proximity with as many people as possible. Those terrorists that do not want to sacrifice themselves, instead need to find a way to release an aerosol of droplets into air that people are breathing (which is technically more of a challenge than infecting people the old-fashioned way, but nevertheless a well-understood process). The problem for the authorities is even to *realize* that there is a problem. Early detection prior to any rapid response is extremely difficult to arrange. Healthcare systems that track reports of infectious diseases are now far more sophisticated – but ultimately they depend on the timely input of accurate medical data, and that varies across hospitals and doctors' surgeries.

In due course, new approaches that combine multiple sources of data ranging from A&E admissions to school-absenteeism may offer a far better finger on the pulse of public health than any single source. But even then, an infection-carrier that visits an international airport-hub might significantly delay detection by any national early-warning system because the first wave of those infected would be distributed across different systems in many countries and might not initially be recognized as an attack at all.

Unfortunately, even if a bioterrorist attack is recognized immediately (for instance because the organization behind it alerts the press) many of the terrorists' goals will have already been achieved because, even if people do not panic, they are nevertheless likely to do whatever they think it takes to protect themselves. Those sorts of changes in behavior are what terrorism is all about. And that is why major cities tend to be the best targets. Few people actually have to die if nevertheless parts of an urban center grind to a halt. Wall Street, the financial Square Mile in London and the Tokyo stock exchange do not need to be bombed to stop the global banking system in its entirety. Employees simply need to be persuaded not to go into work for a month. However big the bonus on offer, few bankers will chose it over the possibility of contracting a potentially fatal disease that may kill not only them, but also their families.

## ADVANCED BIOTERRORISM

Bioterrorism risks being more devastating even than that. A carefully-introduced disease like Foot-and-Mouth could disrupt a whole country not so much because of the interruption of the food supply, but because of the fear that went with it – which would inevitably be fuelled by the media.

# HIGH-TECH CRISES

Any even moderately-well-researched journalist would raise concerns such as: 'If meat can be affected, what about water supplies? What about crops? If we can be attacked by germs we have all heard about, what about other less well-known substances like naturally-occurring Aflatoxins, which are some of the most cancer-inducing substances known, and which can easily contaminate cereals and nuts and spices and vegetable oils? What is left that is safe?' The simple answer, if a nation is under concerted attack, is: Nothing.

It gets even worse than that. *The Convention on the Prohibition of the Development, Production and Stockpiling of Bacteriological (Biological) and Toxin Weapons and on their Destruction* was formulated in 1972 and currently commits almost two hundred states to its terms. This wordily-titled Biological Weapons Convention explicitly outlaws germ-warfare. But the treaty does not include any formal verification process. And what few members of the public realize is that it does not even preclude countries from legally developing small quantities of incredibly dangerous biological substances for medical and defensive purposes. I have met some of the experts that do indeed conduct such work. What would surprise most people, is how ordinary these labs look. Unlike factories for nuclear weapons, it is almost impossible to distinguish a lab that is trying to create a 'designer killer-virus' from a perfectly legitimate research facility. That makes it almost impossible for Security Services to recognize such labs also.

Then again, a lab that is in reality a threat to national security might in fact be formulating a 'designer drug' instead. After all, a hostile government or terrorist group – or indeed organized-crime cartel – might consider it would be better to focus less on classic biological warfare and more on something 'recreational'. Ideal for such an attack would be a recreational drug that was so very addictive and yet also debilitating that whole economies could suffer as a result, much as China's did during the 19th-century as a result of opium deliberately introduced by the West. Ironically, in a historically-balanced tit-for-tat of truly epic duration, there is currently a proliferation of illicit recreational drugs being manufactured in China, and being exported to the West.

The upshot of all these factors is that around the world there are not only collections of supremely dangerous biological substances, but also researchers who are experimenting with creating even more of them (either the 'classic' sort or the 'addictive' sort). Even if no one is trying to develop biological material for a future weapon 'just in case' they need it – and based on past experience that may be overly optimistic – there are certainly numerous labs that are developing such substances for the sole purpose of working out how to vaccinate their citizens against anything similar that a bioterrorist might release. Most labs have extremely high security. But it is difficult to see how those few research facilities in less-stable countries can be guaranteed to be utterly secure against all eventualities. The saddest irony of all will be if global chaos descends because an unstoppable killer-infection gets released from a research lab – not as the deliberate result of ideological aggression – but because someone somewhere makes a really dumb mistake.

## 24. HOW HIGH-TECH RISKS DIRECT CRISES

Thuggish riots and looting

Spontaneous peaceful rallies and online protests

**BOUNDARYLESS PEOPLE-POWER**

Increasing risk of bioterrorist attack or super-addictive recreational drugs or accidental release of pathogens

Biotech factories increasingly affordable to moderately-funded groups and controllable by basic-level scientists

Progressive infrastructural vulnerability to hostile-state or terrorist attack

Near-total lack of civilian shielding against electromagnetic-pulse damage to micro circuitry

**Exponential SIMULATION**

**Exponential DIGITIZATION**

**Exponential MINIATURIZATION**

**Exponential NETWORKING**

Healthcare R&D coalesces around exciting fields such as nanotech in preference to mundane fields such as antibiotics

Trend toward widespread software standardization to encourage broad uptake by casual users

Uncontrollable infection as resistant strains of bacteria emerge faster than science can develop new antibiotics

Increasingly acute vulnerability to largely-untraceable cyberattack by political activists hostile states or terrorists

# WHEN EVEN THE SCIENTIFIC METHOD RISKS FAILING

## The riskiest High-Tech crises arise from unintended consequences throughout the world economy escalating too fast and being too interconnected for conventional responses to work

THE ULTIMATE CAUSE of what may be the most dangerous crises to emanate from High-Tech is also in many ways the most hidden. Certainly, few politicians or global leaders can even see that it is a threat, despite being involved with it every day. Their blindness results from an assumption that they do not realize they are making. The point is that the worst backlashes threaten to arise because national governments and world institutions all habitually tackle global problems in only one way – and in an increasingly interconnected world, it cannot actually work.

What has happened is that, in a strange way, High-Tech has been too successful. As a result, almost without thinking, educated people take for granted that the overall problem-solving approach that made it all possible will potentially solve *any* problem. The trouble is, it will not. The reason for this goes to the very heart of the problem of 'not seeing the forest for the trees'. As such, it is core to appreciating why an interconnected world inevitably brings hidden consequences in the form of global crises.

### UNABLE TO JOIN THE DOTS

It is indisputable that the Scientific Method that underpins High-Tech is one of humanity's greatest inventions. Civilization is approaching the dawn of a Global Renaissance greater than at any time in history, and it is very largely thanks to the way that society tackles otherwise overwhelming problems: It breaks them down into more manageable challenges. It is a brilliantly sophisticated approach to problem-solving that over the centuries has become the cornerstone of science, technology and medicine. Everyone uses it. When a company like Microsoft writes a new generation of an immensely complicated operating-system like Windows, it deconstructs the problem into different parts, and then splits each of those again, and so on until it ends up with a set of largely self-contained modules that different people can write software for. When researchers planned to decode the human genome – despite some scientists stating it was an impractically ambitious goal – they split the challenge down and down until each individual task was achievable. The trouble is, these days anyone who has even-informally been trained in problem solving automatically tries to apply this same approach to every challenge they face. Yet often, when problems are broken down in this way, important insights fall between the cracks.

The reality of modern life is that there is now a massive amount of interconnection between global economies, ecologies and technologies. But as a result, politicians and business people can no longer see the full implications of changes to their super-large, super-complex, super-interconnected environments. Consequently, there are sometimes major unintended backlashes, typically after a long delay. The credit crunch was one of them. Global warming is another. Both are delayed side-effects. Avoiding those sorts of backlashes is a fundamentally different type of problem than today's organizations are typically set up to handle.

Tackling highly-interconnected systemic problems is a bit like trying to predict what the challenges may be if you connect your digital camera to a friend's home-cinema. If you are confused how their complex system works, it does not help to pull out all the wires and break everything down into its smallest components. Then you *really* cannot see how things might impact each other. But that is exactly the approach to problem-solving and management that society's progress over many centuries has conditioned governments (and everyone else) to adopt.

National governments split the massive communities of their civil servants into smaller and smaller groups – each still responsible for complex tasks but working largely independently. That approach no longer fully works for modern governments because issues such as global warming have huge interdependencies between not just different departments but different nations. Forming something like a National Security Council (as the USA and the UK have) that comprises the heads of critical government departments and services is a highly-appropriate response. However, it can only achieve so much. At best it encourages coordination of national responses to more-conventional security issues.

But it remains insufficient to address *globally-defined* threats to national security that, by definition, derive from complex systems within which a given nation is but one small component (directly analogous to the potentially-misaligned and miscommunicating government-departments for which the National Security Councils were themselves set up to compensate).

## UNFAIR HIDDEN CONNECTIONS BACK TO CHINA

The impact on ordinary citizens from the global economic downturn that began in 2007-8 is particularly unfair if you imagine yourself as a hard-working member of the Chinese public. For a long time, prudent Chinese workers did not live beyond their means. Instead – typically earning less for fulltime employment than their equivalent Western counterpart earned on the dole – they saved their money. Without them typically being aware of it, the surplus of their savings was loaned at cheap rates to international banks that in turn then bought what they claimed was a mathematically-safe combo of US-certified 'Prime' loans cleverly wrapped around riskier 'Sub-Prime' mortgages. Next, US-house-prices fell exposing the banks to unknown levels of defaulted loans, so they all stopped lending, causing a credit crunch for consumers and governments that had borrowed too much, which led to a global downturn that three years later translated into a Eurozone sovereign-debt crisis that further impacted global performance and increasingly cut demand for Chinese exports, which ultimately penalized the innocent Chinese workers – even though they in general had been the only ones in that long chain of cause and effect who had been sufficiently prudent actually to save enough.

The complex undertakings of major corporations are similarly split into sets of far simpler activities. But that approach likewise cannot work in a global economy because splitting the widespread interconnections – say in the banking industry – merely hides the danger of complex consequences and leads to dangerous lack of control. As we saw in the chapter on Capitalism Crises, that sort of lack of control is dangerous enough in isolation, a whole generation will suffer for it. But it is potentially catastrophic if too many equally-damaging global backlashes all occur at the same time, and all fundamentally for the same reason, namely, because there was insufficient joined-up thinking to 'link all the dots'.

## HIGH-TECH SPEEDS UP EVERYTHING

That is really important in the context of a global community that is now influenced by, and in turn influences, practically everything on the planet – certainly more than just the human portions. For practical purposes the international community can no longer view itself as completely separate from the planet as a whole. That alone makes things very complicated. But the standard corporate and political problem-solving approaches necessarily confuse things even further because leaders habitually break the global system into little pieces that each seem more-easily managed but that in reality link up with each other in really important ways, ways no one sufficiently understands.

As a direct result of 'not seeing the wood for the trees', Capitalism risks undermining the very society that depends upon it, Industrialization risks destroying the industrial economy, Population-changes risk social collapse, Religion risks destroying what it seeks to save, and – as we will see in the next chapter – Globalization risks backlashes beyond the power of global institutions to control.

Even if High-Tech were not tied into so many other important trends, its prolonged exponential growth would increasingly risk major unwanted side-effects, many of them leading to major backlashes. However, in reality High-Tech has become the dominant *enabler* of modern civilization. That means that it enhances not just opportunities – but also potential threats. The most dangerous large-scale systemic risks are unintended backlashes resulting from apparently-separate but actually deeply-intertwined trends. This is occurring because, as a result of High-Tech, these other powerful forces embedded in global society (Capitalism, Industrialization, Population, Religion and Globalization) are starting to interact more directly and faster than ever before.

Although the worst potential backlashes are in no way inevitable, how well corporations, major institutions and governments avoid the risks over the next two or three decades will in fact very largely be determined by what they do over only the next ten years or so, prior to the most dangerous crises even occurring. As will be detailed in the subchapter *If not now – then when?* (page 432), after that it will tend to cost too much and take too long to make enough difference. It is a simple message: *To avoid the worst backlashes, organizations need to take pre-emptive action.*

The primary reason for this is speed-of-response. I have already pointed out how counterintuitive exponential growth is. But the High-Tech supertrend *is* exponential – and as High-Tech grows, so too do the crises that High-Tech brings directly. So also do the crises it is stirring up as a result of its interactions with Capitalism, Industrialization, Population and Religion. And, because High-Tech accelerates Globalization, it also further escalates all the other five clusters of crises because they are all amplified by the increasing global interconnectedness that High-Tech is also driving. Consequently, the pace at which crises are formed is dominated by the exponential pace of High-Tech itself. And that means there is not the time to react that governments, corporations and global institutions typically assume.

There is a classic illustration that those of us who teach the dynamics of complex systems often use to illustrate this type of problem: Pondweed. The 'background facts' that are usually woven into the example are not strictly accurate, but the mathematics is. The set-up is that pondweed consists of vast numbers of tiny aquatic plants, each of which splits in two every twenty-four hours (in other words, the number of tiny plants doubles each day). For a large village pond it can take three years – to make it easy, let us call that 'a thousand days' – for a very small amount of pondweed to grow sufficiently to eventually completely cover the surface of the water. The simple question is: From the start of the three-year period, how many days is it likely to take before the villagers realize they have got a pondweed problem?

The correct answer is that it will probably take about nine hundred and ninety-nine days – because only then will the pond be half covered. The day before, it will only be a quarter covered. And the day before that, the pondweed will be a small green patch in one corner. That is why exponential problems are so difficult to avoid. That is why they typically feel like a backlash that seems to strike out of nowhere. That is why the hidden consequences of an interconnected world are of such concern: By the time leaders take note of these sorts of dangers – it is typically already too late.

# Uncontrollable escalation

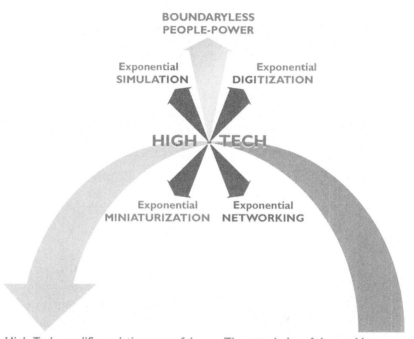

**BOUNDARYLESS PEOPLE-POWER**

Exponential **SIMULATION**

Exponential **DIGITIZATION**

**HIGH-TECH**

Exponential **MINIATURIZATION**

Exponential **NETWORKING**

High-Tech amplifies existing powerful components of the world economy
**BUT**
that includes previously-manageable side-effects that threaten economic stability

The remainder of the world economy fuels the development of High-Tech
**BUT**
if this is ever interrupted then the virtuous cycle will break down catastrophically

INDUSTRIALIZATION

POPULATION

RELIGION

**REMAINDER OF WORLD ECONOMY**

CAPITALISM

GLOBALIZATION

# REDUCING THE THREATS:
# PRE-EMPTIVE RECOVERY

High-Tech crises need *Pre-emptive Recovery* – devising responses to risks as part of the overall development-process

BY THE VERY fact that all of the deeply-interconnected systemic backlashes covered in this book are in some way affected by High-Tech, for most of them it is pretty meaningless to consider any particular aspect of High-Tech as being a 'root cause'. After all, move around the complex system and many other aspects (maybe Capitalism-induced-competition or Population-growth) can be seen to be equally significant in triggering a given crisis. However, it is a lot easier to find shared causes for the small subset of crises that are driven directly by High-Tech – namely those crises that derive straight from Digitization, Networking, Miniaturization and Simulation (such as cyberterrorism and superbugs). The risks of those crises can all be minimized by realigning activities in order to include *Pre-emptive Recovery.*

## THINKING THE WORST

The logic behind this approach to realigning an organization's strategic goals is that the current exponential growth in High-Tech means that new discoveries and developments are already coming so thick and fast that attendant problems are inevitable. But in general, advanced economies invest vastly more into pushing forward exciting disciplines such as social networks, AI, nanotech, biotech, GM-crops and advanced healthcare than they ever do into exploring what the possible negatives could be – let alone working out how to deal with such problems far in advance of them ever occurring, or thinking how to engage widespread support.

As a result, public debate and possible regulation typically come too late and in too negative a fashion. Strident and anxious lobbyists tend to try to block, stifle or hold back potentially very-attractive developments.

But that is because it is always easier for people to block something they do not fully understand – or that they worry is being allowed to run away with itself unchallenged – rather than find a way to optimize it. It is not really the fault of the lobbyists. It is primarily a result of scientists, developers, corporations and governments not doing sufficient groundwork beforehand to ensure that all exciting advancements come complete with their own safety-net.

The people most capable of devising the best defenses against potential negative side-effects such as virulent forms of internet malware, GM contamination, bioterrorism or malevolent AI, are often those with the greatest knowledge of High-Tech in the first place. Yet very few developers consider that one of their foremost professional obligations is to ensure mechanisms to overcome as many potential problems from their work as possible. Nor do governments or professional bodies or employers typically encourage them to do so.

There is another reason Pre-emptive Recovery is so important. Some people suggest that, even though there risks being a 'perfect storm' of global crises within the next few decades, there will also be a virtuous equivalent made up of mutually-reinforcing positive developments in Digitization, Networking, Miniaturization and Simulation that will more than compensate. But these people misunderstand the true nature of the trends involved. The reality is that the crises are themselves *created* by the largely-unstoppable High-Tech trends interacting with the other largely-immovable trends considered in this book. It is misleading to suggest that the Positives are somehow independent of the Negatives they create, let alone that by concentrating on those Positives alone then they will prevail and be sufficient to counter the growing threat of devastating backlashes.

## EARLY WARNING SO LEGISLATION PREDATES CRISES

Governments need to be advised (far more and far earlier than they currently are) of the forms of Pre-emptive Recovery they must ensure are in place – relating to everything from the escalating power of the internet to research on life extension. Government legislation must then anticipate those changes. Privacy laws, for instance, must evolve *ahead* of computer processing and archiving technologies, and yet also be sufficiently well defined that there is not an over-correction causing excessive applications for the equivalent of 'super-injunctions' (which force the media to keep private even the fact that there is something being kept private).

## SUPER-INJUNCTIONS

A so-called super-injunction does not in fact exist as a separate concept in law. It is merely a court-order (an injunction) that specifies that even the fact that an injunction has been granted – along with the name of the person applying for it – must be kept secret. High legal fees mean that super-injunctions are typically expensive to obtain. As a result, most people cannot afford them.

To take another example, that is far-less-extreme than many politicians assume, it is well-recognized amongst advanced-computing scientists that systems capable of Machine Intelligence that will seem comparable to human-levels of intellect are likely to emerge by 2040 – and more-specific versions may appear significantly before that. Indeed, for defense and security applications the most advanced governments are themselves active in such research. The advantages, as well as many of the conceivable threats that such research brings, are well documented and the need for suitable forms of Pre-emptive Recovery are obvious.

However, long before advanced research systems begin to look like serious contenders to win the Loebner Prize (indicating that a computer system has to all intents and purposes demonstrated human-level intelligence) a major ethics issue needs to have been solved. At what stage does deleting an earlier-version of some machine-intelligence software constitute deleting what under different circumstances would be viewed as a defenseless form of 'life'? At what level of sophistication are basic animal-rights relevant?

Over the last several decades, it has usually been assumed that if a machine ever claims that it has consciousness then it probably must be treated differently. But many mentally-handicapped humans could not communicate such a claim, yet are nevertheless protected by rigorous legislation. In the absence of responsible legislative decision-making *in advance* of its need, the risk is that – fairly or unfairly – the general public will later turn on those governments perceived as having had a conflict of interest in regulating the very AI research in which they were themselves heavily involved.

## RESPECTING SCIENTIFIC DEBATE FOR WHAT IT IS

Scientific debate must be accepted as the province of scientists; but scientists then have an obligation to explain themselves well enough that the public trusts them. Given the importance of politicians and others making the right judgments over the next several decades, deliberate falsification of science should be strictly illegal and carry far greater penalties – it is hard enough to do the right thing without vested interests deliberately confusing issues. And the media should be encouraged to question the credibility of anyone without a *relevant* PhD passing judgment *on the science* of a contentious issue such as climate change or GM-crops or nuclear risk (as opposed to commenting on anything else about the issue).

Similarly, the scientific community – with funding from science-based corporations – must feel responsible for pushing-back far stronger against unbalanced or misrepresentative coverage of scientific issues by the media. Scientists have a deep obligation to argue their case, because if they do not then others less qualified will. This is especially true for politically-charged issues such as GM-crops or climate change where science needs constantly to earn people's trust.

In addition, scientists also have a requirement to *anticipate* what may cause concern to the general public in the first place. Avoiding 'unnecessary' backlashes against science is just as much an issue of Pre-emptive Recovery as is developing defenses against something like cyberattack. Foisting a rapidly evolving and powerful idea or technology on the public without due consultation or an open and honest debate makes people worry that their government does not have enough oversight or understanding to protect them – or worse, is hiding things from them. So they react accordingly. Universities, corporations and scientific institutions must invest far more in training scientists to interact with the public and talk to the media as a matter of course. If they do not, then their ideas and ideals will be trashed by those with political and ideological agendas who *do* know how to behave in front of a camera.

## BROADENING RESPONSIBILITY OF COUNTERING ATTACKS

Responsibility to help counter threats such as cyberattack, nuclear terrorism and bioterrorism must rest not just on government but also parts of the private sector. With regard existing computer software used in forms of cyberattack, the international community is already considering 21$^{st}$ century Rules of War. Are there institutions such as hospitals that must not be attacked with malware? Are some forms of cyberattack simply too uncontrollable to be acceptable? Should some cyberweapons be banned by international treaty?

Such agreements must be made by governments – but it is largely only people in academia and software companies that can advise governments what the emerging issues are, let alone do anything about them. And alongside governments, it is the business community and civil society that must accept shared responsibility for minimizing cyber risks. The state alone cannot possibly do all the heavy lifting. Every form of relevant expertise needs to be coordinated into a combined counter to cyberattack. Computers need to be designed to be more secure. Schools must be more vigilant and encourage in their pupils far-more-responsible attitudes to unprotected sharing of software. Companies other than just the obvious targets (such as defense contractors, suppliers of piped water and tube-train services) need to up their game with regard cybersecurity because it is they rather than their well-protected colleagues that are increasingly likely to be targeted. On top of all this, designing or using computer malware should carry far stiffer penalties under international law, and governments should cooperate in a global clampdown.

Increasingly-rigorous monitoring must be used to secure against access by terrorists or rogue states to nuclear materials – with the aim that eventually every nuclear container is tracked electronically. Developments in 'nuclear forensics' (decoding the signatures of materials sourced from different fabrication facilities) should be integrated into a process of international law under which countries are held accountable for any aggressive use of their nuclear material. A worldwide rapid-response system should be set up to monitor for bioterrorist attacks or accidental release of pathogens. And in order to help counter-terrorism generally, far more sophisticated mechanisms should be created across the international banking system to locate and block terrorist fund-transfers flowing electronically from one account to another.

## INTERVENING SO HEALTHCARE HAS THE RIGHT SUPPORT

Systemic healthcare threats such as increasingly antibiotic-resistant bacteria must, if necessary, be countered by active government intervention rather than left solely to market forces. Far better, though, is that pharmaceutical corporations themselves take the lead (rather than wait for governments or others to 'encourage' them) in focusing more of their research on antibiotics, so as to keep pace with the progressive mutation of resistant bacteria. And they should lobby hard to ensure that global guidelines and regulation are tightened to avoid the current cavalier attitude in some countries to using antibiotics indiscriminately. Genetic manipulation, whether of crops or humans, should be actively managed at a global level rather than blocked at the national level – any attempts by individual countries to ban particular aspects will simply create a black market as well as set back their own nation's ability to compete in the global economy.

If politicians are serious about improving the health of their citizens, then they need to take a far firmer stand against tobacco – including counterfeit tobacco, which can have far higher toxic levels. Samples of counterfeit tobacco smuggled from China, for example, have been found to contain thirty times the lead content of regulated tobacco. Increasing numbers of smokers buying cheap under-the-counter cigarettes risk creating a healthcare time-bomb. For similar reasons, politicians and civil groups need seriously to tackle air pollution.

That leaves fatness. In developed countries above everything else, governments and retailers really need to get their act together to tackle obesity. In many advanced countries, eating far too much and exercising far too little has the potential within a couple of decades of becoming the biggest preventable killer. Yet surprisingly little is done to address the issue head-on. To many of us, raising the subject – even with close friends and family – feels a bit embarrassing. As a result, we tend to use the word 'obese' instead of 'fat'. But most of the time we say nothing. As a result, it is not just politicians that keep quiet. Studies are finding that even doctors avoid commenting about their patients' weight until it is far too late.

As part of this collusion, advertising aimed at average members of society adapts its choice of images to reflect the average shape – so an increasingly-overweight population continues to feel comfortable. Standard clothes-sizes grow. Parents begin to think that a child of ideal weight actually looks 'skinny and unhealthy'. And some who are morbidly obese protest their right not to be 'picked on'; meanwhile, their healthcare costs unnecessarily escalate. Everybody involved needs to find the courage to begin some straight talking.

## PROTECTING HIGH-TECH

Some other policies that follow from Pre-emptive Recovery are very high-level and can only really be enacted at international level. For instance, as already detailed on page 154, fusion-power is potentially an extremely attractive energy source thirty years out. Despite the major international projects underway, overall research is underfunded. It should be made a very-high priority as soon as current national deficits have been sufficiently reduced.

Similarly, as the 'supernet' emerges and massive archiving becomes routine, users will need a level of parallelism in search-routines that cannot even theoretically be achieved by the type of computer designs currently in use. Quantum-Computing research is partially funded for government communication-monitoring agencies such as the NSA and GCHQ. But such radically-different approaches will be crucial to more than just cryptography. This sort of research is currently under-prioritized in relation to the urgency that there will be within a couple of decades to realize its potential.

Finally, to avoid global economic collapse from Moore's Law slowing too fast, it is necessary to prioritize High-Tech computer-chip manufacture (and everything that flows from it) even above traditional sectors such as the automotive industry – politically sensitive though such a policy is. When famous-name car companies liquidate, there are massive job losses. If the world's chip designers cannot find the money to create the next generation of integrated circuits on schedule, much of the global economy risks unraveling.

In due course, just as with peaking-oil, the international community will indeed eventually need to manage a globally-orchestrated slowing of Moore's Law (because the technical challenges will at last be becoming insurmountable). But the world economy is absolutely nowhere near that time yet. Long, long before then, High-Tech will have accelerated a final major trend of the world economy to such a degree that extreme backlashes caused by the unfathomable interactions of all the other trends risk becoming both inevitable and unstoppable.

It is this last trend more than any other that hard-wires the interconnections of our world economy and amplifies the hidden consequences that clash within it. Out of sight, it builds uncontrolled feedback throughout the economic system until the overload to our established infrastructure eventually blows the weakest link – in what we perceive as a global crisis. In this chapter we explored the relatively-calm eye of the storm – the very heart of the explosive High-Tech vortex that is stirring up such turbulence further afield. In the next chapter we will see what ultimately constrains that spiraling and increasingly-unstable vortex within its ultimately self-destructive path: Globalization.

# HIGH–TECH CRISES

**In addition to triggering crises in otherwise-benign global trends the four established exponential trends in HIGH-TECH generate crises directly and require Pre-emptive Recovery as a counter-measure**

The combined dominance of the four established High-Tech trends makes the global economy vulnerable to any disruption to them

Each of the four established High-Tech trends carries major risks to economic stability in its own right
- *Although many perceived risks of overdependence on Digitization are unfounded there is a severe vulnerability to technologies such as Pulse Bombs*
- *Many risks from Networking are already well-addressed but Cyberattack remains a major threat because of acute vulnerabilities in civilian targets*
- *Miniaturization crises primarily relate to healthcare – especially if advances in antibiotics and other treatments do not keep pace with emerging risks*
- *The Simulation trend brings major risks of crisis from deliberate bioterrorism and accidental release of pathogens*

The riskiest High-Tech crises arise from unintended consequences throughout the world economy escalating too fast and being too interconnected for conventional responses to work

High-Tech crises need PRE-EMPTIVE RECOVERY – devising responses to risks as part of the overall development-process
- *Those who devise an exciting new technology should also try to forecast even its less-likely potential problems and work out how to deal with them well in advance*
- *Governments must have far better early-warning of potential High-Tech crises so that legislation can anticipate technological trends rather than react to them*
- *Scientific debate must be accepted as the province of scientists but scientists then have an obligation to explain themselves well enough that the public trusts them*

# Chapter summary

- *Responsibility to help counter threats such as cyberattack, nuclear terrorism and bioterrorism must rest not just on government but also parts of the private sector*
- *Systemic healthcare threats such as increasingly antibiotic-resistant bacteria must be countered by active government intervention rather than left to market forces*
- *The High-Tech sector must be protected above traditional manufacturing and very-long-term research into fusion-power and quantum-computing must be prioritized*

## 26. DIRECT AND INDIRECT RISKS OF HIGH-TECH CRISES

**HIGH TECH**

**BOUNDARYLESS PEOPLE-POWER**

Thuggish riots and looting

Spontaneous peaceful rallies and online protests

**Exponential DIGITIZATION**

Progressive infrastructural vulnerability to hostile-state or terrorist attack

Near-total lack of civilian shielding against electromagnetic-pulse damage to micro circuitry

**Exponential NETWORKING**

Trend toward widespread software standardization to encourage broad uptake by casual users

Increasingly acute vulnerability to largely-untraceable cyberattack by political activists hostile states or terrorists

**Exponential MINIATURIZATION**

Healthcare R&D coalesces around exciting fields such as nanotech in preference to mundane fields such as antibiotics

Uncontrollable infection as resistant strains of bacteria emerge faster than science can develop new antibiotics

**Exponential SIMULATION**

Increasing risk of bioterrorist attack or super-addictive recreational drugs or accidental release of pathogens

Biotech factories increasingly affordable to moderately-funded groups and controllable by basic-level scientists

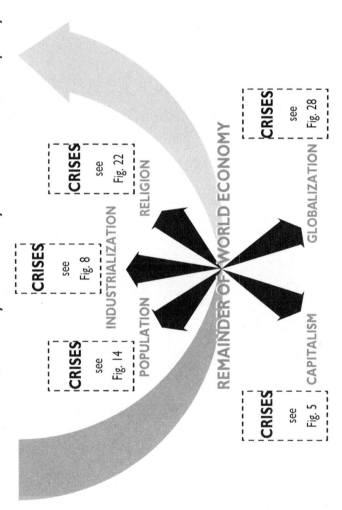

High-Tech amplifies existing powerful components of the world economy

**BUT**

that includes previously-manageable side-effects that threaten economic stability

The remainder of the world economy fuels the development of High-Tech

**BUT**

if this is ever interrupted then the virtuous cycle will break down catastrophically

CRISES see Fig. 22

CRISES see Fig. 8

CRISES see Fig. 14

CRISES see Fig. 28

CRISES see Fig. 5

RELIGION

INDUSTRIALIZATION

POPULATION

GLOBALIZATION

CAPITALISM

REMAINDER OF WORLD ECONOMY

# GLOBALIZATION CRISES overview

Globalization so heightens other threats that the international community now has no mechanism to evolve effective responses and requires Holistic Perspective as a counter-measure

- Globalization exacerbates the risk of *all* globally-defined threats to economic stability – including 'wildcard' events

- Despite generally high competence of individuals, national government decision-making is misaligned with addressing globally-defined threats

- Unfortunately, supranational bodies are also unsuited to exerting sufficient global governance leaving the world economy at severe risk

- Globalization crises need HOLISTIC PERSPECTIVE – seeing issues in the context of both the global arena and a 30-year time-horizon

*Threats of backlashes to: GOVERNMENT, the ESTABLISHMENT and UN*

# GLOBALIZATION

# CRISES

# EVERYTHING SIMULTANEOUSLY BETTER AND WORSE

High-Tech-Globalization exacerbates crises already stirred up by High-Tech interacting with Capitalism, Industrialization, Population and Religion

ALREADY, MUCH OF the world is more uniform than – until quite recently – many of its individual *countries* were. For increasing numbers of people around the globe, everyday life is becoming remarkably similar. From the 1980s onward, explosions in communication and transport, widespread deregulation of international trading, and unprecedented movements of people between different cultures increasingly led to a form of global standardization. That progressive interconnection is not set to slow any time soon. World air-traffic is due to double by 2030; China alone will build almost one hundred new airports over the next ten years.

As a result of all this, large numbers of those living in very different places nevertheless tend to use comparable products and share related ideas. International telephone traffic, worldwide tourism and migration have all shot up, and their costs have plummeted. International banks are interconnected as never before as they borrow billions of dollars from each other every day. Cheap Chinese goods have – directly or indirectly – driven down the living costs for almost everyone everywhere. The gap between the richest billion people and the poorest billion on the planet is growing, but that same pattern is playing out just as much in countries like China and India as in the USA and UK. And despite the huge differences in wealth, around the world people often watch the same films, listen to the same music, play the same games, and even dress in the same styles of clothes.

## PHYSICAL INTERCONNECTIONS

Behind the scenes, much of this has been made possible by an extraordinary global-transport infrastructure of which the general public is

350

hardly aware. A large container-ship can carry up to 15,000 separate 20-foot-long containers, there are roughly 20-million containers making several international trips every year, and each container can potentially be filled with utterly different products. These simple facts have changed the unwritten rules of commerce.

Before globalization really got going, up to 30% of the cost of an imported product might be the cost of shipping it around the world. These days it is typically closer to 1%. The cost of delivering a plasma-screen TV from a local warehouse to your home may be more than shipping it all the way from China. What is more, manufacturers now have the chance to keep far less of their products in a central warehouse, and instead they use the huge container fleets as a form of mobile distributed-warehouse.

## LOST AT SEA

Roughly 0.05% of containers are lost at sea each year (around ten thousand). What is rarely mentioned is that many of those are *deliberately* jettisoned by captains because high seas are making their ships sufficiently unstable that some of the upper-containers must be sacrificed. Unfortunately, on the occasions that most customers transport something by container there is no way of asking for it to be stowed low-down in a ship – so when members of the public are asked if they want to take out insurance 'in case of loss at sea' they should not so much evaluate the chances of the ship going down as the likelihood that their container is unlucky enough to have been stacked on top prior to a particularly rough storm.

Different parts of even quite a simple product may these days be manufactured in different countries and only brought together in the final stage of assembly Just In Time for delivery to the final purchaser. But it is not simply manufacturing that gets dispersed. An automobile 'made' in one country may have its engine, tires and other components each made in different countries to each other, while in addition the designing, marketing and financing of the whole operation may themselves each take place in different parts of the world.

# GLOBALIZATION CRISES

As a result of sophisticated distribution networks it has been possible for factories and even whole communities to become very specialized. The town of Yiwu in Eastern China has become known as Sock Town because it produces billions of the low-cost socks, tights and pantyhose that are now sold in bargain-value packs in retail stores throughout the Western world. That level of specialization for a commodity-product like socks is only possible because of the utterly-fundamental – but largely unrecognized – transformation there has been in how the world interacts. It is easy to see the trend of progressive standardization around the world. But it is the often-hidden processes behind that increasing uniformity that truly define High-Tech-Globalization. Just as with the other complex but camouflaged trends that are escalating threats to our economic and social stability, there are numerous Globalization backlashes that are building. However, *their* cumulative effect risks global chaos.

## NO PLACE LEFT TO HIDE

These unintended consequences tend to be even-more worrying that many of the others we have already looked at. The reason is because, by its very nature, Globalization is all about linking activities together in ways that are far more complex, and much less understood, than in the past. Nearly all countries are conducting the same global experiment all at the same time. None has prior experience. No government can check-up on where such rapid and widespread interconnection of materials and information has worked (or failed) in the past because it has never happened this way before, so history is of less help than usual. Even major powers such as the USA, EU and China will increasingly struggle to cope because the underlying nature of the combined crises that we now face – the hidden consequences of an interconnected world – are completely unprecedented.

More daunting even than that is the fact that when we analyze how the five previous clusters of crises in this book actually interact with each other, it becomes clear that all five are in fact being forced together and magnified by the containing explosion of Globalization. Many of the more-dangerous Globalization Crises are themselves amplifications of risks already triggered by the otherwise-benign trends of Capitalism, Industrialization, Population and Religion – which have themselves already 'gone critical' as a result of their contact with High-Tech.

Moreover, the increasing interconnection of everything with everything else across the international community means that our conventional mechanisms for defending society are already unfit for purpose. The boundary between a national economy, national security and overall national government is even now hopelessly blurred. The role of Foreign Affairs in every government is becoming increasingly fraught. And its sharp historical distinction with Domestic Affairs will soon be illusory. Indeed, the very-greatest threats to national security relate to governments' inabilities to *counter* the amplified risks brought by Globalization.

As this overall chapter will detail, High-Tech-Globalization highlights fundamental restrictions that governments now face in trying to protect their citizens within a tightly-interconnected world. In reality, each country is far more exposed than its general population – or indeed much of its government – typically realizes. As you will learn by the end of the chapter, as things currently stand, our governments no longer have any practical mechanism left that can be used to stop an inexorable and potentially-devastating drift toward progressive anarchy.

# WILD MARKET SWINGS, ECONOMIC CRASHES AND SOCIAL MELTDOWN

High-Tech-Capitalism crises exacerbated by High-Tech-Globalization enhance threats such as wild market swings, economic crashes and social meltdown

GLOBALIZATION REINFORCES NUMEROUS concerns raised by Capitalism. For instance, the global trade on the internet not only fuels Capitalism itself but also makes it easier to buy everything from illegal baby lions and poached ivory to polar-bear pelts and endangered red and pink coral. But the backlash that everyone will feel the effects of will come from Banking. However much governments around the world endeavor to tighten regulation (even despite the huge Legacy Effects within the financial-services industry that resist such changes) politicians are in fact trying to tighten controls at the same time as the world is becoming increasingly interconnected. Delays are shorter. Feedback is faster. That means that many of the dampening effects throughout the global economy are progressively disappearing. Swings potentially become wilder. Over-reactions become more extreme – even if regulation is improved.

For instance, because competitive News coverage is so all-pervasive, an unguarded comment by a politician at the end of the working-day in Asia can be instantly misinterpreted by the British media and cause a buying or selling frenzy in the London market, which later in the day gets picked up by Wall Street and runs unabated until Asia wakes the next morning and a government bureaucrat issues a clarification of the earlier statement. Seeing how their Western colleagues traded, and knowing that it will now be corrected, Asian traders react accordingly, sending another wave through the system that is picked up by European traders several hours later, and later still by Wall Street. All the wild fluctuations eventually settle down to where they were before. They corresponded to nothing real other than the overreaction of an excitable under-damped system.

354

# Escalation of all globally-defined threats

Despite attempts to regulate the banks, as Globalization continues so the largely-unregulated media and internet will nevertheless exacerbate a gradual shift toward increasing turbulence in the financial markets. As things stand, the global economy will be increasingly susceptible to crises comparable to the Credit Crunch that resulted in banking receiving more state aid than any other industry in history. It is just that next time there may not be so much money to bail the economy out. That risk is made more likely because, in practice, controlling banking (as explained in the subchapter starting on page 8 about *Why escalating global financial crises are inevitable*) is going to prove very difficult. Despite plans by politicians to avoid banks ever again holding countries to ransom by being 'too big to fail', the reality is that the banks are extremely skilled in playing cat and mouse with regulators, politicians and the general public.

I have previously mentioned how quickly huge bonuses returned to the financial community following the near-collapse of banking. But what is telling is what happened straight after that. The response to complaints that banks were once again paying major bonuses was that – at least for the next round – many banks appeared to cut the size of bonuses. People who had previously received 'a whopping $1.4-million bonus' (actually rather feeble in terms of bragging rights amongst fellow financiers), now only got a 'vastly-reduced' bonus of 'hundreds of thousands'. It looked responsible. What few realized was that several banks increased the base-pay of their senior people to compensate. Someone who had previously earned a base of $200,000 now earned $600,000 as well as a bonus of *just under* $1-million. Behind the scenes, nothing important had changed.

Nor in many countries did the revolving-door between Banking and Government slow down, with top officials moving from one environment to the other and back again, just as also occurs between Government and the upper-echelons of the Oil and Pharmaceutical industries. With this sort of cross-fertilization so prevalent, it is difficult for the State not to be influenced by the self-interest of the Banks and others. Particularly in the USA and the UK, such 'regulatory capture' is a feat of which some banking, oil and pharmaceutical top-executives are privately rather proud.

## HOW FINANCIAL CRISES TURN INTO SOCIETAL MELTDOWN

All of that is understandable. As explained on page 72, many large corporations no longer view themselves as being there primarily to help the community. Instead they view themselves as being there to make a profit for their shareholders. Their remuneration packages are typically designed to reinforce that belief very strongly. Like many corporate leaders, top banking executives are often granted huge stock-options that pay out more and more as share-price goes up. Their bonuses are typically dominated by financial performance. Under those circumstances, despite what politicians tell them to do, banks are not particularly predisposed to lend to 'risky' businesses or entrepreneurs – it has historically just not been as lucrative as instead lending that money for private mortgages or commercial real-estate development.

Banking is still locked on pretty much the same path as is has been for the last two decades. And the major banks still tend to be so large that there is relatively little competitive pressure on them fundamentally to change direction. On top of that, the damping effects on the global economy are progressively evaporating as proliferating formal media and informal internet-chatter offer near-instantaneous feedback. Banking regulation – however well-coordinated internationally – cannot possibly moderate those parts of the global system that are outside the banking industry and yet heavily impact how it behaves. The whole system is increasingly at risk of becoming unstable. Just because the financial community unintentionally brought the global economy crashing down in such a catastrophic way that (just as in the 1930s) governments promised 'It must never happen again', does not of itself mean that the risk is now any less. On the contrary, not only has little changed in banking, but the global context in which banking operates is predisposed to ever-wilder ricochets than in the past.

Toxic debts that ultimately related to unsafe private-mortgages were the cause of the initial global economic-crisis in 2008. Within three years that had escalated into financial crises relating to 'sovereign debt' (that is, public debt owed by a state government) in countries such as Greece and Portugal that borrowed heavily in order to protect their banks and fund their public sectors during global-recession and then were deemed unable to repay their debts. Rich countries within the Eurozone stepped in. Within only months, the Eurozone itself became at risk.

Large member-countries such as Italy then came into the spotlight – and were viewed as having deep structural problems in paying off their escalating debts. France found itself unduly exposed to Greek debt. German citizens increasingly found themselves committed to contribute the lion's-share of bailouts for countries that they considered had not worked as long or as hard or been as disciplined as they had (although, to be fair, Germany had itself earlier broken the rules of the Euro, and its substantial exports had benefitted from a decade of lower exchange-rates than would have been possible under the Deutschmark). At the end of 2011, national leaders of the Eurozone committed to greater fiscal unity. But even attempting to force-fit all their countries into a straightjacket of conformity will of itself create inevitable backlashes. At the end of the day, inherently unstable complex-systems are *always* exceptionally unlikely to succeed in the long-term. Political 'commitment' does not change the laws of system dynamics. It just delays the inevitable.

As with nearly all politicians and civil servants, too many European leaders have completely underestimated how remarkably difficult it is in practice to change cultures. Even merging-corporations find it an uphill struggle. Countries that do not even share the same leaders, let alone a common heritage or joint aspirations, will find it impossible to change fast enough. The general population of Greece or Italy will not act as if they were Germans. Nor even will Germany's closest economic ally the French. And if political leaders disregard the sustained democratic wishes of their people for too long – their people will remove them. One way or another.

That is the pattern of how the interconnected financial world now works. After each major crisis, politicians and banks promise each other that it is the 'last time' it will ever happen. Then they continue largely as before. But one way or another, in their on-going abusive relationship with The Market, governments *will be* hit again. What there may not be is the public money needed to heal the resulting wounds. And it is that difference that will generate a more-extreme form of crisis.

When nations no longer have enough money, and when The Market effectively blocks them from borrowing any more, then those countries whose governments have been living beyond their means and doling out money to paper-over cracks in their social-structure will have to stop. They will have to renege on The Deal that has kept their public happy. In some places, Nationalist or Fascist movements will attempt to fill the void – just as happened in the 1930s in countries like Germany and Italy and Spain and Hungary and Romania and Brazil. Other places will see a resurgence of Communism or religious-fundamentalism. And many countries will suffer bitter clashes between *all* those extremes. Whereas in 2007-8 the High-Tech-Capitalism crisis was a credit-crunch, with a bit of help from Globalization it can all-too-easily lead to societal meltdown.

# THE UNINTENDED LACK OF CONTROL BROUGHT BY MULTINATIONALS

## High-Tech-Industrialization crises exacerbated by High-Tech-Globalization enhance threats of government lack of control unintentionally caused by the net effect of multinationals

SOCIAL-DISRUPTION AROUND the world is also being worsened by the impacts of Globalization on a combination of Industrialization and Capitalism side-effects. The previously-mentioned container shipping, for example, provides inexpensive manufactured goods to massive retail conglomerates. But those same huge outlets have already destroyed the local social infrastructure of numerous town centers previously served by small shops. That trend is set to continue, not least because the large corporations involved can quite correctly always claim 'market forces' as the justification for why they do what they do. But, although in some ways the loss of vibrant centers in a few urban communities may seem a relatively minor issue, it is the pattern behind that example that indicates what is going on below the surface of social infrastructure as a whole.

When both Capitalism and Industrialization combine with Globalization it means that the largest companies – especially multinationals, which base themselves across several countries – no longer have a particular loyalty to any given locality. They feel a primary loyalty to their shareholders (and to varying degrees their employees), but in reality they can play one country off against another because massive wealth that is not irrevocably tied to any one nation brings great political clout.

That means that as covered in the subchapter proposing *Unelected Responsibility* (starting on page 72), unelected though corporate leaders are, these days they have a major influence that on occasion competes with government officials. Some of this is broadly understood even though it is largely out of sight of the general public. The largest corporations all tend to engage heavily in commercial lobbying of politicians, many make substantial contributions to political campaigns, they influence unions, and often they run their own diplomatic missions in developing countries.

In addition, and far more than politicians tend to acknowledge, some multinationals adopt bullying tactics along the lines of: 'If you don't accommodate our wishes we'll move elsewhere.' But all this has been going on for several decades. What is far newer is the combined global impact that Big Business is increasingly having. As already explained in the subchapter about *Rolling News* (page 44), it is extremely easy for individual choices – for instance by journalists – to result in a *collective* result that no one controls, intends or even wants. The same is happening with unelected Corporate Power.

## BEYOND EVEN 'UNELECTED RESPONSIBILITY'

Each large corporation makes decisions in its self-interest. Ultimately that is what its top executives tend to be paid to do. Although there are a few important companies – primarily in continental Europe and Latin America – that quite deliberately balance making profits with improving the quality of life in the greater community, most do not. That is not because of greed; it is because of a genuine belief that a company's primary obligation is to work for those who ultimately are risking their money by investing in the company in the first place.

I have had a very large number of conversations with the CEOs and top executives of many of the largest multinationals around the globe. And most of those people fervently, and honorably, believe that (at least in an official capacity) *their* duty is to maximize shareholder gains whereas it is the duty of *politicians* to consider the wider population. As a result, a given corporation makes decisions that may prove crucial to how a particular society functions, but those choices are not typically driven according to their social impact. Instead, they are usually dictated by purely commercial considerations. The decision-makers may take a long view (though sometimes, as in banking, they strongly tend toward short-termism), however they will usually focus on the company above all else.

Because these corporations are so big, and because they are not tied to any particular country, they will operate to a large extent as if they were separate nations in their own right. Almost every major corporation adopts that same pattern. As High-Tech-Globalization increasingly frees multinationals from being based in any particular city or state, or even continent, the collective effect is that society is progressively being dominated (completely unintentionally) by the combined sum of all the highly-influential decisions of numerous corporate executives all looking out for their own 'virtual country'.

## HOW BUSINESS STUDENTS LEARN TO BE SELFISH

The belief that a company's overriding responsibility is to its shareholders is often already ingrained in young managers. Over the years, I have taught thousands of post-graduate students studying for a Master of Business Administration (MBA) qualification in leading international Business Schools in the USA, UK and the Netherlands. In my experience, students born in the USA and UK often take for granted that shareholder-value is paramount, whereas those from, for instance, family-owned companies in Latin America or society-oriented countries in continental Europe often start with more-open minds. However, throughout their courses and subsequent business careers, nearly every business textbook or journal or case-study that the students read comes from authors in the USA or UK. And it is *that* exposure that tends to make the strongest eventual impact on them.

Unlike their political counterparts, the Presidents of these elite Executives are unelected by the nations they impact, lack any real legitimacy to influence so heavily the countries they operate from, are largely unaccountable for any negative side-effects they cause, in the extreme can exit a country that is of no further use to them, and can depart with no recourse for the population left behind. But there is a more-important dynamic going on than that. Even if, as proposed in the subchapter starting on page 72, individual corporations do indeed adapt far-greater Unelected Responsibility, that does not imply that their *collective* impact will automatically be beneficial – any more than is the misrepresentative overall impression sometimes left after a feeding-frenzy by journalists, or the global impact of misaligned nations depleting natural resources.

With no international mechanism for politicians to coordinate their (sometimes more-powerful) Corporate Opposition, global governance is shifting toward far more of a corporately-self-serving, non-transparent and non-social focus than most governments realize. And under those circumstances it is almost impossible to apply the True Costing or achieve the Collective Sustainability advocated in the subchapters starting on pages 145 and 217 respectively.

An increasingly-unmanageable number of powerful multinationals are making fully-professional but largely-uncoordinated decisions that are simply not intended to harmonize into something that is collectively best for society as a whole. Typically they are not doing anything wrong. Sometimes – as individual corporations – they are even deliberately trying to 'give something back' to the communities in which they operate. But their disjointed actions increasingly risk swamping the abilities of governments to maintain and improve the overall well-being of the international community as a whole.

Full Globalization is propelling multinationals into the unprecedented league of a loose confederation of Virtual Countries more flexible, more dynamic and often more politically-powerful than many of the nations within which they operate. Yet none of them have membership of the United Nations – or an equivalent. In contrast, it is national governments that *do* belong to the UN – stuck as they are with only one country, one set of depleting natural resources, one polluted environment, one national economy – that risk being left to try to pick up the pieces.

# UNMANAGEABLE PANDEMICS

## High-Tech-Population crises exacerbated by High-Tech-Globalization enhance threats such as uncontrollable pandemics

THERE ARE MANY Population backlashes that are amplified by Globalization. One of the most visible is uncontrolled migration. Effectively linking the world population with world resources – which in many ways is what the world economy is all about – is important to everybody. And when those links are not strong enough, populations tend to migrate. As an example, by 2020 the Arab population in the Middle East is expected to match that of the European Union. Most will be young. If, over the following decade, affordable oil and water begin to become scarcer, many will want to leave their homelands. Exactly the same will be true in many parts of Africa. As deprivation and conflict build, migration into Europe risks becoming unstoppable. Just as does Mexican migration into the USA.

However, backlashes in the form of mass migration are not just caused by famine and war. At the moment, the global economy severely underperforms its potential because of a profligate waste of human talent – for instance, once again, across major regions of Africa and the Middle-East. In each location (though for different reasons) there are large populations operating far below their capabilities. In much of Africa, many are incredibly poor and they struggle to survive. In parts of the Middle-East, there is currently so much oil-money that whole generations risk wasting their lives. That is a far-more-current reason to move.

There are many other Population backlashes that are exacerbated by the homogenization that Globalization tends to bring. For instance, the increasingly widespread use of the same monocultures of particular high-yield strains of crops and species of livestock places agriculture around the world at risk from natural (or bioterrorist) epidemics that affect animals or plants. As a result, any potential risk of Malthusian Collapse from famine is artificially increased. However, there is a far greater concern.

## GLOBALIZED GERMS

Nowhere is the amplifying effect of Globalization more pronounced than when it comes to communicable diseases. As already highlighted in the subchapter that started on page 325, Bioterrorism is a growing concern – not least because it might not be the result of extremism but might instead be caused by someone with the mind-set of a 'spree killer' or an arsonist. However, the diseases-of-choice for terrorists (and the recreational drugs-of-choice for organized crime) are the types that remain relatively contained within a selected community.

A far greater biological threat comes from naturally-occurring diseases that spread uncontrollably. Technically, if an infectious disease has spread so far around the globe that people are getting ill from it almost everywhere, it becomes formally reclassified from Widespread Epidemic to Pandemic. And it is the danger of pandemics that High-Tech-Globalization has elevated into a whole new level of threat. Forgotten today, by the end of 1918 it was becoming increasingly impractical to continue World War I – because of Spanish flu. The previous year, only a hundred or so people died from it. But over the next couple of years, around a third of the world's population became infected. At least one in ten of those infected died, that is about 50-million deaths. It may even have been double that number. If the same mortality-rate occurred with today's far-larger human population, it would result in between 200-million and 400-million deaths.

That is not as preposterous as it seems. Even with today's advances, Spanish flu's unusual severity and very-high infection rates would make it exceptionally hard to control. Antibiotics would be completely ineffective because it is a virus, and antivirals are not always practical. What is more, being fit would not help either. Spanish flu predominantly kills strong young adults. Children and the old often survive. Today the Spanish-flu outbreak is largely overlooked by general historians. But not by public-health officials. That is why these days they will always tend to err on the side of caution with regard threats like the 2009 H1N1 'swine flu' outbreak. They know very well just how dangerous a modern pandemic could be.

The real problem is caused by High-Tech-Globalization mixed with mutation. Modern-day travel – whether by road, rail, air or sea – means that within a couple of days a disease can spread throughout the world. And once it has spread, even modern medicines in sophisticated and rich countries may struggle to get rid of it. But that is only part of the issue.

363

# GLOBALIZATION CRISES

## WHY SPANISH FLU KILLED THE FITTEST

Normally flu kills the very-young and the old, so with Spanish flu it was highly-unexpected that healthy strong adults should die far more frequently than those with weaker immune systems. Very recent research on a virus recreated from the decoded DNA of a tissue sample from a Spanish-flu victim suggests that deaths occurred as the result of an overreaction of the immune system known as a 'cytokine storm'. Young adults with the strongest immune systems would, ironically, be most likely to overreact to the infection – and their bodies burned-out as a result.

## WHY SMALLPOX WAS FAR EASIER TO CONQUER THAN AIDS

Eradicating smallpox around the world was, at least in principle, relatively simple because the virus hardly mutates at all. Once enough people had been immunized, smallpox died out. In early 2003, Severe Acute Respiratory Syndrome (SARS) broke out of China and rapidly infected around forty countries. The world's labs combined their expertise in an unmatched demonstration of collaborative effort, and within four weeks they had decoded the virus' genetics. Luckily, SARS was hardly mutating. After a mass quarantine, the outbreak was over and a pandemic avoided.

Something like the AIDS virus – HIV – is very different. More than a quarter of a century ago, scientists hoped quickly to develop a vaccine. Back then, long before it was possible to decode a virus' DNA within mere weeks, they estimated a vaccine would take a couple of years. Despite all the exponential medical advances since then, there is still no vaccine for HIV or cure for AIDS. It is now a pandemic. Tens of millions are infected worldwide, with a few million added each year – many of them babies infected during pregnancy or via their mother's milk. The trouble is that the AIDS virus keeps mutating. That means the medical profession cannot yet even eradicate it from a single individual, let alone from the global population. Classic immunization just will not work. Even for an individual, the best – expensive – treatments at the moment just manage to keep AIDS in check. At least for a while. Usually with unpleasant side-effects.

# Escalation of all globally-defined threats

If patients live in a rich country then AIDS can often now be treated as a chronic disease. If they live in a poor country, infection with HIV is typically still a slow and miserable death sentence. About three-quarters of AIDS deaths are in sub-Saharan Africa, in impoverished and failing countries. In such regions, in addition to killing people, AIDS accelerates societal-collapse. When someone contracts AIDS it means another family-member has to look after them. Maybe a child has to drop school to help their one remaining parent. Some girls resort to what is referred to as 'survival sex' – which often spreads the disease still further. At many levels, it is an utter tragedy. Yet, despite some religious extremists continuing to preach about AIDS as if it were a 'new' plague that started in the 1980s within the US gay community, the truth is that the AIDS tragedy has been playing out in Africa for about a century.

## AIDS IN AFRICA

In sub-Saharan Africa around 25-million people are infected with HIV although only 1-million of them receive anti-viral treatment. Life expectancy in the thirty-eight AIDS-afflicted African countries has dropped by about ten years to an average of only forty-five years old. As a result, although it was largely kept quiet at the time, some medical authorities in developed nations were privately concerned about the eventual impact of the 2010 World Cup in South Africa (where 6-million residents have AIDS) – given that for countries like the UK more than two-thirds of heterosexual men and a quarter of women who contract HIV do so through unprotected holiday sex.

Genetic analysis of the virus now suggests that it first crossed from chimpanzees to humans about a hundred years ago in the central African region that is now the Democratic Republic of the Congo. Those regions that are suffering the worst today are, broadly, the same environments from which AIDS first originated and then grew into an early epidemic that spread from the poorest nations to the richest states in the USA (probably via extremely-poor Haiti). There is a crucial lesson in that – potential-pandemics tend to get their first foothold in the world's poorest communities. Then they spread.

# GLOBALIZATION CRISES

## WHERE PANDEMICS COME FROM

Most human killer-diseases come into existence quite randomly. They often mutate from a strain of the disease that has adapted to infecting a particular animal. Of all the random mutations that the disease makes, hardly any one of them may have a chance of surviving in humans. But it only takes one. And then the disease has in effect jumped across species. H1N1 swine-flu came from pigs. H5N1 bird-flu came from chickens. AIDS originally mutated from chimpanzees. Living closely with animals comes at a cost. Yet not all possible-pandemics start in developing countries. 'Mad-cow disease' is thought to have been spread by Western farmers feeding cattle with food-supplements that were themselves derived from slaughtered cattle. But no one fully understands how the disease first originated.

Although few members of the public worry about Mad Cow these days, maybe they should. The human variant – Creatzfeldt-Jakob Disease (CJD for short) – is invariably fatal. And you can catch it in a way that medical-science hardly understands. It is transmitted not by a virus but by a weird type of protein called a 'prion'. CJD is the most common type of 'spongiform encephalopathy' found in humans, basically your brain ends up looking like a sponge. The type found in cattle is bovine spongiform encephalopathy (BSE). The prions that cause CJD are still not fully understood but they are believed to be transmitted to humans by eating meat from cows infected with BSE. Although BSE was originally assumed to have mutated from the sheep equivalent (scrapie), many now consider it as likely that BSE originated spontaneously.

But one of the many problems about Mad Cow and CJD is the lethal prions. They are extremely difficult to destroy. Sterilizing surgical instruments sometimes does not work. Cooking meat even to Well-Done certainly is not sufficient to destroy prions and avoid infection. What is more, the incubation period of the disease is not known, though it is estimated it could be many decades. Although it now seems highly unlikely that CJD will in fact become a major problem, it is an important wake-up call because it is an illustration of a whole type of degenerative-disease transmission that science knows little about and that breaks many of the rules that doctors – and the public – take for granted about avoiding infections. No one knows what the next prion disease will be.

The trouble is that no one knows what any of the future killer-pandemics will be. It is hoped that it is unlikely, but there is no fundamental reason why AIDS could not mutate into a more-easily-transmittable form. Far more probable is a virulent form of killer-flu for which science cannot design a suitable antiviral treatment. Despite what the general public tends to assume, it is currently very difficult to design safe antiviral drugs. In order to replicate itself, a virus actually takes over cells in the infected person's body. So it is often extremely hard to disrupt the virus without also disrupting important cells the patient needs to keep alive. For now, there is no guarantee that researchers can find an effective antiviral treatment for a specific virus that does not seriously harm the patient. And there is currently no equivalent treatment for prions at all.

However, although we do not know what the worst pandemics will be, we *do* know where most of them will come from. New diseases will continue usually to take root in the poorest communities in the world – partly because healthcare standards are so low but also because the poorest people tend to live in very-close proximity to each other and to animals. It is estimated that around one billion people currently live in slums and shantytowns. The forecast is that by 2050 the number will be two billion.

Even the emergence of antibiotic-resistant bacteria – discussed in the subchapter on *How pharmaceuticals risk being overwhelmed* (page 319) – is much more likely in slums. The potentially-incurable strains of tuberculosis announced in 2012 were first recognized by Indian doctors at the Hinduja National Hospital where they had been treating TB patients for as long as two years on a battery of antibiotics, and yet failed to cure them. Those patients all came from the huge shantytown that sprawls across Mumbai. In the current age of economic austerity and public-service cutbacks, some question the logic behind foreign aid. Advocates of Survival-of-the-Fittest suggest that the highest priority is for developed countries to look after themselves first. There is a catch though. Charity may begin at home – but killer pandemics begin in slums.

# IMMIGRATION TIME-BOMBS

High-Tech-Religion crises exacerbated by High-Tech-Globalization enhance threats such as immigration 'time-bombs' exploding into civil unrest and international conflict

RELIGION CRISES ARE being brought to a head as High-Tech-Globalization forces apparently-incompatible views together. Real-time TV News coverage of Israeli action against Palestine inflames anti-Semitism in some Moslem communities at the same time as Islamophobia builds in some Christian and secular communities because of perceived cultural or terrorist threats.

## BURQA OR NIQAB

When non-Moslems hear about 'banning the burqa' they often get confused about exactly which bit of clothing is being referred to. Technically, a burqa is the traditional all-enveloping loose garment that covers a woman head to toe with a slit for her to see through. It is the niqab that is the slit face-veil part of the burqa that some people want to ban. But in the West the term 'burqa' and 'niqab' are often used to mean the same thing. The majority of Islamic scholars rule that both the burqa and niqab are merely traditional forms of dress and are not a religious obligation in the way that, for example, a turban is for a Sikh.

As New Yorkers try to prevent a mosque being set up near Ground Zero, Switzerland attempts to stop the construction of minarets, France tries to prevent people wearing the burqa and niqab in public places, and the Netherlands voices concerns about an anti-Moslem backlash, so second-generation African, Arab and Pakistani youths living in the USA and

368

countries right across Europe feel progressively alienated and radicalized, with Islam becoming more important to their sense of identity than their nationality – of a country that, after all, seems increasingly to reject them.

Meanwhile the Anglican church splits over gay-rights and female bishops, the pope offers the more-conservative Protestant church leaders a 'fast-track conversion' to Roman Catholicism, and – against fierce opposition from the Vatican – Argentina becomes the first country in Latin America to legalize gay marriage. Then in May 2011, Brazil (the world's most populous Roman Catholic country) adopts same-sex civil partnerships. Some of the same dynamics that risk destabilizing the global economy are already destabilizing global religions and are creating schisms both within the religions themselves and the wider community. Alienation is leading to polarized intolerance as a new generation becomes radicalized. As religious riots once again flared in Northern Ireland during the summer of 2010, stones were being thrown at the police – by children.

As already detailed in the chapter on Religion Crises, growing polarization risks extreme reactions that threaten the social fabric of all communities. It is primarily High-Tech-Globalization that is escalating that potential flare-up. And in many countries, the greatest risk of explosion comes from an earlier well-intentioned partial-mixing of different religious groups. Unknowingly, the governments of those countries have packed some of their major cities with an incendiary cocktail of inadequate social-cohesion mixed with intolerant religious dogma. Over several decades they have been building a stockpile of Immigration Time-Bombs.

## INNER-CITY RELIGIOUS GANG CULTURE

Some of the more-unstable examples are currently in a handful of European cities. And any one of these inner-city Time-Bombs is quite capable of triggering a chain-reaction that explodes throughout the whole world economy. Yet the reason they have become so unstable is not really anything to do with Immigration *per se*. Or even Religion. On the contrary. Nations like the UK have been forged by millennia of successive waves of migration, and the USA comprises almost nobody *but* immigrants. New ethnicities can invigorate a country, just as multiple religions and religious sects and non-believers can all co-exist and enrich each other's lives.

However, as already explained in the subchapter that starts on page 262, if a society tolerates self-segregating *intolerant* factions within it then those factions tend to become increasingly polarized and hard to manage. Within the tinder-box of deprived inner-city areas, that dynamic of polarized intolerance reveals itself in the form of inner-city gangs – including inner-city *religious* 'gangs'. Derivatives of gangsta culture imported from the USA are now prevalent throughout many European cities, as are gangs and gang-culture of many other types. However, buried within this overall social dynamic has been the emergence of sectarian factions that, in many important ways, were created by the same forces, and operate according to the same sort of code, as all the other gangs.

For almost a century, Belfast – the capital of Northern Ireland – has suffered from gang warfare between The Republicans and The Loyalists (the gang names adopted by the rival Catholics and Protestants). This sort of Rival-Christianity has a long history across Europe even though, as with all city gangs, most of the more-moderate community have had little or no direct gang involvement. But recently there have been new types of religious gangs forming in European inner-cities, this time around Islam. As with the longer-established sectarian gangs, most of the public are not active members of Islamist gangs. But, at least for now, their tightly-knit and self-segregated local Moslem communities do tend to tolerate them.

Unlike, for example, in Canada where Muslims are well-integrated with the general community, in countries such as Spain, France, Italy, Germany and the UK there are cities with significant Muslim populations that are not yet integrated. Sometimes this has fitted with a deliberate government policy of multiculturalism based around the philosophy of 'live and let live'. Sometimes it has simply been the result of new immigrants coalescing into a community of like-minded people. But this lack of cohesion with the values and identity of the cities and countries in which they live is showing signs of weakening the fabric of broader society.

Exactly the same is true, of course, for many other non-Islamist inner-city gangs as well. But there is what many perceive to be an important difference. And in this instance, perception is reality. If it were not for the frequently-publicized threat of Islamic fundamentalism and associated terrorism, such segregation would not carry anything like the same implications to the 'average' member of the general public. Nor would any of that public perceive a symbolic threat when they saw someone in a burqa. But as it is, uncertainty, instability and insecurity leads to intolerance – on both sides – that is easily further amplified by populist propaganda.

## GLOBALIZED ESCALATION

Meanwhile, most politicians really would prefer not to have to get involved. Addressing an issue that necessarily ties into both religion and (by implication in most people's minds) into race is a political hot-potato. No politician tends to want to touch it lest they be seen as racist or Islamophobic or both. But, unfair and touchy as many politicians feel these issues are even to raise, if the growing tensions are not rapidly defused then such unstable examples of Immigration Time-Bombs will inevitably explode. And any one of them risks triggering a chain of similar explosions all the way back to the Middle East.

Once that happens, it is an easy route to progressive conflict. As already pointed out, Globalization can potentially link together *everything*. Even a relatively-minor incident caused by an immigration backlash can help trigger another. And that can kick off a cascade of further incidents all reinforcing each other. Maybe Muslims and their non-Muslim supporters in a European city march against a ban on the burqa. 'In the interests of balance' there are incessant media reminders that although radical members of that same Muslim community insist on their own claimed rights they nevertheless deny the female-equality and they condemn the gay-rights that are written into the country's laws. Anger builds. Riots ensue. Someone is killed, many are injured.

Police intervene in the glare of World News. Riots flare in other cities. With the support of the wider public, politicians encourage their police to clamp down on rioters, hard. The Arab world interprets this as its fellow-Muslims being under attack. Playing to an Arab public increasingly frustrated by 'Western intolerance' – and also wanting a justification to hike up the price of overstated (and rapidly diminishing) oil reserves – Arab leaders of major oil-producing states react with a coordinated show of outrage.

In a public News conference they posture by playing the West at its own game and threatening punitive sanctions, primarily in the form of cutting off oil to 'anti-Muslim extremists'. Within the hour the global markets are in convulsion. A US official declares on TV he considers this a threat to national security. Iran counter-claims that it now has nuclear weapons and Western aggression against Islam must stop. Within days of what was supposed to be a peaceful rally about a headdress, the world is edging toward catastrophic brinkmanship.

# AN INTERNATIONAL COMMUNITY ON PERMANENT ALERT

The combined impact of every crisis – and 'wildcard' event – exacerbated by Globalization increasingly places the international community on near-permanent alert

THAT IS THE hidden-problem that Globalization brings – the world is increasingly on a hair-trigger. Even a few decades ago, people were joking that 'if the USA catches a cold, the rest of the world starts sneezing'. But already, if something ever happened in somewhere as unknown to most people as Bangalore in India – with all its telephone call-centers and outsourced IT – the global economy would be directly affected.

Major catastrophes could therefore pull down everybody. As many excited documentaries and blockbuster Hollywood-movies have pointed out, there are some kinds of events (ranging from a regional arms-race leading to nuclear holocaust, all the way to a massive asteroid-strike or megatsunami) that would be sufficiently disruptive they could trigger global chaos. However, as I will now briefly explain in this subchapter, dramatic as these apocalyptic scenarios are they remain for the most part 'wildcard' events – namely, ones that are indeed theoretically possible (and would have a massive impact if they did happen) but are unlikely, or often *exceptionally* unlikely, to occur within the next several decades.

For example, despite the forecasts of some political commentators, I tend to rule out the idea of a regional coalition of, say, Russia, China and India forming against the USA and leading to an arms race with risks of escalation comparable to the Cuban Missile Crisis. For a start, there is simply too much economic downside for those involved. But there is another reason. The people who consider such a scenario is likely massively underestimate the political and managerial complexity of setting up such a regional coalition in the first place. Yes it is possible, but the hidden inertia that would need to be overcome (deeply-embedded Legacy Effects once again) means it would be highly impractical.

In the context of joining Federations, it may be worth putting on record that I have also discarded any threats arising from contact by aliens from outer space or human time travelers from the future. The consensus among astrophysicists and physicists I talk with seems to be that the likelihood of both is now very-slightly higher than thought a few years ago (though, to be fair, travelling back in time was previously ruled to be utterly impossible even theoretically). Nevertheless, vastly more likely is that first-contact with a new form of intelligence will be the result of an earthbound computer–system becoming sufficiently advanced.

Similarly, although nuclear proliferation remains a deep concern, it is now extremely unlikely that within the next thirty years there will be a nuclear holocaust that takes out the whole planet. The basic logic behind Mutually Assured Destruction still just-about holds whichever relatively-stable nations or confederations get arsenals of nuclear bombs and missiles. For the majority of the world, the logic against nuclear war has increasingly been strengthened the more far-reaching and interdependent the global economy has become, so even the illusion of a 'limited nuclear arena' has become a bit meaningless. Naturally, none of this logic applies to suicidal fanatics – but although fanatics may on occasion get to rule a country with nuclear capability it is unlikely (though not impossible) that they will be the suicidal ones. Fortunately, however, there is an added protection.

Given that established nuclear powers are well aware of the dangers of nuclear proliferation, it is in all their interests to try to ensure that the current balance is not destabilized – which is, understandably enough, why Iran and North Korea receive such serious attention. Iran gaining nuclear WMD would, for instance, trigger an arms-race that Saudi Arabia, Turkey and Egypt would also each try to win. The extreme threat of destabilization of the Middle East that such a regional arms-race would bring might easily lead a country like Israel to attempt a pre-emptive attack, if only in the forms of sabotage and cyberattack.

However, China, Europe, Russia and the USA have between them significant economic and diplomatic influence over smaller countries – even if these days they will not necessarily choose to be seen to take direct action themselves. On balance, therefore, wholesale nuclear Armageddon is no longer likely, not so much because it is not still a very real threat, but because *it is a genuine and well-understood threat.* Unfortunately though, none of this logic rules out the risk from nuclear terrorists acting on behalf of dispersed or hidden groups.

The danger, for instance, from Al Qaeda getting hold of nuclear material if the Afghanistan Taliban encroached much further than they have been into nuclear-capable Pakistan (which probably already has around a hundred nuclear warheads, adding about ten a year), is far less manageable than old-fashioned nuclear brinkmanship. The long-term residence of Osama Bin Laden within Pakistan was blamed on either the incompetence or collusion of some senior Pakistani officials. But if that was possible, then it raises question over many other aspects of security. Those sorts of risks necessarily remain far more likely to occur than wildcard events.

## INEVITABLE EARTHQUAKES

In terms of natural disasters, it is not worth planning too much for a massive asteroid-strike – just because such an extinction-event is quite possible at any time, it is nevertheless extremely unlikely. More likely, but also worth ruling out is a megatsunami. Although there are a few unstable land masses we know could theoretically create sufficient of a landslide to submerge Wall Street under the Atlantic, such an event is just not vaguely in the same league of probability as any of the potential crises analyzed in this book.

Likewise, no account should be taken of an eruption of one of Earth's supervolcanoes. Even though the one under Yellowstone seems to go off every 6-700,000 years and an eruption is 'due' and the caldera floor is rising faster than previously, no one should change their vacation plans in anticipation. In contrast, it is inevitable that massive earthquakes *will* relatively soon occur in cities such as Tokyo, Istanbul and Los Angeles. Ten out of the world's twenty largest cities are located in areas of seismic danger. One or more of these cities suffering The Big One is by far the most likely of the wildcard events. Some of these quakes may result in local chaos similar to the LA Riots in 1992 and the looting after Hurricane Katrina in 2005; not all cultures are as stoical and community-oriented under pressure as the Japanese proved themselves in March 2011.

Damage-costs from an extreme city-quake of around half a trillion dollars will cause pressure on the insurance industry that could trigger economic aftershocks that echo around the globe. Indirect disruption to the global economy – for instance from interrupted manufacturing or services – may ultimately be even more severe. Most damaging, however, may be the longer-term impacts and psychological trauma of somewhere like Los Angeles (including Hollywood) effectively shutting down for business. And, depending on timing, that may further undermine already-excessive State borrowing.

## EARTHQUAKES IN BOSTON AND SAN FRANCISCO

Having lived in Boston, I am well aware that most residents are blissfully unaware that they are at any risk from earthquakes at all. That is probably the most sensible attitude to take. But technically, Bostonians are at about as much *danger* from earthquake damage as their trans-continental cousins in San Francisco. The main reason is that although the likelihood of a serious earthquake is *very much less* than in San Francisco, the damage caused by a less-serious quake would be vastly higher. That is because it was only in the mid-1970s that earthquake protection got incorporated into Boston building codes. Most buildings in the gentrified center of the city are far older than that. My home, like every Victorian building around it, was in fact built on infill that would effectively 'liquefy' during an earthquake.

If the devastation is directly to a financial center such as Tokyo – unlike the earthquake and tsunami that hit Fukushima – it will impact the operation of the world financial markets. If the earthquake is in a center of scientific research like Boston (where, technically, residents are estimated to be as at much risk as if they lived in San Francisco) the financial repercussions may be far slower but even more far-reaching. However, irrespective of the source of a global shockwave – whether real or metaphorical – the overriding implication of Globalization is that the world economy will feel the force of it. Every nation is now indirectly connected to every major crisis, 24/7. The net effect is that *globally-defined threats to national economic security and social stability are growing exponentially.* And as a result, these days the international community is on near-permanent alert. Unfortunately, as the remainder of this chapter now details, government bodies are increasingly unable to cope.

## 27. HOW GLOBALIZATION EXACERBATES CRISES

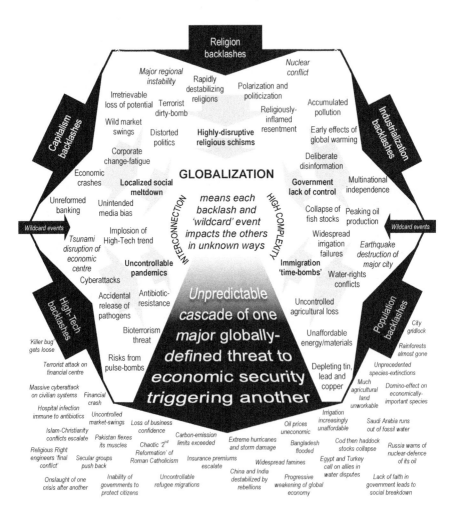

# WHY THE ESTABLISHMENT APPEARS TO SUFFER FROM BAD PEOPLE

## Contrary to popular misconception most inadequacies attributed to The Establishment as a whole in fact only relate to a few outliers

AROUND THE WORLD these days, much of the public views people in positions of authority – whether politicians or police or civil-servants – as inadequate or corrupt. But the truth about The Establishment is not that simple. I have spent my adult life being asked to dissect all types of organization to see how they really operate (as opposed to how they are supposed to behave). I have been allowed to peel back layer upon layer of façade until at last the reality of modern civilization stands naked before me. What I am left looking at is often not especially pretty.

Even my clients only get to see the overall outline. But I have to look at it all. Every sordid detail of human selfishness and frailty – as well as every inspiring example of human dignity and imagination. Day in, day out, since the 1980s. Professional footballers, janitors, Senators, postal staff, members of the House of Lords, anonymous bureaucrats, household names, production-line workers on their factory floors and music moguls on their private jets. But this has revealed a very important overall pattern: The broader population is remarkably like the Establishment figures it is so cynical about. Not better. Sometimes worse. The following is what I have found.

### THE TRUTH ABOUT US ALL

In every community – corporate, political, publically-funded or charity – I have found, as might be expected, a spectrum of personalities. Usually it is nothing like as broad a spectrum as in the general population, but it is still a spread. In each environment, there are a few people who are incredibly dedicated, self-disciplined and willing to self-sacrifice for the cause to which they have devoted themselves. Ironically, in my experience, these individuals do not necessarily make it to the very top jobs but, if they do not, they nevertheless tend to become trusted and valued seconds-in-command to the ultimate leaders.

At the other end of the spectrum there are – nearly always – those who are intensely self-serving, out to get what they can, sometimes lazy but often more devious than lazy, greedy and arrogant enough to believe that it is alright for them to 'bend' the rules (by which they mean either exploit the rules in ways that were never intended or contravene them in ways that are unlikely to get caught). The good news is that, from what I have observed, these individuals rarely make it to the very top jobs either. Although they can get worryingly close.

The vast majority of people are between these two extremes. They are hardworking, try to be professional, and they believe in what they are doing even if they do not necessarily think that it is the most important thing in their lives. They certainly want to do well for themselves, but they know there are always trade-offs involved. They follow their enlightened self-interest not because they are selfish, but because they are human. And like each other person, they sometimes make silly mistakes and errors of judgment – though deep down they are not malicious or incompetent. Like most people, they can sometimes be insecure, vain, pretentious, unthinking, self-opinionated. And like everyone, most of the time they will not even recognize that they are doing it.

The people that everyone tends to focus on, though, are that minority who are abusing their positions. Such an apparently-automatic fixation on the worst offenders is to do with how our human brains are wired. We are all pre-programmed to focus on the negative; what is going wrong usually disproportionately grabs our attention. It is a survival trait from our distant ancestors. As a result, just as with all other media coverage, the severity of problems and corruption in politics or the police (or in religion or science or anywhere else) is inevitably overstated – not because any journalist necessarily claims that there is more than a small number of offenders, but because the public quite understandably locks onto those examples. What is more, as these reprobates are in public office or positions of respect there is a legitimate argument they should be held to higher account, not least because they so easily can damage faith in the State, and if that collapses then so does society.

All this is inevitable. As a result of there being a spectrum of different personalities in every community and organization, there will always be a small group within The Establishment that does not meet the same standards as the majority – and, by the way, who will frustrate like mad those of their colleagues at the opposite end of the spectrum. If the behavior of the offending few is not just below-standard but is also unacceptable then they absolutely need to be weeded out, which is why the media spotlight on them is so crucial even if it is potentially misrepresentative of the whole. But it is important not automatically to assume that the behavior of those few is an accurate indicator of what is broadly going on below the surface, the tip of a fundamentally corrupt iceberg. It almost certainly is not. No community works that way. There are always outliers in both bad and good directions. And the majority in the middle occasionally just get a bit too swayed by one end of the spectrum rather than the other.

## RISKS TO THE ESTABLISHMENT

All this has implications for how we misinterpret many public institutions. In the past it was far easier for members of The Establishment. That was not because the success rate for political initiatives or other activities was any higher than today, but because the public did not know so much, and it often respected politicians and other establishment figures just because of who they were – rather like A-list movie stars and other top celebrities are lauded today. In many countries, citizens now have the right to access state records, they scrutinize public expenses, watch videos made on mobile phones of politicians saying what they 'really thought' when they were in private, the public is repeatedly shown the sound-bites of politicians, police chiefs and religious heads promising to do something, reassuring that they themselves never did something, committing never to do something.

And yet that same public these days knows that many times all those promises turned out to be lies. He did attempt a whitewash at The White House. He did have sexual relations with that woman. The expense claims were wrong. The children in their care were indeed being abused. No one would ever have learned the truth without the whistle-blower. The sleaze was real (and hypocritical given the 'family values' they had been preaching). Current generations have grown up with this. Everyone is now far more sophisticated in how they view Establishment figures, even if some of those figures still treat 'the average person' as gullible and easily fooled. It is no surprise that the general public has become cynical about The Establishment in general.

In addition to politicians being held in disrespect, in many developed nations the police and the legal-system as a whole have also dropped in public estimation. In several developing nations they have *never* held people's respect. That is not surprising either. Those two components of the Establishment are themselves nearly always old institutions with deeply-established ways of doing things that – because of Legacy Effects – are therefore incredibly difficult to change.

What is more, modern police forces can face unimaginably difficult situations. Some of them on occasion act genuinely heroically, even though it can be a thankless task. And that can easily foster an 'us against the world' mentality that puts internal loyalty above most else. That sometimes leads to problem behavior that, when picked up by the media, can appear much worse or more institutionalized than it necessarily is. Even so, 'getting it seriously wrong' is a real and inevitable risk that all contemporary police run. Not least because in practice it is so difficult to overhaul such complex institutions and bring them back into synch with evolving society. And all this can lead to an undesirable 'truce' between the Police and the Media. The police need good PR because they cannot function effectively without the broad support of the public. The media can get useful leads (and even, potentially, illicit information) from friendly police contacts. It can be very easy for a working relationship to develop in which neither side particularly wants to rock the boat. Just as with Politicians and the Media.

The relatively secret and ancient and elite world of the judiciary is at even more risk – although in many developed countries it so-far has largely been immune to scandal.  Abuses by the judiciary (especially if in concert with the police or government) undermine even greater public trust than an outrage by the police or by politicians alone. If people lose faith in State Justice then they lose faith in the State's right to rule at all. Because the stakes are very high, the risks of something going wrong are if anything *increased* – as with the Roman Catholic Church scandals, there are very strong pressures to keep things quiet. At the moment, it is a growing risk that no one is talking about.

For the same reasons, some have had concerns that the Security Services run even greater risks of corruption – with the added worry that unless something went extremely awry, the general public (and even most government officials) would never get to hear about it. The reality, however, is that rival countries' services keep an extremely close watch on each other, and often have every incentive to blow the whistle on any conveniently-embarrassing revelations about their competition. Paradoxically, the shadow-world of secret intelligence is one of the most effective self-regulatory global systems that there is.

## ATTRIBUTION ERROR

However, despite the inherent risks that parts of The Establishment genuinely run, it is a bit of a cop-out to suggest that the reason why politicians and The Establishment as a whole seem incapable of solving even basic problems like crime, education and healthcare is because – unlike the rest of the community – they are unfit, out to get what they can, or part of some secret conspiracy. It is just not true. From what I know, if business executives were put under as much public scrutiny as modern politicians, the general public would be utterly horrified. If the general public were put under as much scrutiny as modern politicians, the reaction might be one of utter depression. But that is no fairer to the general public than it is to politicians.

The reality is that as human beings we each have a natural tendency to assume that when someone else acts in a way we do not like it is because they are either stupid or evil. However, if we ever act in a similar way we tend to believe there are mitigating circumstances. We very easily attribute to other people motivations and causes that may be completely inaccurate. Someone cuts us up on the road and we are immediately angry at their aggressive driving. We accidentally cut someone up on the road and we immediately feel embarrassed for our silly mistake.

Around the world, some members of The Establishment *are* close to being stupid or evil. But in most countries it is an extremely small minority. The reason why the remaining 'good' people nevertheless often do such a bad job has little to do with incompetence or ill intent. As detailed in the next subchapter, it is a specific series of hidden problems caused by the nature of their environment. Most inadequacies in The Establishment relate not to bad people – but to The System in which they all operate.

## A CAUSE FOR OPTIMISM

Through my work I have seen more of the detailed reality of how human civilization secretly operates than most. What is more, unlike – say – a psychotherapist (who necessarily sees a skewed section of society) my cross-section of a given population has always been chosen to be as representative as possible of the community concerned. So in my line of profession there has been no chance for me to escape from drawing conclusions about society as a whole. As a result, it might be expected that I have been left a little bit cynical.

Quite to the contrary. I am left with a deep optimism – not least because I have seen just how very 'flawed' the *whole* of society is and yet how, despite that, civilization usually progresses. It is a big secret. Movies and television shows conspire to maintain the myth that most people have many fewer human frailties than they really have. As a result, most of society probably tends secretly to feel a little inadequate. What is worse, unless individuals have for instance a caring partner who – typically as a lone voice – points out their foibles and failures in ways that convince them, over time they become just as delusional about their own capabilities and behaviour as those (relatively few) bullying CEOs and autocratic dictators who are surrounded only by people who agree with them.

Yet despite so many of the general population being so deeply flawed as individuals, society as a whole has most times moved forward. Despite there always being a few rotten apples in the metaphorical barrel, the bulk of society has always tended to win out. And despite members of The Establishment being just as human as the general public – with just as many outliers for good and for bad – it should not be unduly distressing when it proves necessary to weed out those few who are not up for the job, because they will always tend to be matched by those equally-rare individuals with a level of honor and altruism and passion that truly can change the future for the better.

# IMPOSSIBLE CHALLENGES THAT GOVERNMENTS NONETHELESS ACCEPT

## The hidden reality of The System means state-influence is increasingly difficult to exert and politicians are ill-prepared to address complex globally-defined threats

NATIONAL AND INTERNATIONAL initiatives necessarily face far greater challenges, and carry a much greater potential for failure, than corporate initiatives. In most countries it is only necessary to examine Healthcare or Education or Crime to find an archaeological dig of layer upon layer of dashed hopes. No one should be surprised. Even assuming that politicians are in general as hardworking and competent as those in the private sector (which they typically are) their goals are in many ways far less achievable. For a start, unlike most long-established corporations, many of the official rules by which a country or state is run – namely The Law – are viewed as wrong. As a result they are constantly changing because they are out of synch with what many citizens want. Even if laws were perfectly aligned with the majority, there would still be many outliers who wanted different things – age of consent, tax thresholds and speed limits, for instance.

But laws and regulation are mainly doomed to be out of alignment because they are typically either trying to set or to catch up with public opinion and behavior. Issues such as the rights for minorities are classic examples. And if laws are already out of alignment, then how can a politician hope to change legislation in a way that will get the whole of society to move in a new direction, when it is not all moving in the same direction to start with? It is much more difficult even than that. Many of the consequences of changing the Rules of State are often deeply hidden as well as seriously delayed – the impact of tax laws for instance – so it can be very hard for politicians to fine-tune their policies. It is certainly far harder than within the relatively short-term environments of most corporations, and it is hard enough there.

# GLOBALIZATION CRISES

What is more, in the business environment it is recognized that sometimes the only way to zero-in on the best set-up is to try something, see how it goes, and then either adapt the initial idea or give it up if it is seen not to be worth the disruption of continuing. But if politicians adapt a policy, or change their minds on something, the public and the government's official Opposition criticizes them for being indecisive or making a U-turn.

Another reason why it is so much tougher to exert influence as a politician than as a corporate leader is that compared with a company, where employees are recruited according to various preselected profiles, the general population to which State leaders are ultimately answerable (even in dictatorships) is vastly more diverse. That means that in practice it is often impossible to find a single policy or law that will affect people's behavior equally across all the different facets of society. When wielding State Power over communities even just the size of a city, let alone a whole country, one size does not – and can never – fit all.

This is complicated by the fact that in their everyday lives individuals in reality each belong to several further communities. Most people are part of at least one formal power structure, typically that is their place of work or education. But they are also members of numerous informal communities such as families, social gatherings, neighborhoods, recreational groups – even inner-city gangs. In general, people tend to avoid a feeling of powerlessness (unable to change the rules of their workplace or the laws of their country) by focusing instead on the mini-universe of people closest to them where they can at least hope to be protected and maybe even make a difference. Inevitably that very-human tendency creates islands that often then become even more insular. That is true of internal family rivalries, neighborhood disputes, cliques at school, local gangs, in-company departments, ghettos in cities, battles between corporations, factions in religion, and wars between nations.

The roots of nationalism and race-riots (as well as Islamophobia and Anti-Americanism) are remarkably similar to the reasons why as teenagers we hung out with some kids and not others. Individuals tend to cope with a complex world by keeping their loyalties within their 'tribe'. That way they can at least try to keep safe and get things done within their clan. But, especially if they identify themselves too narrowly, it means it is far harder for all the tribes to agree, let alone act as one. As we saw earlier, that dynamic can lead directly to urban tensions so strong that they risk tearing apart the social fabric needed to hold the city-streets safe from anarchy. That is the set of challenges that all politicians face when they try to exert influence in the immensely-complex modern world. And those challenges are becoming almost insurmountable.

## REFORMING THE ESTABLISHMENT SYSTEM

To have any chance at all, today's politicians need not only to be exceptional individuals (as at least a few of them are) but also to work within an Establishment that maximizes their chances of a successful outcome. And it is here that we find the greatest reason why the modern Establishment is failing. It is not so much the IQ or motivation of the members of The Establishment. It is not the cliquishness of the non-members outside of The Establishment – the general population – diverse and split into very-dissimilar clubs as they all are. It is not even The System by which The Establishment operates that is pulling it down. The fundamental problems arise from The Establishment's *inability to reform fast enough The System in which it operates.*

As I will explain in the next subchapter, many of those problems are caused by how politics is organized, but some of the inability to improve things relates to the previous-exposure that politicians themselves tend to have had. Today's politicians have a rather narrow set of backgrounds. That is not to do with their social origins or even their formal education, it is because typically they have been involved in politics most of their adult lives. They have typically never run a corporation, never been groomed in management, and then are put in charge of a major government department. It should be no surprise that many of them struggle and are, frankly, managerially amateurish in comparison with even mid-level executives in the private sector. Likewise, they usually do not have scientific backgrounds but nevertheless some can seem to take the view that science is simple enough that with a bit of expert-briefing they are quite capable of deciding the merits of fraught scientific issues such climate-change and fishing quotas.

Moreover, the skills needed to get voted into office tend to be very different to those needed to run a country. The former often requires a thick skin, a high sense of self-worth, an ability to reduce complex ideas to a sound-bite, and the skill to sway the emotions of large numbers of anonymous strangers – whatever the true facts. The latter, amongst other things, needs a politician genuinely to keep listening.

Finally, debating style (egged on by media coverage) is possibly the greatest handicap unnecessarily imposed on today's politicians. I have worked with the top-executive teams of many of the world's most successful corporations. *There is not a single one of them* that would discuss important issues in the archaically-confrontational style that public political 'debates' usually take. The tribal-politics and snide rebuttals are more akin to the posturing in a school-yard than intelligent adults attempting to construct the best solutions to complex problems. Unlike nearly all party-political debate, the most sophisticated business-dialogue these days is measured by the quality of the eventual solution.

In top-executive meetings around the world, there is typically an expectation that multiple points of view will be needed in order ultimately to come up with something that is better than any of the initial proposals because it combines the best of all of them. Individual contribution is measured less by who comes up with which original building-blocks, so much as who best can build upon and refine other people's ideas and help construct a solid action-plan. In contrast, in the USA during televised sessions, Senators and Congressmen playing up to their voters appear more interested in crudely forcing their pre-prepared sound-bites into their comments than actually trying to build on other people's ideas. In the UK, the evasion and baying that constitutes the weekly overacted-theatre of Prime Minister's Question Time is justified by the suggestion that without such spectacle the viewing public might find the event boring. Adopting these debating styles, in 2003 both countries voted to go to war.

But it is unfair to single out the USA and UK. They in fact appear neither better nor worse than most other large groups of politicians. And if the same people were put into different environments they would likely interact very differently. However, as things stand, national government decision-making systems are increasingly misaligned with today's immensely complex issues – especially those whose causes stretch outside national borders, such as terrorism, religious conflict, pollution, global warming, depleting oil, overfishing, progressive drought, and pandemics. And, as we will now explore, that is a severe problem.

# HOW THE EU, NATO AND OTHER SUPRANATIONAL BODIES ALL FAIL

There are numerous failed approaches aimed at dealing with issues that affect one or more nations but over which none has sufficient influence

FEW MEMBERS OF the general public (or even most politicians) know much at all about how the major issues of global politics are actually handled. The simple answer is, despite the outstanding ability of many of those involved, Not Very Well. One of the basic reasons is that the human brain is simply not particularly good at thinking about extremely-complex problems made up of lots of largely-self-contained components that are each themselves complex and interact with each other in obscure ways that involve long delays between doing something and it having an effect. It is the ultimate 'forest and trees' problem.

As already explained in the subchapter that covers *When even the Scientific Process risks failing* (page 330), such interconnected complex problems – including all the potential global crises considered in this book – simply are not susceptible to the 'reductionist' approach of breaking difficult problems down into simpler ones. And that is why, however exceptionally skilled the politicians involved, an issue such as a given-county's Food Security cannot even theoretically be solved by its politicians acting independently of other nations. The combined impact of the actions of other countries will ultimately dominate.

Yet that is a difficult message for many politicians to accept, let alone convey to their citizens. It risks making 'leaders' seem ineffective. So some of them bluster and over-commit. A few link this with a form of macho-management that frankly makes them a destabilizing influence. But most top-politicians in fact recognize how constrained their options are to influence the global stage. Unfortunately this can all-too-easily become deeply embedded into people's attitudes. Every country, and everyone within them, can quite legitimately claim that the biggest problems in the world are 'not our fault'. This can become entrenched all the way down to individuals on the street blaming their problems on foreigners, The Establishment, local politicians, the police, their poor education, the neighborhood they grew up in, their bad luck. Everything but themselves.

National governments often fall into exactly this same trap when they become fazed by the enormity of the major problems that are only made worse by Globalization. But despite that tendency, there have nevertheless been numerous attempts at dealing with issues that affect one or more nations but over which none of them has sufficient influence. I will now quickly go through the basic approaches that have been tried. None work.

## SUPERPOWERS

As (quite sensibly) there is probably not a single country willing to give up its sovereignty to a President of the World who could impose solutions for such planet-wide problems, instead nations have resorted to three broad ways to aim to exert 'Global Governance', that is, the management of global issues in the absence of a global government. None of these techniques has ever yet come up trumps, although countries keep trying.

The first approach is also the oldest. It is the Superpower Solution. If a community is powerful enough (whether it is the ancient Roman Empire or the current USA) it can follow the philosophy that 'might is right'. It can continue to do what it wants, and by one means or another force other countries to comply. When President Bush, Sr. informed the world that, despite the average US-citizen being responsible for twice the $CO_2$ emissions of the average European, 'The American lifestyle is not up for negotiation' – he succinctly conveyed the philosophy behind the first part of the Superpower Solution. When his son, without express UN backing, invaded Iraq allegedly to reduce terrorist threats to the USA (and to an extent to secure important oil deposits) – he completed the illustration of how the Superpower Solution is supposed to work.

Unfortunately, although invasion is a major undertaking, it is relatively ordered. In that sense at least, war is simple. Peace, in contrast, is very complex. And the Superpower Solution alone can never sufficiently reduce the massive complexity of global issues to solve them sustainably. Even a coalition of two superpowers cannot get very far. The hypothesized 'G2', made up of the USA and China, would between them represent a quarter of the world's population, but even together they could not demand, for example, reductions in pandemics from Africa and the end of religious terrorism from the Middle East.

## A COALITION OF THE TOP-TWO SUPERPOWERS

Although the USA is quite understandably now attempting to improve relations with the future superpower China, the proposed G2 is unlikely ever to be formalized. China is well aware that it needs to build and maintain close links with *many* nations. Chinese leaders expect that within a few decades the USA will be just one of several powerful nations or multi-nation groups – such as the EU – that will then be courting China as the dominant superpower. In former times, China had many centuries' experience of being top-dog. Many of its politicians assume that relatively soon their nation will be again – and that, like it or not, the USA will drop down the league-table. Under those circumstances, why formalize a G2?

## EUROPEAN UNION AND THE EUROZONE

The second attempted-solution to Global Governance has been to form a variety of 'clubs' of different nations. One of the most successful is the European Union. In its modern form the EU comprises 27 member states and has over half a billion citizens. Most people these days have forgotten that the EU in fact originated from an international organization called the European Coal and Steel Community formed in 1951. The ECSC was set up by France and West Germany with the deliberate goal of making future war between them impractical. Belgium, Italy, Luxembourg and the Netherlands also decided to join in. In terms of avoiding internal war, the EU has been a success.

More than that is less clear. After sixty years, the 27 EU countries are certainly better aligned than ever before. But even so they are still sometimes hopelessly disjointed. Even such a tightly-coupled and powerful group of countries really struggles to act for the common good. A tremendous amount of the political activity involves 'doing deals' with fellow European Members of Parliament in order to gain sufficient votes to pass the motions a given country wants or block those that it does not. Very few seem able to break free from the constraints of national self-interest and instead ask what would be best for Europe as a whole. Partly as a result, many working in EU politics tell me they find the bureaucracy

**389**

and waste unnecessarily high whereas they find the effectiveness of decision-making to be depressingly low.

Even the Eurozone sub-group of seventeen countries that have all adopted a common currency finds it almost impossible to put collective interest above national interest. As an example, Germany – with the East and West now fully re-unified – is a highly-successful country whose citizens and politicians have worked really hard to generate one of the world's most impressive economies and also to hold Europe together. But they nevertheless have problems, in the form of other Eurozone countries.

A recently well-publicized example is fellow-member Greece. That country's ancient history has possibly contributed more to modern civilization than any other. But for a long time, Greece has also been a country where you hand over a bribe to get ahead in a hospital waiting list or to pass your driving test. And by the admission of those within it, the Greek government has been far more corrupt even than that. Because Greek politicians did not get around to solving the problems they were being paid to address, Greece effectively went bankrupt. Yet as they were part of the Euro, both politically and economically that could not be allowed to happen. So German citizens (more than anyone else) had to bail out Greek citizens, who consider it their right to retire earlier than Germans do, pay less tax, and who rioted against the austerity measures their country was being forced to adopt, primarily by Germany.

Across a club of just seventeen countries, each with its own self-interest and with no-one in overall charge, it is in practice impossible to solve the sorts of issues where one or more members can pull everyone down. As a result, with extreme concerns over Greece (let alone Spain, Ireland, Portugal and Italy) the Euro is already a weak-link in the global economy. And Greece is the weakest link in the Euro. Financial traders are increasingly betting against overstretched countries that it believes will eventually be forced to default (or at least heavily 'restructure' their debt) leading to a progressive, and ultimately unaffordable, cascade of politically-motivated Euro bail-outs. Meanwhile, banks that loaned to financially-suspect countries try to reduce their exposure. And in many ways the easiest way of them doing that is to pass the risk of default onto the Eurozone as a whole or, even better, onto the International Monetary Fund (IMF) – similar to the pattern foreign banks experienced during the 1997 Asian financial crisis.

## PIGS

Although many assume that the acronym PIGS (for Portugal, Italy, Greece and Spain) is a recent pejorative that was coined because of the sovereign-debt concerns about those southern European countries, in reality the term was already being used on financial trading floors in the early '80s to cluster the four countries because they had similar cultures and economies. Only recently has Ireland been interchanged with – or added to – Italy as the 'I'.

## FROM G8 TO INTERNATIONAL WHALING COMMISSION

Other Clubs of Nations also find it impossible to avoid complex backlashes. The G8, made up of the heads of government of the industrialized countries of Canada, France, Germany, Italy, Japan, Russia, UK and USA, could consider Competitive-Overuse problems such as a collapse of global fish-stocks or uneconomic oil-reserves. But they certainly could not solve them, even as a group. At least the crucial expansion of the G7 finance ministers – representing all the G8 countries except Russia – into the G20 means that the main economic council of wealthy nations at last includes massive countries like China and India. But the G20 is basically a meeting of the financial (and often also the government) heads of rich countries. That is not a broad enough context to wrestle with issues like religiously-inspired terrorism or pandemics. In practice, the G20 finds it very tough even to agree global banking reform.

Meanwhile, based in Washington, the IMF aims to oversee the global financial system by attempting to amalgamate the macroeconomic policies of its 187 member-countries. But the IMF's voting structure (dominated by the USA) no longer even vaguely reflects the relative economic importance of major countries such as China. And anyway, it has a track-record of tending only to respond to economic crises rather than prevent them. In a similar way, NATO is all-too-often a fallback for its members when they cannot obtain full UN support for a desired military action (which is nearly always). And decisions made by the twenty-two members of the Arab League are only binding on those countries that voted for them in the first place anyway. Furthermore, as with its unequivocal collective-decision to support Libyan rebels in 2011, the League's ability actually to deliver on anything it decides is, at best, rather constrained.

Even when international groups are extremely focused, they still prove incapable of taking the global view. The International Whaling Commission (IWC) today has around 90 member-states. In 2008 it began what was hoped would be a methodical negotiation about how best to manage whale populations. The negotiation-period had originally been meant to be one year, but – as many had expected – not enough had been achieved after only twelve months so the period was extended. In 2010, after two years had elapsed, the IWC annual meeting nevertheless once again failed to agree a way forward. Some countries had insisted on an end to whaling in Antarctica. Others had refused. Willingness to compromise on both sides had not proved sufficient. Now it seemed it would be at least three years before an acceptable compromise was agreed.

But instead, in 2011 the meeting almost collapsed. Latin American nations tried to force a vote on a proposal to form a whale sanctuary in the South Atlantic. Pro-whaling countries walked out. The vote was postponed by yet another year. As a result, for at least four years since 'negotiation' began, whales will have continued to be slaughtered as before. And neither the IWC nor those countries that object can do anything at all about it. Worse, that explicit impotence relates only to the *subset* of species that the IWC has chosen even to try to regulate. There are almost eighty species of 'cetaceans' (that is, the group of marine mammals that includes whales, dolphins and porpoises) that the IWC does not typically attempt to regulate – including the Dall's porpoise, of which around 15,000 are harpooned by Japanese fishermen each year. By any objective measure, and despite really-sincere efforts by many of its members, the IWC (and, just as importantly, the Global Governance model on which it is based) is a depressing failure.

## THE PROMISE OF THE UNITED NATIONS

That leaves the third attempted solution to resolving globally-defined problems. There are actually a total of 203 countries in the world (204 if you include newly-emerging South Sudan) that claim sovereign status: the 192 states that almost everybody accepts, Vatican City, and ten further states that claim independence but are not diplomatically recognized by most other states. The third attempt at Global Governance is to bring together the 192 recognized countries of the world, create a forum for them to talk with each other, and call it the United Nations.

It would appear to be the best hope of addressing global backlashes. Not only does it draw together almost every member of the international community but it is already explicitly addressing many of the globally-defined threats. The UN currently focuses on climate change, disarmament, financial crisis and poverty, global health, peace and security, and the rights of women. It also accepts its Responsibility to Protect. Often written as R2P or RtoP, this is the principle adopted by the UN at the World Summit of 2005 and confirmed by the Security Council in 2006 that any state has the obligation to look after its people – and that the international community has an obligation to step in if those people are being unduly abused (as was considered the case in March 2011 with Libya).

Overall the UN's combination of goals and opportunities is incredibly impressive. It offers the promise of a forum collectively capable of addressing every aspect of the crises covered in this book. That seems extremely exciting. The UN's ability to deliver is lot more sobering. In practice, the capacity of the UN to take action tends to be heavily influenced by the strength and economic or political importance of the abusive regime – as demonstrated almost exactly a year after the successful UN actions against Libya when, with complete disregard to a request from the Arab League, and flying in the face of world opinion, Russia and China blocked UN attempts to stop the escalating abuses by Syrian leaders against the Syrian people.

## THE REALITY

Old-fashioned invasions still happen without redress (provided those involved are powerful enough), and historically abusive and autocratic regimes are tolerated provided they have kept enough friends because they offer stability and oil or other natural resources. Modern-day terrorism, sponsored by some member-states against others, continues. And future forms of attack, for instance using computer malware or even artificial intelligence, are not on most delegates' radar screens.

Despite the impacts of potential future economic crashes on global poverty, things like banking regulation let alone the increasing volatility of the global economy are not seen as topics for on-going debate. As the Anglican Church splits, backlashes against the symbolism of the burqa threaten social stability, and Papal directives on condoms condemn millions to AIDS and tens of millions to unwanted pregnancies – religion tends to be given a wide berth by the UN. The implication (or even the imminence) of peaking-oil is not a central issue, any more than overfishing or depleting aquifers.

Even when issues *are* addressed, progress is usually painfully slow. In 2005 the UN World Summit was unable to issue a statement on nuclear disarmament and non-proliferation because there had simply been no movement forward. In 2001 the World Trade Organization began negotiating the so-called 'Doha Development Agenda' to lower barriers to trading across the globe. But there were severely-conflicting views between developed nations and developing nations regarding trade barriers, as well as between the EU and the USA (and pretty-well everyone else) over agricultural subsidies acting as trade barriers. The Doha negotiations have been stalled since 2008.

At a Johannesburg summit back in 2002, the UN Convention on Biodiversity agreed targets to be achieved by 2010 to curb the unprecedented extinction rates around the globe. Those targets were not met by a single country. The international community continues to maintain the 'thousand times higher extinctions than historical rates' that it had before. None of the twenty-one subsidiary targets set in 2002 have been met globally either.

The Convention on International Trade in Endangered Species (CITES), also known as the Washington Convention, is administered by the UN Environment Program and focuses on wild fauna and flora. In 2010, its wildlife meeting rejected a proposal to ban the slaughter of Giant Bluefin tuna, because Japan, Canada and several small nations protested it would hurt their economies. The market proved too lucrative. The fishing lobbyists were too powerful. It was yet another illustration of how Competitive Overuse plays out in modern global politics.

And then came the 2010 Nagoya biodiversity talks. Almost exactly the same dynamic played out; countries put national interests far above global interests. Although sufficient compromises were made eventually to achieve what was claimed as a successful outcome, what in reality happened *during* the meeting is far more indicative of how Competitive Overuse works in a UN context. Some countries proposed weaker rather than stronger targets for protection. Some governments argued that the UN Convention of Biological Diversity should not even discuss conservation on the high seas. Others proposed that the existing target for marine protection of 10% of the world's coastal waters should be reduced to only 1%. These kinds of self-interests have not suddenly gone away. It is, in practice, how those unresolved conflicts play out that will determine what actually happens to biodiversity – rather than the glowing Press Release issued at the end of the talks.

## WHAT WENT WRONG WITH THE UN AND CLIMATE-CHANGE

Politicians worldwide tend massively to underestimate the power of all these sorts of undercurrents that pervert attempts at managing global threats. The most public recent example of this was the 2009 UN Climate-Change Conference held at the Bella Center in Copenhagen. If ever the conditions were right, it was then. Politicians were fired up. Significant sectors of the general public wanted to see progress. Hopes were high. But whatever was said publically afterwards, for many of those directly involved in the Summit those hopes were in truth subsequently dashed. And because the most important gathering of world leaders ever to address global warming ended in such chaos and acrimonious disagreement, behind the scenes the political climate is now more hostile to a deal than ever. It is easy to feel frustrated about the outcome. What is vital to understand, though, is *why* Copenhagen hit such problems.

As was well-publicized at the time, at the highest level the conference failed because countries like Venezuela, Bolivia and Sudan blocked the deal since it seemed unfair. Developing countries viewed a cap on global emissions as implying an unreasonable cap on them. After all, once the emissions that developed countries sign up to are deducted, what is left are the emissions the developing countries can make. When these poorer nations ran the sums, they felt that they were getting less of a chance to benefit from the 'one-time energy boost' from fossil fuels than those who had industrialized before them. So they felt that the rich countries were basically telling them: 'Do as we say, not as we did.'

What few have heard about, though, is what was going on down in the detailed negotiations throughout the Bella Center. It was a bureaucratic nightmare. For a start, the UN had accredited about three times the number of people to attend Copenhagen than could fit within the center. There were huge lines. People waited for hours to get in, and some key negotiators did not make it inside for several days. They and their delegations were furious. Already efficiency was low and emotions were high. Then the story circulated that the G77 had dropped out of discussions on long-term commitments. The G77 is an informal group of developing nations that was originally made up of 77 founding-member states but has now expanded to 130 (even though in diplomatic circles it is still referred to as the G77). So, when this group dropped out, it was interpreted as meaning that a really important bloc of developing nations had no desire to be involved. But that simply was not true.

In reality the G77 strongly *supported* the need for long-term commitments but they felt that some of the developed nations were wriggling out of agreeing hard numbers. The G77 wanted to tie any new targets into the emission-reductions already set out in the previous 'Kyoto Protocol' agreed by most nations in 1997 (though refused by the USA). Widespread misinterpretation of the motivations behind the G77's actions meant that trust-levels sank. Into this already-chaotic setting, must now be factored-in Translators. Whatever was happening in a room, even if it was a heated debate of top delegates, when lunchtime came or the end of a normal working day arrived, the translators left. Without them, delegates could not debate any more. So they split into cliques.

On other occasions suitable translators were missing because the timings of sessions had been changed. Before one important debate the individual translation devices everyone was issued were unusable because they did not have headphones attached. By the time the headphones arrived many of the delegates had left the hall in disgust and the meeting had to be postponed. If many of those present had not felt that the fate of the world was at least to some degree at stake, all these sorts of farcical barriers to a productive outcome might have been laughed off. As it was, they were sadly symbolic of exactly how shambolic modern global politics all-too-often can become.

Although lessons were learned for running the 2010 UN Climate-Change Conference held in Cancún, the eventual commitments that were agreed in Mexico remained modest, short on detail, less ambitious than many scientists advocated, and were not binding anyway. The deal that was struck ended up achieving far less than many countries had hoped would have been committed to at Copenhagen. A year later, in Durban, the conference finally agreed a deal: To go away to agree a legally-binding deal to be presented in 2015 with commitments for 2020. Once again, that was not the fault of the highly-committed attendees. It was, as we will now see, the fault of an insurmountable problem in the design of the UN itself.

## WAYS TO DEVISE RESPONSES TO CRISES ARE FAILING

- 2005 UN World Summit unable to issue any statement on nuclear disarmament because no progress
- Despite near-ideal conditions 2009 UN Climate-Change Conference in Copenhagen was largely a failure
- Commitments at 2010 Cancún UN Climate-Change Conference were not binding – and less than hoped
- 2011 Durban UN Climate-Change Conference agreed a deal to agree a legally-binding deal to be presented in 2015 for 2020
- Eurozone proved incapable of aligning members such as Greece and Ireland enough to avoid bailouts
- World Trade Organization attempts since 2001 to lower trade barriers have been stalled since 2008
- Despite UN 2005 confirmation of its Responsibility to Protect it is slow and inconsistent (as in Libya 2011 and Syria 2012)
- 2002 UN Biodiversity Convention agreed 2010 targets to curb rate of extinctions – every country failed
- 2010 Nagoya biodiversity talks revealed that extreme conflicts still underlie the newly 'agreed targets'
- 2010 UN wildlife meeting rejected proposal to ban the slaughter of endangered Giant Bluefin tuna
- After three-years' negotiations 2011 International Whaling Commission again failed to agree a way forward
- Largely governed by formal and informal cartels the oil industry is decoupled from global interests
- In the absence of any effective global governance world-religions further polarize and destabilize

# THE INEVITABLE BUT FUNDAMENTAL INADEQUACIES OF THE UN

## Even the UN is inadequate to the task because it is structured more for countries to protect local interests than global interests

AS THINGS STAND, no better mechanism exists than the United Nations to avoid the sorts of global crises that will increasingly form as High-Tech-Globalization intensifies the backlashes already generated by High-Tech clashing with Capitalism, Industrialization, Population and Religion. But there is a real problem with The System within this ultimate UN Establishment. The UN reflects the world as it was after World War II. It is not aligned with the reality of the early-21$^{st}$ century. Although it is still moderately good at doing what it was set up to do – in effect, regulating and limiting the power of individual states – it is simply not designed to orchestrate the kinds of collective action needed to protect global civilization as a whole (as opposed to the self-interests of individual nations). It is currently incapable of preventing the multiple global examples of Competitive Overuse represented in Industrialization and Population crises. And it is likewise unable to protect against the potentially-debilitating escalations of destabilized Capitalism and Religion.

To understand the many reasons for the UN's powerlessness, you first need to appreciate just what the UN is really like. People who have not experienced it tend to assume that it must be a really impressive and august organization. But the reality can be a bit disillusioning. For a start, there is a general lack of trust. Everything is about power, and games-playing, and deals, and trade-offs, and impenetrable bureaucracy. There are numerous largely-opposed factions that out of sight are locked in a high-stakes political melee. But on the surface it all appears relatively civilized and polite, not least because people never know when someone may turn out to be 'useful' to them.

Below the etiquette, however, no one is ever quite sure what everyone else truly thinks. Or even what they are really trying to achieve. There is deference to the powerful, but being candid is often seen as overly-aggressive. The culture tends to be conservative and risk-averse, stultifying and partisan. And everyone in the UN tends to be defined by the 'gangs' they hang out with. For instance, although the term is getting a bit dated, many people within the UN still refer to the North versus the South to describe the fundamental split of the UN into its two major political groups, the richer developed nations that are largely in the Northern hemisphere and the poorer developing nations largely in the South. Within UN circles, Australia and New Zealand are always geographically relocated to the North.

There are also the unofficial regional voting-blocs: the Africans, the Asians, the Latin Americans and Caribbeans, the Eastern Europeans and the 'Western European and Others'. Then there is the Organization of the Islamic Conference made up of fifty-seven Moslem states. Then of course there is the G77 and G20 and still the G8. And, although historically G5 represented the five leading economies of the world, the term is now used for the Group of Five largest *emerging* economies, namely: Brazil, China, India, Mexico and South Africa. And then there are always the Annex I and Annex II countries. And so on.

## U N ANNEXES

The 'Annex 1' and 'Annex 2' countries derive their label from the original Kyoto Protocol on climate change that listed in Annex I all the industrialized countries and 'economies in transition' that signed up to the agreement, and listed in Annex II the subset of those signatories that were 'developed' and that therefore would pay for costs of developing countries.

## THE UNREPRESENTATIVE SECURITY COUNCIL

By far the most important gangs, however, are actually dictated by the UN's overall organization structure. Indeed, the way that the UN is fundamentally organized is the single factor that, above all else, at present makes it incapable of dealing with many of the imminent problems the world economy faces. Unfortunately, the structure of the UN is almost impossible to change.

The Secretary General, based on the 38th Floor of the UN headquarters in New York, has a huge Secretariat to run things. He and they are guided by the UN-Charter's focus on 'We the peoples...' In general, they – largely alone – aim for a fully-global perspective. But incongruously the Secretary General's post is surprisingly powerless. He watches over a group of broadly-autonomous feudal kingdoms (such as UNICEF and the WHO) but he has relatively little authority to change anything.

The most powerful group is actually the Security Council. It is the only group with the power to make binding agreements that all members are, at least in theory, committed to carry out. There is no other group in the world with that level of apparent authority. The Security Council is made up of only fifteen people. The 'P5', that is, the five Permanent members of the Security Council – China, France, Russia, UK and USA – are the only ones that have right of veto on any Council-vote (to be precise, they cannot actually block a decision to debate something, but they can always block what is called a 'substantive resolution', in other words a decision actually to do something other than talk).

What upsets many people is that the ten non-permanent members of the Security Council are elected for only two years each and are chosen out of all the remaining 185 members of the UN. At any one time there are always three Africans, two Asians, two Latin-Americans (who can come from the Caribbean), two Western-Europeans (which for historical reasons may include a Canadian, Australian or New-Zealander), and one Eastern-European. Some on the P5 tend to want to maintain that status quo. For all the other members of the UN, almost everything about the whole set-up of the Security Council seems really unfair.

Japan and Germany, for example, because they are such successful economies contribute more funding to the UN than any other country bar the USA. Yet they are not on the P5, in essence for the historical reason that they lost World War II. In contrast, France and the UK (which did win) have permanent seats and right of veto. The members of the European Union contribute more to the UN budget than anyone including the USA. But, although there are important UN-centres in Geneva, Vienna and Nairobi, it is the Headquarters overlooking the East River in Manhattan, on land originally donated by John D. Rockefeller, Jr. and now designated as international territory, that is the undisputed heart of the

# Failing supranational bodies

UN. Similarly, there is no member of the P5 who represents Europe as a whole, and indeed the EU is not really reflected in the UN structure at all – because it did not exist when the UN was founded. As a result, in the established metaphor of the UN, Europe 'punches below its weight' whereas both the UK and France 'punch well above their weight'. No wonder many countries feel frustrated.

## IRRELEVANCE OF THE GENERAL ASSEMBLY

The second major UN structure that is creaking at the seams is the General Assembly made up of one representative for each of the 192 member-states. It is a huge debating group that has the power to pass so-called Resolutions – which, unlike those of the Security Council, are in reality non-binding 'recommendations' to all the member states. Each country, whatever its size, has one vote within the General Assembly. Major decisions, for instance relating to military action, require a two-thirds majority. Less important decisions only need over half the votes. This all seems like detail. But in fact it is crucial to understanding why global politics is often incapable of tackling today's truly global issues. 'Governance' in its broadest sense is all about who gets to make what decisions. So Global Governance in the form of the UN is in practice dictated by the apparent trivia of who is in which group and what the voting rules are.

And those voting rules are skewed. In less than fifty years the General Assembly has grown in size by 70%. The Security Council has hardly altered. Back in 1963, the size of the Security Council was increased from eleven seats to the current fifteen, which was the last time it changed. At that time, there were only 113 countries represented in the General Assembly, so almost one is seven was part of the Security Council. Today, with 192 member-states, the ratio is closer to one in thirteen, so it is much more difficult to get most countries feeling they are properly represented.

What is more, because each member of the General Assembly carries the same voting power, in principle the 64 least-populated countries can block a two-thirds majority vote. That means that less than 1% of the world's population can force the rest of the world to compromise. And the 127 smallest countries can similarly win a two-thirds majority vote, even though they only represent around 8% of the world's population. In practice, given that the General Assembly can only ever make recommendations to its members, those members representing about 92%

of the world's people probably simply would not pay attention to such a two-thirds majority vote. Which is just one illustration of how the current system is so very ineffective.

## NEAR-IMPOSSIBILITY OF REFORM

That would not of itself be such a big problem except for one thing: Reform of Global Governance as exercised by the UN is exceptionally difficult. It may, in practice, even be impossible. By the rules set down within the UN's own Charter, changing something like the size or membership of the Security Council would require support by a two-thirds majority of the General Assembly *and* of the Security Council itself *and* the unanimous support of every member of the P5 (any one of which can veto the decision). How likely is that?

It is made even less likely by the options for reform that different groups are pressing for. Many countries want to expand the size of the Security Council. But some on the P5 worry that the larger the Council the less effective it is likely to become; certainly, that dynamic tends to be true of any corporate Board of Directors. It is already a major challenge for even fifteen people to have a sensible discussion. Similarly, within the General Assembly, the North tends to want debates to focus only on pressing issues. The South worries that this is merely the developed nations trying to push them out of the way. And when one group proposes a mechanism to expand the membership of the P5 – usually by getting themselves added to that elite band – there is immediate resistance from almost everybody else because even though they may think the P5 should be more representative, they do not want to see their rivals get special privileges when they do not. And anyway, small and medium-sized countries have little incentive to strengthen further the power of the larger countries (or coalitions like the Moslem states) that they already worry can walk all over them.

Meanwhile, within the General Assembly, there is a chronic lack of focus with debates being easily distracted by details that no equivalent top-executive body in the corporate world would ever waste its time on. But far worse, the search for consensus is often interpreted as a need to have *everyone* agree. So wording of Resolutions becomes diluted, differences get camouflaged, and aspirations tend to sink to their lowest common denominator. It is almost impossible under these circumstances for the General Assembly to take bold decisions. Nor can there be any true leadership. Not because of an absence of great leaders in the hall. But because there is no appetite for followership.

Because of the insurmountable political roadblocks that are in essence embedded within the Charter of the UN itself, nothing alters. For decades there has been talk of reform. Everybody knows that the existing system is not working. Yet nothing changes because within the UN system it is almost impossible for any changes to be voted in. In 2005, Kofi Annan (the then Secretary-General) attempted major reform of the UN. However, partly because it was seen by many as a way of 'bringing the USA back into line,' there was strong opposition from those who might otherwise have backed it. No major nation supported change. Worse, as a result of its failure, Grand Reform is now felt to be off the UN agenda for the foreseeable future.

Consequently, these days the UN has lost its way. As an institution, its very creation is one of the most spectacular achievements of the modern age. But wonderful though its ideals are, glorious though its potential remains, the sad reality is that it is currently unfit for purpose and apparently incapable of reform. Powerful countries may still go through the motions of submitting themselves to the supposed-authority of the UN. But in the economic reality of today's Globalization, they know perfectly well that within reason they can largely do whatever they choose. And no one in practice can stop them. That, in a nutshell, sums up the institutionalized global selfishness that is the United Nations: Each delegate feels the obligation to fight for his or her own country's interests above all others. *None* of them is fighting for humanity as a whole.

# An Entire World-Economy in Peril

## Because of all these factors there are for now insufficient ways to devise counters to globally-defined threats – so the entire world economy is in peril

THE SECRETARY-GENERAL of the UN in 1992 was Boutros Boutros-Ghali. Two decades ago he correctly identified many of the global threats that the international community continues to face today: terrorism, weapons of mass-destruction, poverty, pandemics, environmental degradation. He tabled an ambitious paper to tackle them entitled 'An Agenda for Peace'. Nothing happened. Only recently, now in his late-eighties, he has been campaigning for a radically new Parliamentary Assembly at the UN, democratically elected by citizens around the world. The general feeling is that the member-states of the UN are not in the mood for it.

Even if they were, there is no longer time to get it working before the next wave of crises. And even if there was, the inherent competition between UN member-states would *still* remain. That is because the root cause of our potentially-catastrophic failure in Global Governance is not restricted to the UN at all. The structure of the UN is merely an accurate reflection of a far-more-fundamental structure that is in practice utterly unchangeable: The world is organized by territory. The laws, taxes and regulations that drive everyone's lives are dictated by national governments. People's rights are the rights of their country, and no one will willingly give those up to a higher regulatory authority. That is why UN members do not fight for the world economy above their own state.

To do so would require not just giving up power but potentially also committing their citizens to losing out relative to some of their rivals in other countries. And those citizens are relying on their UN Ambassador to protect them. Turning against national interests for the good of others is a very-tough call. Yet increasingly, as I will now explain, neither Ambassadors nor local politicians are in fact able to defend even their *national* interests any more.

## GLOBALLY-DEFINED THREATS TO NATIONAL SECURITY

National Security is every government's highest obligation. And yet something that was completely unpredicted has happened over the last few decades. Without most even realizing what was going on, every country – even the USA – progressively lost control over aspects of its national security. Bioterrorism and cyberattack are well-recognized risks. But just as threatening now are looming issues relating to energy-security, collapsing fish-stocks, depleting aquifers, polarizing religious-intolerance, pandemics, uncontrolled species-extinctions, wild swings in the global economy, exhausting mineral deposits, climate change, and the unintended consequences of increasingly-powerful but unelected and unrepresentative multinationals with no particular allegiance to any given country.

## THE C I A AND CLIMATE CHANGE

A few individual global crises (though not their combined impacts) have recently been formally recognized as dangers to national security. In 2009, for instance, the CIA set up a small unit to focus on climate change and bring together into one place expertise on the effects environmental factors could have on political, economic and social stability outside the USA.

The point is that although there is widespread public concern (at least in some countries) about the issue of global warming, governments are seriously at risk from many *other* globally-defined threats to national security as well. And many of those dangers are far more imminent. Yet not one of those threats is under the control of any given nation-state. Instead, they are all determined by the complex interaction of *all* nation-states. Between them they are a new breed of security risks that although they bring severe threats nationally, are nevertheless defined globally. The most-hidden dangers in fact come from complex global interactions of more than one of the individual perils, any of which is already hazardous in its own right.

For example, in a decade or so the USA might hypothetically be threatened by social chaos resulting from a virulent pandemic spreading from Haiti. But that plague perhaps arose during an earlier famine that resulted from wild hikes in food prices triggered by London-based commodity-speculators responding to drought in grain-producing Russia, which was made more critical because of depleting Chinese fossil-water aquifers needed for irrigation of crops used for biofuel to substitute for increasingly scarce and expensive Middle-Eastern oil. The crises examined in this book have crept up on national governments so slowly and with so much camouflage that even today there is not a collective term for them. Yet as soon as issues such as climate-change, depleting oil, religious conflict and overfishing are reframed as 'globally-defined threats to national security', various issues become clearer.

On the one hand, it highlights that national governments in fact carry an explicit obligation (in many countries it is a legal and constitutional obligation) to take a lead in dealing with such threats – not to do so is a dereliction of their most basic duty of protecting their citizens. On the other hand, no national government can possibly fulfill that obligation to protect against such globally-defined threats without achieving some form of alignment with other governments, as well as with numerous non-government organizations, multinationals and global media; in contrast, a fortress mentality has no chance of success. However, assessing globally-defined threats has been made far harder for governments, and indeed all of us, because of the confusing mix of hidden interconnections and hidden complexity on which this book has focused.

## SERIOUS FLAWS IN RISK ASSESSMENTS

Previous risk analyses have been unable accurately to reflect how some of the important aspects of the global economy *really* work (as opposed to how they are supposed to work). Crucial examples include the hidden dynamics of financial-services companies, oil and energy corporations, the media, business generally, religions, the scientific community, fisheries, agricultural groups, general populations, national governments, supranational bodies such as the UN, as well as the obscured interactions of fundamental trends such as digitization, networking, miniaturization and simulation.

Decoding all of these hidden inner-workings of the international community is, in practice, vital to understanding the true root-causes of threats to national security. However, in the absence of such knowledge, existing well-intentioned and seemingly highly-professional threat-assessments merely list *already-recognized* risks to the world economy, rank their likelihood and impact based on people's *subjective perceptions*, and attempt to link them to each other according to their similarity of *symptom*.

Apparently-comprehensive though such surveys are, in the absence of sufficient systemic insight, compilers are forced to cluster things like Environmental Risks all together even though the *root-causes* of Air Pollution are importantly different to Biodiversity Loss – let alone Earthquakes and Volcanic Eruptions, which are not even manmade. Such analyses end up being unintentionally simplistic and incoherent. Lack of accurate data on how key aspects of the world economy work 'below the surface' makes it impossible to predict *unrecognized* risks (for instance the national-security impacts from a too-rapid slowdown of the High-Tech cycle of two-yearly upgrades, or from the polarization that will occur from inevitably-increasing destabilization of dogmatic sects in Christianity and Islam but not in Buddhism or Hinduism).

Previous analyses likewise have been unable to take account of the high degree of hidden reinforcement built into some components of the world economy, such as across the international banking community. Only with such knowledge is it at last possible to rank likelihood and impact of risks *objectively*. Most importantly, without a better systemic understanding of how the international community actually operates, any recommendations of counter-strategies to defend against threats to national security risk being naive because they focus on symptoms not *root-causes*. If risks are clustered only according to superficial similarity (such as Economic Risks, Societal Risk, and so forth) it is not just unhelpful but potentially dangerous.

Without an understanding of how risks of backlashes link together, and therefore where they are particularly susceptible to intervention, responses are attenuated and potentially ineffectual. In some cases (such as reactions to religious polarization) uncoordinated and non-strategic approaches can actually make things worse. What is more, lack of systemic understanding also makes it far harder to realize that many of the highest threats to national security are in fact *side-effects* arising from otherwise-benign trends that are vital to *maintaining* national security. In the absence of such knowledge, governments can take actions that risk 'killing the golden goose'. They also risk falling into the trap of thinking that although certain threats may be Crucial they are not yet Urgent, and so they may leave their reactions too late to respond well enough to exponentially-growing threats.

Worst of all, they risk becoming so blasé about the doom and gloom of so many Apocalypse Scenarios that they convince themselves they are already addressing all the main threats, and that existing plans are sufficient. Unfortunately, that is probably the most accurate description of the mind-set of almost all governments today. It is an attitude that is more than just an unintentional dereliction of duty; it risks destroying the very economies for which such politicians are responsible.

## INABILITY OF GOVERNMENTS TO PROTECT

This is where globally-defined threats to national security end up – governments either so unaware or so sure of themselves that they, like everyone else, cannot see the forest for the trees. The growing *complexity* of Globalization makes unanticipated crises inevitable. And increasing *interconnection* means not just that everyone globally may be impacted by a local crisis, but that every crisis potentially *triggers a further crisis* – just as falling house-prices in the USA triggered a global recession that ultimately triggered Sovereign-debt crises that led to problems with the Euro (which in the future will lead to problems with the political unity of the European Union as a whole).

Yet, as I have discussed, all classic problem-solving techniques depend on dividing complex issues into manageable parts, and all political problem-solving structures depend on dividing the world into manageable territories. For a hugely interconnected system like global civilization, those approaches unintentionally hide interdependencies from everyone's view and prevent even recognized solutions from ever making sense for individual countries to adopt. As a result, all countries are left precariously exposed. Paradoxically, the most powerful cross-border organizations these days are multinationals, with unelected leaders maximizing their global interests, sometimes at the cost of local economies. Yet elected UN-leaders cannot protect global interests in the same way. Talks on climate-change and fishing quotas and nuclear testing do not fail because of lack of resolve. *They fail because there is no mechanism for them to succeed.*

Such failures build on each other. By far the greatest globally-defined threat to economic stability is the cumulative impact of an increasingly uncontrollable onslaught of systemic crises. The current powerlessness of countries to take other than a broadly-reactive stance to such a build-up

**408**

risks too little eventually being attempted by too few too late. Within that context, it is quite artificial to prioritize specific threats because, by their inherent nature, apparently separate crises are in fact deeply interconnected. It is nevertheless possible to rank some of the importantly-different dimensions that global crises have. Excluding threats such as nuclear proliferation (because although they are extremely dangerous they are well-understood and already well-addressed) reveals examples of some of the most important types of global crisis that currently risk overwhelming governments worldwide.

One of the most threatening dimensions relates to *Exploding Internet Repercussions*. The exponential growth of the internet is so counterintuitive that governments are inevitably under-prioritizing the associated risks. In addition to the obvious threats of cyberattack and even pulse-bombs, exceptionally-rapid worldwide feedback brings wild economic swings and uncontrolled surges of Boundaryless People-Power. Social fabric will come under severe strain as virtual reality and social-networking progressively polarizes factions. Privacy will break down as it in effect is traded for on-line access. There will be an escalation in misrepresentation and flouting of authority by News Media and on-line communities, lack of political control, growing irrelevancy of education systems, and structural mismatching of workforces with job opportunities. Yet any undue slow-down in internet-growth risks massive economic disruption.

Just as worrying, but on a different dimension, are global crises relating to *Ungoverned Competitive-Overuse*. In the absence of any supranational mechanism of global governance capable of addressing worldwide examples of Competitive-Overuse, and in conflict with the net-effects of self-interested optimization by unelected multinational corporations, threats will escalate relating to overexploited fish-stocks, fresh water and land use, as well as peaking oil and pollution (including manmade global warming). Government inability ultimately to protect its citizens – or indeed the international community as a whole – against such crises will undermine confidence and increasingly risk revolt.

On yet a third dimension are the global crises relating to *Destabilized-Religion Politicization*. Religion-inspired threats such as Al Qaeda terrorism and the indirect repercussions of Middle-Eastern conflict (such as oil disruption or the need for military intervention) are well-addressed. Far less so is the escalating destabilization, fuelled by exponential trends, of numerous intolerant and exclusive sects that is leading to progressive politicization not just of hardline Islamists but also of the well-organized Religious Right, Pentecostals, and Vatican orthodoxy. Each will increasingly feel trapped into trying to dominate each other and all those who oppose them, resulting in progressively heightened threats of civil instability.

Even just those three dimensions of very-different forms of global crises highlight one of the fundamental problems of addressing *all* global crises. The ultimate High-Tech-Globalization side-effect is an inescapable dilemma: The actions of the few can hurt the many, but usually the many cannot stop the few without hurting themselves. Which means that, as things are, the only hope of Global Governance – the United Nations – will fail. If nothing new is done to compensate for that shortfall, then national governments will find that they have insufficient means to devise counter-strategies to globally-defined threats to their national security.

As a result, they will be powerless to solve those kinds of crises originating beyond their territorial influence and, increasingly faced with such unsolvable problems, they too will fail. Politicians will feel progressively stressed because they know they cannot offer the security that their public demands but they will also know that the public will penalize them if they are told that truth. Either way, the politicians will fail. And under those circumstances the full onslaught of unrelenting global backlashes threatens to begin.

## THE WORST-CASE LIKELY SCENARIO

Based on all my analyses over the last few decades of catastrophic breakdowns in complex and interconnected systems, I have to conclude that although in many ways an unstoppable onslaught of punishing global crises is a 'worst-case' scenario, it is – as things stand – nevertheless reasonably likely. Perhaps as likely that it happens as not. That may be alarming. But it is not alarmist. Such a cascade of extreme crises is a genuine and very-severe threat.

It is impossible to know how such a threat would unfold or even which crisis would come first. Maybe it will be something to do with High-Tech. Maybe a bioterrorist attack or a dirty bomb in a financial center. Maybe a cyberattack using a particularly virulent form of malware. Or maybe a completely different type of 'killer-bug' accidentally gets released from a developing-country's research lab. Or maybe salmonella or MRSA continue their current trend and a strain becomes fully-resistant to all known antibiotics. Maybe someone lets off a pulse-bomb and fuses every computer chip across a whole city. Or maybe Moore's Law simply slows down too quickly and triggers an implosion of the global economy.

Perhaps it will be a Capitalism Crisis in its own right – another crash caused by yet another hidden risk, combined with a general malaise caused by progressive change-fatigue sapping the resilience of corporate and government endeavor. Perhaps it will be a radical loss of financial confidence as unintended media-bias reinforces increasingly wild swings across an out-of-control marketplace, and the cumulative effects of sustained short-termism finally hit too many corporations devoid of any genuine long-term strategy, and too many governments addicted to short-term gratification at the expense of future generations.

It might be one of the Religion Crises. It could be triggered by a radical-Islamist terrorist attack that triggers an Islamophobic overreaction, which within Moslem states triggers extreme Anti-Semitism, Anti-Christianism and Anti-Westernism. And on the Indian sub-continent, Pakistan could flex its nuclear muscle against Hindus as well. It could be a different form of extremist disruption will be engineered behind the scenes by the Religious Right in the USA. It could be that increasing conservatism in the Vatican triggers a second Reformation in Roman Catholicism at the same time as the Anglican Church also splits. It could be that secular societies begin to fight back against them all.

At least many of the Industrialization Crises are far more predictable. Pollution will continue to build, and a general lack of public support for extreme measures will mean that politicians find it impossible to avoid the current momentum taking the global economy toward the higher estimates for carbon emissions over the next several decades. Existing proposed targets will then all be missed. What is less clear is whether any of the Positive Feedback cycles will kick in. Even if they do not, extreme hurricanes and storm surges will on average become more severe. Florida and the East Coast of the USA will suffer. Bangladesh will be devastated.

Oil costs will increase, and the absence of sufficient alternatives risks pushing-up electricity prices too high for many irrigation systems in developing countries to remain economic, leading to widespread famine. In developed nations, suburbia risks becoming steadily more expensive to run, house prices will then irretrievably drop into negative equity leading to growing resentment and unrest. Major cities risk first clogging, and then beginning to fail at the same time as container-shipping slows and global distribution breaks down. Russia will, if necessary, defend its oil reserves by using its nuclear deterrent.

Many of the Population Crises also now seem unavoidable. Within a few decades the rain forests will largely be gone and much of today's agricultural land will be damaged. Fish stocks of cod and then haddock will collapse leading to massive unemployment, as well as starvation in fish-dependent developing countries. Rich sushi-aficionados will remorselessly eat the Giant Bluefin tuna into extinction. Water-rights disputes over the Nile and over the Tigris and Euphrates will escalate, and both Egypt and Turkey will call on their allies for support. There will be major water shortages caused by depleted aquifers in Northern China, North-West India, Pakistan, Mexico, North Africa, the Southwest of the USA, and nearly all of the Middle East. The richer nations will buy-in food. The poorer will starve.

China and India face progressive destabilization and attempted rebellions. And as China is at the core of the global economy, that instability risks unraveling the economy of every nation. There will be an unprecedented number of species-extinctions. There will also be a domino-effect of unpredictable and unexplained impacts similar to Colony Collapse Disorder in bees. Widespread starvation in developing nations will lead to uncontrollable migrations. Meanwhile, developed nations face too little government-money to fund either pensions or healthcare, as well as a fundamental mismatch between people's ages, their education, and available jobs. With high fuel costs, inadequate food stocks and a fundamentally-misaligned population, many communities will become unsustainable. Unlike those in less-developed countries, advanced communities hit by societal collapse – will simply be unable to cope.

High-Tech-Globalization only makes all these risks higher. Escalating dangers from pandemics, from banking's imperviousness to regulation, from polarized intolerance, from uncontrollable corporate self-interest, from immigration time-bombs, and from statistically-inevitable natural disasters, all exacerbate the individual risks of each of the other crises. But far worse than that, Globalization links all those crises together into an inexorably-destructive Perfect Storm. It is that Perfect Storm that reveals the true nature of the hidden-consequences created by our newly-interconnected world. The combined impact is far more than just the sum of all the separate components within it.

## ADOPTING A VICTIM MENTALITY

Over the last few years there have been growing numbers of sometimes sensationalist – sometimes well-considered – warnings about an almost unlimited range of supposedly-imminent catastrophes: Mad-Cow Disease, Tsunamis, Swine Flu, Volcanic Explosions, Meteorite Near-Misses, Threats of Worldwide Economic Collapse, Global Warming. We are now almost immune. It is like living in a major earthquake zone; we no longer think too much about The Big One. Instead, as the general public, or as politicians, or as business executives, or religious leaders, or heads of communities, we focus on our day-to-day lives and we take on those challenges that feel achievable – things at which we feel we can make a difference. And we increasingly warn against 'unrealistic idealism'. And we counsel ourselves to be 'pragmatic'. And we increasingly find ourselves thinking some of the same thoughts as a younger generation that has become 'apathetic' and 'lost faith' in politicians and The Establishment as a whole. And we feel a little embarrassed by the 'naivety' of times past when individuals dared to aspire to change the world. Without even noticing, large numbers are beginning to act like victims who are on the point of giving-in to the inevitable – who are unknowingly preconditioning themselves to give up without a fight.

Any single global crisis will knock the world economy. But such a blow risks weakening the international community for a sustained period – just as the damage caused by the Credit Crunch is set to continue for the best part of a decade. When the next shock hits, many nations will already be in a weakened state. And – in such a worst-case likely scenario – it is that progressive enfeeblement that above all else is set eventually to pull the world economy down. Globalization dictates the overall dynamics of what for now is the 'default' future that every country currently faces. Whatever the specific details, the overall pattern is already quite clear. The extreme worldwide backlashes to be endured over the next few decades are not going to be intermittent and isolated events. Instead, one crisis will trigger another. The international community faces not just a progressive cascade of a selection of the potential global crises examined in this book. As

**413**

things stand, it may well be hit by a relentless and unstoppable assault of nearly *all* of them. And with each blow, countries will become less capable of withstanding the next, leading to a gradual but inexorable and irretrievable slide into increasingly destructive global chaos.

## WHEN IT HAPPENED ONCE BEFORE

It seems completely unthinkable that a sophisticated global civilization like ours can end. But to put that into a historical context, global chaos destroyed human progress once before. Seventeen-hundred years ago, humanity seemed set to soar. There was moderate progress in China, India and the Americas, but the greatest potential at the time was around the Mediterranean. Incorporating the sum of all Greek and Egyptian knowledge that had come before it, this highly-developed society proudly called itself The Roman Empire.

## THE LIBRARY OF ALEXANDRIA

The Ancient-Egyptian port of Alexandria (one of many cities of the same name founded by Alexander the Great) was the scientific capital of the world, and its Library was its greatest treasure because it contained the essence of all the wisdom of centuries – there was no repository of knowledge to match it anywhere on Earth. At the time of Cleopatra's death, it claimed to hold a copy of every book in existence, maybe 700,000 scrolls of papyrus in total. The library's voracious appetite for papyrus (which proved increasingly difficult to satisfy) was only surpassed by its demand for books. Locals claimed that customs officers had a standing order to commandeer any new book they found on board a ship passing through the port so that the scribes at the Library could duplicate it before, ideally, returning the copy – rather than the original – to its rightful owner.

It was a vast complex world economy that was technologically advanced and managerially sophisticated. Indeed, the Roman Empire was not only *complex*, but also *interconnected*. The network of extremely well-engineered major highways could stretch more than twice around the equator, and the smaller roads went still further. Even more than in today's world, the whole of the 'global economy' had become remarkably uniform in terms of highways, coinage, language, laws and even fashion – with successful people around the empire all trying to dress as if they lived on the West Coast of the United States of Italy. A century-and-a-half later it was all but finished.

Humanity took around twelve-hundred years to recover, and then largely only thanks to the Arab and Asian scholars who had kept copies of a few fragments of the vast collection of ancient documents lost in the West. Today, in the early $21^{st}$ century, we are only about four-centuries more technically and scientifically advanced than the Ancient World was when the main Library of Alexandria burned down and much of the archived knowledge of the previous thousand years was lost. In many aspects we are little more than two-centuries more advanced artistically and socially. In other words, although humanity is seventeen-hundred years older, we are not very much further forward. If Roman civilization had continued progress at the rate at which things picked up again in the $17^{th}$ Century (without the long stagnation that actually occurred) then nuclear power would have been discovered during the period that we instead associate with Viking marauders. The first computer with human-level intelligence would have appeared around the date that we now celebrate as the Norman invasion of Britain by William the Conqueror. *That* is the impact of global economic and social chaos.

# REDUCING THE THREATS:
# HOLISTIC PERSPECTIVE

## Globalization crises need Holistic Perspective – seeing issues in the context of both the global arena and a 30-year time-horizon

IT IS THE hidden planet-wide connectivity of apparently unrelated aspects of the world economy that raises the greatest globally-defined threats of major crises. This is also what makes many of those challenges the hardest to overcome. Ultimately it is High-Tech-Globalization that has pushed the international community into what can feel like an end-game – an apparently neck-and-neck race between the extremes of Global Renaissance and global chaos. That is why the realignment that governments and major corporations and others must undertake necessarily includes adopting a *Holistic Perspective*.

There are two components to this realignment, the most obvious of which involves deliberately viewing even apparently-domestic issues in the context of the whole global arena. One of the implications of Globalization that politicians tend not to focus on publically is that there are no longer remaining parts of a nation's activities that are fully isolated any more – they impact other countries and are themselves influenced by numerous decisions made elsewhere around the world.

Only by attempting to reflect fully that relatively-new reality is it possible to unleash all the potential of existing governments operating in concert together as well as with corporations and civil organizations. For instance, it is far easier for the government of a massive emerging economy such as China to explore how to rebalance its cash and trade surpluses by encouraging local consumerism (despite the often-claimed cultural aversion of the Chinese to consumption) if it first considers the threats to its national future if the global economy suffers as a result of China *not* rebalancing.

# Holistic Perspective

## ADOPTING A 30-YEAR TIME-HORIZON

The second component of a Holistic Perspective is far less obvious to many people. In addition to interconnecting across space, the massively-complex system we think of as the Global Economy also interconnects across time, often with major delays that span decades. The human mind struggles on the best of occasions to associate cause with effect if two events are geographically separate (for instance, the eruption of an unpronounceable volcano in the middle of nowhere that nevertheless causes chaos at major international airports thousands of miles away). However, extreme time-delays are even harder to process. Smoking may have been proved seriously to damage health, but the connection never feels as real as the idea of drinking strong acid.

Important commodities such as oil, tin and copper may all be rapidly depleting, pension-ages may be unsustainably low, and many national-economies may be addicted to budget deficits that are edging the whole world economy toward crisis; but these issues are not set to go critical for perhaps a few decades. Whereas the threat of a major act of terrorism, even though it might potentially ruin the lives of 'only' a few thousand families at most, can feel like almost the worst thing that could happen to a country. It is especially important therefore to compensate for the natural tendency of all politicians, business heads and other leaders to focus on the Urgent (in other words, imminent and local) in place of what may be equally Crucial but is far away in distance or time or both. The easiest way of encouraging this discipline is to force a time-horizon that, other than in professions such as the oil-industry, is rare to consider in the modern world. At the moment, approximately 30-years works well as a window on issues relating to major trends in the global economy because by around 2040 some of the exponentially-driven developments within AI, the 'supernet', materials-science and biotech are set to change things so much that to try to forecast much further becomes increasingly pointless.

Yet within that 30-year window it is vital to explore implications of the more likely threat scenarios (which is a key role for collective-action by corporations working with governments and others, as detailed in the final chapter of the book). For example, as commodity-prices of depleting resources nudge upward, what will be the likely effects on migration away from some countries and into others? And therefore how sustainable are current international border-controls, especially for huge 'borderless' zones such as most of the EU.

# GLOBALIZATION CRISES

## REASSESSING THE SCHENGEN AREA

The so-called Schengen Area that includes 25 EU countries (that is, all of the EU except for the UK and Ireland) acts like a single state as far as travel is concerned, with border controls needed only for those entering or leaving the zone, but not usually for those moving within it. That may not be sustainable in the long-term.

## PREPARING FOR WILDCARD EVENTS

Realigning activities consistent with a Holistic Perspective also highlights the importance of pre-planning for certain 'wildcard events' that, even though unlikely, would be hugely disruptive if they happened. If for example any of the events covered in the subchapter about *An international community on permanent alert* (page 372) do in fact occur within the next few decades, they will only reinforce any pressures toward increased global chaos. Of course, by definition, wildcard-events although catastrophic are rare. However, something like an asteroid strike is certainly sufficiently plausible that it is highly appropriate to maintain the existing arrangements for monitoring Near-Earth Objects, such as NASA's recently launched Spaceguard Project.

In tandem, once sufficient numbers of countries can again afford extra expenditure, the international community should supplement global funding of programs aimed at devising practical responses to the discovery that a very large object is indeed heading our way. Even theoretically it is a tough problem to crack. Although it might, for example, be helpful to fire nuclear missiles at – or detonate them near – a few types of space-object, in many cases that would simply result in breaking them up into multiple large objects that were all still heading on a collision course for Earth.

A far more probable crisis within the next few decades is that a major earthquake strikes an important city. The seismic risks to major cities in China's western region were not systematically surveyed at the time rapid expansion began, only now are they being fully appreciated. Likely targets elsewhere in the world (such as Istanbul) are badly prepared because very-few buildings have adequate earthquake protection. In addition to the major loss of life and property that will result, there may be far-wider

418

economic impacts to the global economy if, for example, Turkey has by the time of such major city earthquakes already joined the EU. Other cities at high risk (like Tokyo, San Francisco and Los Angeles) have many more modern buildings designed to withstand severe quakes. But that does not necessarily mean that an extreme earthquake in those cities will not still cause massive disruption.

## TRANSFERRING LESSONS FROM GREECE TO TURKEY

There are strong political attractions to Turkey joining the European Union as its first predominantly Moslem (yet secular) member. However, as with for example Greece, cultural attitudes to taxation and corruption may also turn out to be important factors affecting its subsequent economic integration, and therefore the means by which it can best be assimilated. Similarly, costs of the apparently-inevitable major earthquakes due in Istanbul and elsewhere in Turkey – including the longer-term impacts on Turkey's economic performance – may also need to be factored into a hard-headed evaluation of the terms of Turkey's membership.

As was found at Fukushima in March 2011, although few buildings in the vicinity fell as a result of the earthquake, and although tsunamis are sufficiently common in the area that a sea wall protected the nuclear power-plant, and although in the event of a crisis graphite-rods automatically lowered in order to shut-down the reactor, and although there was even a battery back-up for the cooling system in the unlikely event that the main generator failed – it was still a disaster. What went wrong was that the sea wall proved slightly too low, so the tsunami knocked out the generators, with the result that there was no cooling for the still-hot reactor after batteries ran out eight hours later. That sort of unforeseen cascade of unfortunate and unlikely events is typical of major industrial accidents. It is also likely to be the pattern in Tokyo, San Francisco and Los Angeles.

Current research suggests that there may never be ways to predict earthquakes sufficiently accurately to justify evacuating cities. However, it is nevertheless already possible to set up a sensor network that can give ten or twenty seconds' warning. That may not sound like long – but with the correct electronic communications network it is sufficient time for all elevators to stop at a floor and open their doors, for road signs to flash 'Slow Down', for mainframe computers to store what they are doing, and for surgeons to take their scalpels out.

## EXPLAINING THE COMPLEX TRADE-OFFS OF FOREIGN POLICY

Despite member-states of the UN accepting their collective Responsibility-to-Protect populations that are being abused, delivering on that obligation is not so simple. Behind closed doors, and based on long-standing overseas-policies regarding globally-defined threats to national security, diplomats continue to argue the *Realpolitik* of bolstering certain unpleasant regimes almost whatever they do. The countries that historically have been selected for such special-treatment have tended to be those that offer regional stability as well as access to oil or military bases or diplomatic support, and more recently, repression of claimed Islamist extremists. The sometimes-reluctant judgment to display public friendship to certain countries that in practice act as bullies (to the outside world just as much as to their people) has been justified as being on-balance better than risking losing their oil or access to territory or restrictions on terrorism or influence over some ever-bigger, even-longer-term issue.

The tension over Syrian human-rights violations begun in April 2011 is an example. Syria holds the equivalent of only 1% of Saudi oil reserves (so from that point of view was of relatively-low strategic importance), but it was seen as potentially crucial in the on-going negotiations over Palestine (which is central to Middle-Eastern stability and much of Western foreign policy for the region). Few members of the news-media or general public appreciate just how much even enlightened 'ethical foreign policy' has to balance such long-term big-picture factors, many of which are often hardly even in the public domain. Yet in today's world of intense public scrutiny, such a stance increasingly risks nevertheless being portrayed by the media, and accepted by the general public, as unpalatably hypocritical. As a result, it threatens to undermine public trust in the 'moral compasses' that their politicians are following and, amplified by Boundaryless People-Power, form a backlash against governments.

As the more-general 2011 events across Arab states demonstrate, when the international community tolerates human-rights violations in order to secure stability, it only *postpones* instability. In the modern interconnected world it cannot avoid social systems from changing, whether by evolution or revolution. And when an inevitable backlash to undue suppression of change occurs, disruption risks rippling throughout the global economy and causing repercussions that potentially then threaten the national security (if only in the form of economic stability) of those very countries that adopted the policy of appeasement in the first place.

In addition to their assumed UN Responsibility-to-Protect abused populations, state governments also have an explicit responsibility to protect their own nations from the instability caused by artificially sustaining autocratic regimes that then implode in uncontrollable ways that directly or indirectly disrupt the world economy. Even powerful nations these days have reduced funds to spend on major foreign interventions, military or otherwise. So, it is well-understood within diplomatic circles that there are some aspects of real-world international politics (including the need sometimes to do business with unpleasant regimes) that necessarily open any government to the criticism of double-standards if they become known to the general public, especially if taken out of the immensely-complex context of modern Foreign Affairs.

However, the current diplomatic stance is probably unsustainable. Whatever the economic and strategic logic behind tacit-support of autocratic and abusive regimes, the mood of the general population throughout much of the international community (not just the West) – fuelled as it is by unprecedented media and internet coverage – seems set to harden against those of their governments that are increasingly depicted as being 'on the wrong side of history'. That overriding attitude appears to be as true for the new generations that have grown up in the Middle East as for those in Europe, Asia and the Americas. As a result, it is becoming necessary for governments to lay out far more explicitly the complexity of trade-offs they face in Foreign Policy. In the past this has often been seen as being too complicated for the general public to understand, or at least to agree with. But that is an increasingly risky stance for governments to take – because it is publically indefensible.

In contrast, in the long-term it is those governments that are seen to lead the diplomatic pack away from historically-unpleasant pragmatism toward a more (at least apparently) open and transparent style of Foreign Policy that seem most likely to sustain public support. Ironically, because of this these same governments are also likely to find that, in the intense spotlight of modern Globalist 24/7 news, their new approach is actually *more* pragmatic than the one they cautiously leave behind. By adopting a truly Holistic Perspective *and then sharing selected parts of it with the general public*, the international community has the potential to act far more concertedly in its Foreign Policy, not least because the general public across numerous nations can be persuaded to provide far greater support.

## OVERHAULING EDUCATION FOR A VERY DIFFERENT FUTURE

Media will play another crucial role in how the Holistic Perspective plays out – it will help large numbers *achieve* such a viewpoint. But that process is not restricted to the News Media or to New Media. In many countries, for example, some of the most effective ways of communicating ideas on family planning or HIV have turned out to be Soap Operas. Even 'pure entertainment' is useful in educating a general population to think broader and longer-term.

That is itself a component of a far-more-fundamental realignment that is needed of Education generally. Unfortunately, although Education is one of the most powerful potential levers for sustained change across the international community, education-processes overall are in fact extremely difficult to adapt. The trouble with attempting to transform society by using the formal education system is that, in every country, the ways that youngsters are groomed for the future tends itself to be one of the most deeply-established – and therefore difficult to change – aspects of a culture. A child's learning is impacted by many different factors. Whether for example it is an Islamic madrasah, a Roman-Catholic convent, or a Beverly-Hills High School, every education system has at its core the accumulated body of knowledge that educators select to pass on. And that selection alone has an extraordinary impact. But almost as influential are the means by which learning is transferred, and the skills and background of those responsible for the teaching – as well as how all that fits with what children learn from family-members, friends, the TV and (above all these days) electronic-games and the internet.

Within this Complex-and-Interconnected context, governments must urgently reform their education systems to prepare children for the globally-integrated High-Tech world that is around the corner. And educators themselves need to be aggressive in circumventing the overly-traditional approaches often still adopted in classrooms everywhere from Nursery Schools to Business Schools. Even students (even young children) posting educational games on the internet would be more relevant and effective than some of the current educational approaches, which are little more than relatively-superficial upgrades to a talk-and-chalk approach inherited from the Victorians.

Just as importantly, universities must face up to the implications of all prior knowledge soon being almost-instantly available on-line. PhD students must learn how to track down obscure insights from other institution's electronic archives and work effectively in a virtual global-research community. Medical trainers must decide what the future skills of a GP need to be – given that the internet often already provides patients with more detailed insight into their illness and treatment than any family doctor can remember or keep up-to-date with. Exponential trends are set fundamentally to transform the world over the next few decades. The graduates and trainees that will enter the radically-altered jobs market then, are today just entering the education system. Yet – despite the sometimes-inspiring dedication of their teachers – almost everything about that system was designed in the past, it is educating pupils using techniques from the past, and it is preparing them for a future that by the time they reach it will already feel like the *distant* past.

## RE-EDUCATING POLITICIANS FOR AN UNGOVERNABLE WORLD

Politicians themselves must also be re-educated to fit a world that is ungovernable, even at the national level, using only the oratory, tribal politics, intrigues and public-manipulations of the past. Whatever the rights or wrongs of the recent Iraq war, few if any would suggest that the national decisions to support or oppose the invasion, let alone the absence of any clear decisions on how to 'win the peace' afterwards, were sufficiently well-informed, appropriately scrutinized or effectively debated by all the world's politicians.

That unintended unprofessionalism has to change. The current widespread disillusionment with politics is not, from what I observe, primarily caused by apathy as many have suggested. It is instead the partial-rejection of a system that is increasingly seen as disconnected from the world of the general public. It is also a reaction against politicians whose viewpoints, or unwillingness to answer questions directly, all-too-often come across as transparently self-serving. Yet countries face unprecedented and growing challenges to globally-defined national security. The public now expects (and in truth would anyway need) politicians to operate in the most efficient and effective possible manner going forward.

That includes staggering their vacation times. It is utterly absurd for any modern government effectively to 'shut down for the summer'. In the past, when travel was difficult, it made sense for politicians to stop sitting at various periods throughout the year. That logic has long been superseded. Likewise, top government posts can no longer automatically be handed to politicians who have neither a background in the subject nor experience in running a large department; however bright they are, and whatever they claim, it is simply too risky. No major corporation would dream of being so offhand. The general public should expect no less professionalism in its own governments.

Similarly, debates must be exactly that: Debates. It is unacceptable that in many countries politicians do not even attend the discussions about the issues they then vote on. It is just as inappropriate that those who do attend while someone tries to sell an idea to them, rather than carefully listening to the detail instead resort to rhetorical barracking and political point-scoring. That is not the way that members of professionally-run organizations conduct themselves when they care about achieving the most valuable outcome from a discussion. Neither now can politicians. Effective dialogue is a skill. It can be trained to politicians just as it has been for decades to many top-executives.

## BALANCING ADVOCACY AND INQUIRY

Having been asked to facilitate the interactions of innumerable top-teams over the years, there is one guideline to effective discussion that I have has found more useful (and universal) than any other. It is to try to ensure that there is a reasonable balance between people selling a point of view and people genuinely trying to understand the problem. In academic circles this is referred to as 'Balancing Advocacy and Inquiry'. It is impossible to come up with the best outcome from a debate if everyone is only pushing their own pet idea. Likewise, the debate gets nowhere if everyone is only exploring the problem and no one is proposing a potential solution. For dialogue to be effective, it needs a bit of both.

# Holistic Perspective

And finally, politicians during interviews must stop resorting to the increasingly-obvious avoidance techniques encouraged by outdated media-trainers. A sophisticated viewer sees it for what it is, and these days even uneducated societies in poor nations run by tyrants are becoming sophisticated viewers. However, it should go without saying that government reform that merely entails a bit of training of politicians and a few organizational updates is – on its own – little more than glorified tinkering. It will never, of itself, resolve the fundamental disconnect between national self-interest and globally-defined threats. Any more than a bank realigning its strategy to encompass the principle of Unelected Responsibility will avoid another global financial crisis. Any more than an oil-company applying True Costing and a retail-chain adopting Collective Sustainability will minimize climate change or prevent depletion of the ocean's fish.

To achieve those things demands something extra. It certainly still needs a widespread realigning of corporate, government and institutional strategies around appropriate combinations of Unelected Responsibility, True Costing, Collective Sustainability, Mirrored Tolerance, Pre-emptive Recovery and Holistic Perspective. But it requires more. It is time for some grown-up discussions. Time for joined-up thinking. Time for genuine leadership. As the final chapter of this book now reveals, this is the opportunity for private individuals, groups, communities, companies, major corporations, multinationals, whole industries, institutions, governments, supranational bodies and the international community at large to make a difference. It is time for the true leaders in society to stand up and *take the initiative.*

CHAPTER SUMMARY
# GLOBALIZATION CRISES

**Globalization so heightens other threats that the international community now has no mechanism to evolve effective responses and requires Holistic Perspective as a counter-measure**

Globalization exacerbates the risk of *all* globally-defined threats to economic stability – including 'wildcard' events
- *High-Tech-Globalization further exacerbates crises already stirred up by High-Tech interacting with Capitalism, Industrialization, Population and Religion*
- *High-Tech-Capitalism crises exacerbated by High-Tech-Globalization enhance threats such as wild market swings, economic crashes and societal meltdown*
- *High-Tech-Industrialization crises exacerbated by High-Tech-Globalization enhance threats of government lack of control unintentionally caused by the net effect of multinationals*
- *High-Tech-Population crises exacerbated by High-Tech-Globalization enhance threats such as uncontrollable pandemics*
- *High-Tech-Religion crises exacerbated by High-Tech-Globalization enhance threats such as immigration 'time-bombs' exploding into civil unrest and international conflict*
- *The combined impact of every crisis – and 'wildcard' event – exacerbated by Globalization increasingly places the international community on near-permanent alert*

Despite generally high competence of individuals, national government decision-making is misaligned with addressing globally-defined threats
- *Contrary to popular misconception most inadequacies attributed to The Establishment as a whole in fact only relate to a few outliers*
- *The hidden reality of The System means state-influence is increasingly difficult to exert and politicians are ill-prepared to address complex globally-defined threats*

# Chapter summary

Unfortunately, supranational bodies are also unsuited to exerting sufficient global governance

- *There are numerous failed approaches aimed at dealing with issues that affect one or more nations but over which none has sufficient influence*
- *Even the UN is inadequate to the task because it is structured more for countries to protect local interests than global interests*
- *Because of all these factors there are for now insufficient ways to devise counters to globally-defined threats – so the entire world economy is in peril*

Globalization crises need HOLISTIC PERSPECTIVE – seeing issues in the context of both the global arena *and* a 30-year time-horizon

- *To help unleash the full potential of existing governments to operate in concert, they must assess even apparently-domestic issues in the context of the overall global-arena*
- *To compensate for the natural tendency to focus on the Urgent in place of what is Crucial but a long time away, international strategic assessments must adopt a 30-year time-horizon*
- *Wildcard events that are extremely doubtful though catastrophic can largely be discounted from evaluations of economic stability but likely global impacts of city earthquakes cannot*
- *For national Foreign Policies to be strong and viable in the long-term they must be based on a Holistic Perspective and their complex trade-offs explained to the public*
- *Education systems – which inevitably have delays of up to a few decades built into them – must urgently reform to prepare pupils for an almost-unrecognizable future*
- *Politicians must themselves be re-educated to suit a world that is increasingly ungovernable – even at the national level – using only the political skills of the present*

## 28. WHY EXISTING GLOBAL GOVERNANCE IS SO POWERLESS

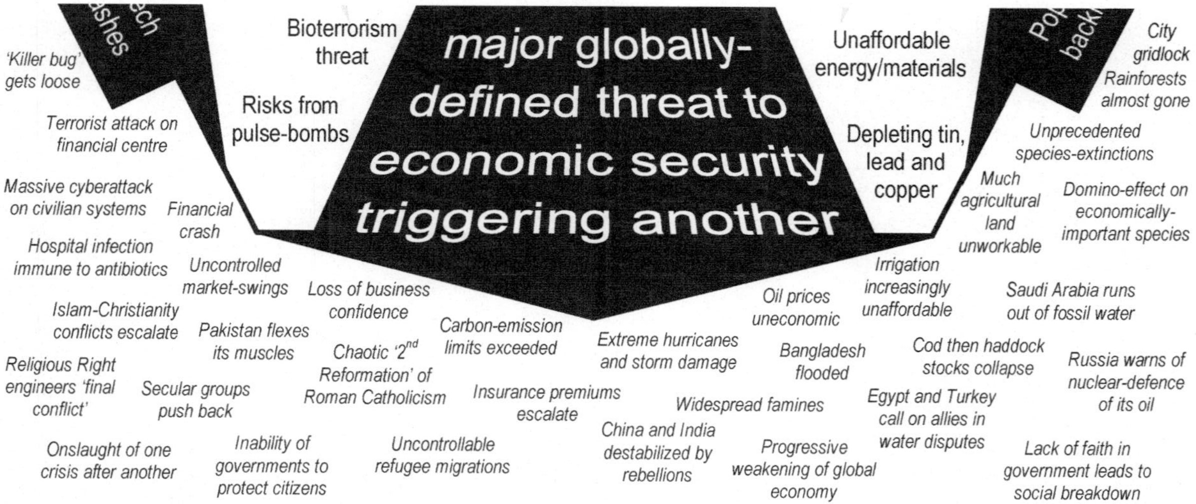
ech
ashes
Pop
back
major globally-defined threat to economic security triggering another
'Killer bug' gets loose
Terrorist attack on financial centre
Massive cyberattack on civilian systems
Financial crash
Hospital infection immune to antibiotics
Uncontrolled market-swings
Islam-Christianity conflicts escalate
Pakistan flexes its muscles
Religious Right engineers 'final conflict'
Secular groups push back
Onslaught of one crisis after another
Inability of governments to protect citizens
Bioterrorism threat
Risks from pulse-bombs
Loss of business confidence
Chaotic '2nd Reformation' of Roman Catholicism
Carbon-emission limits exceeded
Insurance premiums escalate
Uncontrollable refugee migrations
Extreme hurricanes and storm damage
China and India destabilized by rebellions
Widespread famines
Oil prices uneconomic
Bangladesh flooded
Progressive weakening of global economy
Unaffordable energy/materials
Depleting tin, lead and copper
Irrigation increasingly unaffordable
Cod then haddock stocks collapse
Egypt and Turkey call on allies in water disputes
Much agricultural land unworkable
City gridlock
Rainforests almost gone
Unprecedented species-extinctions
Domino-effect on economically-important species
Saudi Arabia runs out of fossil water
Russia warns of nuclear-defence of its oil
Lack of faith in government leads to social breakdown

***BUT*** – because current systems of global governance inevitably encourage each country to prioritize its own interests above collective interests – ***all the existing mechanisms to evolve counter-strategies are failing***

- 2005 UN World Summit unable to issue any statement on nuclear disarmament because no progress
- Despite near-ideal conditions 2009 UN Climate-Change Conference in Copenhagen was largely a failure
- Euro-zone proved incapable of aligning members such as Greece and Ireland enough to avoid bailout
- World Trade Organization attempts since 2001 to lower trade barriers have been stalled since 2008
- Commitments at 2010 and 2011 UN Climate-Change Conference were less than hoped and postponed
- Despite UN 2005 confirmation of its Responsibility to Protect it is slow and inconsistent (as in Libya 2011)
- 2002 UN Biodiversity Convention agreed 2010 targets to curb rate of extinctions – every country failed
- 2010 Nagoya biodiversity talks revealed that extreme conflicts still underlie the newly 'agreed targets'
- In the absence of any effective global governance world-religions further polarize and destabilize
- 2010 UN wildlife meeting rejected proposal to ban the slaughter of endangered Giant Bluefin tuna
- After three-years' negotiation 2011 International Whaling Commission again failed to agree a way forward
- Largely governed by formal and informal cartels the oil industry is decoupled from global interests

# TAKING THE INITIATIVE overview

For their enlightened self-interest key players in the world economy must form the equivalent of Global Guilds to fill the current leadership-vacuum and trigger the far-reaching changes needed to minimize global crises

- Despite current widespread disruption there will never be a better time to trigger the changes needed to secure against different forms of escalating systemic-crisis

- In the absence of any effective global governance – industries cannot wait for outside help but must realign their activities and form 'Global Guilds' to create a practical way forward

- Global Guilds must trigger a viral strategy that has the ultimate goal of accelerating the collective responsiveness of their members to growing crises

- Rather than wait for protracted international agreement – self-improving *prototype* Global Guilds will immediately improve the odds of those organizations that form them

*Opportunities for GLOBAL REALIGNMENT to minimize crises*

*GROWN-UP DISCUSSIONS...*
*... LEADERSHIP...*
*... GLOBAL GUILDS...*
*... ACCELERATING RESPONSIVENESS...*

# TAKING THE
# INITIATIVE

# IF NOT NOW – THEN WHEN?

Despite current widespread disruption there will never be a better time to trigger the changes needed to secure against different forms of escalating systemic-crisis

BIG BUSINESS MAY turn out to be the good guys after all. For some people, that may not seem a welcome suggestion, but the fact is that against all the odds, and contrary to the increasing sway of popular opinion against them, multinationals and faceless conglomerates have the potential for an extraordinary comeback. Unpopular, despised and derided by the general public as Banking, Oil, Energy, Pharmaceuticals and Media corporations have sometimes become, they and their fellow corporate-giants in other industries – along with Little Business – nevertheless have the power to edge the global economy away from progressive chaos. Furthermore, it may be that they *alone* have that power. In a global economy in desperate search of heroes the biggest surprise of all may be that, unloved and unwanted, it is Big Business that despite everything saves the world.

## INADEQUATE POWER STRUCTURES

Territorially-focused governments can never address globally-defined crises effectively. And the United Nations is incapable of changing itself into a body that could. Yet just as formal religions once claimed overriding authority over state sovereigns, so today national governments and supranational bodies such as the UN claim exclusive authority over running the planet. To maintain that right they must continue to fulfill the highest obligation of all governments – to protect their people. However, when it comes to the global crises covered by this book, neither national governments nor bodies like the UN can deliver on that responsibility. They are increasingly floundering. Through little fault of their own, when it comes to global crises such as climate-change or depleting natural resources or financial crashes they are inherently and unavoidably unfit for

432

purpose. And that means that they can no longer automatically claim an exclusive right to govern.

Naturally, in democratic countries most citizens rightly expect that issues that *are* controllable by their politicians should remain exclusively governed by duly-elected leaders. But it is those issues that are *not* controllable by them that are in question. At the moment, in addition to the historical impact of governments and formal-religions, the growth of global crises is in fact primarily influenced by the uncoordinated actions of a select number of powerful and global industries. The most impactful are High-Tech (including IT, telecoms and pharmaceuticals), Banking, Media, Energy (covering oil corporations as well as power utilities), Marine industries (especially fishing), and a range of Land industries (primarily relating to agriculture and mining). Between them, these six sectors dominate how global crises are forming. Collectively, the leaders within these industries *already* have, in principle, the power to steer what those in national and supranational governments cannot. It is these business leaders alone who currently have the potential to offer effective global governance.

At the moment, in contrast, these leaders often do not even recognize that with unelected power comes Unelected Responsibility – let alone do they view such implied responsibility in the context of a Holistic Perspective. As a result, their combined impact on global crises is at best misaligned and ineffectual and at worst anarchic and dangerous. That needs to change. As this final chapter of the book now lays out, individual businesses and whole industries have an unparalleled opportunity to take the initiative. What is more, it is in their enlightened self-interest to do so.

But they need to act fast. Being subjected to a progressive series of uncontrolled global crises is like being forced to keep playing Russian-roulette – it is only a matter of time before a fatal version of Game Over. However, the pace of the Spin-Click of our global game of jeopardy is accelerating. Based on the exponential nature of the High-Tech trends driving the worst global crises, if today the international trigger was getting pulled only once a year, by 2040 we would have to face the risk of a bullet in our collective brain once every sixteen seconds.

## FIGHTING ON TOO MANY FRONTS

We certainly do not have thirty years to get our act together. As things stand, even within fifteen-to-twenty years the world economy will come under extreme threat from the globally-defined crises covered earlier. But that is a very short time to get ready. By then the international community must be far more resilient, and must have slowed those trends likely to cause the worst trouble – as well as removed whatever obstacles to a potential Global Renaissance that are possible. Moreover, it will get steadily harder to make a difference. As a result, the most influential industries and nations probably only have little more than ten years left to improve our odds significantly. That is because of a two-pronged argument: The global economy will not be able to withstand more that a small number of fundamentally-different crises at the same time, and there are more than that small number that are already likely to occur within the next fifteen years or so.

Dealing with the first element of the argument, it is remarkably easy for government and corporate decision-making to become catastrophically overloaded during times of crisis. It is a surprisingly consistent pattern. Indeed, across my confidential analyses of numerous top-level governance structures I have found that leadership teams tend to flounder when confronting more than just *two* fundamentally different crises at the same time. There are many contributing factors to this, but basically it comes down to the leaders not being able to hold sufficient detail in their heads at the same time. They resort to briefings that are necessarily only about a subset of what is going on. They put off issues that may in time turn out to have been crucial, but were never urgent enough to become a high priority. Anyway, their freedom of action tends to be significantly reduced by the immediate impact of the crises themselves. On top of that, the interconnections between problems and solutions and potential unintended consequences get missed, and then cause further problems later on.

I have been privileged to observe some of the most talented top-leadership teams in the world, often at times of great turmoil. Only the very best were truly able to handle two completely different major crises at the same time. From everything I have witnessed, managing more concurrent urgent crises than that – even with the best political, business and social leaders working in the best environments – is likely in practice to be impossible to sustain. Even at the moment, on those days when there are not any truly-urgent crises breaking, governments nevertheless have to cope with the aftermath of a world recession at the same time as related Sovereign-debt worries in parallel with revolutions in North Africa and the

Middle East. Understandably, dealing with the failure to address climate-change has tended to drop in political priority from where it was just before the 2009 Copenhagen Climate-Change conference. However, imagine if the initial financial collapse and Arab rebellions had all occurred in the same month, along with a natural disaster such as the 2011 Japanese tsunami raising concerns over nuclear meltdown. Addressing climate-change would probably not have got any top-level attention at all.

## THE THREE-STRIKES RULE

There is another problem with too many urgent global threats – global crises demand global leadership. Yet as examined in the chapter on Globalization Crises, the international community does not even have effective infrastructures for dealing with those sorts of problems. As a result, even two truly-major global crises (comparable, say, to the global-banking crisis of 2008) will be very tough to handle at the same time. Three concurrent such crises is too much to expect existing systems to be able to manage. The partly-parochial, unintentionally short-term solutions that would inevitably result would themselves then cause *even more* uncontrolled crises that would eventually lead to further unrecognized damage.

This risk of triggering further problems is made even worse by the fact that, on top of everything else, global systems tend to respond painfully slowly to attempts to change course. Even if leaders somehow could keep a clear head and maintain a clear view of the full implications of all their actions, which in practice they never could, they would still be unable to cope. The longer you leave it before responding to global crises, the more that options to change direction become overly restricted. Everything takes too long. It is an extreme instance of the often-quoted example of steering massive oil-tankers – if captains try to change direction too late there is absolutely nothing they can do to avoid crashing.

In terms of multiple globally-defined threats to the national economies of numerous individual states, the metaphor is closer to trying to steer several fleets of often-competing oil tankers through a sea of uncharted and largely-hidden icebergs. Before the tanker captains can even *begin* to steer a course to safety without getting in each other's way, they must first agree with their rivals what avoidance strategy they should adopt. That will cause still further delay, which risks making things even worse.

# TAKING THE INITIATIVE

In conclusion, even though it would be hard enough for corporate and government leaders to handle multiple crises within the same 'family' of threats (for instance, all Capitalism Crises – like the current Sovereign-debt crises on top of the world economic slow-down), it would nevertheless be a lot easier than multiple crises driven by backlashes of largely *separate* global trends (say, uncontrollable worldwide Religion-inspired urban terrorism and a devastating global Industrialization-pollution crisis) that necessarily shared few if any common solutions.

As a first approximation, governments and corporations can reassure themselves that multiple crises all arising from the same basic trend still only count as One Strike against them. Parallel urgent crises driven by two largely-separate trends, however, are sufficiently hard to address in harmony that this scenario represents Two Strikes. The implication is that as countries are tested by crises generated by any of the trends detailed in this book, leaders should keep track of the number of distinct clusters of threats they are urgently tackling. Three Strikes – and they risk being out.

## WHY THE NEXT DECADE IS SO IMPORTANT

The second element of the logic as to why we have only about ten years or so to get our act together is that, if we do not, then soon after that time we can reasonably expect the Three-Strikes rule to come into effect. Given current trends, food scarcity caused by aquifer depletion and other water shortages are likely to begin to cause disruption in around fifteen years' time. But only five years after that, oil-restrictions combined with collapses in fish-stocks are set to coincide with a massively-increased world population demanding ever-more from those diminishing resources. Five years would be too short a time to steer away from the inevitable crash from Competitive Overuse.

Anyway, long before that there are likely to be other major crises. The international community will be lucky if a religion-inspired crisis, such as another terrorist-attack comparable to 9/11, can be averted for as long as even ten years from now. Hopefully the next dangerous pandemic and the next global economic crisis (as opposed to the continuation of the current one) will not occur until at least then – nor will any major natural disaster hit a large city directly. And hopefully, widespread cyberattacks via the internet will continue to be held in check, as will antibiotic-resistant strains of bacteria.

Combining all these threats, a reasonable working estimate is that one way or another the world economy may have around ten to twenty years before three or more extreme crises risk all hitting at the same time from substantially different directions and swamp the ability of governments and corporations to respond effectively. It *could* happen within only the next five-to-ten years – but that would mean we had been unlucky. It is also possible that there will not be three major parallel crises until twenty years or more from now – but on the world-economy's current course that seems overly optimistic. Naturally, it is not 'all or nothing'. More-minor crises should be manageable in greater numbers. And even in ten years' time the international community will still have plenty of opportunity to reinforce further and refine any changes in direction that are underway. But by then it will be too late to *begin* the process of a major change in direction.

## PERFECT TIMING

The global disruptions since 2007 have ironically *improved* the odds of the international community avoiding multiple global crises in the future. The unexpected wild repercussions have concentrated everybody's minds, and as a result the time is now right for change. The slew of world crises is not necessarily the prelude to the often-proposed New World Order – a term beloved of leading statesmen and conspiracy theorists alike – but it can certainly help.

We will never get a better time than this. Prior to the Credit Crunch that kicked off in 2007-8 and prior to the relative failure of the Copenhagen Climate Change conference in 2009, we were all probably too arrogant and overconfident to challenge the root causes of globally-defined threats to our collective security. We did not think we needed to. We felt we could pretty-well get away with anything, even if that did require a heroic global effort with world statesmen flying into Denmark on their private jets to save the world. It was all very Hollywood. But it did not work. With the very best of intentions, and with the very best of humanity playing their very best shots – it did not work. And if things are left as they currently are, it never will.

But that now seems unlikely. Without its recent bruising from unprecedented economic crises and unresolved manmade global warming, the international community would likely have just carried on regardless. Business, institutional and political leaders would have left it too late to try something new. But not now. Instead, the new-found humility of the world economy's leaders and their recently-recognized vulnerability grant us all a very real chance to break free of the old ways of doing things. The continuing shockwaves from the 2008 recession, and governments' sustained failure to address climate-change satisfactorily, and the uncertain long-term outcomes of the 2011 swell of Arab rebellions – could not have all come at a better time.

# IF NOT THE MOST POWERFUL –
# THEN WHO?

In addition to realigning their activities to create the conditions needed to counter their particular types of systemic crisis – the most powerful industries must align themselves as 'Global Guilds'

FEW PEOPLE REALIZE that when modern tankers need to steer, the rudder is in fact so large that even turning that alone would take an unrealistic effort. Yet on the trailing edge of the huge rudder is something called a Trim Tab. It is that small trim-tab that steers the enormous ship. Long before the tanker needs to change course, a minor shift to a control on the bridge sends a tiny electrical signal to a hydraulic system at the stern. An actuator then bit by bit adjusts the relative angle of the trim-tab to the rudder. The seawater rushing past it creates a pressure that in turn slowly helps pull the whole rudder to a new position that eventually – after a long delay – very gradually steers the massive tanker. To avoid the metaphorical hidden-icebergs of global crises, the fleets of the international community need to find and activate their own 'trim tabs'.

## WHAT GOVERNMENTS CANNOT PROVIDE

If the world community had an effective mechanism for world-governance then it would at least be possible to try steering the world economy directly. Examples of Competitive Overuse, such as oil, fish and water, would still be tough to handle, but by managing the depletions from a global perspective it would be far easier to avoid chaotic collapse. And addressing worldwide issues such as the ultimately-unsustainable exponential growth of High-Tech, progressive destabilization of Religions, and the growing need for optimized regulation of banking and multinationals would, again, at least be possible.

But even the UN does not provide an effective mechanism for world-governance. At the global level the international community is in many ways engaged in a rather polite form of civil war, collectively pulling itself down despite countries' shared individual long-term interests. And realistically the UN is not going to be able to reform itself fast enough to fill the world-governance gap within those very few years left for action.

Yet, from everything I have uncovered, even individual governments are not capable of succeeding either. Their infrastructures are enormous. Their reach is extensive. And even today, their budgets are huge. What is more, many political and military leaders and civil servants really do care passionately about fulfilling their duty of due-care and making a difference. And some of them have formidable intellects and leadership skills. They simply do not have an effective means of addressing globally-defined threats to economic security and social stability. Nor do they have any shared solutions to any of the specific threats. Nor even do they have an effective way of coming up with potential global solutions, let alone ones with a good chance of success.

The overriding problem that any government faces is not so much that the hugely-sophisticated diplomatic, political, economic and military processes that it typically uses day-to-day are not already geared to handle these sorts of issues at the national level. They usually are. It is just that, as things stand, when issues interconnect at the global level, those processes become far too slow and unreliable to be effective. Everything degrades into little more than a bloated diplomatic debate in search of a consensus that rarely emerges. It is a system that never even begins to tap the full potential of the people and institutions that constitute it. But the fact remains that despite all the rhetoric and good intentions and motivated individuals, the systemic-failures within national and supranational bodies make it impossible for them alone to rise to the challenge of avoiding global crises.

Instead, they need the support of Big Business. It is corporate executives, not politicians, that are set to be the Trim Tabs that will help steer the fleets of oil tankers safely through the shifting icebergs. But not Big Business in its current incoherent form. Not the existing groups of self-interested multinationals and conglomerates. Governments desperately need the help of broadly-aligned groups of industries striving for common goals that suit not just businesses themselves but also to a large extent the international community at large. Governments – individually and collectively – need an alliance with the as-yet-unformed 'Global Guilds'.

## RISE OF THE GLOBAL GUILDS

The concept of what I think of as Global Guilds is as much a Process as it is a loose confederation of Organizations. And, in terms of world governance (as opposed to the self-interests of its members) it is a process of last resort – because only globally-defined crises are unsolvable using existing political setups. Everything else can, at least in principle, stay as it is. Realistically, the unelected power of Global Guilds over national governments would only be accepted within that context anyway.

The primary purpose of the Global Guilds is to create the conditions needed to allow businesses to reduce their vulnerability to backlashes *by minimizing the global crises that exacerbate them*. That is of immediate benefit to the organizations themselves. But minimizing global crises ultimately benefits everybody. In order to make enough difference though, the Global Guilds must be formed around not just those components of the world economy that are at greatest risk, but at their core must be the *most powerful* organizations that are at risk. Based on all the crises analyzed in this book, that suggests that the six most important Global Guilds for the foreseeable future will be the *High-Tech Guild*, the *Banking Guild*, the *Media Guild*, the *Energy Guild*, the *Marine Guild* and the *Land Guild*. It makes more sense for less-powerful industries that are nevertheless exposed to extreme threats of backlash, such as Education, to belong to one of the powerful Guilds (in Education's case, probably Media) rather than form a weak independent Guild that cannot hold its own.

As it is, in the spirit of maintaining a Holistic Perspective, any given organization should probably have a primary affiliation with one Guild, but also maintain two secondary affiliations with other Guilds. For instance, an oil-multinational would have its first allegiance to the Energy Guild, but might also belong to the Land Guild and the Marine Guild. Similarly, a computer-software multinational might major in the High-Tech Guild but also minor in Media and Banking. And an automotive manufacturer might major in High-Tech and minor in Energy and Land.

More broadly, Global Guilds must not only tie into the most critical corporations, but also into the most relevant government institutions, civil groups and even religious bodies. By the very nature of what is driving the growth in turbulence across the world economy, all Guilds must link strongly with the High-Tech Guild. And, given that sustained change can only ever happen when sufficient numbers of the general population start behaving in new ways, all the Guilds must crucially also tie into key members of the Media Guild so that the public can be directly involved.

Part of each Guild's role is to help members realign their activities to minimize backlashes in the ways already discussed in the previous chapters of this book. In practice, all industries need to embrace a Holistic Perspective and, to slightly varying degrees, accept their Unelected Responsibility. However, the priorities of the other Principles (True Costing and so forth) will vary across the different Guilds. Nevertheless, the overarching role of the Global Guilds is far more than just instilling the Guild Principles. Forming Global Guilds is a means of providing sufficient world-governance to align efforts aimed at avoiding dangerous crises, *despite* the shortfalls in our existing political infrastructure. Sticking with the oil-tankers metaphor, the Global Guilds are not the various fleets or even the groups of rival tanker-captains. Nor do they represent Seamen's Unions or Naval Schools. They act for the global economy, as I will now explain, like a sophisticated set of Sat Nav systems.

## 29. PRIORITY OF GUILD PRINCIPLES FOR DIFFERENT GUILDS

### GUILD PRINCIPLES

| GLOBAL GUILDS | Unelected Responsibility | True Costing | Collective Sustainability | Mirrored Tolerance | Pre-emptive Recovery | Holistic Perspective |
|---|---|---|---|---|---|---|
| High-Tech | ✓✓ | ✓ | ✓ | ✓✓ | ✓✓✓ | ✓✓ |
| Banking | ✓✓✓ | ✓✓ | ✓ | | ✓ | ✓✓ |
| Media | ✓✓✓ | | | ✓✓ | ✓ | ✓✓ |
| Energy | ✓✓ | ✓✓✓ | ✓✓ | | ✓✓ | ✓✓ |
| Marine | ✓✓ | ✓✓ | ✓✓✓ | | ✓ | ✓✓ |
| Land | ✓✓ | ✓✓ | ✓✓✓ | | ✓✓ | ✓✓ |

# TRUSTED OBSERVERS

Global Guilds must act like *Trusted Observers* by which organizations gain an undistorted overview of globally-defined threats without breaching confidentiality

FOR A GLOBAL Guild to act as a figurative Sat Nav for its members it must fulfill three distinct roles. The first is as 'Trusted Observer'. In effect, this role behaves like an undistorted mirror that accurately reflects current reality. A Global Guild needs to provide an unbiased and trusted insight into what exactly is going on with regard to globally-defined threats to economic stability. At the moment, no individual corporation (or government) knows these things – although between them they hold all the keys needed to unlock the answers. Members of a given industry need a *shared* 'head-up display' of where the international community truly is, not where for political and commercial reasons members have to say that they are.

Yet different corporations cannot learn the full truth directly from each other, any more than countries can, because so many of the facts provide commercial and diplomatic leverage that none of the interested parties wants to give away. No profit-oriented organization, for instance, is going to tell another organization the whole unadulterated truth about topics such as peak-oil or overfishing any more than different governments will tell each other the whole truth about what *they* know.

That is why corporate members within a given Global Guild need an alternative way for them to learn the full facts and appreciate the complex uncertainties, free of spin. To be fully effective, the whole integrated set of industries within a given Guild needs to see the same unobstructed view. For members to benefit from an undistorted reflection of what is truly going on (in, for example, global warming or banking abuses or finning or water depletion or cyberterrorism), they need a trusted inside third-party to gather potentially-sensitive data and then share the *patterns* that can be synthesised from such otherwise-confidential insights.

By analogy with the fleet of competitive oil tankers traversing a sea of shifting icebergs, the Trusted-Observer role is like an accurate Sat Nav display that shows both icebergs and the GPS-locations of rival tankers but without any of the tanker-names being attached. And there is a further very-important element to the Trusted Observer role: It provides a mechanism for members and others to *understand* the motivation behind apparently-unreasonable actions taken by different industries and governments. Only in this way is it possible to find aligned solutions to otherwise intractable standoffs.

Across innumerable examples, and consistent with decades of prior analysis, I have found no examples whatsoever of national or corporate *group-behavior* – however seemingly irrational, unfair or ultimately dangerous – that did not in reality turn out merely to be the result of 'enlightened self-interest' for the most-influential players. However confusing or objectionable the resultant actions are to outsiders, what all such groups do *makes sense*, at least to those people who are on the inside.

## NO ONE DOES WRONG WILLINGLY

Although the phrase attributed to Socrates 'No one does wrong willingly' is typically portrayed as one of his paradoxes, in reality it appears to be an accurate description of the behavior of *groups* of people who on balance adopt a given set of perfectly-rational and internally-consistent Unwritten Rules that – in the absence of an explanation – outsiders may nevertheless find impenetrably 'irrational'.

Whether it is the insistence by successive US-governments of the rights of its citizens to consume profligate quantities of low-duty fuel despite the environmental impacts, or the maintenance by the EU of unsustainable fishing quotas for heavily-subsidized fleets, or the attempts by some religious groups to deny women and gays basic human rights, or even the adoption of terrorism by some Islamic extremists – there is always an understandable (though typically hidden) logic that justifies the behavior in the minds of those groups involved.

# Global Guilds

To decode such hidden logic, and then convey it to outsiders in a sufficiently comprehensible way that they can temporarily get inside the heads of those who think that way, is a crucial contribution for Global Guilds to make. Without it, the all-too-human interpretation by other industries, governments and the general public of the behavior of those whose actions exacerbate global crises is to dismiss the perpetrators as being supremely selfish, dangerously stupid or fundamentally evil. None of those assessments tends to be correct. As a result, the counter-strategies taken by businesses, governments and others risk being precariously misguided.

# VIGILANT COUNSELORS

Global Guilds must act like *Vigilant Counselors* monitoring globally-defined-crisis scenarios, alerting about changes and facilitating integrated counter-measures

BASED ON CONFIDENTIAL insights into what different countries, industries and institutions actually intend to do, a Global Guild must fulfill the role of 'Vigilant Counselor'. In this capacity it must not only feed member-organizations a continuous forecast – free of commercial, media or political bias – of what is most likely to happen regarding global crises over the next few decades, but it must also help members align their responses accordingly.

More precisely, a Global Guild needs to help the international community gain a shared understanding of the most likely composite *scenarios* of how backlashes will develop (in other words, the different ways that backlashes may unfold), the reasoning behind each scenario, the indicators that will suggest that one scenario rather than another is coming true (that is, the Leading Indicators of a scenario), and the opportunities to pre-plan coordinated responses to those of the crisis scenarios that – if they occur – may develop extremely rapidly, as with the Pondweed example on page 334.

It is, even in theory, impossible to set up a forecasting system that can predict and monitor all potential crises. It is also impossible to catch every major crisis in time. But it is perfectly possible to predict many (probably most) of the extreme crises, predict their most likely triggers, and predict the measures that will best indicate an imminent rise in the threat-levels they represent. As a result, although a few crises will always risk appearing to explode out of nowhere, the odds against that occurring can be dramatically improved. What is more, because such threats are *globally* defined and typically bring widespread threats to multiple organizations, there is very largely only downside for a corporation to attempt such forecasting alone.

446

# Global Guilds

Whether the overall analysis of global crises is conducted by a multinational headquartered in the UK, the USA, China, Russia or even Saudi Arabia – the basic trends and the overall conclusions remain the same. The findings are true for all. Corporate responses may, of course, vary considerably. But even then, the logic that determines which industry can most usefully coordinate its members' chosen strategies will be determined at the global (not individual-business) level.

Although the role of Vigilant Counselor benefits from the confidential access that a Global Guild has as Trusted Observer, it is an importantly-distinct activity. By analogy, it is like the oil-tankers' shared Sat Nav system alerting the rival captains to projected collisions – at risk of occurring maybe several minutes later – not only with icebergs but also with rival tankers that are in the process of changing course in ways their competitors are unaware of.

Within a Global Guild, the Vigilant Counselor role demands strong forecasting capability *combined* with the judgment and skill needed to encourage appropriate groups to work with each other so as to coordinate particular plans. The alternative option of all potentially-relevant parties all attempting to align all of their plans on everything is simply not practical. Worse, such an attempt would probably result in such a logjam that some of the most crucial integrations would never even get prioritized. In contrast, one of the less-obvious benefits of the Vigilant-Counselor role is that it promotes selectivity and focus in attempted coordination activities across industries and beyond.

## THE POWER OF TRANSPARENCY

There is also another dynamic that comes into play. One of the reasons that formal ties into a Global Guild are potentially so beneficial relates to how people behave when their actions, and the consequences of those actions, are visible – at least to other members of an inner-group. I have consistently observed this across all types of corporate and social communities. And importantly, the findings are also confirmed by 'Game Theory', a broad term to cover a branch of applied mathematics that models human behavior in situations in which a successful outcome is based upon the decisions of others.

The reason why transparency is useful is because in a situation, for example, of Competitive Overuse (maybe overfishing or overlogging) people tend to take less from a common resource if their actions are relatively public rather than private. What is more, the least greedy then build a positive reputation as a result of their behavior, which in due course can help them gain support on other issues. Broad public pressure, in addition to peer pressure, builds up against those who increasingly appear selfish. Those that are showing restraint begin to band together, because they now view themselves as being taken advantage of by the others. The more that they then communicate with each other, the more that the different factions identify themselves as part of the larger group, which makes it even less likely that any of them will act as 'free riders' and take advantage of the sacrifices made by the rest.

But all this only tends to happen if the full reality of who is doing what is kept public, at least within a group such as a Global Guild, especially if the different parties do not really know each other very well. And this is even truer if the reality is publicized to a far larger audience than just the main players themselves. However, that publication must be seen to be completely even-handed (ideally orchestrated by an independent party) because otherwise it is often seen as an attack by one party against another. This same overall pattern is observed playing out in global agreements where, even if there is no practical sanction against countries that break a deal, they will nevertheless be far less trusted on future issues. If their actions are fully reported by the world press then widespread domestic and international pressure also comes into play. And if, as a result of one country reneging, an overall global deal begins to unravel then – fairly on not – it is the first country that reneged that tends to be held responsible by the public. It is this same dynamic that the Global Guilds will by design have to engineer.

# GLOBAL ADVOCATES

## Global Guilds must act like *Global Advocates* so organizations can better justify unpalatable measures needed to avoid collective (and so also individual) crises

THE THIRD DISTINCT role for a Global Guild is to act as a 'Global Advocate' – that is, an advocate for the global community in its entirety (as, for example, the UN Secretary-General is typically expected to be) *not* an advocate for a given multinational, or even a given industry, let alone any of the roughly-200 individual countries that make up the world economy. That is a crucially important distinction when system-dynamics such as Competitive Overuse bring benefits to individual territories at the same time as threatening the collective performance of all. Under such circumstances, a shared advocate for each of the component nations or industries tends to come at the problem from the point of view of defending individual rights of exploitation, whereas an advocate for *all the nations and industries taken as one* will approach the same issue from the perspective of defending the rights of the whole international community to collective stability within a mutually-dependent world economy.

Inevitably, given the current pre-eminence of national governance over global governance, individual states can always choose to disregard the diplomatic lobbying of a Global Advocate. From that point of view it is like the oil-tankers' Sat Nav advising all captains on the optimal avoidance courses for the whole fleet – but then automatically recalculating if some captains do something else. Nevertheless, that is a far better situation for the international community than the current one in which the perspective of The Whole as opposed to the sum of The Parts is never even heard. Diplomats and commercial lobbyists have, in practice, no interests to disregard other than those of other nations and different corporate interests.

Up until now, there has been *no one* at Ambassadorial level responsible for pointing out what would work best for the international community if it were (in effect) just one country. Whereas national governments are often expert at managing medium-term trade-offs between one part of their country and another for the long-term good of their nation as a whole, there is no formal international equivalent. Informally, trade-deals and military aid tends to be given to regimes that provide oil and other resources (or that claim to offer regional stability, for instance by keeping extremist groups in check). It is given rather less to the leaders of countries that have little that richer countries want. In that sense the international community already prioritizes the development, or at least funding, of some countries over others. But formally, and in the more-general international arena, there has been no counter-balance to collective national self-interest at all.

Exactly the same is true for multinationals. Yet if individual corporations do not even know which of their corporately-optimized decisions run contrary to what would be globally-optimized collective decisions of innumerable organizations, then how can they possibly be expected to contemplate any potential trade-offs that might improve things for others? By the very nature of globally-defined crises, global interests ultimately cycle back to affect industry and corporate interests as well. Under those circumstances, even long-term sacrifices at the corporate level may still be justified by a Board if as a result it gains important long-term benefits in the form of lessening the likelihood of potentially debilitating backlashes.

To increase the likelihood of these sorts of crucial trade-offs between medium-term corporate interests and long-term global (and as a result *also corporate*) interests, the Global Advocate role needs to build some constructive tension into the proceedings of the international community linked to a Global Guild.

## BUILDING TENSION

That is automatically partly achieved simply by clearly communicating the massive corporate opportunities offered by a lucrative (ultimately High-Tech-driven) future, at the same time as highlighting the cumulative threats from global crises. That same contrast works equally well at a personal level as well. After all, for anybody – whether in a corporate or private role – it is only natural to feel attracted to the positive but want to get away from the negative. As a result, people tend to try to do something that moves them from one to the other. Governments, advertisers, religions and nutritionists all use the same approach to try to shift the behavior of the general public.

However, the chance of entering a Global Renaissance by around 2040 contrasted with (at worst) the risk of global chaos is simply not sufficient to break the logjam that is blocking effective world-governance. That is why the Global Guilds also need to stand up for the international community as a whole, and against that measure hold the world's individual governments to account in a completely unbiased and non-partisan way. Actively representing and advocating and lobbying for the long-term interests of global performance *as a route to collective corporate performance* forces a different perspective on the actions or inactions of governments and religions, just as much as corporations.

## CORPORATE VISIONS

Strategic visioning has become a classic approach to instigating change (in everything from a single individual to a huge multinational or whole country). The key is simultaneously to communicate both a compelling vision of what could be, as well as an unrelentingly honest reflection of current reality. This contrast might be as simple as an image of the fit and toned person someone wants to become versus the couch-potato they see when they look in the mirror. This sets up in people's brains a 'creative tension' between the two contrasting images. It usually does not feel very comfortable: 'I want to look like that but I actually look like this.' There are only two ways to remove the discomfort. Deny reality (and maybe stop looking into full-length mirrors) or strive to realize the vision.

It highlights short-termism and selfishness but just as importantly highlights corporate or national policies that are unintentionally counter-productive because they are ultimately self-defeating. It offers a standard against which to measure the proposals that individual corporations and governments make. It also provides a natural mechanism for the Global Guilds to introduce additional proposals that no individual business or nation feels able to raise without upsetting some of its allies. Highlighting those kinds of disconnects to governments as well as to members across the Global Guilds – and, when appropriate, to the general public – means that global misalignments can no longer be quietly disregarded. More positively, it also helps those corporations or governments that genuinely want to act from a global perspective, albeit partially in order to secure their own commercial performance or national security.

Even though they perhaps for instance know that in the medium-term a given approach risks harming their corporate or national interests, the more explicit that the conflict becomes the easier it is for them to gain the support of others (including shareholders or citizens) who feel drawn to add their weight behind the World lobby. International negotiation integrated with far-more-tightly-aligned international public debate, is a form of diplomacy that can at last begin to address otherwise irresolvable issues of Competitive Overuse such as overfishing and climate change.

## 30. THE RIGHT RESPONSE AT THE RIGHT TIME

| Escalating threats of backlashes | Key governments already worried | Inadequate global governance | Insufficient time for protracted reforms | Need to unleash potential of existing bodies | Global businesses especially well-placed to take a lead |
|---|---|---|---|---|---|

### IDEAL TIMING

# GLOBAL GUILDS

| TRUSTED OBSERVER | VIGILANT COUNSELOR | GLOBAL ADVOCATE |
|---|---|---|
| through which members gain an undistorted overview of globally-defined threats without breaching confidentiality | monitoring globally-defined-threat scenarios, alerting about changes and facilitating integrated counter-measures | so organizations can better justify unpopular measures needed to avoid collective (and so individual) backlashes |

*DESIGN GUIDELINES* that successively refine a Global Guild's effectiveness and relevance to its members

- *Rigorously INDEPENDENT and as a result accepted as completely unbiased and confidentially secure*
- *Unimpeachably GLOBALIST so a Guild Ambassador can believably claim: 'I speak for no country; I speak for all'*
- *Deeply PARTICIPATIVE in its interactions with other bodies – partly to enrol them and partly to leverage their capabilities*
- *Fundamentally MINIMALIST in its interventions to avoid counter-measures resulting in further threatening backlashes*
- *Supremely PRAGMATIC with its effectiveness unconstrained by conventions and bureaucracies of other similar bodies*
- *Consistently EXCEPTIONAL in terms of the intellect and talent of its staff as well as the pre-eminence of its insights*
- *Inherently ADAPTIVE to built-in feedback mechanisms that progressively refine tactics, operating guidelines, strategy, goals*

# ACCELERATING RESPONSIVENESS TO CRISES

Global Guilds must create conditions for *Accelerating Responsiveness* in order to refine and customize decentralized tactics and to counter specific crises directly

BIG BUSINESS IS not just currently well-placed to form Global Guilds, it is also very much to its advantage to do so. The overriding reason for this is that the strategic goal of all the Global Guilds is effectively one of the strategic goals that Big Business must itself adopt: *Accelerating Responsiveness* to growing threats of backlashes. The need for 'responsiveness' to such newly proliferating threats is self-evident. But the need for 'acceleration' is dictated by the exponential nature of the otherwise-benign trends that are creating those backlashes in the first place. Conventional corporate strategies for countering them – overhauled at best every few years – may appear to work in the short-term, but ultimately such classic centralized and top-down approaches can never keep up with the escalating variety and spread of crises.

In contrast, the Global Guilds must, by design, trigger a form of 'viral' strategy that is constructed to spread throughout the international business community and beyond. Very importantly, like the Global Guilds themselves, that viral strategy must be self-improving. As I will now explain, it is a combination of 'Progressive Refinement' and 'Viral Spread' that substantially improves the odds of successfully countering the damage caused by global crises.

## PROGRESSIVE REFINEMENT

The dynamics that keep progressively refining a Global Guild should operate at many levels. For a start, even just the core 'Sat Nav for global crises' function of a Global Guild should be designed to be automatically self-improving. For instance, an embryonic Global Guild will bring immediate benefits, but only to its founding-members. That makes is attractive for more new members to want to join, which in turn enhances the Global Guild's ability to address global crises, which accelerates its responsiveness to such threats, which brings still-greater benefits to those that are members, which makes it more attractive to join, and so on.

Similarly, as detailed further in the subchapter that starts on page 471, feedback mechanisms must be built into all the Global Guild's processes so that tactics, operating guidelines and even strategy and goals are continuously improved. At first glance that just seems like standard 'continuous improvement', which would suggest steady rather than accelerating refinement. However, it is important to realize that the processes within a Global Guild that are subject to such improvement must *include the improvement processes themselves*. In other words, Global Guilds – and even the details of their own strategies – must be designed to improve the very way that they improve their own designs. It is that feedback of the improvement-process onto itself that strongly reinforces Progressive Refinement.

## VIRAL SPREAD

There is another dynamic within a Global Guild's strategy of Accelerating Responsiveness that not only strengthens Progressive Refinement but also creates the foundation for a Viral Spread of that strategy. From the start, a prototype Global Guild must employ increasingly-sophisticated IT to support analysis of globally-defined threats. This in turn will allow greater synthesis of a progressively wide range of inputs, including ideas and feedback collected from the internet.

However, it also allows improved channeling of information in *both* directions, in *and out* of the Global Guild. In addition to highly-specific information exchange to member-organizations, some channels will be directly to governments and the public (such as via the open internet or other broadcast media such as the Press). Other channels will be more indirect (such as via chosen authority figures, relevant celebrities, appropriate journalists, leading politicians, members of civil bodies). But in all cases, the improving information exchange will be designed to create more and better locally-customized responses to growing threats of backlashes.

For its own long-term preservation, any major corporation needs to minimize threats of backlashes by stimulating exactly this proliferation of customized-but-aligned counter-measures around the world. Moreover, if it had to attempt it alone, a top multinational would still have to realign its activities in much the same ways as a rival corporation would be attempting in parallel. Under those circumstances, to maintain too much separation does not make a lot of sense.

## THE GLOBAL-GUILD PRINCIPLES

When corporate realignment is conducted as part of a Global Guild, it becomes a lot easier to learn lessons from others about how best to proceed. And the broad guidelines of the realigning-process become, in effect, the Principles that everyone in the Guild is following. Unelected Responsibility, True Costing, Collective Sustainability, Mirrored Tolerance, Pre-emptive Recovery and Holistic Perspective (the 'Guild Principles' detailed in the earlier chapters of the book) are a coherent set of largely-distinct strategic-realignment guidelines. They mutually reinforce each other in pursuit of the overall strategic goal of minimizing backlashes by means of Accelerating Responsiveness. In other words, the Guild Principles are what is often termed a 'strategic thrust'.

By analogy with the tanker-fleet, these Guild Principles are the equivalent to Rules of the Sea – such as which tanker should give way to which others, what direction two head-on tankers should steer to avoid a collision, and so on. Ideally, every tanker-captain should abide by these principles, but it is immediately helpful even if the captains of only a single company's fleet of tankers initially agree to follow them.

There are innumerable aligned actions that the Global Guilds need to encourage corporations and others throughout the international community to take, and it is the six Global-Guild Principles that help translate the grand strategy of Accelerating Responsiveness into those coherent actions. But the Guild Principles alone are not enough. I have already suggested some of the guidelines that businesses, institutions and governments need to follow. However, to be effective across a very large number of different circumstances, the details of such counter-tactics must be refined and customized around the globe. As I will explain in the next subchapter, that is where Viral Spread plays a crucial role.

## 31. DYNAMICS OF ACCELERATING RESPONSIVENESS

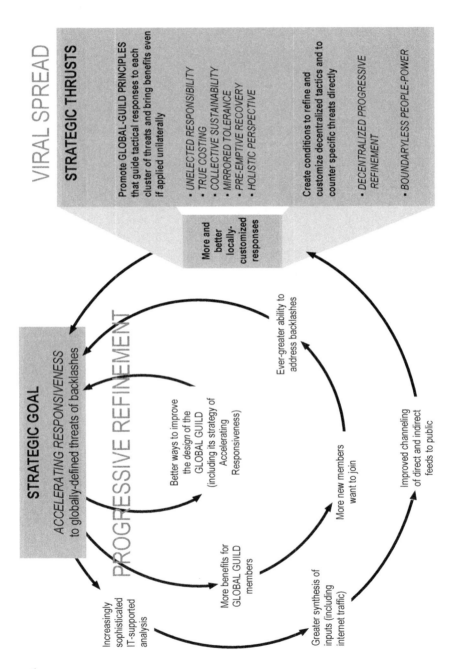

# FOCUSING ON HIGH-IMPACT-BUT-DIFFICULT CHANGES

Similar to how Wikipedia grows and upgrades accuracy so Global Guilds must enable a decentralized focus on High-Impact-but-Difficult issues – and find patterns across those solutions

EVERY GLOBAL GUILD needs to embed a strategy of Accelerating Responsiveness throughout all its members so that in diverse ways each corporation helps to minimize the collective risk of backlashes to the whole Guild. Yet to achieve that, there can be no 'one size fits all' approach. Broad-brush solutions simply will not work. Instead, each Guild must create the conditions under which Progressive Refinement and Viral Spread *are applied to the Guild Principles themselves.*

This is analogous to crew-members of a variety of ocean-going vessels – not just the tankers – having the facility to go online to participate in various Sat Nav chat-rooms in which they can feed-in their own sightings of other tankers, corrections to charted iceberg positions, suggestions for new or better Rules of the Sea, newly-discovered shortcuts and (most importantly) *potential* shortcuts that just need enough crew-members of other tankers to alert their captains to join-in in order to help break through an ice-sheet.

The conditions under which Global Guilds can encourage all the inconceivably complex optimizations needed to reduce each member-organization's contribution to stirring up collective crises are similar to how something like Wikipedia gets written: create a shared vision, maintain a high degree of openness and transparency, allow almost anyone to get involved, impose very few rules, and keep things flexible. These are the general conditions needed to create what, in a book I wrote with a colleague in 1996, we referred to as an 'Accelerating Organization' – namely one that can keep learning and adapting in ways that steadily improve both its ability to fulfill its overall purpose *and* its ability to keep learning and adapting. It is a virtuous reinforcement of 'learning to change' combined with 'changing to learn'. Far more traditionally, it is also the way that vendors self-organize their stalls in huge markets. No one specifies what it is that people can sell or what stalls should look like or where particular vendors can set up. But for millennia the process has nevertheless led markets to adapt themselves until they best-satisfy the complex and often conflicting needs of local buyers.

Initially, this kind of decentralized Progressive Refinement can best be stimulated by a Global Guild setting up intranet wiki sites for its members that allow flexible creation and editing of web pages within very-loose constraints. From the start, carefully chosen sections of those wiki sites can be made available to broader specialist groups such as government bodies, and some areas can even be made accessible to contributions from the general public over the internet. This should eventually build to a full AI-based system that can synthesize contributions from extremely high numbers of sources and extract meaningful patterns from them. At the highest level the wiki sites should initially be organized around the six Global-Guild Principles – Unelected Responsibility, True Costing, Collective Sustainability, Mirrored Tolerance, Pre-emptive Recovery and Holistic Perspective – in order to provide coherence to what everyone individually elects to do.

In that sense the six Guild Principles are acting in a similar way to the *shared-values* across any given community. When potentially everything else is up for grabs, shared-values act like stabilizers that hold a community steady. In contrast, if a large group is more disjointed, and values are not broadly shared, it is far harder for the community as a whole to remain stable in the midst of turbulence. As mentioned on page 268, this has implications for multiculturalism. In the context of Global Guilds it means that the shared Guild Principles will help glue the loose confederations of Guild-members together.

Over time, the original Guild Principles will be steadily improved and maybe even completely superseded as a result of decentralized Progressive Refinement. But, however they evolve, their initial existence will act as a means of channeling (without stifling) uncontrolled widespread creativity, experimentation and innovation. It is also a way of ensuring that constructive revolution does not unintentionally degrade into counterproductive anarchy.

# Accelerating Responsiveness

## MULTIPLE LEADERSHIP ROLES

Formal – and just as importantly, self-appointed – leaders of every type and at every level potentially have vital roles in devising local tactics consistent with the Guild Principles. However, some backgrounds will be particularly useful in aligning specific components of the world economy. For instance, Unelected Responsibility is a standard against which potentially all unelected leaders should test themselves in many aspects of their lives. But those working in commercial companies have a particular ability to make a major difference in minimizing Capitalism Crises. Those in Banking and in the News Media have tremendously important leadership roles in this. And multinationals as a group naturally have vital inputs to make.

Industrialization Crises can best be managed by widespread adoption of True Costing. As consumers of energy and fossil-fuel products ranging from plastics to gasoline, every member of the public can have a direct impact simply by the consumer-choices that they make. But governments, economists, ecologists, manufacturing corporations and, naturally, oil and energy companies themselves, have the greatest opportunity to smooth the path to the international community weaning off oil and reducing carbon-emissions without unduly hampering the progress toward Global Renaissance.

Population Crises will necessarily be handled differently in different societies because, more than ever, one size cannot fit all. But all approaches can nevertheless adhere to Collective Sustainability. In general, the public in developing nations have the power to avoid Malthusian Collapse by regulating birth-rate, and women in particular can indirectly be helped by teachers who take a lead in improving female education-standards and by religious authority-figures who encourage birth-control. In developed nations, birth-rates are less of an issue. There, in addition to consumer purchasing choices and the leadership of environmental organizations, the special-connection to Collective Sustainability is in major corporations tied to agriculture and fishing.

In a similar way, although everybody can make an important difference by living their lives according to the Principle of Mirrored Tolerance – always welcoming generous diversity but immediately standing up to intolerant bullies even if they happen to belong to a minority – it is primarily religious and social leaders (at every level) who bring a uniquely powerful influence and who have a deeply-important and potentially-courageous role to play in tackling Religion Crises. However, within the Global Guilds, it is those High-Tech corporations that come under attack from more-extreme religious sects that must push back. And the News Media also have a key role to play in supporting the overall dynamic of Mirrored Tolerance that all the groups involved are endeavoring to apply.

Unleashing the potential of the High-Tech supertrend is an area that can especially benefit from the unique skills of politicians, entrepreneurs, scientists, technologists and computing experts (including those experts who are kids). Similarly, countering direct risks of High-Tech Crises by living up to the Guild Principle of Pre-emptive Recovery is a particularly powerful contribution that can be made by academics researching into science and medicine, as well as those who lead major commercial operations such as IT, telecom and pharmaceutical corporations and cutting-edge organizations such as defense contractors.

And finally, upholding the Principle of Holistic Perspective is something that every member of the international community has a direct ability to impact. Many citizens often have a special fondness, loyalty and pride for the country they live in, or originally are from, or maybe both. People may prize the ethnic, religious or social community to which they feel they most closely belong. But they also each belong to an older family that uniquely binds them all together – Humanity as a whole.

Politicians, teachers, writers, those in film, radio and TV, musicians, artists, athletes and sports personalities all have a special ability to remind the international community of its common roots and of its shared future. But ultimately, that sense most strongly must come from how people view themselves, their self-identity. Celebrating the multiple facets of identity (say, as an American female Moslem member of Humanity, or as a gay black professional-basketball playing member of Humanity) is a far richer as well as more accurate way of viewing individuality than artificially choosing any one element over another.

## EASE AND IMPACT

As soon as the Global Guilds begin to form, the Viral Spread of decentralized Progressive Refinement will begin to realign countless systems throughout the global economy. In a very similar way to how decentralized Boundaryless People-Power can achieve complex coordination – even in revolutions or riots – that no single group orchestrates (a phenomenon technically known as Emergence), the international community will, in effect, informally 'agree' how to reduce the probability of the most likely global crises. In the process it will boost the collective security of the Global Guilds.

## 32. PRIORITIZING DIFFERENT CHANGE-OPTIONS

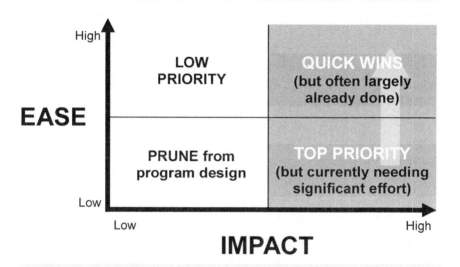

The best approach I was ever able to devise for my clients to think about prioritizing different change-proposals was to distinguish Ease and Impact. I visualized this for them by drawing a two-by-two matrix. On the vertical axis is Ease going from Low at the bottom to High at the top. On the horizontal axis is Impact going from Low on the left to High on the right. Each of the four quadrants describes different types of initiatives. Top-Right are Quick Wins – but they have often largely already been done. Top-Left are Low Priority initiatives. Bottom-Left are initiatives you should Prune from any plans. It is the Bottom-Right quadrant that often holds the Top Priority initiatives, even though they may currently need too much effort to make them practical. As a result you need to see what the common-denominators are of the reasons the Top Priority initiatives are so hard to implement – and then devise an *extra* initiative to remove those barriers *before* attempting the Top Priority actions.

# TAKING THE INITIATIVE

Many ideas already exist for countering most *individual* types of backlash. But to coordinate all those together in ways that do not undermine each other – such as proposals for addressing peaking-oil that in fact end up resulting in increased carbon-emissions – it is necessary to understand linkages that currently remain either completely hidden or are so complicated as to be unintelligible. Here is where the Global Guilds can speed the process by injecting some pragmatism into the initial selections made of proposals suitable for decentralized Progressive Refinement (proposed by member-corporations, the general public, governments and others). It all comes down to Ease and Impact.

Some proposed initiatives will only ever be expected to have a low impact on Guild-members – others, a high impact. Similarly, once people take account of the full reality of how a Guild's industries actually operate, some initiatives will be seen to fit well and so will be easy to implement – whereas others run counter to all sorts of Legacy Effects, so will be hard to make work. Most corporate (and government) plans ideally aim to tackle problems that will be Easy but also High-Impact. The trouble is, those types of initiatives have nearly always *already been done*. They were the 'low hanging fruit' of earlier programs. What happens as a result is that eager planners then propose all sorts of follow-up initiatives that are Easy but are in fact Low-Impact. Unfortunately, those sorts of initiatives can never get to the root of the problems the community faces.

This is a very common challenge that the Global Guilds need to overcome. Over the years, I have evaluated several hundred proposals for major change-initiatives and, although they each tended initially to look good on paper, when I analyzed how well they would mesh with the hidden workings of the communities they were destined for, I often found that those proposing the ideas had fallen into the trap of addressing Easy but Low-Impact initiatives. Typically they had completely missed any chance of finding *shared* ways of removing barriers common to several High-Impact-but-Difficult initiatives.

Global Guilds need to encourage their members to coalesce around solving High-Impact *but Difficult* problems – namely countering the combined impacts of Capitalism, Industrialization, Population, Religion, High-Tech, and Globalization backlashes all taken together. It is that highly-complex but deeply-interconnected problem than the Global Guilds have the collective ability to solve, far better than any territorially-focused governments ever can.

# Accelerating Responsiveness

## DECENTRALIZED PROGRESSIVE-REFINEMENT

This book has already taken a first step by categorizing the major systemic-threats of global crises into just six clusters that (typically below the surface) share similar root-causes and so are potentially broadly susceptible to similar counters. That is an easier starting point than analyses that cluster according to relatively-superficial *symptoms* and therefore offer little guidance in finding underlying solutions. But the Global Guilds will be able to go very much further because, rather like the process of evolution, Emergence will then come into play.

### 33. DECENTRALIZED PROGRESSIVE-REFINEMENT OF GUILDS

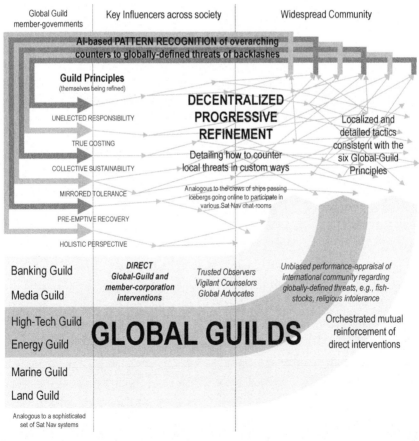

# TAKING THE INITIATIVE

As a result of unrestrained hoards of people trying an incredible number of local attempts at solutions, some unpredictable combinations of actions will work better than others. Those solutions that work best, different Guild-members may apply elsewhere (albeit in a locally-relevant form). But that is just the beginning. There will inevitably turn out to be common-denominators that link many apparently-separate clusters of crises. Shared mutually-relevant solutions will gain momentum, but they will also reveal something extremely important. Their very success will uncover the more-general pattern of how to manage *groups* of crises.

That solution cannot be worked out in advance any more than it is possible to predict how a particular animal will evolve over the next several million years. But as AI-based computer analysis decodes the pattern of what works, and why it works, then – just like looking back *down* the evolutionary tree and seeing how humans evolved from earlier primates that in turn came from still-more-primitive mammals – decentralized Progressive Refinement will lead to a far deeper understanding of how to realign the global economy so as to *keep* on a course away from cumulative global crises (and as a result, toward Global Renaissance).

In this way, it is at last a realizable goal to achieve joined-up thinking across the enormous range of counter-tactics needed throughout the international community. Although the immense complexity of the detailed solution is utterly beyond the capability of any individuals to work out centrally or disseminate top-down – so too are the extraordinarily harmonized flight-paths of flocks of birds, or the uncontrolled sophistication of marketplaces. That is how Emergence works.

# GOOD-ENOUGH TO GET STARTED

Governments are unlikely to take the initiative – although they should – so it is more effective for a pioneering organization to sponsor a prototype Global Guild than attempt much the same alone

FROM MY ANALYSIS of the UN and other supranational bodies, it is completely impractical to rely on suitable reform of political institutions occurring in time. They will not address the global-governance shortfalls that currently confound attempts to counter the growing threat of uncontrollable crises. Unfortunately, it is also unreasonable even to expect government organizations to be able to set up a political equivalent to the Global Guilds. In many ways, it ought to be expected of them. After all, what appear as Major Backlashes for businesses and institutions are Globally-Defined Threats to National Security as far as a state government is concerned. Any government's citizens have the right to expect that the politicians they elected (or even the autocratic dictators they cannot unelect) will fulfill their primary duty to protect them. And that includes protection from global crises. It is possible. Some governments might show the leadership to do something more than they currently are. But it is not very likely.

As already explained in the subchapter on *How the EU, NATO and other supranational bodies all fail* (page 387), there are currently major obstacles to the UN being able even to agree the *design* of a supplementary body that could fulfill an equivalent role to the Global Guilds – say, some form of 'World Embassy' that spoke for the whole of humanity. It is even less likely that the UN could implement and then operate that design effectively. As with so many other considered reforms within the UN, the design-process would inevitably become dominated by political gamesmanship and the design-goals would be severely compromised in pursuit of diplomatic trade-offs. Any resultant outcome, if implementation ever got that far, would be unfit for purpose. Far more likely is that the initiative would stall.

Nor should we expect that in due course the extreme global threats that cumulative crises represent will prove sufficient to cause UN member-states to pull together in an unprecedented way. If the crises were allowed to develop sufficiently to cause such extreme backlashes then, in addition to their immediate impact, they would necessarily also cause wide-reaching and unknowable further crises. Consequently, despite any pulling-together that the initial slew of global crises encouraged within the international community, it would on balance be hugely destabilizing to the global economy. It is certainly not a scenario worth 'engineering' in order to bounce the UN into reform. And any attempt to exaggerate the imminence and danger of existing threats of global crises would rapidly be found out and result in an even-less-cooperative global community than before.

Yet, despite the infeasibility of such forced-cooperation, there is nevertheless also totally insufficient time to pursue the more-conventional diplomatic routes to founding a World Embassy. Not only would the concept risk being seen as sufficiently Important that it warranted far-reaching and long-drawn-out international debate (with all the national self-interests that implies), but there appear to be insufficient mechanisms to enroll and align every country anyway – at least, without the cost of their participation being a design blurred to the lowest common denominator and a World Embassy compromised into total inadequacy.

## INDIVIDUAL GOVERNMENT SPONSORING A WORLD EMBASSY

In the absence of the UN, it is certainly possible for one or more individual governments to take the lead and sponsor an early-form of World Embassy, as a more-desirable and acceptable alternative to Global Guilds. For many countries, such an approach would be the most practical, and cost-effective, way for them to enhance their defenses against globally-defined threats to their *own* national security. Ultimately, to sponsor a World Embassy is in a government's enlightened self-interest (just as Global Guilds would be for major industries). Even though, as a result, the countries involved would also improve the odds for everybody across the whole of the international community.

This could happen in a variety of ways, but perhaps the most attractive – and certainly the one to try first – would be to take the lead in promoting the formation of an independent organization intended ultimately to end up under the umbrella of the UN. After all, although there are several

# Getting going

potential homes for a World Embassy, by far the most natural (although not the easiest to engineer) is for it to be strongly associated with the UN. One way this could develop would be if the idea was instigated by one or both of the two P5 countries that 'punch above their weight' on the UN Security Council but that no longer dominate competing national interests – namely the UK and France. That step would in turn open the doors to explicit sponsorship by the USA. As one of the truly-powerful P5 members, the USA's premature public support might otherwise be misinterpreted as a self-interested power-play and damage the World Embassy's prospects of gaining the tacit support and eventual membership (or at least avoiding the active obstruction by veto) of the remaining two P5 members.

Pursuing a UN-route directly would inevitably prove too slow. But from the start it would be useful to begin lobbying for general support from the Secretary General and key members, with the goal that the World Embassy later eventually got closer to the UN once it had 'proved itself', and after it had become immune to some of the obstructions that the UN itself represents. In the extreme, if the UN proved completely unsupportive then a World Embassy could nevertheless operate perfectly well in many other environments, moving to a new home only if it became especially attractive to do so. Indeed, the very fact that alternative eventual homes to the UN were completely possible would only increase the pressure on the UN to do what was necessary at least to support the idea or risk being seen as 'once again unfit for purpose'.

There are also numerous other government-routes by which a World Embassy could be formed as an alternative or supplement to Global Guilds. Either Canada or Switzerland, for example, could form a multi-nation coalition as a neutral and centralist international body. Any European country could sponsor the idea within the EU (although the EU carries its own bureaucratic hurdles). Or a well-positioned country could use its diplomatic links to broker a semi-formal coalition of China, Europe, India and the USA to experiment with a joint organization. There are, in reality, a large number of legitimate routes that all potentially lead to an effective form of World Embassy. In practice, and to the great discredit of global politics, *none* of them is likely.

## GOVERNMENT IN NEED OF COMPETITIVE STIMULUS

Far more likely than that inspired political intervention will lead to some form of World Embassy is that politicians instead expend their energies portraying the potential power of Global Guilds as a threat to the claimed monopoly of state government. Big Government risks viewing Big Business as a usurping rival. In reality, such concerns completely miss the point. Any cross-territory power that the Global Guilds wield will be because *the governments cannot exercise it themselves.* Anyone who thinks that the power of Global Guilds to cut across one dimension of the world economy (territory) with another dimension (industry) is about 'Big Business taking-on State Government' is dangerously simplistic. In practice, optimizing such a matrix power-structure is what nearly all multinationals have internally been experimenting with for decades. Governments have simply proved incapable of conducting their own trials.

When politicians have come together in supranational groups such as the UN, they have (rather amateurishly in comparison with multinationals) been completely unable to balance individual territorial considerations against collective global ones. Instead, forced by their governance structures rather than lack of intellect, they have habitually fought for their own country's self-interest almost whatever the eventual collective cost. There has been no counterbalance, no opposing power. Although government organizations are unlikely to welcome the prospect, the truth is that their relative impotence in harmonizing the multiple dimensions of the global economy is increasingly dangerous. A new power needs to fill that vacuum. Whether we like it or not, and despite the obvious risks inherent in any undemocratic body, the only power that looks like it can be ready in time is the power of something like the Global Guilds.

What is more, government bodies should not forget that it is no bad thing for a monopoly to feel the threat of what it views as competition. Healthy rivalry stimulates improvement. As it is, up until now citizens have had no alternative to having their world run by a combination of politicians – who, it should be noted, in bodies such as the UN are completely unelected – and behind-the-scenes equally-unelected civil servants. Neither of these groups generally have the same skills and experience of top executives from the private sector. In the past that has not of itself been an obvious handicap. But in many countries, leading politicians come to power having spent most if not all of their careers within politics, yet they convince themselves that they nevertheless have a sufficient understanding of how the 'real world' works and what up-to-date 'professionalism' feels like. Similarly, senior civil servants tend to have been in their often-old-fashioned and rather inefficient work environments for all their careers, surrounded by others like themselves that consider that they have a 'job for life' that may not be cutting-edge but is at least secure.

Yet these are the same people and systems that are expected to help optimize the performance of a global economy of unprecedented complexity and sophistication. With the best will in the world, most current government organizations are simply not up to the task. They need major upgrading, of people *and* management systems, not just evolutionary reform. Atypically amongst politicians, the Chinese government has proved willing to reassess its operations every few years and, as appropriate, shut down whole Ministries and Government Departments and create very different and better-suited ones in their place. In contrast, most other countries have maintained largely the same government structures as they used fifty years ago.

At every level and in every way the political infrastructures around the world that currently claim a monopoly over global governance are in need of an extreme shake-up if they are to become fit-for-purpose. They need to get their acts together so that they are at least as professional as the comparable organizations in the private sector that over the last few decades have been honed by unrelenting competition. Until the very cleverest and most ambitious and most creative people routinely choose a life in government rather than business, which is far from the situation today, then it is very healthy that politicians and civil servants and the systems they take for granted feel the full force of competitive pressure from the equivalent of the Global Guilds. After all, so far governments have not managed to achieve the necessary changes on their own. And now there is insufficient time to wait to see if they can.

## DOING WHAT POLITICIANS CANNOT

Given the urgency of getting some stimulus from the Global Guilds, there is probably insufficient time for the protracted international agreements needed to create a set of fully-formed Global Guilds in one go. However, there is another way. One of the reasons that multinationals and businesses as a group have the potential to move far faster and more effectively than governments is because they are familiar with an advanced form of Prototyping.

# TAKING THE INITIATIVE

It has long been recognized within the corporate environment that in order to circumvent the 'analysis paralysis' that can forestall major change initiatives, the most effective tactic tends to be the toe-in-the-water approach of locally prototyping a change initiative in such a way that it increasingly encourages a progressive roll-out of the overall change. To achieve this dynamic, the detailed-design of the prototype is crucial. It must, of course, be a useful trial that represents a microcosm of what is planned to be the eventual full change. And it must also be designed in a way that lessons-learned can readily be fed back into the overall design both of what the eventual change will look like and also the *way* that the change is rolled out. Even governments occasionally adopt this form of prototype.

However, there is another less-obvious design criterion that often makes a fundamental difference: The prototype must be designed not only as a trial but also as an intervention in its own right that is explicitly aimed at making it *increasingly attractive for the overall initiative to be rolled-out.* In other words, its most important role is often to help create a 'pull' for the overall initiative. To do that, the prototype must typically be designed to bring immediate benefits that the wider community sees, and wants. That tactic will also work for the formation of Global Guilds. In place of attempting to push with a floppy string of commercial lobbying-meetings the governance-structure needed to help counter global  crises, one or more influential corporations can instead create the conditions under which other key players in the world economy begin to pull *themselves* toward the idea of Global Guilds.

As with any successful change-prototype, the design will include mechanisms by which the initial prototype brings sufficient benefits to its first users (however few) that others want to get involved, and in so doing help improve security against backlashes still further. A prototype Global Guild must therefore adhere to design-guidelines that help successively to refine its effectiveness and relevance to founder-members, and so the attractiveness for others to join. Those design-guidelines are what I will highlight next.

# THE SEVEN RULES OF GLOBAL GUILDS

The effectiveness and relevance of a prototype Global Guild will keep rapidly improving if it remains Independent, Globalist, Participative, Minimalist, Pragmatic, Exceptional and Adaptive

THERE ARE NUMEROUS guidelines that flow even from the high-level definition of Global Guilds as 'Trusted Observers, Vigilant Counselors and Global Advocates'. But, in their simplest form, the effectiveness and relevance of prototype Global Guilds will keep rapidly improving if they adhere to just seven specific design-guidelines.

## INDEPENDENT

For a start, although a Global Guild can in part be a virtual organization that taps into the capabilities of several existing corporations, and takes full advantage of the best that each can contribute, it must remain rigorously unbiased and ultimately *Independent*. As a result, at its center it needs dedicated people and resources that not only can stimulate and maintain the multiple interactions that a Global Guild needs, but who also can as necessary maintain strict confidentiality between the different corporations and other bodies with which those interactions take place.

After all, as with the numerous confidential sources accessed for this book, crucial patterns often emerge that do not themselves need to be classified at the same level of secrecy. For the Energy Guild, as an example, the true overall status of global oil reserves would be one useful insight. The broad pattern of the genuine intentions of governments regarding greenhouse-gas emissions would be another. Similarly, any common denominators across different corporations' successes (and failures) in tackling backlashes would be useful for any of the Global Guilds.

## GLOBALIST

Associated with the guideline of independence is that a Global Guild must also be unimpeachably *Globalist* in operation and outlook. No individual corporations (or governments) should be able to claim better insight into the overall global reality than they can gain from their ties to the Global Guilds. And any representative of the Global Guilds should, whatever their origin, credibly speak with the moral authority of a representative of humanity as a whole. For a Guild to assert and maintain its Globalist positioning, the true test – itself fully-consistent with the Guild's basic role of Global Advocate – will be for a Guild Ambassador believably to be able to claim: 'I speak for no country; I speak for all.'

## PARTICIPATIVE

The need to accelerate the process by which corporations and others come up with globally-aligned initiatives that actually work implies various design-guidelines. For instance, a Global Guild must be deeply *Participative* in its interactions with other bodies because the reality is that people who have a choice in designing proposals tend to accept the consequences whereas those who are not involved usually just blame others. Such a Participative approach will also help constrain the size of a Global Guild, which otherwise will have a tendency to bloat even though it needs to remain flexible and dynamic by keeping its center relatively small. In a world where government departments can employ tens of thousands of people, a Global Guild should not ever grow to have an inner-core of more than around two-hundred people. To put that size in proportion, it is the typical upper-limit of an efficient department in the private sector.

For the hub of a Global Guild to remain that small it will, of necessity, be forced to tie tightly into the best of the existing corporate and non-corporate bodies that are already focused on individual threats. These include fully-governmental organizations such as the IPCC for issues of climate change or the WHO for global public health. But that is as it should be. Duplication is inefficient. And any attempt at centralizing into a Global Guild some of the key activities of other institutions, would almost guarantee resentment and lack of cooperation from the very organizations with which the Global Guilds need to participate most closely. Good management-practice these days dictates that any activities that two-hundred highest-caliber individuals do not have time for (assuming they all use top-of-the-range computing and high-tech support) are far better handled by more-specialized components anyway, which is exactly what the operating-guideline of being Participative would also suggest.

# Getting going

## MINIMALIST

A Global Guild must aim to cause the bare minimum of disruption, even if the 'bare minimum' is sometimes substantial. The point is that at the global level of complex interconnectivity, any intervention whatsoever inevitably causes unintended consequences. So, all proposed changes should be as focused as possible – rifle-shots rather than scatter-gun approaches.

## LEGACIES OF MACHO-MANAGEMENT

Despite the desire that many leaders have often conveyed to me that they want to 'shake things up a bit' or 'start from a blank sheet of paper', the reality is that in any well-established community it is incredibly difficult to make major interventions without risking equally major repercussions. The larger and older the community, the more of a challenge this becomes. Countries are the most extreme example. Major corporations are the most common. I was bought in to analyze the aftermath of some of the more draconian Business Process Reengineering (BPR) projects conducted in various large corporations during the mid-1990s – especially in the USA. The most heartless examples had adopted the philosophy promoted by BPR-advocate Michael Hammer that 'You can't make an omelet without breaking eggs' and combined it with a particularly arrogant form of Macho Management that considered it not just legitimate but also appropriate to 'disregard the human side'. Some of the reengineerings that resulted came close to professional malpractice and created eviscerated corporations that never fully recovered. It was not corporate management's finest hour.

After all, in terms of world governance the Global Guilds are supposed to be a process of last-resort. And anyway, it is generally good practice in a complex environment that issues should be resolved as locally as possible, which is a long-standing 'Principle of Subsidiarity' that has successfully been adopted in communities ranging from multinationals to governments to the Roman Catholic Church. Moreover, a Global Guild has little direct power of its own, only the opportunity of influence within member corporations and via the public. That means, once again, the Global Guilds' involvement should be as minimal as is needed to manage the risks of global backlashes to its members.

## PRAGMATIC

The international community does not have a lot of time to improve its odds against global crises, so 'good' now is very much better than 'almost perfect' later. What is more, the only reason the Global Guilds are needed at all is because the existing systems are not working well enough. That means that every aspect of the design of a Global Guild should solely be chosen to make it as effective as possible, rather than because of any existing conventions in similar organizations. It has to be highly autonomous, unhampered and focused so that it can do whatever will best amplify the capabilities of the organizations that have a formal relationship with it. Conceptually this is exactly the approach adopted by, for example, IBM when it set up a team to design its first personal computer, adopted by General Motors to create the revolutionary small-car codenamed 'Saturn', and adopted by Lockheed Martin for its Advanced Development Programs (the truly original Skunk Works).

As an example, although some staff-members within the Global Guilds will need multiple-language skills in order to interact with corporations, governments and institutions around the world, inside the Global Guilds (in common with many multinationals in the private sector) they should only use a single language – probably the default world-language, English. What is more, to be considered for a post, each potential staff-member must first demonstrate the level of exceptional fluency needed to appreciate and communicate very-subtle nuance. In contrast, nationalistic sensitivities are not sufficient justification to allow a range of poorly-spoken languages, as many existing supranational government bodies do, which mean people do not deeply understand each other.

## EXCEPTIONAL

The Global Guilds must leverage exceptional computing, internet and other High-Tech resources in order to model and partially-compensate for the extreme complexity and interconnectivity of global issues. And they need the flexibility and culture to attract and keep the 'best of the best' – people who will typically be drawn from the private sector but who need to have skills and profiles very different to that of a typical corporate executive. In some areas, a PhD or equivalent will be the minimum academic qualification needed to manage the intricacies of a Global Guild role. But academic and intellectual excellence alone is insufficient. Supreme interpersonal skills and high-level practical experience in business, government or elsewhere is also crucial. After all, Global Guild staff must be capable of holding their own with everyone from heads of state to chief executives to media correspondents to religious leaders to influential celebrities, academics, scientists and artists. In addition, senior staff-members also need a 'clean record' as far as the media are concerned because (on top of being deeply knowledgeable and trusted by companies, governments and civil-groups around the world) they must potentially also be trusted by the general public.

## ADAPTIVE

In terms of its own performance, a Global Guild needs constantly to learn and respond. And its responses need not just to improve its performance but also improve *how* it improves its performance. As explained in the subchapter about *Focusing on High-Impact-but-Difficult changes* (page 457), a Global Guild in effect learns how to change better, uses that knowledge in order to change how it learns better, as a result learns how to change even better, and so on – constantly refining its performance.

That sort of Progressive Refinement is one of the ways that a Global Guild can itself accelerate sufficiently to keep pace with the exponential trends that it is designed to help address. However brilliant that design becomes, it can never remain static. Nothing can be sacrosanct. An added advantage of this approach is that, tying into the 'Pragmatic' design-guideline, the initial design of a prototype Global Guild only needs to be 'good enough to start'. Protracted debate about even quite fundamental issues can be ended simply by trying things out and seeing what happens. Provided that founding-members fully appreciate that their Global Guild is inherently adaptive then, rather than take too long off-line, it will always tend to be quicker and more effective to add a prospective refinement to the working prototype Global Guild (or indeed to *one part* of the prototype and not to the rest) and then observe what happens.

This flexibly experimental approach, potentially with many competing experiments running in parallel, is very different to the approach adopted by governments. Yet, not only does such in-built Progressive Refinement mean that a Global Guild will rapidly evolve into a design that is better than even the best minds were initially able to construct (and continue to accelerate its performance still further), but it also means that a Global Guild is very much easier to kick-off in the first place. After all, it is 'only a prototype'. By the time that any initially-obstructive governments and unsupportive multinationals realize that the Global Guild prototypes have effectively become embedded into the fundamental operations of the international community, the Global Guilds will have sufficiently proved themselves that those same corporations (and even governments) will begin to consider that it may be preferable to join up rather than remain on the outside and risk becoming increasingly isolated against growing backlashes.

# GLOBAL REALIGNMENT

Fundamental change can be triggered by a relatively small number of organizations throughout the world economy – and now is their opportunity to rise to that challenge

THE INCOMPREHENSIBLE COMPLEXITY of the myriad local decisions needed to minimize global crises can all be held in alignment. It merely requires enough people to adhere to steadily-improving versions of the six Guild Principles, while still tweaking their specific actions according to local circumstances. Monitoring the overall pattern of what works best then provides feedback into the Guilds' overall strategy of Accelerating Responsiveness.

The Principle of Unelected Responsibility will realign the worst of the undesirable traits in capitalism without stifling the global economy. Meanwhile, True Costing will take account of the full hidden implications of industrialization, so that the world economy can transition away from depleting and damaging resources in a controlled manner that does not destabilize the international community. Collective Sustainability will likewise address the overexploitation of everything from fish to water to rainforests that results from unprecedented global population. Mirrored Tolerance will clamp down on religious bullying, at the same time as cultivating social integration. Pre-emptive Recovery will provide a balance to the High-Tech supertrend. And finally, a Holistic Perspective will, amongst other things, steer countries away from the dangerous threats caused by nationalism and protectionism clashing against globalization.

Holding everything together, the Global Guilds – cutting across the territorial silos of state governments – will not only stimulate coherent responses throughout high-powered global industries, but also provide a visionary focus that encourages individual contributions to coalesce into Boundaryless People-Power that directly addresses specific crises (by the general public, say, stopping eating an endangered species) and nudges society toward Global Renaissance and away from global chaos.

## 34. GLOBAL GUILDS AND BOUNDARYLESS PEOPLE-POWER

To do so requires deliberate rebellion. Not against (most) governments. Not against the law, although a few laws will no doubt need to be changed. But a form of public rebellion is indeed needed against the pervasive attitudes and habits and interpretations throughout society that are trapping whole countries on an unintentionally-disruptive course. Leaders in every forum must rebel against the Legacy Effects that unnecessarily are holding the international community back from harmonizing-changes. Most importantly of all, they must rebel against the feelings of powerlessness, of inevitability, of incomprehensible complexity that risk stifling any thoughts that they dare to dream of a better future.

# Getting going

Everybody – in corporations, governments, religions, civil groups and as private individuals – needs to break free in a broadly aligned way, largely within the same one or two decades, and while keeping most of the rules of society intact so as to maintain stability. It is a massive undertaking. But so is the progress that our interconnected world achieves every single day. The hugely-intertwined infrastructure of people and technology and business and aspiration that is powering our global economy has the potential to channel exactly that same collective activity. That means that, however powerless everybody may sometimes feel, the reality is that there is nothing stopping us but ourselves. Global realignment is in principle totally achievable. It is under no one's control but our own. It is up to us.

## GENUINE LEADERSHIP

Up until now there can be no blame. No government, past or present, deliberately created the global crises that increasingly threaten the national security of our countries. None of the corporate business-decisions taken in previous years were recognized as likely to cause the severity of unintended consequences to the world economy that they did. The only blame will be if, knowing what we now know, we do too little or act too late. Unlike all our predecessors, it is we alone who carry that newly-forged responsibility.

The opportunity to set things in motion will never get better than it is now. By about 2020 the global economy will have reached a point of no return. But by then the international community can already be in a far better position. There is enough time to stimulate the beginnings of a worldwide gradual transition that will encourage alignment to emerge out of the growing chaos. Yet, without the equivalent of either corporate leaders forging Global Guilds or political leaders founding a World Embassy, it will prove exceptionally difficult to avoid the perfect-storm of multiple backlashes that risks destroying what otherwise is set to be a mind-stretching leap forward for humanity around 2040. Today's global warming and world economic crises are merely distant rumbles from something far more destructive that is heading our way. But having recognized what is coming, leaders of all types now have time to take charge. And corporate leaders across Big (and Little) Business may be the best-placed of all to lead the way.

# TAKING THE INITIATIVE

In addition to their ability to trigger the formation of cross-territory Global Guilds that protect their industries against backlashes (and as a result defend the wider world-economy), business leaders can also take full advantage of their collective expertise in interacting with the wider public so as to stimulate Boundaryless People-Power that tackles particular global crises directly. Only by mastering those two new non-geographic dimensions of power can we break free of the straightjacket of territorial governance that currently renders the best-intentioned politicians incapable of effectively addressing the increasingly complex interactions that generate global crises.

Only by understanding in detail where those crises come from and how they grow and reinforce themselves can we at last begin to construct defenses that match, rather than deny, the crises' true form. And as a global community we are now ready to do that, because, twinned with the world economy that we created, we too are growing up.

## A GLOBAL ECONOMY COMING OF AGE

Ours is an adolescent world. Its onset of metaphorical puberty was triggered by initial stirrings of the exponential High-Tech supertrend in the early-20th century, accompanied by defiant shrieks of 'I Hate You' hurled between most of the world's nations, economic ideologies, races and religions. A century later governments are trying to act a lot more grown up, in between occasional temper-tantrums and battles of will. Like any adolescence, our journey toward maturity has been bitter-sweet. Wide-eyed enthusiasm for science or for religion did not solve everything. A juvenile feeling of invulnerability and disregard for consequences did not stop countries maxing out their credit, taking things they did not replace, and wrecking their shared home. Nor did stubbornness make naive ideas any truer. Throughout all of this, Mother Nature sporadically made even powerful governments feel stupid and useless. And on some occasions they behaved as if they were.

In the last several decades, our most successful nations have become increasingly-wild teenage prodigies. Nourished by a heady cocktail of new-found strength, inflated ego, lack of experience, passion, frustration and desire, we have become addicted to fossil fuels, real-time information, accelerating change, and unlimited food whatever the time of year. But no addictions are free of consequences. We now face a self-inflicted Rite of Passage that no one really understands, no one wants, and – in the far extreme – no one may survive. It turns out that the exponential gift of High-Tech has exacted a fearsome price. Yet the uncontrollable backlashes that are forming because of the escalating misalignment of hidden-interactions are not inevitable.

To avoid the worst crises, we must now enter into a mature debate that recognizes how the balance of power between national government and international business and boundaryless groups of people is already inevitably shifting. Existing authority figures must accept that their previously-unquestioned right to wield ultimate power must adapt; they no longer have the ability to lay down the law on everything. But those gaining previously-unprecedented influence must also accept that part of the deal for a more grown-up relationship is that with greater power has to come greater demonstrated responsibility. Most importantly we must each accept that as our world economy begins to fulfill its potential, so we too must adapt with it. The roles of governments, businesses and the general public all must change. If we are to curtail future crises then there is no alternative. There is no going back. And there is no longer the option of simply keeping things as they are. The need to realign our global governance is not a choice. It is an implication.

It inevitably follows from the triumphant coming together of our planet-wide civilization. It is a sign that our adolescent world at last is Coming of Age. Despite all the forthcoming struggles, the uncertainty, the long road toward Global Renaissance that still stretches ahead, ultimately the full recognition of what our current circumstance actually means should be the cause of immense pride. For it signals the crossing of a unique threshold reached by civilizations on, at most, only a very few precious planets scattered across the universe: The need for global realignment of the power structures and governance of a whole species is the single most important hidden consequence of a *truly interconnected* world.

More than anything else, *that* is the reality of Global Crises.

# TAKING THE INITIATIVE

**For their enlightened self-interest key players in the world economy must form the equivalent of Global Guilds to fill the current leadership-vacuum and trigger the far-reaching changes needed to minimize global crises**

Despite current widespread disruption there will never be a better time to trigger the changes needed to secure against different forms of escalating systemic-crisis

In the absence of any effective global governance – industries cannot wait for outside help but must realign their activities and form 'Global Guilds' to create a practical way forward

- *In addition to realigning their activities to create the conditions needed to counter their particular types of systemic crisis – the most powerful industries must align themselves as 'Global Guilds'*
- *Global Guilds must act like TRUSTED OBSERVERS by which organizations gain an undistorted overview of globally-defined threats without breaching confidentiality*
- *Global Guilds must act like VIGILANT COUNSELORS monitoring globally-defined-crisis scenarios, alerting about changes and facilitating integrated counter-measures*
- *Global Guilds must act like GLOBAL ADVOCATES so organizations can better justify unpalatable measures needed to avoid collective (and so also individual) crises*

Global Guilds must trigger a viral strategy that has the ultimate goal of accelerating the collective responsiveness of their members to growing crises

- *Global Guilds must create conditions for ACCELERATING RESPONSIVENESS in order to refine and customize decentralized tactics and to counter specific crises directly*
- *Similar to how Wikipedia grows and upgrades accuracy so Global Guilds must enable a decentralized focus on High-Impact-but-Difficult issues – and also find patterns across those solutions*

482

# Chapter summary

Rather than wait for protracted international agreement – self-improving prototype Global Guilds will immediately improve the odds of those organizations that form them

- *Governments are unlikely to take the initiative – although they should – so it is more effective for a pioneering organization to sponsor a prototype Global Guild than attempt much the same alone*
- *The effectiveness and relevance of prototype Global Guilds will keep rapidly improving if they remain Independent, Globalist, Participative, Minimalist, Pragmatic, Exceptional and Adaptive*
- *Fundamental change can be triggered by a relatively small number of organizations throughout the world economy – and now is their opportunity to rise to that challenge*

## 35. GLOBAL GUILDS AND ACCELERATING RESPONSIVENESS

**GLOBAL GUILDS**

**IDEAL TIMING**

| Escalating threats of backlashes | Key governments already worried | Inadequate global governance | Insufficient time for protracted reforms | Need to unleash potential of existing bodies | Global businesses especially well-placed to take a lead |
|---|---|---|---|---|---|

| TRUSTED OBSERVER | VIGILANT COUNSELOR | GLOBAL ADVOCATE |
|---|---|---|
| through which members gain an undistorted overview of globally-defined threats without breaching confidentiality | monitoring globally-defined-threat scenarios, alerting about changes and facilitating integrated counter-measures | so organizations can better justify unpopular measures needed to avoid collective (and so individual) backlashes |

*DESIGN GUIDELINES that successively refine a Global Guild's effectiveness and relevance to its members*

- *Rigorously INDEPENDENT and as a result accepted as completely unbiased and confidentially secure*
- *Unimpeachably GLOBALIST so a Guild Ambassador can believably claim: 'I speak for no country; I speak for all'*
- *Deeply PARTICIPATIVE in its interactions with other bodies – partly to enrol them and partly to leverage their capabilities*
- *Fundamentally MINIMALIST in its interventions to avoid counter-measures resulting in further threatening backlashes*
- *Supremely PRAGMATIC with its effectiveness unconstrained by conventions and bureaucracies of other similar bodies*
- *Consistently EXCEPTIONAL in terms of the intellect and talent of its staff as well as the pre-eminence of its insights*
- *Inherently ADAPTIVE to built-in feedback mechanisms that progressively refine tactics, operating guidelines, strategy, goals*

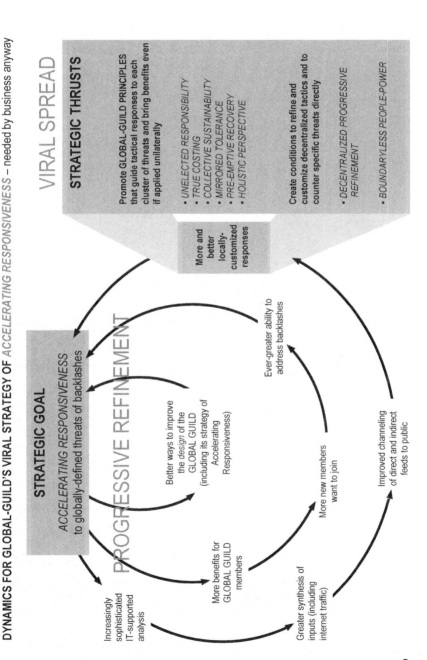

**DYNAMICS FOR GLOBAL-GUILD'S VIRAL STRATEGY OF** *ACCELERATING RESPONSIVENESS* – needed by business anyway

VIRAL SPREAD

**STRATEGIC THRUSTS**

Promote GLOBAL-GUILD PRINCIPLES that guide tactical responses to each cluster of threats and bring benefits even if applied unilaterally

- *UNELECTED RESPONSIBILITY*
- *TRUE COSTING*
- *COLLECTIVE SUSTAINABILITY*
- *MIRRORED TOLERANCE*
- *PRE-EMPTIVE RECOVERY*
- *HOLISTIC PERSPECTIVE*

Create conditions to refine and customize decentralized tactics and to counter specific threats directly

- *DECENTRALIZED PROGRESSIVE REFINEMENT*
- *BOUNDARYLESS PEOPLE-POWER*

More and better locally-customized responses

**STRATEGIC GOAL**

*ACCELERATING RESPONSIVENESS* to globally-defined threats of backlashes

PROGRESSIVE REFINEMENT

Better ways to improve the *design* of the GLOBAL GUILD (including its strategy of Accelerating Responsiveness)

Ever-greater ability to address backlashes

More new members want to join

Increasingly sophisticated IT-supported analysis

More benefits for GLOBAL GUILD members

Greater synthesis of inputs (including internet traffic)

Improved channeling of direct and indirect feeds to public

485

## 36. VIRAL SPREAD APPLIED TO PROGRESSIVE REFINEMENT

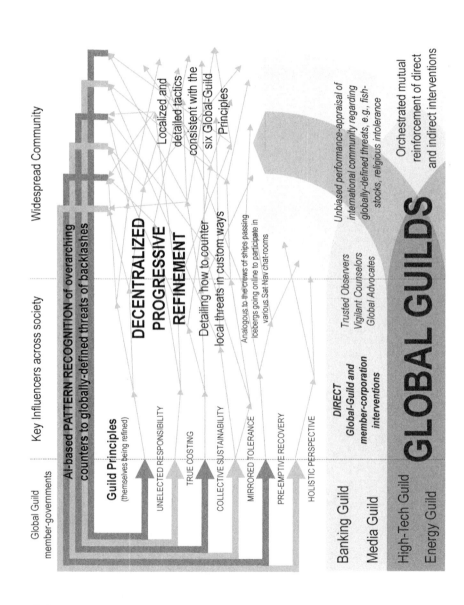

Marine Guild

Land Guild

Analogous to a sophisticated set of Sat Nav systems

**INDIRECT**
*Global-Guild and member-corporation interventions*

*Selection, recruitment and support of celebrities and thought-leaders*

*Supported contributions to websites and briefings of chosen members of broadcast and news media*

*e.g., banks held accountable for the economic contributions to the growth of countries they serve*

*e.g., developing countries curtail population explosions*

*e.g., news media held accountable for their impacts*

*e.g., shared Foreign Policy better supported by international community*

*e.g., political skills upgraded*

*e.g., national governments accept short-term local losses to counter long-term collective threats*

*e.g., unstable regions persuaded against nuclear proliferation*

*e.g., oil and energy corporations work with governments to help wean economies off carbon*

**BOUNDARYLESS PEOPLE-POWER**

Countering specific threats of backlashes directly

Analogous to the crews of nearby ships alerting their captains to steer to join other vessels already helping each other to break through an ice-sheet and form a shortcut

*e.g., members of a religion become intolerant of their own religion's intolerance*

*e.g., more responsible use of antibiotics (to lessen resistant strains)*

*e.g., public stops eating unsustainable fish species*

*e.g., nuclear power seen as a valid and necessary supplement*

*e.g., greater energy efficiency and less food wastage*

Global Guild member-governments

Key Influencers across society

Widespread Community

487

# ACKNOWLEDGEMENTS

I am immensely grateful to my unnamed corporate, institutional and private clients around the world who since the 1980s have invited me to evaluate the always-confidential and often-embarrassing innermost workings of their organizations. It is they who provided me with the otherwise inaccessible insights on which this book is based. Although I am obliged not to identify any but a small handful of these clients, and must anyway protect certain people within even the organizations that I *can* mention (which is often best achieved simply by not mentioning the client-name at all), there are many astute, highly connected – and in some cases, rather courageous – individuals who will hopefully recognize their fingerprints on different details within this book. In practice, I had to corroborate all such details from multiple independent sources. So, for each detail, there are in truth many people to whom I would like to extend my thanks – albeit in a blanket statement that maintains their anonymity.

In terms of producing *The Reality of Global Crises,* I can thankfully be far more explicit. Since 1984 I have had six books published by traditional publishers. Each time has been very productive – but the process has felt unduly protracted and old-fashioned, aimed at somewhat-different goals than mine, and controlled by individuals with little insight into my specific book topics. This time I wanted an experience suited to the $21^{st}$ century. I am extremely grateful to all the folks at Amazon who have transformed an archaic production rite into a joy. Theirs is definitely the way of the future.

With any books written over a long period, the greatest sacrifices are inevitably made *not* by the authors but by their family and friends. And for the last couple of years that has certainly applied to this book. Above anybody and everybody deserving of heartfelt gratitude is the wonderful and ever-supportive Francis (without whose motivation and encouragement the project would have stalled at least twice), as well as Mar and Da (who, both in their nineties, nevertheless every day made a point of demonstrating their caring interest by happily discussing whatever topic, however abstruse, that I happened to be writing about).

To everyone, named and unnamed: Thank you.

# INDEX

## A

Abortion, 202, 237, 269, 272, 276, 287

Abu Ghraib, 268

Acid rain, 92

Advertising, 55, 156, 312

Afghanistan, 196, 198, 268, 272, 374

Africa, 121, 164, 174, 181, 183, 185, 206, 212, 237, 252, 362, 365, 388, 399

Agenda for Peace (Boutros Boutros-Ghali), 404

AIDS, 258, 276, 277, 364, 365, 366, 367, 394, 422

Air Force One, 60

Air pollution, 92

Al Qaeda, 374, 409

Algal blooms, 91, 178

Algeria, 119

Allergies, 322

Amish, 249

Anglican church, 278, 284, 369, 393, 411

Angola, 119, 206

Annex I and Annex II countries, 399

Anonymous (hacktivists), 313

Antarctic, 105, 111, 114, 392

Antibiotics, 319, 320, 321, 322, 323, 341, 363, 411

Anti-Semitism, 411

Aquifers, 182, 183, 204, 212, 215, 221, 394, 405, 406, 412, 436

Arab League, 391

Arab populations, 61, 88, 119, 122, 137, 142, 199, 210, 231, 270, 279, 316, 362, 368, 371, 391, 415, 420, 435, 438

Arab Spring, 14, 15, 68, 69, 210, 264, 279

Aral Sea, 181, 182

Archbishop of Canterbury, 250, 267

Arctic, 97, 110

Aristarchus, 242

ARPANET, 309

Artificial Intelligence (AI). *See* Machine intelligence

Asia, 61, 93, 97, 110, 211, 354, 421

Association of Small Island States (AOSIS), 110

Asteroid strike, 372, 374

Australia, 140, 189, 318, 399

Automobiles, 65, 67, 87, 107, 127, 135, 149, 203, 305, 310, 342, 474

## B

Bacteria, 49, 320, 321, 325, 340, 341, 436

Baghdad, 306

Baltic Sea, 178

Bangladesh, 110, 178, 411

Banking, 5, 8, 18, 20, 21, 22, 23, 24, 25, 26, 27, 28, 29, 30, 31, 32, 33, 35, 37, 40, 42, 54, 59, 61, 63, 64, 76, 77, 80, 88, 135, 149, 221, 300, 313, 316, 327, 332, 340, 350, 354, 355, 356, 359,

# Index

# Index

# Index

# THE REALITY OF GLOBAL CRISES

## M

## N

# Index

# Index

# Index

# ABOUT THE AUTHOR

As foremost authority on the hidden inner-workings of the world economy, Dr. Peter B Scott-Morgan has been invited to decode the complex reality behind all the main components of the international community. For more than 25 years and across the USA, Europe, Asia Pacific and Latin America he has been offered exceptional access to institutions, government organizations and corporations (including many of the major players in banking, pharmaceuticals, oil, energy, IT, telecoms and media) to analyze their systemic threats and advise their leaders how to respond. He is one of very few that has ever gained so much confidential insight into such a wide-ranging sample of the world economy.

Dr. Scott-Morgan has given more than a thousand speeches, presentations and workshops in over thirty countries and has spent approximately the same amount of his career based in the USA as in Europe. He has an expert knowledge of technology, sociology and management science, and a detailed grasp of history and politics. With specialist expertise in system dynamics, organizational strategy and change management he has built a track record of published thought-leadership, authoring over a hundred articles and refereed papers, as well as several reference materials and six books.

Within academia he has taught numerous post-graduate MBA courses in London, Boston and Rotterdam, as well as been Professor of Business and Chairman of the Board of Trustees at a Boston-based international Business School. In corporate life he has been Senior Vice President of a 3,500-person professional-services firm and the Managing Director of a 150-person international management consultancy.